Music and Gender

MUSIC AND GENDER:
PERSPECTIVES FROM THE MEDITERRANEAN

Edited by Tullia Magrini

The University of Chicago Press
Chicago and London

780
Music
2003

3 1712 01068 9399

Tullia Magrini is associate professor of ethnomusicology at the University of Bologna. She is the author or editor of seven books in Italian, most recently *Introduzione all'etnomusicologia,* and is founder and editor of the Web journal *Music & Anthropology.*

The University of Chicago Press, Chicago 60637
The University of Chicago Press, Ltd., London
© 2003 by The University of Chicago
All rights reserved. Published 2003
Printed in the United States of America
12 11 10 09 08 07 06 05 04 03   5 4 3 2 1

ISBN (cloth): 0-226-50165-5
ISBN (paper): 0-226-50166-3

Library of Congress Cataloging-in-Publication Data

Music and gender : perspectives from the Mediterranean / edited by Tullia Magrini.
      p.   cm. — (Chicago studies in ethnomusicology)
   Includes bibliographical references and index.
      ISBN 0-226-50165-5 (cloth : alk. paper) — ISBN 0-226-50166-3 (pbk : alk. paper)
   1. Gender identity in music.   2. Women musicians—Mediterranean Region.
   3. Music—Mediterranean Region—History and criticism.   4. Ethnomusicology.
   I. Magrini, Tullia.   II. Series.

   ML3838 .M949   2003
   780'.82'091822—dc21
                                                                    2002151281

♾ The paper used in this publication meets the minimum requirements of the American National Standard for Information Sciences—Permanence of Paper for Printed Library Materials, ANSI Z39.48-1992.

Contents

Acknowledgments   vii

Introduction: Studying Gender in Mediterranean Musical Cultures   1
Tullia Magrini

A Man's Game? Engendered Song and the Changing Dynamics   1   33
of Musical Activity in Corsica
Caroline Bithell

Body and Voice: The Construction of Gender in Flamenco   2   67
Joaquina Labajo

Those "Other Women": Dance and Femininity among   3   87
Prespa Albanians
Jane C. Sugarman

The Gender of the Profession: Music, Dance, and Reputation   4   119
among Balkan Muslim Rom Women
Carol Silverman

Come into Play: Dance, Music, and Gender in Three   5   147
Calabrian Festivals
Goffredo Plastino

The Female Dervish and Other Shady Ladies of the Rebetika   6   169
Gail Holst-Warhaft

Archivists of Memory: Written Folksong Collections of   7   195
Twentieth-Century Sephardi Women
Edwin Seroussi

Representations and Female Roles in the Raï Song   **8**   *215*
Marie Virolle

Poetry as a Strategy of Power: The Case of Riffian Berber Women   **9**   *233*
Terri Brint Joseph

Nashaṭ: The Gender of Musical Celebration in Morocco   **10**   *251*
Deborah Kapchan

On Religion, Gender, and Performing: Female Performers   **11**   *267*
and Repentance in Egypt
Karin van Nieuwkerk

Male, Female, and Beyond in the Culture and Music of   **12**   *287*
Roma in Kosovo
Svanibor Pettan

The Tearful Public Sphere: Turkey's "Sun of Art," Zeki Müren   **13**   *307*
Martin Stokes

"And She Sang a New Song": Gender and Music on the Sacred   **14**   *329*
Landscapes of the Mediterranean
Philip V. Bohlman

List of Contributors   *351*

Index   *355*

A gallery of photographs follows page 146

Acknowledgments

I owe thanks first of all to the Fondazione Levi in Venice, and in particular to the Scientific Board and its chair, Professor Giulio Cattin. Since 1992, the Fondazione Levi has supported the foundation and activity of the Study Group on Anthropology of Music in Mediterranean Cultures of the International Council for Traditional Music. I owe thanks as well to the members of that group: this volume could not have been conceived without the fruitful collaboration of the scholars who gathered in Venice several times to explore the complex issues of Mediterranean musical anthropology. In 1998, the Fondazione Levi organized a meeting of the study group, "Music as Representation of Gender in Mediterranean Countries," which proved to be the starting point for this book. The meeting, successfully realized through the participation of scholars from Mediterranean countries, northern Europe, and the United States, many of whom have contributed to this volume, provided the first occasion for a careful consideration of the issue of gender in the territories surrounding the Mediterranean Sea. The debates initiated at the meeting continued on the pages of the Web journal *Music and Anthropology,* thanks to the support of the University of Bologna and the University of Maryland at Baltimore County, which hosts the mirror site of the journal. Around the same time, the editors of the series "Chicago Studies in Ethnomusicology" encouraged me to think of a volume on the topic discussed in Venice. I am deeply grateful to them for their constant support and suggestions during the long road to publication of this work. Finally, I must thank the authors of the studies presented here for their scholarly contributions, for their permission to include them in this anthology, and for their patience. A special thank-you to Piera Sarasini, who was ever ready to help me in the editing process.

Tullia Magrini

Introduction: Studying Gender in Mediterranean Musical Cultures

Tullia Magrini

In the past few decades, music scholars have grown increasingly aware of gender as a major feature of musical life. It has become essential to consider the "gender" factor in order to understand, describe, and interpret a given musical culture and to discover further elements of continuity or differentiation among musical cultures. The theoretical premises of such studies—in particular, the distinction between the biological reality of sex and the cultural category of gender—have been repeatedly emphasized: "Whereas sex refers to biological phenomena, *sex role* or *gender* denotes their cultural, psychological, and social correlates: the rules, expectations, and behavior appropriate to being male or female within a particular society" (Hanna 1988, 7).[1] The research carried on in recent years, particularly within the disciplines of ethnomusicology and music anthropology, has demonstrated that gender roles strongly affect musical behavior and related concepts all over the world (e.g., Koskoff 1987; Herndon and Ziegler 1990; Citron 1993; Cook and Tsou 1994). Gender has come to be recognized as one of the main factors shaping individual and group identities—thus also the practices that construct and express these identities. Women's repertoires and musical practices that for a long time had remained at the outskirts of anthropological and ethnomusicological research because of their "private" or "marginal" character are now at the center of the scholars' critical inquiries.

It should be emphasized that women's musical activities had not previously been examined as an expression of specific social situations and cultural responses, even when these activities were well known to scholars. In Italy, for example, music anthropology originated at the end of the 1950s thanks to several pathbreaking studies on phenomena that were essentially centered on women, such as tarantism and funeral mourning (De Martino 1958, 1961). But the focus of these works was mainly on the existential and historical dimension of the rituals, taking somewhat for granted (and failing to problematize) their feminine character.[2]

To expand our knowledge of women's musical behavior and of the values they express by engaging in musical events is no doubt an important goal, one that figures prominently in this anthology. In my opinion, however, the main objective of a gender-oriented study should go beyond this level, and beyond the need to complete our picture of the musical world by accounting for women's musical practices. In a wider perspective, it seems to me that attention to the role of gender marks the beginning of what might be considered a new phase in the study of the musics of the world. Whereas early contributions in the field of comparative musicology and folklore studies had privileged the sonorous document and its analysis, and whereas ethnomusicology, conceived of as anthropology of music, has focused on "music as culture," today one can no longer avoid investigating the role played by gender—of both the music makers and their audiences—in determining essential aspects of a musical activity and its cultural meaning. In this new phase, one of our discipline's prominent goals is to approach music "as gendered culture." In this way, we can develop a vision of the human dimension of musical activity that is increasingly richer and more complex, constantly aware of the fact that each musical practice may be used to represent, convey, and elaborate specific values for the individual genders in particular contexts (see Magrini 2002, 211–29).

The scholars represented in this anthology take as their object of investigation the territories that border the Mediterranean. Their goal is to discover and emphasize the richness of various concepts of gender as they relate to Mediterranean cultures and to examine how certain musical practices in these countries have been effective in creating and perpetuating or transforming specific ideas and roles related to issues of gender. In this introduction, I wish to outline both the main premises of the chapters gathered here and a common context for the work. I will also reconsider the view of genders that has been proposed by the classical Mediterraneanist anthropological literature and discuss a few preliminary questions related to the very idea of a "Mediterranean" culture.

Researching Gender in Past and Present Musical Life

The literature on music has long neglected the existence of a relationship between music and the dynamics of gender. Indeed, as Ellen Koskoff has claimed, "Until recently, few of us were aware of the impact of our own or any other society's gender structure on all sorts of behavior" (Koskoff 1987, 2). This does not mean, however, that the musical phenomena studied in the past cannot be reexamined from new perspectives, or that they must be thought of as necessarily outside the domain of gender studies. To the contrary, musical scholarship has produced an enormous amount of data on the sound objects of the oral traditions: although such data may at first sight appear foreign to a study of the issues of gender, on careful analysis they may turn out to be quite relevant to a reinterpretation of musical practices that are now in many cases extinct—a reinterpretation that attempts to comprehend the ways in which certain documented musical practices were in the past directly related to divisions or interactions between genders within society.

Let us consider, for example, a "classical" genre such as the ballad, documented by a vast amount of data. The ballad of the oral tradition has customarily been viewed as a unified musico-poetic genre with a huge number of textual and musical variants.[3] We know the formulaic expressions, the ways to combine them, the different musical systems employed, and many other aspects of this genre. But is it possible to determine, for each specific context of performance, whether or not ballads also conveyed an ideology of gender? On this point, I would like to refer to a recent study of mine on the Italian repertory (Magrini 1995), in which I argue that the existence of different male and female performance practices of the ballad has to do with the fact that the music making had very different goals and meanings for men and women.

There is no doubt that the practice of singing ballads was once predominantly female in northern Italy. This conclusion is confirmed by the ballad collectors' sparse notes on their informants—mostly women—dating from the nineteenth century onward (e.g., Nigra 1974), as well as by fieldwork completed after the 1950s, that is, at a time when the "feminine ballad" was declining. But even more significant is the analysis of the poetic texts of the ballads sung by women. It is well known that the narrative ballads are emblematic, rather than historically accurate; but, following Ricoeur, we can assume that fictional narratives assist us in our being "in history" and emphasize our need to cope with reality in imaginative ways. "By its mimetic intention, the world of fiction leads us to the heart of the real world of action" (Ricoeur 1981, 298). As I have argued, the worldview of northern Italian ballad texts is quite female: "ballads are mainly concerned with stories of women and in particular with the representation of the dangers coming from men (abduction, rape, murder, betrayal, mistreatment, abandonment), with the terrible consequences coming from a conflict with family or authority for questions of love (imprisonment, death) or from breaking the law, and virtuous female behavior. . . . Ballads narrate women's emblematic life experiences, paradigmatic sequences of events that may stem from a relation between a woman and a man, where men are often depicted as dangerous and are never heroes" (Magrini 1995). In the large households once typical of northern Italian peasant societies, ballads were performed by women in small groups: through the practice of singing, women transmitted values and models of behavior, reflected upon the appropriate strategies to follow in their relationships with men, developed imaginative activity, and worked out their own representations of life and the world. Within this context, ballad singing was the most important instrument that women had to reflect upon themselves and their relationship with society, and to construct their identity. However, the breaking up of large households, migration into the cities, and the gradual entrance of women into the workforce, among other changes, transformed peasant society and disrupted the repertory's patterns of transmission (previously guaranteed by women's mobility under the custom of virilocal residence). In this new context, the particular meanings of and the occasions for the singing practice vanished, and consequently female ballad singing faded out.

The male practice of singing ballads is not documented in the remote past in the forms that we know today. Male ballad singing lasted until recently, probably because its function, unlike that of the female tradition, was not one of transmitting and reflecting on certain narratives. Some ballads could simply belong to the mixed repertoire of songs performed by large groups of men gathering in taverns in the countryside or, more recently, by organized choruses. For these groups of men, a ballad was a song like any other: they would often sing only a few verses of the texts worked out with many repetitions, thus losing the general meaning of the narration. Men were mainly interested in singing per se, in emphasizing the social and cohesive nature of singing, and in developing a polyphonic style characterized by physically demanding, prolonged and impressive performances that emphasized vocal strength and fusion. (In contrast, women's performances of ballads were generally lively and fast.) In short, male groups used ballads like any other song that could be accommodated in their peculiar vocal style, the meaning of which seems to have resided chiefly in the affirmation of the members' ability to merge into a collective action—that is, to perform through music their inner symbiotic relationship. Indeed, this is one of the basic psychological properties of a group (Corbella 1988).

The example of the Italian ballad highlights the possibility that, on renewed analysis, the same repertories that have been transmitted to us as collections of mere literary and sonorous objects may turn out to be essential instruments for the reconstruction of gender identities in a more or less remote past. Furthermore, the example shows that the same repertory could be used by both women and men in different contexts and with different performance practices, thus acquiring deeply diverse meanings. It follows that these meanings are to be located not in the repertory itself, but rather in the complex social and cultural situations from which the different male and female performance practices originated. Such an approach informs some of the chapters in this volume, for example, those that reconsider genres such as flamenco or *rebetika* songs, in an attempt to emphasize certain aspects that, thus far, have been completely or partially ignored.

If it is possible to rediscover the gender-based meaning of past musical practices, it seems even more fruitful to investigate the musical life of our time from the same perspective, and to wonder how the gender roles of a given social group may be examined through a study of its musical practices. Musical occasions are traditionally a privileged venue for the public construction and representation of individual gender identity, as well as of the relational models between genders within particular communities. A study of the enormous variety of musical practices may yield an extremely nuanced picture of the extent to which such gender relationships vary, and of the ways in which the words, the gestures, and the sounds of music are capable of expressing different gender identities.

Indeed, a discourse on gender should not only move beyond the traditional binary view grounded on the biological male-female dualism, but also realize that gender, far from being an incontrovertible natural phenomenon, is rather a changing construct in space and history. "More exactly, it is a never-ending process of constructing ideas about male and female characteristics and differences. This constructionist process is likely to be regulated by, as well as expressive of, those discourses on gender that are most powerfully represented in one's cultural setting at one or another historical moment." As a consequence, "gender is an unstable mix of socially conformist beliefs and practices and individually varied, often hidden and marginalized forms of both submission to and rebellion against normative pressures" (Schafer 1994, 1–2).

As cultural constructs, the views on the feminine and the masculine are context-bound and, in general, complementary, so that they regulate the encounter and the relationship between male and female in a given setting. For example, we can consider the rules that discipline the use of the body in the dance, an event that in many societies constitutes not only a means of self-display for the individual, but also, and especially, the traditional occasion for a public relationship between men and women (as well as between persons of the same gender). These rules offer a typical example of the synthesis of ideas on the feminine, the masculine, and on the "proper" interaction between genders (or within a single gender) that distinguish a given community at a given point in time. Dancing provides a faithful expression of the most diverse and nuanced meanings, since its rules specify who can take part in the dance and how the body is to be used, also allowing or denying specific forms of bodily contact, and regulating other aspects in such a way as to highlight shared ideas on what constitutes an acceptable physical relationship between men and women in the public sphere. As Judith Lynne Hanna has claimed, "Feelings and ideas about sexuality and sex roles (also referred to as gender) take shape in dance. These visual models of which dancer (male or female) performs what, when, where, how, why, either alone, or with or to another dancer reflect and also challenge society's expectations for each sex's specific activities, whether dominance patterns or mating strategies" (1988, xiii). It should also be emphasized that the same kind of dance may take on different meanings in different contexts. The *tarantella* danced in Polsi, described by Goffredo Plastino in chapter 5, illustrates how traditional southern Calabrian society employs dance both as a ritual of socialization within a group (*rota*) and, at the same time, as performance of a relationship between two partners. On the basis of my own fieldwork in northern Calabria (see Magrini 1986), I can add that when the partners are a man and a woman, the tarantella takes the meaning of a danced courtship rich in sensuality, although according to the traditional way of dancing, no bodily contact between the two dancers is allowed. When the partners are two men, the tarantella becomes a much more animated dance where bodily messages of defiance are mutually sent by the dancers while a subtle homoerotic relationship between them may also be hinted (sometimes it is clearly suggested for fun when one of the men imitates the female dance behavior). Dance may also become a way to represent generational identity and changing gender roles, a topic also explored by Plastino with reference to tarantella. Similarly, in chapter 3, Jane Sugarman contrasts the old dance style of Prespa Albanian women with the new fad for the çoçek, a type of solo dance that was formerly performed by professional entertainers, particularly Roma, at weddings and other festivities (see also chapter 4, by Carol Silverman). The old style is characterized by the display of female modesty: "By moving her body as a unit and carefully controlling the movements of her limbs, a woman assures that the attention of onlookers will not be drawn to the more 'private' and sexual parts of her body. Through her subdued manner, she presents herself both as sexually proper and socially deferential, and she demonstrates her self-control by deflecting attention from her personal emotional state through a downward or blank gaze." In contrast, the new fad for çoçek is typical of young people (in particular young women), who resort to it as a marker of their generational identity and as a way to project a more "sexualized" image of femininity consistent with ideals that they are absorbing from Western popular culture. Nevertheless, because of the dance's Ottoman origins, they can also affirm their sense of a localized (Balkan/Muslim) identity.

It is well known that dance is also often concerned with the representation of relationships of "power, dominance, defiance, and equality" (Hanna 1988, xvi). In chapter 2, Joaquina Labajo examines how the evolution of the style of flamenco dance may be interpreted in terms of changing power relations between male and female dancers. She argues that over the past century women asserted greater power and authority in the world of flamenco by progressively appropriating dances and attitudes previously reserved to men: they claimed their right to develop that kind of artistic virtuosity "based on rapid motions of the legs and heel-tapping" associated with the male style of dance, and in this way also tried to understate the potential sexual meanings of their own movements. As a consequence, "men have tried constantly to work out new types of movements and representations in order to rival the dynamic and impressive female repertoire," and today they are sometimes "looking for new hypermale roles." Although the display of the body in dance may often have sexual meanings—as exemplified by Silverman's, Plastino's, and Deborah Kapchan's arguments in chapters 4, 5, and 10—with reference to male dance, Sugarman argues in chapter 3, for instance, that "a blatant physicality is . . . an express component of men's performances, although it is a physicality that stresses strength and agility rather than sensuality." Gail Holst-Warhaft's observations in chapter 6 on the Greek zebekiko suggest in addition that the goal of male dance may be as far as it can be from eroticism. Dance may be far more concerned, for example, with a sophisticated use of the body aimed at the public expression of a man's mood, as shown in the zebekiko performed in the closed world of the hashish dens and underworld haunts of Piraeus where the rebetiko was born. This introverted dance, as Holst-Warhaft states, "carved out a territory within which the dancer was free to interpret the music as he wished and which was violated by another man at the risk of serious bodily harm." The space belonged to the dancer who paid for it and was used for a solipsistic representation of the dancer's existential pain. The dancer "could be admired not for being macho but almost for its opposite: for his willingness to weep secretly in public."

If dance offers the most valuable visual representation of gender identity, in a broader perspective, music provides as well a wide range of opportunities for the expression of those nuanced sets of ideas on genders that are typical of every social group. Factors as different as repertory and its relationship with the performers' gender, the particular occasions of music making, performance practice, singing style, the lyrics and their elaborations, instrumental practice, the more or less segregated character of performance, and still other aspects of musical behavior may become the occasion for an in-depth analysis of the value of musical expression "as gendered culture." Kapchan, for example, argues in chapter 10 that in Morocco the state of *nashaṭ,* that is, the attainment of a particular emotional condition in the context of a musical event like the celebration of a wedding or a circumcision, is "coded as feminine" and "relies on a recognition of feminine difference and desire." By examining three celebrations at the level of diverse social classes, she observes that, notwithstanding the many dissimilarities between the specific contexts of the celebrations—same sex or mixed participants, musical performance entrusted to female professionals or a male group, and so forth—the catalysts of nashaṭ are women, either performers or guests, whose performance of seduction in a sexualized and musical ambiance is deeply involved in the creation of this particular festive condition.

Other chapters in this volume show how in the past, in many Mediterranean societies, men and women usually performed different repertoires with a strong gendered character, so that crossing the boundaries between female and male musical practices could be stigmatized as improper and socially unacceptable behavior. But, most interesting, in many contexts during the past century, the strictly gendered character of several musical practices has been challenged (or has simply disappeared), for example, through the cross-appropriation of musical repertoires or practices that had caused a shift in their previously established feminine or masculine nature.

In chapter 1, Caroline Bithell looks at a case of female appropriation with regard to the traditionally male practice of polyphonic singing in Corsica. Bithell emphasizes its basic aspect of "celebration of male togetherness," aimed at "creating a sense of intimacy and spiritual bonding" within a men's group. During the 1970s and early 1980s, in the context of the folk music revival, the masculine character of Corsican polyphonic singing increased even more because of its association with nationalism and political militancy. These soldier-singers were thus caught unaware by the appropriation of polyphonic singing by recent female groups who, following the model offered by the *Mystère des voix bulgares,* stepped onto the "world music" stage and obtained considerable international success. Not only did these female groups question the exclusive male property of Corsican polyphony and shift the strictly gendered nature of this musical practice, but they also worked toward its evolution, detaching it from values such as the continuity of Corsican tradition, nationalism, and militancy, which had remained the point of reference of the male groups: female performers "opened the way for a creative as opposed to a purist or conservationist approach to 'the musical heritage.'" The opposite happened in the history of Algerian raï. Throughout most of the twentieth century, female singers had a leading role in the birth and diffusion of this genre. However, in spreading throughout France and enjoying a huge popularity as a "world music" genre in the last decades of the century, raï lost its former largely feminine character. Nowadays, the most popular singers of raï are three men: Khaled, Cheb Mami, and Faudel. In chapter 8, Marie Virolle wonders ironically whether the market system of the major record and entertainment companies will succeed in reducing the women of raï to silence, which "a particularly hard patriarchic system did not manage to accomplish." One might also wonder whether the strongly transgressive role of female raï singers in Muslim society (which has no apparent impact in permissive France) favored their success in Algeria and throughout the Maghreb. Not only do they openly challenge Muslim beliefs through their audacious song texts, where sex and alcohol are no taboo, but they also play with gender signs in their behavior: "masculine and feminine signs are superimposed, inverted, corresponding and mutually nullifying," so that the singers appear as androgynous personalities who blur gender distinctions. This could have particular significance in a changing Islamic society, since "female singers may be said to deconstruct and reconstruct the relation between the sexes and genders, orchestrating the expression/repression of this divided society."

In a European context, the marginality and underworld character of the social environment where the rebetiko was composed and performed also furthered transgression of mainstream gender roles at the beginning of the last century. This was true not only for the men, the *rebetes* or *manges* of Piraeus, but also for the women who participated as artists or fans or poetic fancies, as Holst-Warhaft argues: these women adopted "masculine" behaviors, such as drinking and smoking *arghilé,* showed "disdain for societal norms," and were depicted in songs as daring personalities. Later, Sotiria Bellou, the most celebrated female rebetiko singer in the post–World War II period, emphasized in her story and personality the unconventional temperament of the women involved in the rebetiko world. Before beginning a career as rebetiko singer, Bellou was active in the Resistance, and in later life too she was ready to fight for her political ideals. As a singer, she not only had a deep, masculine voice, but she also possessed a masculine attitude and occasionally even adopted mannish attire. Finally, she was openly lesbian in a time of prevailing homophobia. In a sense, sexual "deviance" fitted and stressed both her own *rebetissa* character and the social deviance connected to the musical genre she sang.

Disregard for mainstream gender systems, however, has not been so unusual on the musical stage, since, like theater, "its space is specially licensed to harbor unorthodox individuals and otherwise inadmissible conduct" (Selenick 1992, xi). It is certainly more surprising to find contexts where women's transgressing gender roles did not arouse disapproval: Svanibor Pettan argues in chapter 12 that Balkan "sworn virgins" (transgendered individuals who are biological females and become social men) were accepted with no embarrassment in their communities, since their existence "reflected the society's economic and social needs." Their double gender identity also allowed "sworn virgins" to overcome the traditional separation of the female and male musical spheres: the literature gives evidence that they performed both men's and women's repertoires and instruments and, as professionals, could make music for both male and female audiences. In other words, at any given time they could take advantage of their original (female) sexual identity as well as of their acquired (male) gender role in order to participate in two differently gendered musical practices. This was not perceived as transgressive behavior, since the very existence of these transgendered individuals was a socially accepted custom (probably in part because the transgendered identity was not connected to "deviant" sexual behavior but to abstinence from sex). It represents, however, a rather unique reality. In the same context, performance of the women's repertoire by male musicians was understood as an index of gender ambiguity: in fact, among the Roma of Kosovo, the homosexuality ascribed to the first male *talava* musicians in the 1990s sprang mainly from the genre they performed, which belonged to the private female domain. By singing lyrics to frame drum accompaniment, they behaved like women and aroused mixed reactions among male audiences, who disapproved of them as men but liked their performances. Pettan argues that thanks to these musicians, who acted as mediators between the private female world and the public musical scene, the talava was eventually accepted also in the male musical repertoire, where it was somewhat transformed and gained great popularity among both men and women.

The cases examined in this volume make it clear that the musical world has frequently been a privileged field for expressing, challenging, and transgressing local models of gender identity. It is no surprise, therefore, that today's musical scene, playing to a global audience, is again an ideal place for emphatic presentation of any kind of "deviance" from the binary system of gender/sexual identity and for the triumph of the "ambiguous." The popular music icon Madonna, whose performances celebrate gender fluidity and ambivalence, has been seen as the embodiment of Judith Butler's postmodern feminist text (1990), which is credited with introducing "queer theory" to the world. In Mediterranean countries, transsexual singers have recently enjoyed great popularity, among them the Israeli performer Dana International (whose much discussed victory at the Eurovision Song Contest in 1998 unleashed in Israel "an incredibly complex response [regarding] religious, national, and international identity" [Bohlman 1998]) and Turkish performer Bülent Ersoy, discussed by Martin Stokes in chapter 13. In a sense, the association between stage and unorthodox behavior furthers the public representation of a whole gamut of ambiguous, weird, kinky, whimsical gender identities. The representation is typically spectacular and artificial as it destabilizes existing conceptions about gender as well as offering something different and by design shocking to the omnivorous mass-media audience. "The display of gendered opulence, luxury, and superabundance" leads Stokes to state that in this context "gender, in effect, becomes hypergender." In conclusion, how gender is represented turns out to be more interesting than gender itself. But it should not be overlooked that it is indeed the musical context of the performance that makes this representation possible and alluring.

Honor and Shame?

An investigation of gender issues in Mediterranean cultures is bound to address past studies on this subject, and in particular the influence exerted by the theories of the Oxford school of social anthropology on subsequent research. At the end of the 1950s, a group of anthropologists, led by John G. Peristiany and Julian Pitt-Rivers, initiated a discussion about the Mediterranean as a territory characterized by a set of common features that assured its cultural homogeneity. One of the founding publications of the anthropology of the Mediterranean was the anthology *Honour and Shame: The Values of*

Mediterranean Society (1966), edited by Peristiany. Although Peristiany and Pitt-Rivers recently claimed that they had never meant "to establish the Mediterranean as a 'culture area'" (1992, 6), their previous statements about "the continuity and persistence of Mediterranean modes of thought" (Peristiany 1966, 9) were clearly understood by the scholarly world as an implicit acknowledgment of the existence of such a unified entity. The so-called honor and shame syndrome was one of the most important "modes of thought" that Peristiany and his colleagues assumed to be pan-Mediterranean: they argued that "there exists a sex-linked, binary opposition in which honor is associated with men and shame with women" and saw honor and shame as "inextricably linked, tied to one another in cognitive as well as affective terms" (Brandes 1987, 122). As a result, this "syndrome" became constantly associated with Mediterranean studies.

It could be argued that the chapters included in the Peristiany volume are less unanimous than the editor states; they focus on different societies, chosen from among the most marginal in the countries bordering the Mediterranean so as to "tribalize" them; and finally, they exemplify the classical shortcomings of Mediterranean anthropology, namely, the "failure to compare, to make use of history, to work in cities, to relate part to whole" (Boissevain 1979, 81–82). In spite of these shortcomings, the concept of a pan-Mediterranean "honor and shame" syndrome soon became the flag of Mediterranean anthropology. As Stanley Brandes observed, "We must beware of discovering honor and shame, as such, everywhere simply because we have learned that they are by definition Mediterranean. Until now, scholars felt duty-bound to encounter manifestations of these moral Bobsy twins when carrying out fieldwork any place in the Levant, North Africa, and Southern Europe" (1987, 123). Still today, there are almost no anthropological studies of Mediterranean societies that fail to mention "honor and shame," sometimes simply as a link to previous literature (e.g., Abu-Lughod 1993), sometimes to support it (e.g., Gilmore 1987), or finally to criticize it (e.g., Dubisch 1995). I will not comment here on the "honor and shame" syndrome itself. Many scholars have already done so, calling our attention to the following points: the two concepts of male honor and female shame are not consistent throughout the Mediterranean (e.g., Herzfeld 1980, 1987; Marcus 1987); they do not appear everywhere in these countries, while, on the other hand, they may be found elsewhere (e.g., Pina Cabral 1989; Lever 1986; Henderson Stewart 1994); above all, these values today appear largely obsolete in many Mediterranean regions (e.g., Davis 1988, 1993).

I can only add that ethnicity, religion, class differences, contrasts between lifestyles in the cities and in the country, opposition between systems based on monogamy and polygyny, preference for endogamy or exogamy, the contractual or sacramental nature of marriage, and related issues are all factors that, among others, should be taken into consideration in accounting for the deeply differentiated male-female relationship in Mediterranean societies today as well as in the past. As regards the chapters included in this volume, it may be stressed that, far from confirming the existence of a uniform "honor and shame" syndrome, they point out the multifaceted "modes of thought" about gender that we encounter in examining the musical life in the countries bordering the Mediterranean.

In spite of its limitations, the first literature on Mediterranean "honor and shame," when compared with most anthropological literature on non-Mediterranean countries that appeared in the 1960s, represents an interesting early example of research on gender-based values. Since the "male" value of honor was thought to be inextricably linked to the "female" value of shame, the authors of that period had to take into consideration women as well as men, their roles in society, and their mutual relationships. But how did the pioneers of Mediterranean anthropology portray women and men?

Throughout the anthropological literature, women were represented as silent, passive, and marginal figures who were secluded in their houses, modestly covered head to toe in order to exorcise the potential sensuality of their bodies, and removed from any outside activity or role. This representation soon became a stereotype that hindered a more thorough examination of the roles of women in Mediterranean societies. More important, this representation prevented many scholars from realizing that, while a part of the literature insisted on representing the chaste, secluded, mute "Mediterranean woman," the position of women was undergoing a dramatic change in most countries of the region, as John Davis, for instance, has pointed out (1987, 22–34; 1988). Gilmore recognized twenty years ago that the customary representation of women as "somehow foreign or isolated from the 'real life' of the community" ignored half the story: "we are caricaturing 50 percent of the Mediterranean world" (1982, 195). More recently, Jane Cowan noticed, with reference to a town in Greek Macedonia, that "the selective insistence on the girl's confinement to the house is all the more striking in the context of the historical participation of Sohoian girls . . . in agricultural production and in waged work outside the house" (1990, 117). Similarly, Keddie has pointed out that the lifestyle of Middle Eastern women (sexual segregation, veiling, etc.) changes according to class and ethnicity (1991, 2–3). Such remarks show how important it is for us "to distinguish societal ideals from the experiences of real women and recognize that strategies of gendered representation typically treat ideals rather than lived experience" (Citron 1993, 121).

We can thus argue that female passivity and the image of cloistered women turn out to be elements of a discourse that aimed at silencing half of the Mediterranean world. This "silence" is nothing else than the concrete image of the low social weight assigned to women's words and activities (see Méndez 1988, 187), of the recurrent pattern of undervaluation of Mediterranean women as social, economic, and cultural actors.

In contrast, the chapters in this collection emphasize how women customarily played an important cultural role as transmitters and elaborators of their musical tradition. In some cases, they even acted as archivists. For instance, within Sephardi society, not only did women orally transmit the old *romances* that, as is well known, have their roots in medieval Spain, but also compiled notebooks documenting those oral repertoires. In chapter 7, Edwin Seroussi reconstructs the story of one of these collectors, Emily Sene, a Sephardi Jew born in Edirne, Thrace, who grew up in Istanbul and later lived in Cuba and the United States. Sene documented what Seroussi calls the "new Sephardi song," a largely forgotten repertory created by professional Sephardi artists and widely performed during the period between the world wars. The Sene collection is thus a very valuable historical record of the Sephardi song in the twentieth century: "Emily succeeded in presenting to us one of the most unique and comprehensive documents of the Sephardi song conceived and realized by a Sephardi woman without any institutional support or scientific background."

Other chapters in this volume deal with women who could assert their economic role as professional singers and dancers. In many Mediterranean countries, professionalism in female musical activity has a long tradition both in the field of art music and in the world of musical entertainment. Concerning folk music, the role of Rom women in this field should be remarked, since music has historically been a privileged field for Roma, who have often been accepted in many places as the best professional interpreters of local traditions. Discussing the Balkans in chapter 4, Silverman states that "female artistry as an occupation has a long history, as witnessed by Ottoman çengis and early-twentieth-century frame drum players and singers." Women's income has usually been recognized as essential to survival in Balkan Rom families, notwithstanding the somewhat inconsistent stigma associated with female dancing and singing in public. The interesting life story of Esma Redžepova, who became the first renowned Rom singer in this region, is a story of struggle against gender and racial prejudices that eventually "legitimated Rom music and dance as a female art form." Similarly, in chapter 2, Labajo traces the first documentation of a specific Gypsy dance style in the sixteenth and seventeenth centuries: "For a long time one of the main sources of income for

women in the Gypsy community was the money that they received for dancing at country festivals and market fairs." From the late nineteenth century
onward, a woman could perform professionally as *bailaora* or *cantaora* in the
context of flamenco shows. Elsewhere, professional women singers performed
in *cafés-aman* in Asia Minor at the end of the nineteenth century and became
popular also in Greece in the 1920s and 1930s. Finally, the spread of different forms of popular musics in the twentieth century gave women the opportunity to perform successfully as professional musicians throughout the
Mediterranean.

Besides pointing out the role of women as cultural and economic actors in the field of music, this volume focuses on what Mediterranean women
themselves can tell us about their roles in society, expressing their feelings,
ideas, and protests through the symbolic forms of song, dance, and ritual. In
this way, it becomes clear that it was possible to contradict the stereotyped
view of men and women proposed by the "honor and shame" theory even in
marginal and archaic societies. In chapter 1, for example, examining the old
practice of the female lament in early-twentieth-century Corsica, Bithell argues that "lament texts reveal that [women] were far from silent or passive in
terms of their political influence." In particular, as regards violent death, "the
singer heaps terrible threats and curses upon the family of the aggressor and
in some cases positively goads the men of her own family to action, mocking
them for their lack of courage and their hesitation in taking up arms and embracing their duty to avenge the death," so that, in conclusion, "the tables are
almost turned as women show themselves to be as much concerned with
honor as their menfolk and . . . it is the men who are most vulnerable to being shamed."[4] In chapter 9, Terri Brint Joseph similarly argues that among
the Riffian Berbers of the Beni-Waryaghar and Ibbucoya tribes in Morocco
"songs constitute strategic devices, weapons which can help women have a
voice in the community and gain control over their lives." In this context, by
performing their songs publicly at weddings, young women present themselves to the whole community and express their opinions freely: through
singing a woman can "defend herself, attack others, encourage suitors, announce an engagement, remind young men of the tribe that she is in love,
shame and ridicule an unwanted swain, or justify her decision to break an
engagement." These cases show that music can empower women even in societies where they are believed to be totally under male control, and even as
regards the crucial issue of premarital relationships.

The chapters dealing with change in musical behavior related to the widespread transformation of women's status in contemporary society are perhaps
still more relevant in showing how the claims of conventional controls over

female sexual behavior are frequently challenged in traditionally repressive contexts. In chapter 5, Plastino's interpretation of the different ways of dancing the tarantella at religious festivals as an expression of different ways of being a woman in contemporary Calabria is very telling in this regard. Unlike the dancers of the traditional tarantella at Polsi, the young women who dance for Saint Rocco at Gioiosa Ionica exhibit the freedom they have achieved through a bodily language that is no longer subject to male control and censorship and use the dance in an erotic display that expresses a physical relationship with their male partners inconceivable in a not so remote past. These young Calabrian women, like the young Albanians described by Sugarman in chapter 3, use their dancing bodies to declare their independence; they are no longer simply objects of male desire, but rather subjects who can display their own desires, sensuality, and sexuality. In Algeria as well, the diffusion of raï over the past two decades has worked to overcome the customary sexual segregation in dance: now young women and men can dance freely together in public, exchanging erotic messages in their performance. However, the Algerian situation is complex. Female raï singers have always enjoyed great freedom and placed themselves outside the "tribal" code of honor of Algerian society, although in order to do so, they have had to lose their patronymics and their individual identities within the patrilineage. This is just one sign of the inherent contradictions in the condition of women in today's Algeria: one can perhaps begin to grasp these contradictions, as Virolle suggests in chapter 8, simply by picturing "a wedding in which dozens of women of all ages yell in chorus," dancing to a raï hymn to sexual freedom "around a stiff, still, and strained bride."

We have seen how, according to the view proposed by the Oxford school, the image of the "shameful" Mediterranean woman was inextricably linked to that of the "honorable" Mediterranean man. Even if the authors of the Peristiany volume were more careful in examining the multiple meanings of the concept of male "honor" than those of the concept of female "shame," later studies adopted their restricted notion of the term evidenced in the following quote by Pitt-Rivers on the division of roles within the Andalusian family: "[Such a division] delegates the virtue expressed in sexual purity to the females and the duty of defending female virtue to the male. The honour of a man is involved therefore in the sexual purity of his mother, wife and daughters, and sisters, not in his own" (1966, 45).

If we include musical behavior in the notion of "honor" described by Pitt-Rivers, it is possible to confirm that in selected regions of the Mediterranean some singing practices did reveal a male concern for the sexual purity of women. In southern Italy—for example, in Calabria—a man was expected to serenade his fiancée with a group of friends as a public acknowledgment of their engagement (see Magrini 1986). Through this practice of "bringing the serenade," the entire community was able to exert a strict control on premarital relationships within the village, in such a way as to ensure complete adherence by both the man (whose task was to court his fiancée) and the woman (whose task was to be courted) to the complex set of social conventions that regulated the institution of engagement. Even the breaking of an engagement was effected and communicated by means of a serenade: in this case the man and his friends did not perform a love song, but rather a song of "disdain" in which they openly accused the woman of shameful behavior. By breaking up the relationship so publicly, the men avoided the possibility that their honor would be "contaminated" by the woman's shame. Obviously, this practice gave men considerable power over unmarried women, since the former were in charge of establishing the reputation of the latter. However, just as women could respond to love songs, they could also respond to songs of disdain. They could not sing in the village, but they were allowed to sing outside, mainly while working in the fields. Through singing, women could accept or refuse a suitor, rebuke them for betrayal, and also react and protest against their suitors' charges, as well as mocking and accusing them in turn.[5] The songs thus constituted a sort of dialogue at a distance between young men and women, which was otherwise impossible because of their customary segregation in everyday life. Male performances of songs of love and disdain, however, were justified not only by the need to control premarital relationships, but by their function as a model of interaction between men—that is, the singers themselves. Indeed, these performances survived for a long time, after the practice of serenades had disappeared, as an exclusively male form of entertainment endowed with deep social and psychological meanings (Magrini 1986, 1989).

If the old practice of the serenades in the agro-pastoral communities of southern Italy is an indication of the weight of social control that used to be placed on women's sexual behavior, other male musical traditions in the Mediterranean highlight the centrality, for the male community, of values that are quite unrelated to relationships with women. For example, the dominant singing tradition in western Crete is the exclusively male practice of *rizitika* songs, generally reserved for convivial occasions. The meanings of this musical practice have nothing to do with the social control of women's sexuality; instead, they are connected with the establishment of relational networks among patrigroups. It is the *parea*—the group of friends and allies who gather to eat and sing together—that is manifested and celebrated in these collective musical performances. Moreover, the extolling of male friendship in communal singing, as well as the subjects of conflict and death confronted in the songs, reflects the centrality of social and existential themes in the musical construction of male identity in western Crete (Magrini 2000).

The differences between the serenade in Calabria and the rizitika in western Crete thus point to varied interests and priorities, at least in regard to the public expression of men's gender identity. At a more general level, the case studies examined in this volume indicate that the notions of gender conveyed by the musical practices of Mediterranean countries are far more diverse than previously suggested by the classic "honor and shame" anthropological literature. In conclusion, the stereotyped figures of the Mediterranean man and woman proposed by the Oxford school fade out and make room for a more realistic representation of human groups who live femininity and masculinity according to a more nuanced—and ever changing—range of models.

Music and the "Mediterranean"

One of the aims of this volume is to further the research on the human and social aspects of music in Mediterranean countries, that is, of musical repertories that have generally been studied mainly from historical and theoretical/analytical perspectives, or according to the philological and documentary methods of musical folklore. With few exceptions, the music of Mediterranean countries has not traditionally been studied as a medium for understanding men, women, and society, and it seems to me that this constitutes not only a lacuna in ethnomusicological and anthropological literature, but also a lost opportunity.

The choice of Mediterranean musical cultures as a context for the study of the manifold relations between music and gender did not originate from the idea of the Mediterranean as a culturally homogeneous territory, but rather from the decision to research an environment that is extremely complex, thus particularly challenging, from a cultural point of view (see Magrini 1993). Studying the "Mediterranean" does not imply belief that the peoples living in this territory resemble each other, for instance, because of their proximity to the sea:

> Not all peoples living on the shores of the Mediterranean have been
> affected to the same degree by their proximity to it; and even if we
> take groups like the Catalans and the Lebanese, who *have* been
> deeply affected by their relationship to the Mediterranean, this fact
> does not entail that they should resemble each other more than they

resemble their inland neighbors to the north and the east, respectively. For one thing, different human groups can react very differently to similar circumstances; and for another, the fact that people have been deeply influenced by their location does not mean that this has been the only, or even the main, influence on them." (Henderson Stewart 1994, 78)

If Mediterranean peoples do not necessarily resemble each other in this, then, what do they have in common? In my view, what is most important is that they share some six thousand years of history. As they came into contact with one another, as they fought with and dominated each other, they also exchanged goods, studied the artworks and the monuments of neighboring communities, spread religions, and developed the most diverse syncretisms. The depth of information we have on this history is remarkable and significant for our study, first, because it enables us to deal with the issue of time, which has not been raised for many years in anthropological and ethnomusicological studies. Furthermore, the history of the Mediterranean is extraordinarily rich: if among the regions of the world there is one geographical area that can be said to have prefigured the postmodern condition, it would have to be the Mediterranean, where Hellenism developed into what might be called the first historical experience of "globalization." The Mediterranean region thus offers us the possibility of conducting research on music as a human and social phenomenon through a unique historical perspective, as well as of acquiring critical instruments toward a better understanding of the transformations and continuities of its cultures in our own time. We have only to remember, for example, that practices of ritual mourning such as the ones discussed in this volume are documented in the Bible and in the *Iliad*, as well as illustrated in the monuments of ancient Egypt.

Moreover, as a consequence of its complex history, the Mediterranean is a fascinating place where countless diversities converge. It offers us the chance to observe the ways in which diversities may coexist, mix, become familiar with one another, preserve the long historical memory of their relationships, or simply ignore one another.

If we look, for example, at the music of the elites in the Mediterranean territories from the end of the Middle Ages, the region appears to be divided into halves. The north is turned completely in the direction of continental Europe by virtue of the interaction between the music of Mediterranean Europe with that of Flanders, Germany, England, and northern France; the south stretches horizontally from Maghreb to Turkey, with strong continuities with the musical worlds of Iran and India. From this point of view, the Mediterranean constitutes a barrier in musical culture, rather than an element of continuity. At the same time, it should be remembered that the countries bordering the Mediterranean exported cultural goods (including musical instruments) and exerted significant influence upon territories that were extremely far away—a scenario that, even in the musical domain, corroborates Braudel's theory of the "expanded Mediterranean" (1949).

At different musical levels, however, the Mediterranean offers a mosaic of strongly localized practices that are rooted in particular social contexts and carry a deep meaning for the sociocultural identity of each locale. In Mediterranean countries, the number of musical practices with strictly local significance is enormous. It is precisely this cultural fragmentation that yields the proliferation of repertories, vocal performance practices, and instrumental practices. From this perspective, "music is socially meaningful not entirely but largely because it provides means by which people recognise identities and places, and the boundaries which separate them" (Stokes 1994, 5).

Finally, the Mediterranean is also a setting for musical syncretisms that result from unique historical vicissitudes and from the ability of certain social groups to elaborate cultural encounters in original ways. Perhaps in this case it would be appropriate to restrict the meaning of the adjective "Mediterranean" to those musical expressions rooted in cultural interactions between different areas of the geographical Mediterranean—in other words, to those musical phenomena that cross the sea, that have in their DNA a genetic patrimony that unites elements of different cultures, and that carry the historical memory of contacts within the Mediterranean.

I find this perspective particularly interesting because it enables us to study the Mediterranean as a stage of interaction both through history and in the present time. Indeed, contemporary popular music of the Mediterranean often shows a strong tendency toward "contamination" and creation of countless hybrid repertories similar to many other "practices of mixing, syncretic hybridization, blending, fusion, creolization, collaboration across the gulfs" throughout the world (see Feld 1994, 265). Thus, *mizrakhit* music (see Regev 1996), perhaps the most striking example of this trend, blends Hebrew lyrics with Arabic music traditions to produce a cultural fusion that bypasses long-standing ethnic, political, and religious hostilities.

Our concentration on the Mediterranean thus allows us to deal with the opposite phenomena of syncretism and diversification in its music and suggests quite different avenues of study. To focus on diversification, for example, requires an examination of the religious component of the region's musical cultures, because it was in this narrow territory that the three great monotheistic religions developed, often in close relation with one another. Judaism, Islam, and Catholic and Orthodox Christianity are obviously different in many ways. For example, Judaism—as an ethnic religion—does not have the "militant" character of Christianity and Islam, both of which aim at expanding their areas of influence through proselytizing in line with their belief in the redeeming mission of religion. The implied conflict between Christianity and Islam, which according to Braudel (1983) is unavoidable, may rightly be considered as one of the most powerful agents of history in the Mediterranean, starting from the time of the Arab conquest of North Africa and Spain after Muhammad's death in 632 A.D. Since then, the opposition between Christian north and Muslim south has periodically revived in the Mediterranean. The opposition has had, of course, territorial, political, and ideological aspects; however, it has often found its most powerful representation in the confrontation of religious symbols: Cross and Crescent.

In contrast, communities of the Jewish diaspora and Gypsy communities for a long time had no choice but to live under the authority of either Christians or Muslims. The Jews and Roma used religion and culture both to maintain their identity and to mediate with their neighbors. It goes without saying that, in this complex situation (which is becoming more and more complex because of the increasing mobility of peoples within the Mediterranean), the distinctive views of genders belonging to the different religions played an important role in maintaining the identity and cohesion of particular communities, since "religion is eminently concerned with boundedness of social groups and with the anchorage of individuals within them" (Wolf 1984, 3).

One can agree that, in spite of their differences, the Abrahamic religions share a basic discriminatory and sexophobic attitude toward women, who are excluded from power, from the most prestigious religious institutions, and from important forms of worship that have been and still remain the almost exclusive domain of men. Yet each religion has a peculiar view of femininity, a view influenced by many idiosyncratic factors, including "the history of productive and reproductive relations between genders, as reflected in the workings of different indigenous kinship systems" (Kandiyoti 1991, 24). The view of each religious tradition has influenced women's status and lifestyle in Mediterranean countries for centuries, but in the contemporary world, each has had to cope with new concepts about female roles and behaviors that are sometimes provocatively symmetrical to the ones customarily supported.

For instance, Catholic and Orthodox Christianity have traditionally magnified women's reproductive role (e.g., Davis 1984, 24), symbolized by the image of Madonna and Child adorning churches and shrines throughout southern Europe.[6] This notwithstanding, recently both in Spain and Italy,

Catholic countries par excellence, the lowest fertility rates in the world have been recorded,[7] in spite of the Pope's insistent appeals in favor of maternity. According to Fatima Mernissi, Islam views the woman first of all as a sexual being, a seducer endowed with a "rampant disruptive potential" (Mernissi 1975, 13), whose power must be subdued and contained through veiling and seclusion (but see also Fawzi El-Solh and Mabro 1994). However, in Muslim countries where Islamic fundamentalism has not taken hold, such as Turkey or Tunisia, many women have succeeded in attaining a previously unconceivable status as economic and political subjects deeply involved in public life. Finally, the orthodox Jewish view is based on men's and women's asymmetrical religious education (e.g., Siegel 1997), connected to "the androcentric view of Judaism as a text-oriented religion" (Seroussi 1998). The female ideal is thus the young bride—untrained in religious issues—of a man well versed in the Torah, who will be entrusted with the burden of supporting a family and caring for it while her husband, as Israeli women ironically say, "sits and learns." But today women's organizations in Israel fight actively against the monopoly of rabbinic courts on issues of female personal status such as marriage and divorce.[8]

Long before these recent changes in women's status were possible in many Mediterranean countries, music provided occasions for them to challenge the ideals promoted by religious authorities and to assert a different, more empowered female identity.[9] For example, Sephardi women, whose voices were considered "indecent" by rabbis, resorted to singing as a peculiar form of resistance (Seroussi 1998). In chapter 1 of this volume, Caroline Bithell deals with the (now extinct) practice of the Corsican *voceru,* a funeral lament traditionally sung by women that exemplifies mourning's "work of pain" (Magrini 1998). Within the space of religious ritual and "deviant religious practices" (Dubisch 1995; Davis 1984, 18), Catholic and Orthodox women could assert their role as caretakers of the spiritual and physical well-being of their families. In occasions of ritual mourning and song, women could voice their own and their families' sorrows and anxieties publicly, act as mediators between humans and the sacred or magic world, and sometimes exert a form of political influence over men. Women's self-assertion through religious rituals is common also in Islam: for example, the Aissawa of Oujda (Morocco), excluded from orthodox religious practices, still gather weekly to chant religious songs and ask for the intercession of some *marabout,* thus sending "a loud signal to the community at large" that they exist and have "heartfelt grievances" (Langlois 1999).

While these kinds of ritual practices have generally been tolerated by religious authorities, female musical behavior may be stigmatized and provoke strong opposition because of religious beliefs. The case of Egyptian belly dancers studied by Karin van Nieuwkerk in chapter 11 is of particular interest in explaining current Islamist reaction against this dance, widespread in the Maghreb and Middle East. As an emblematic representation of female power to ignite sexual desire, belly dance is condemned by fundamentalists not simply as an immoral activity performed for economic gain, but as an irreligious, even pagan behavior. As the Islamist influence has grown since the 1980s, even in Egypt, which throughout most of the twentieth century was far from a stronghold of fundamentalism, political concerns have moved authorities to pressure dancers toward "repentance" and a "return to Allah." The plight of the dancers shows how "women were and are used in a game that is really more about politico-ideological questions, including relations with the West, than about women per se" (Keddie 1991, 15). Constraints on women's behavior, such as the call to "repentence," veiling, and so forth, show how the Islamist resistance to the Western (Christian and Jewish) political, economic, and cultural offensive has taken up the issue of gender in order to demonstrate control over a critical sphere of social life and to create an emblem of Islamic tradition: as Keddie argues, the fundamentalists "take what they see as the Islamization of women's role as a touchstone of Islam" (17). This attitude is also connected to the strong Islamist opposition to Algerian raï singers, which has led to attacks and even, in the case of Cheb Hasni, among others, to murder. As already mentioned, raï singers, the women in particular, dramatically challenge the Islamic lifestyle and ideal of femininity: according to Virolle, they represent the Eros revolution, which clashes with the Thanatos revolution embodied by fundamentalists.

In conclusion, one sees that female musical behavior in the Mediterranean has been considered across the board, from simply marginal to openly transgressive of religious ideals of femininity. Women's musical behavior, even when challenging religious norms, nevertheless reflected the peculiar concepts of the different faiths about the nature of femininity and women's position and role in society. In this sense, religion, as a crucial component of the cultural and social contexts in which musical life takes shape, must be seen as fundamental to the differentiation of the "Mediterranean."[10]

Let us look at Mediterranean music from an opposite perspective. If the cultural diversification of the Mediterranean is rooted in and well represented by religious diversity, the syncretism of musical styles in these territories manifests itself in various forms. As an example of this phenomenon, I would like to mention a *paneyiri* (an Orthodox religious festival) that I recently attended in a village on Lesbos, a Greek island a few kilometers off the Turkish coast. As it often happens in Greece, this religious festival also included evenings of dancing in which almost the entire community participated. The participants followed the common practice of the *parangelia:* anyone who wants to dance must pay the musicians to play, and then only the payer and guests may perform, while the rest of the party looks on. Thus, the dance becomes a moment of conscious public representation on the part of the performers, who may be groups of friends, groups of family members, or even a single couple. The two nights of paneyiri that I attended were totally dominated by one couple, husband and wife, who carried out a long series of dances, in particular *zebekika* and *karsilamadhes.* These dances, compared to others widespread in Greece—such as the *sirtos* or the *ballos*—are characterized by a relaxed and allusive use of the body. Through their dances— even when only one partner danced while the other looked on—the couple seemed to suggest a harmonious erotic relationship in front of the community, which, in turn, responded in full syntony, expressing admiration, toasting the dancers, or offering them drinks and flowers.

It was obvious to me, even in the midst of this musical event, that it would be extremely complicated to analyze, since it united multiple elements in a single phenomenon: a festive Christian Orthodox religious context; the Greek praxis of public representation through dance by way of the parangelia; and the allusive display of the female body, reminiscent of the eroticism of the dancing body in the Ottoman world. Moreover, the festival included the performance of the zebekiko, originally belonging to Greek-Turkish culture of Anatolia (Holst 1975, 64),[11] later a symbol of the urban rebetiko subculture in Piraeus, Athens, and other Greek cities, and more recently a widely performed individual (mainly male) dance (see also Cowan 1990). The complex array of instruments (*bouzouki,* guitar, keyboard, drums) that also includes a brass wind instrument (the trumpet) is found only in Lesbos and western Macedonia (Dionysopoulos 1997, 31). In sum: the Lesbos festival represents an emblematic case of synthesis of different cultural values from various landing places of the Mare Nostrum. In my view, it stands as a case of real "Mediterraneanness," that is, a coming together of disparate cultural elements in a musical event that is nevertheless perceived as completely coherent with local culture.

Considered from a historical perspective, the syncretic character of this event is not at all surprising. Until the early twentieth century, Lesbos belonged to the cultural area dominated by Smyrna, a city on the coast of Anatolia that, during the last two hundred years of the Ottoman Empire, was the most important economic and cultural Greek center under Turkish rule. Despite its multicultural character, the population of Smyrna was in fact largely Greek (up to 60 percent). It is not by chance that it was at Smyrna and in the surrounding area that the Greek and Turkish musical cultures fused, creating new song genres. This fusion generated a rich repertoire that the Orthodox community—upon being expelled from Turkey after the destruction of the city in 1922, following the failed Greek invasion—took to many Greek locations (including Lesbos), but above all to Piraeus and Athens, giving birth to the repertoire of the *café-aman* and becoming one of the components of the rebetika. The peculiar synthesis of cultural and musical elements realized in Lesbos can thus be understood in terms of the strategic position of this island in the web of relationships developed in and around the Aegean Sea during the centuries of Ottoman rule and afterward. It is also worth stressing that the kind of cultural syncretism represented by Lesbos' paneyiri is particularly interesting because it does not simply characterize a repertoire of commercial music—a genre that is traditionally more open to contamination—but manifests itself in the ceremonial and religious life of the villages.

Syncretic phenomena thus reinforce the impression that "Mediterranean" is far more than a geographical term. The multiple facets of Mediterranean musical realities demonstrate that this body of water has served as the venue of intense cultural interaction between countries in Europe, Asia Minor, and North Africa, a medium for the circulation of ideas and values that cross national and continental boundaries. The goal of studying musical phenomena in their Mediterranean "dimension," then, may prove to be particularly fruitful, as it forces us to be constantly aware in our investigations of the richness of the historical and cultural relations involved in the production of such phenomena.

The aim of this collection is not to provide a survey of gender issues across the whole range of Mediterranean musics, which would exceed the limits of a single volume. Rather, the selection of case studies presented here approaches a series of questions in relation to representative repertories born and developed in European, African, and Asian countries bordering the Mediterranean. Chapters 1–3 form a group, comparing men's and women's roles in the development of various repertories of Mediterranean Europe. Caroline Bithell's "A Man's Game? Engendered Song and the Changing Dynamics of Musical Activity in Corsica" looks first at the Corsican lament tradition and then proceeds to an analysis of the tradition of male polyphony and its more recent developments, which have led to a new practice of female polyphony. In particular, Bithell explores the part played in this process by a younger generation of educated and well-traveled women who have had the opportunity to sidestep the insular association between traditional music and militant nationalism that in the "revival" of the 1970s reinforced the connection between singing and male identity. In chapter 2, "Body and Voice: The Construction of Gender in Flamenco," Joaquina Labajo also deals with both male and female performance in order to reconsider the well-known phenomenon of that Spanish dance. In the performance of this repertory, men and women cooperate in the different roles of singer, dancer, and guitarist, but these roles and their gender associations, Labajo argues, are highly stereotyped and far from the reality of the popular practice of flamenco. Labajo demonstrates that flamenco has a much more complex reality, in particular as regards gender issues, than the one commonly offered to tourists on the stage. In chapter 3, "Those 'Other Women': Dance and Femininity among Prespa Albanians," Jane Sugarman again compares male and female musical behavior. She points out the contrasts in men's and women's ways of dancing according to the tradition of Albanian villages—a world that is now fading away. She juxtaposes this dance style with the urban style of solo dance that has been common in the towns since Ottoman times, from which the çoçek popular among today's Albanian youth derives. The difference between these dance styles is seen as evidence of a deep transformation concerning ideals about gender roles.

The authors of the next two chapters switch attention to the feminine world. In chapter 4, Carol Silverman introduces the Rom women's musical tradition of the Balkans and deals in particular with a popular Macedonian vocalist, Esma Redžepova, whose life story reveals a trajectory of difficulties because of discrimination not only by non-Roma against her because she is a Rom, but also by Roma against her because she is a woman. Goffredo Plastino's argument in chapter 5 concerns three religious folk festivals current in Calabria, a region of southern Italy: the festival of Madonna della Montagna at Polsi, the festival of Saints Cosimo and Damiano at Riace, and the festival of Saint Rocco at Gioiosa Ionica. Plastino takes into consideration the different groups that dominate each festival (thousands of Calabrian worshipers at Polsi, Gypsies at Riace, local youth at Gioiosa Ionica) and surveys the differences characterizing the role of women in the dances of tarantella. It is worth pointing out that the term tarantella indicates not a single dance but a group of dances that are performed in different ways and through which different gender roles can be represented by men and women.

Chapter 6 and 8 are devoted to repertories of pop music. In "The Female Dervish and Other Shady Ladies of the Rebetika," Gail Holst-Warhaft explores the traditionally male milieu of the popular Greek genre of the rebetika by pointing out the role of women as performers, as well as their depiction in certain lyrics. She observes that the women who joined the shady world of the hashish-smoking manges were celebrated for their independence and enjoyed the camaraderie of their musicians, offering us a more nuanced picture of male-female relationships in this segment of Greek society in the first part of the twentieth century. Holst-Warhaft's chapter pairs with Marie Virolle's "Representations and Female Roles in the Raï Song," where again we see that whether women take part in musical performances as singers or as audience, they are able to express transgression from mainstream gender roles and challenge commonly accepted norms of behavior.

Virolle starts to explore questions related to gender in Islamic North Africa, which is the field studied also by Brint Joseph, Deborah Kapchan and Karin van Nieuwkerk. In chapter 9, Joseph's ethnography of Riffian Berber women, based on fieldwork carried out in the 1960s in the Rif Mountains of Morocco, illustrates how in Berber society special occasions and repertories were reserved for the public expression of women's opinions, as we have already seen, for instance, in traditional Corsica. Kapchan also turns to Morocco in chapter 10, but this time the environment is urban. Her topic is the nashaṭ, a state of celebration intricately related to Moroccan ludic events that emerges in moments of accelerated aesthetic stimulation and, as mentioned above, is coded as feminine. Kapchan explores the domain of nashaṭ in Moroccan imagination and the way class determines its enactment and evaluation, thus introducing an issue seldom considered in gender studies. In chapter 11, Nieuwkerk reminds us of the present role of Islamic fundamentalism in Muslim countries. As a result of Islamists' growing influence in Egypt, several forms of art are under attack: in Islamist discourse, being a devout Muslim and a practicing performer is a contradiction, particularly for women. Several famous female performers have repented and are now used in the Islamist struggle against art. Nieuwkerk deconstructs the discourse on the contradictions of believing and performing and compares the Islamist discourse on religion, gender, and art—in which repentant artists play an important role—with views of "non-star" performers in Egypt.

Jewish women are dealt with by Seroussi and Bohlman in chapters 7 and 14. Seroussi offers a unique contribution in detailing female roles in the transmission and documentation of Jewish folk culture. His story of Emily Sene, mentioned above, points out the different agendas of male and female collectors of Sephardi Jewish folksongs in the twentieth century. While male collectors felt deeply the anxiety of cultural dissolution in an era of profound social changes, female collectors, the original carriers and performers of most of this repertoire until the beginning of the century, wrote down the songs for the practical purposes of remembering and passing them along to the next generation, as Emily Sene did, leaving us an impressive collection. In chapter 12, Svanibor Pettan takes us again to the territories of the former Yugoslavia and documents the situation of music in Kosovo before the wars of the

1990s, which undermined all aspects of social life and endangered the continuity of many practices previously observed by the author. Pettan thoroughly explores the division among the different musical repertories according to their association to a specific gender, in particular as regards the Roma. He also goes beyond the male-female duality and examines individuals endowed with "alternative gender designations," pointing out how the gender associated with a particular musical repertory and the performer's gender can be combined in various ways and assume different meanings. Martin Stokes introduces a star of Turkish pop music in chapter 13, "The Tearful Public Sphere: Turkey's 'Sun of Art,' Zeki Müren." While other Mediterranean popular urban genres surveyed in this volume, such as raï and the rebetika, have been associated with subversive forms of gendered identity, Stokes draws on Baudrillard's notion of the hyperreal both to argue for and to consider the limitations of the idea of "hypergender" in the musical performances he considers. Philip Bohlman's conclusion to our discourse occupies a very particular place in the context of this volume. Unlike the other contributions to this collection—case studies dealing with particular repertories in particular places and contexts—Bohlman's final chapter tackles the Mediterranean as a whole. He investigates the notion of "the sacred"—whether conveyed by Christianity, Islam, or Judaism—and how it can be differently gendered through musical activity.

As I have hoped to highlight in this précis, this collection can be read from many perspectives: according to geographic regions, religious affiliation, musical styles, and gender identity. The individual chapters also present a series of internal references that reveal the collaboration that has successfully characterized the relationships of the authors and the teamwork that enabled the realization of this volume, which opens a long awaited debate on the Mediterranean as an area of particular interest for the study of gender, music, and their mutual relationship.

Notes

1. It should not be overlooked, however, that both sex and gender distinctions are in fact culturally and socially constructed: "What is male and what is female will depend upon interpretations of biology that are associated with any culture's mode of life" (Rosaldo and Lamphere 1974, 5; see also Ortner and Whitehead 1981).

2. Anthropologist Annabella Rossi has published the letters written to her in the 1960s

by a tarantist woman (Rossi 1994), and which represent a unique documentation of the tarantists' worldview and identity. Rossi's discussion is, however, more focused on class than gender issues.

3. Here I do not consider the broadside ballad, generally a man's product whose features are in many ways autonomous, also in relation to gender ideologies (cf. Cook 1994).

4. A similar practice has been studied in the Peloponnese by Nadia Seremetakis (1991).

5. I could still record female performances of love songs in northern Calabria in the 1980s (Magrini 1986); women told me also of the practice of responding to male songs of disdain, but did not want to perform their own songs. Such female songs were, however, documented by Raffaele Lombardi Satriani in the early twentieth century (1931–34).

6. According to the Catholic Church, reproduction is the main goal of religious marriage—which is a sacrament and therefore is distinct from civil marriage—and failure to give birth is the main reason for its annulment. However, the role of reproduction in marriage is magnified not only in Christianity. For instance, the Jewish Talmud has made it mandatory to divorce a barren wife (one who has borne no children in a period of ten years).

7. In the late nineties the fertility rate in Italy and Spain has fluctuated around 1.1 or 1.2 percent.

8. See reports of the New Israeli Fund: http://www.nif.org/.

9. The emphasis on motherhood, sexuality, or wifehood that can be glimpsed in the different religious notions of femininity is also interesting in terms of its association with the variable status assigned to women in these different contexts (see Ortner and Whitehead 1981, 23).

10. It must, however, be added that the Abrahamic religions, as Bohlman argues in chapter 14 of this volume, share common practices, such as the pilgrimage, that lead worshipers again and again across the Mediterranean Sea. Although pilgrims may travel along different paths, these routes may nevertheless lead to a common destination, such as Jerusalem, a sacred place for Jewish, Muslim, and Christian believers alike.

11. The karsilamas too was performed in Smyrna in the first decades of the twentieth century. For an example, see the CD *Memory of Smyrna,* series "The Greek Phonograph," Archives 630.

References

Abu-Lughod, Lila. 1993. *Writing Women's Worlds.* Berkeley and Los Angeles: University of California Press.

Bohlman, Philip V. 1998. "The Shechinah, or the Feminine Sacred in the Musics of the Jewish Mediterranean." *Music and Anthropology* 3. http://www.muspe.unibo.it/period/MA/

Boissevain, Jeremy. 1979. "Towards a Social Anthropology of the Mediterranean." *Current Anthropology* 20 (1): 81–93.

Brandes, Stanley. 1987. "Reflections on Honor and Shame in the Mediterranean." In *Honor and Shame and the Unity of the Mediterranean,* edited by David D. Gilmore, 121–34. Washington, D.C.: American Anthropological Association.

Braudel, Fernand. 1949. *La Méditerranée et le monde méditerranéen à l'époque de Philippe II.* Paris: Colin.

————. 1983. *La Méditerranée*. Paris: Flammarion.

Butler, Judith. 1990. *Gender Trouble: Feminism and the Subversion of Identity*. New York: Routledge.

Citron, Marcia. 1993. *Gender and the Musical Canon*. Cambridge: Cambridge University Press.

Cook, Susan C. 1994. "'Cursed Was She': Gender and Power in American Balladry." In *Cecilia Reclaimed: Feminist Perspectives on Gender and Music,* edited by Susan C. Cook and Judy S. Tsou, 202–24. Urbana: University of Illinois Press.

Cook, Susan C., and Judy S. Tsou, eds. 1994. *Cecilia Reclaimed: Feminist Perspectives on Gender and Music*. Urbana: University of Illinois Press.

Corbella, Silvia. 1988. "La terapia di gruppo." In *Trattato di psicoanalisi,* edited by Antonio Alberto Semi, 769–837. Milan: Cortina.

Cowan, Jane K. 1990. *Dance and the Body Politics in Northern Greece*. Princeton: Princeton University Press.

Davis, John. 1984. "The Sexual Division of Labour in the Mediterranean." In *Religion, Power, Protest in Local Communities: The Northern Shore of the Mediterranean,* edited by Eric R. Wolf, 17–50. Berlin: Mouton.

————. 1987. "Family and State in the Mediterranean." In *Honor and Shame and the Unity of the Mediterranean,* edited by David D. Gilmore, 22–34. Washington, D.C.: American Anthropological Association.

————. 1988. "Col divorzio c'è differenza?" In *Onore e storia nelle società mediterranee,* edited by Giovanna Fiume, 47–60. Palermo: La Luna.

————. 1993. "Modelli del Mediterraneo." In *Antropologia della musica e culture mediterranee,* edited by Tullia Magrini, 89–106. Bologna: Il Mulino.

De Martino, Ernesto. 1958. *Morte e pianto rituale: Dal lamento funebre antico al pianto di Maria*. Turin: Boringhieri.

————. 1961. *La terra del rimorso: Contributo a una storia religiosa del sud*. Milan: Il Saggiatore.

Dionysopoulos, Nikos, ed. 1997. *Lesbos aiolis* (booklet and CDs). Heraklion: Crete University Press.

Dubisch, Jill. 1995. *In a Different Place: Pilgrimage, Gender, and Politics at a Greek Island Shrine*. Princeton: Princeton University Press.

Fawzi El-Solh, Camillia, and Judy Mabro. 1994. *Muslim Women's Choices: Religious Belief and Social Reality*. Providence: Berg.

Feld, Steven. 1994. "From Schizofonia to Schismogenesis: On the Discourse and Practices of World Beat." In *Music Grooves,* edited by Charles Keil and Steven Feld, 257–89. Chicago: University of Chicago Press.

Gilmore, David D. 1982. "Anthropology of the Mediterranean Area." *Annual Review of Anthropology* 11:175–205.

————, ed. 1987. *Honor and Shame and the Unity of the Mediterranean*. Washington, D.C.: American Anthropological Association.

Hanna, Judith Lynne. 1988. *Dance, Sex, and Gender: Signs of Identity, Dominance, Defiance, and Desire*. Chicago: University of Chicago Press.

Henderson Stewart, Frank. 1994. *Honor*. Chicago: University of Chicago Press.

Herndon, Marcia, and Susanne Ziegler, eds. 1990. *Music, Gender, and Culture.* Wilhelms-haven: Florian Noetzel Verlag.

Herzfeld, Michael. 1980. "Honour and Shame: Problems in the Comparative Analysis of Moral Systems." *Man,* n.s., 15:339–51.

———. 1987. "'As in your House': Hospitality, Ethnography, and the Stereotype of Medi-terranean Society." In *Honor and Shame and the Unity of the Mediterranean,* edited by David D. Gilmore, 75–89. Washington, D.C.: American Anthropological Association.

Holst, Gail. 1975. *Road to Rembetika.* Athens: Denise Harvey.

Kandiyoti, Deniz. 1991. "Islam and Patriarchy: A Comparative Perspective." In *Women in Middle Eastern History,* edited by Nikki R. Keddie and Beth Baron, 23–42. New Haven: Yale University Press.

Keddie, Nikki R. 1991. Introduction to *Women in Middle Eastern History,* edited by Nikki R. Keddie and Beth Baron, 1–22. New Haven: Yale University Press.

Koskoff, Ellen, ed. 1987. *Women and Music in Cross-Cultural Perspective.* Urbana: University of Illinois Press.

Langlois, Tony. 1999. "Heard but Not Seen: Music among the Aissawa Women of Oujda, Morocco." *Music and Anthropology* 4. http://www.muspe.unibo.it/period/MA/

Lever, Alison. 1986. "Honour as a Red Herring." *Critique of Anthropology* 6 (3): 81–106.

Lombardi Satriani, Raffaele. 1928–40. *Canti popolari calabresi.* Vol. 1. Laureana di Borrello: Tipografia Il Progresso. Vols. 2–6. Naples: De Simone.

Magrini, Tullia. 1986. *Canti d'amore e di sdegno.* Milan: Franco Angeli.

———. 1989. "The Group Dimension in Traditional Music." *World of Music* 31 (2): 52–79.

———. 1994. "The Contribution of Ernesto De Martino to the Anthropology of Italian Music." *Yearbook for Traditional Music* 26:66–80.

———. 1995. "Ballad and Gender: Reconsidering Narrative Singing in Northern Italy." *Ethnomusicology Online* 1. http://research.umbc.edu/eol/

———. 1998. "Women's 'Work of Pain' in Christian Mediterranean Europe." *Music and An-thropology* 3. http://www.muspe.unibo.it/period/MA/

———. 2000. "Music and Manhood in Western Crete: Contemplating Death." *Ethnomusi-cology* 44 (3): 429–59.

———. 2002. *Universi sonori: Introduzione all'etnomusicologia.* Turin: Einaudi.

Magrini, Tullia, ed. 1993. *Antropologia della musica e culture mediterranee.* Bologna: Il Mulino.

Marcus, Michael A. 1987. "'Horsemen are the Fence of the Land': Honor and History among the Ghiyata of Eastern Morocco." In *Honor and Shame and the Unity of the Medi-terranean,* edited by David D. Gilmore, 49–59. Washington, D.C.: American Anthro-pological Association.

Méndez, Lourdes. 1988. *"Cousas de mulleres": Campesinas, poder, y vita cotidiana, Lugo, 1940–1980.* Barcelona: Editorial Anthropos.

Mernissi, Fatima. 1975. *Beyond the Veil: Male-Female Dynamics in a Modern Muslim Society.* New York: Halsted.

Nigra, Costantino. 1974. *Canti popolari del Piemonte.* 1888. Reprint, Turin: Einaudi.

Ortner, Sherry B., and Harriet Whitehead, eds. 1981. *Sexual Meanings: The Cultural Con-struction of Gender and Sexuality.* Cambridge: Cambridge University Press.

Peristiany, John G., ed. 1966. *Honour and Shame: The Values of Mediterranean Societies.* Chicago: University of Chicago Press.

Peristiany, John G., and Julian Pitt-Rivers, eds. 1992. *Honor and Grace in Anthropology.* Cambridge: Cambridge University Press.

Pina Cabral, Joao. 1989. "The Mediterranean as a Category of Regional Comparison: A Critical View." *Current Anthropology* 30 (3): 399–406.

Pitt-Rivers, Julian. 1966. "Honour and Social Status." In *Honour and Shame: The Values of Mediterranean Societies,* edited by John G. Peristiany, 21–77. Chicago: University of Chicago Press.

Regev, Motti. 1996. "*Musica Mizrakhit:* Israeli Rock and National Culture in Israel." *Popular Music* 15 (3): 275–84.

Ricoeur, Paul. 1981. *Hermeneutics and the Human Sciences.* Cambridge: Cambridge University Press.

Rosaldo, Michelle Zimbalist, and Louise Lamphere, eds. 1974. *Woman, Culture, and Society.* Stanford: Stanford University Press.

Rossi, Annabella. 1994. *Lettere da una tarantata.* Lecce: Argo.

Schafer, Roy. 1994. "On Gendered Discourse and Discourse of Gender." In *Psychoanalysis, Feminism, and the Future of Gender,* edited by Joseph H. Smith and Afaf M. Mahfouz, 1–21. Baltimore: Johns Hopkins University Press.

Selenick, Laurence, ed. 1992. *Gender in Performance: The Presentation of Difference in the Performing Arts.* Hanover, N.H.: University Press of New England.

Seremetakis, C. Nadia. 1991. *The Last Word: Women, Death, and Divination in Inner Mani.* Chicago: University of Chicago Press.

Seroussi, Edwin. 1998. "De-gendering Jewish music: The Survival of the Judeo-Spanish Folk Song Revisited." *Music and Anthropology* 3. http://www.muspe.unibo.it/period/MA/

Siegel, Rachel Josefowitz. 1997. "'I Don't Know Enough': Jewish Women's Learned Ignorance." *Women in Judaism: A Multidisciplinary Journal* 1 (1). http://www.utoronto.ca/wjudaism/

Stokes, Martin. 1994. "Introduction: Ethnicity, Identity, and Music." In *Ethnicity, Identity, and Music: The Musical Construction of Place,* edited by Martin Stokes, 1–29. Oxford: Berg.

Wolf, Eric R., ed. 1984. *Religion, Power, Protest in Local Communities: The Northern Shore of the Mediterranean.* Berlin: Mouton.

1

A Man's Game? Engendered Song and the Changing Dynamics of Musical Activity in Corsica

Caroline Bithell

In the words of the Corsican singer Patrizia Gattaceca, "to sing polyphony is to affirm oneself as a Corsican; it is to say 'I exist.'" [1] Certainly the human voice has traditionally served as the privileged instrument of musical expression on the island, with the traditional polyphonic singing styles occupying pride of place. Only in recent years, however, have women been free to affirm themselves in this way. In former times, to sing in public and certainly to sing polyphony was—with rare exceptions—strictly a male prerogative. In this chapter, I aim to offer an insight into the way in which questions of gender have articulated both with song traditions and with singing activity, and to explore aspects of the changing dynamics between the sexes in relation to singing. I begin with a brief discussion of the traditional "gendering of the field" before going on to consider the different ways in which male and female forms of musical expression were affected during the period of social change and cultural decline that the island entered into in the early decades of the twentieth century. I then move on to a more detailed exploration of the musical revival that has been gathering pace since the 1970s, focusing in particular on the new possibilities and identities that have most recently presented themselves to women singers.

Music and Gender in Traditional Corsican Society

In traditional Corsican society as it existed at least up until the time of the First World War and to some extent through into the second half of the twentieth century, male and female singing practices were clearly differentiated with respect to genre, social context, function, and motivation. As far as the range of genres customarily sung by the different sexes is concerned, a glance at table 1 will immediately show that the vocal field has traditionally been heavily weighted in favor of men. While women's repertory has consisted mainly of laments and lullabies, men's repertory has featured polyphonic songs (*paghjelle, terzetti,* and *madrigali*), improvised debate (*chjam' è rispondi*), improvised "songs of circumstance" (*currente*), threshing songs (*tribbiere*), muleteers' songs, balladlike bandits' laments, laments for animals, serenades, and more recently, soldiers' songs and election songs (although the latter might also be composed and sung by women). Polyvocal settings of the Latin mass and other liturgical and paraliturgical material (particularly in connection with Holy Week) are also sung by all-male *équipes*.

Most striking is the fact that polyphonic singing has traditionally been absent from women's musical practices, although in the case of paghjella singing there have been notable, if rare, exceptions. Félix Quilici's extensive collection of field recordings, for example, includes a recording of paghjella singing made in the village of Pié D'Orezza in the Castagniccia in the early 1960s that features the voice of the wife of one of the male singers. In another case that was brought to my attention, three sisters living in a village in the Giussani had been taught to sing "in polyphony" by their father, who had no sons to whom he could pass on his repertory. Such cases of women actually singing polyphony should, however, be seen to represent circumstantial rather than customary practice. (Men, when asked why women do not sing polyphony, might assert that it is simply "too difficult" for them, an explanation I have also encountered in neighboring Sardinia; otherwise the explanation given is simply that "it is not part of our tradition").[2]

The opposition monody/polyphony, together with other aspects of the contrasting singing styles of women and men, for example, timbre and tessitura, can be seen to reflect to some extent other familiar oppositions such as indoor/outdoor or private/public.[3] In general terms, men's songs have traditionally belonged to, and have been organized in accordance with, a more

Table 1 Gender Allocations of Traditional Corsican Song Genres

Song Type	Singers	
	Men	Women
Monophonic		
Chjam' è rispondi	•	(•)
Currente	•	(•)
Miscellaneous improvisations	•	•
Voceri		•
Bandits' laments	•	
Laments for animals	•	
Lullabies		•
Tribbiere	•	
Muleteers' songs	•	
Serenades	•	
Satirical songs	•	
Election songs	•	•
Polyphonic		
Paghjelle	•	
Terzetti	•	
Madrigali	•	
Masses and liturgical songs	•	
Paraliturgical songs	•	(•)

Note: Parentheses indicate that the genre is sung only occasionally.

outdoor, communal lifestyle, while women's musical activity was historically, as in many other parts of the Mediterranean, largely centered on the more intimate world of home and family, where it was also closely linked to women's role as guardians of rites of passage, most notably birth and death. This is not to suggest, however, that past generations of women did not enjoy any kind of collective activity, musical or otherwise. As Salini (1996, 65) has remarked, it is difficult to imagine that, in a society that drew all of its resources from the earth, women would have been excluded from any kind of work outside the home—even if Carrington does speak of some women, especially in the south, as being "virtual prisoners in their homes," being allowed out only in order to attend funerals (1984, 43). The abbé Galletti (1863) reports that women would practice lament singing during the hours spent on communal tasks such as picking olives or chestnuts. They might also sing when gathered together at the village washhouse. Nor is it the case that monodic songs were heard only in the home. They were also sung in company, for example, at *veillées* or *veghje* (informal social gatherings of friends and neighbors, featuring singing and storytelling) or at the fairs (although in the latter case they would almost invariably be sung by men, female singers in such public places again being the exception).[4] The point to be made about the contrast between collective and individual, communal and domestic, polyphony and monody, male and female is perhaps a more subtle one and concerns the circumstances and assumptions that generate the songs and determine the form they take. Essentially, the prototypical male genres, namely, the paghjella and the chjam'è rispondi, to which I will return below, have an inbuilt need for other singers: they cannot simply be sung solo.

The scope of this chapter does not allow for a discussion of all song genres or for a detailed musical analysis of individual genres.[5] In the following sections, I take as my focus the paghjella and the chjam'è rispondi as the most representative examples of male genres—both of which have survived in the living tradition into the present day—and the lament, or *voceru,* as the representative female genre (with brief reference also to the lullaby). In association with these selected singing traditions, a number of observations can usefully be made with the aim of contributing to a deeper understanding of male and female singing practices and drawing attention to the sometimes surprising insights that they can offer into the question of gender identity and the balance of power between the sexes in traditional Corsican society.

Men's Songs: The Paghjella and the Chjam' è Rispondi

The *paghjella* (pl. *paghjelle*) is sung by three voices, *secunda, bassu,* and *terza,* and can be defined as a musical rendition of a series of octosyllabic couplets in a characteristic polyphonic arrangement, three of these couplets, each sung to the "same" musical *versu* (pl. *versi*), making one complete stanza, and each village typically having its own versu or variant of a basic musical prototype. The style might best be described as "drawn-out," with overlapping melismatic meanderings in the two upper voices alternating with long sustained notes. While each of the three voices has its own specific timbre and role within the overall structure of the piece, making a vital and individual contribution to the multidimensional polyphonic texture, the interaction is essentially democratic, with the individuality of each singer being subsumed in the service of the collective endeavor. Laade (1990) notes that the paghjella was in former times the favorite musical form of the shepherds, sung on occasions when they met and spent a night together in the mountains. It belongs to the realm of conviviality, hospitality, and relaxation: meals and family gatherings, evenings around the fire or at the bar, village patron saints' day celebrations, sheep-shearing parties, transhumance, hunting parties, and the mountain fairs.

Some stanzas that appear as paghjelle are in fact extracts from longer well-known monodic songs such as laments, lullabies, and serenades: essentially, any text in the traditional form of the octosyllabic six-line stanza can be resung "in paghjella." In this way, texts pass from one singing context to another—and significantly from women's repertory to men's repertory—and many stanzas from monodic songs that are no longer heard in the living tradition have been preserved in the paghjella repertory. An interesting parallel can be drawn here with the process described by Magrini (see the introduction to this volume and Magrini 1995) with respect to the ballad tradition in northern Italy, whereby female ballad singing with its educative and moral function has died out as women's lives and identities have changed, while polyphonic arrangements of the ballads as sung by men (often in a fragmentary form) have exhibited a greater tenacity, which can be explained by the fact that the context in which they are sung and the function they serve still have a relevant part to play in men's lives. In this connection it is also interesting to note that the secunda line of many paghjella versi is remarkably similar to the monostrophic melody type of what appears to be the oldest layer of women's laments, a curiosity that has been remarked upon in the literature but not as yet satisfactorily explained.

While in the past a paghjella might have consisted of several stanzas, so retaining the original narrative structure of the text, it is sometimes only a single stanza that "becomes" a paghjella.[6] This stanza then assumes a microcosmic quality, serving as a type of "sound bite" in the form of a self-contained statement, often of a proverbial or formulaic nature. As one singer of my own acquaintance commented, "All one needs for a paghjella is thirty seconds of good poetry out of several hours of improvisation." At one level, any stanza will serve the purpose as long as the text "fits well in the mouth" or "is easily singable." At times it would appear that the words are appreciated more as sound units than as lexical units, to the extent that the text can be seen almost as a pretext—an impression that is certainly reinforced by the way in which the text is treated in performance, with breaths being taken in the middle of words, voice entries occurring in the middle of words, words being broken across the caesura, and the bassu on occasion intoning the vowel sounds alone, resulting in an almost calculated obfuscation of the lexical sense. This circumstance would again appear consonant with Magrini's observations concerning the way in which in men's polyphonic ballad renditions the emphasis is on sonic interaction and the "affirmation of the members' ability to merge into a collective action," rather than on transmitting any message explicitly embodied in the text.

Paghjella singers typically adopt a stance similar to that found among singers of polyphony in other parts of the Mediterranean, forming a tight horseshoelike cluster and raising one hand to the ear, while often leaning casually on one another's shoulders. The secunda singer (who launches the song) might appear to withdraw into his own interior world, his eyes closed or glazed over, while the bassu and terza singers focus intensely on his face, following his every movement. Essential to the spirit of the paghjella is an element of spontaneity: the song is born of an inner impulse and is created anew at each performance as the singers interweave their voices, adapting one to another as their musical lines unfold. Equally vital is a sense of complicity: musical harmony can only be successfully achieved if the singers are in a state of spiritual harmony. Polyphonic singing is often described by singers within the culture as *un état* (a state), and indeed the intensity of the experience appears to have an almost mesmerizing effect on the participants. The overall impression is that the singers are singing into one another, penetrating one another's song, creating a sense of intimacy and spiritual bonding, which is often further intensified by the effects of alcohol. Even when the singing is at its most animated and vigorous, there is no sense of competition between the singers within the équipe: any imbalance would be contrary to the spirit of the paghjella and would threaten its successful execution.

Sessions of paghjella singing, once under way, can continue for hours into the night. Once men are seduced by the spirit of the song, it is as if they enter a time-warp, which leaves them oblivious to the rest of the world and in particular uncomprehending of the need to return to the demands of an orderly domestic routine that might ever more urgently beckon any wives present. For the latter, paghjella singing counts as part of "men's business" and, for some at least, as a manifestation of typically incorrigible male behavior. Indeed, the risk of female disapproval might be one of the reasons why men sometimes appear to be inhibited about singing paghjelle in mixed company, preferring to wait until the women have gone home or are preoccupied with domestic tasks. (I am reminded here of an occasion in Malta when I met a singer who was overjoyed to learn that I, like himself, had been at the Imnarja festival—an annual event attracting singers from all over the island—the previous evening. In response to my prompt "And did you sing?" he surprised me by replying, "Me? Sing? But I was with my wife! I had to behave!")

Such singing can, then, be seen primarily as a celebration of male togetherness, the sense of intimacy that is both cause and effect being underlined by the body language. It would be possible to see here aspects of the "homo-erotic" undertones that can be read into certain aspects of Mediterranean gender relations and are addressed in some of the contributions to *Honor and Shame and the Unity of the Mediterranean* (Gilmore 1987, 10), albeit with respect in this case to male rivalry as opposed to male bonding. One of my Corsican informants did in fact comment, somewhat mischievously, that singing paghjelle was the only time in Corsica when men made love together; another similarly remarked that it was the only time when men danced together. This sense of intimacy would again explain in part why men are sometimes reluctant to "perform" in public, often preferring, even at fairs and festivals, to wait until late in the evening when the crowds have gone home and they can create their own more private and intimate space. It is also one of the reasons why some of the present generation of men feel uncomfortable about singing paghjelle on stage.[7] I hasten to stress, however, that despite this aura of liminality surrounding paghjella singers, which might be seen to equate to the "gender-identity ambivalence" discussed by Gilmore (1987, 12)—although again Gilmore uses the notion in a rather different context, that of an often "vehement abhorrence" and repudiation of feminine traits—it would, of course, be incorrect, and, as Gilmore points out, impertinent and offensive, to gloss "homoerotic" as latently homosexual, just as it would be culturally naive and shortsighted to interpret the interaction of male singers in terms of "feminine" behavior. Giacomo-Marcellesi, with specific reference to the Corsican paghjella, speaks rather of "an erotico-musical function connected with the pleasure of singing, of singing with others, of singing in harmony with nature" (1982, 27). It is nonetheless noteworthy that much of the imagery encountered in connection with paghjella singing takes a feminine form. The circle or horseshoe formed by the singers—popularly known as a *conca* (conch [shell])—is, for example, often referred to as being womblike: the circle gives birth to the song.

Despite my earlier observations regarding the way in which the text often appears to serve only as a pretext in paghjella singing, it does nevertheless appear to be significant that the greater proportion of texts sung as paghjelle are in the voice of the first person. There is a high incidence of texts that take the form of a message or letter to a loved one: the speaker might be a shepherd away with his flocks, a conscript, or a prisoner in foreign lands. The texts themselves often begin with a reminder that the poet is illiterate, as in the line "S'eiu sapissi leghje è scrive" [If I knew how to read and write], or with a reference to a letter that the speaker would like to send. Songs of frustrated love can also be addressed directly to the loved one, for example: "Sè tù sapissi u male / Chè tù faci à u mo core" [If only you knew the harm / That you are doing to my heart]. Such texts, with their roots in the world of orality and improvisation, are closer to spontaneous personal utterances than to formally constructed poetry. At the same time, the speaker's situation or dilemma is immortalized as his verse passes into the common repertory where the emotions expressed appeal to a sense of shared experience or sympathetic identification. The fact that these songs are often sung away from the company of women (in the village bar or up on the mountain) would seem to be significant. Sentiments that cannot, perhaps, for reasons of distance or decorum be addressed directly to their object are instead expressed in the company of other men who offer harmonic as well as moral support.

Chjam' è rispondi (lit., "call and response") is the term used to refer to an exchange, or more often a type of debate or verbal joust, between two or more poets who improvise stanzas taking the traditional format of six octosyllabic lines, sung to variants of a single melodic model.[8] The melody itself, which is also used for many other genres of monodic song, both improvised and composed, can be seen as one of the prototypical male melodies: it is often referred to as *u versu currente*.

Chjam' è rispondi is customarily sung at the fairs, during saints' days festivities, or among friends gathered to share in pastoral tasks such as sheep-shearing (see plate 1). More spontaneous exchanges might also take place in bars or over the supper table. In the case of a semiformal gathering of poets (as opposed to a chance encounter), a session of chjam' è rispondi will typically begin with all manner of courtesies: a welcome to those present, an acknowledgment of the hosts and an appreciation of their hospitality, an elaboration on any special reason for the gathering, expressions of homage to the great poets of the past and to others not present on this occasion, and invocations to the muse to inspire the poets and thereby to facilitate a harmonious and successful evening. After these preliminaries, which serve in part for the poets to "sing themselves in," a topic gradually defines itself and the debate proper gets under way. If the atmosphere and general conditions are propitious—if the poets are in a good mood, extraneous noise is not causing too much interference, the temperature is pleasant, there is good food and drink—the exchange is likely to continue well into the night, if not until dawn.

The chjam' è rispondi provides a platform for challenge as well as praise, and a witty retort, often reaching a triumphant climax with an ingenious pun, is highly prized. As the poets warm to their subject, they will often begin to gibe their opponents, casting aspersions on aspects of their general behavior and integrity of character as well as on their present argument and making ever more outrageous jokes at their expense. While such teasing is often taken further in this context than it could be in a normal verbal encounter, allowing for a healthy venting of grudges that might otherwise accumulate to the point of becoming damaging, the ritualized framework ultimately offers a safety net should the exchange start to become too offensive or malicious, and the group as a whole ensures that appropriate etiquette is observed.

As in the case of the paghjella, there have always been exceptions to the norm of male exclusivity, with one or two women in each generation being renowned as improvisers. In my own research, I have encountered two women singers who readily join in chjam' è rispondi sessions with the men, although one complains that she is frustrated by what she perceives as the men's frequent refusal to take her seriously in terms of the debate itself. Part of the problem is that a female presence can be seen to interfere with the element of male bonding inherent in the practice, which is expressed in part through the recurrence of the theme of "women," in itself an expression of a distinctly male ethos and one to which it is obviously difficult for a woman to contribute.[9]

While the chjam' è rispondi and the paghjella differ in a number of essential ways—one is monodic, syllabic, excessively logogenic, and demands the singers' acute concentration, while the other is polyphonic, melismatic, excessively ecstatic, and induces in the singers an almost hypnotic state—they are commonly interwoven in the same singing session or event and are, on occasion, sung by the same people (although the chjam' è rispondi requires an advanced degree of linguistic skill and tends to appeal to a different temperament). In both cases, the emphasis is on process rather than product (a paghjella is "made" rather than "sung"), on participation and communication between the singers rather than performance. The circular or inward-looking formation adopted by the singers in each case, together with their body language, serves to emphasize the sense of togetherness. Attention is strictly focused on the others in the circle, all of whom are participants. Any listeners or audience are firmly located—both physically and in terms of the singers' awareness—outside the group: only rarely will a singer make any physical reference to the wider circle of onlookers. Both of these genres, in their different ways, appear to be born from a natural urge to communicate through song and can be seen to fulfill the function of maintaining peaceful relations among the men, each serving to release tension in different but complementary ways. Together, they offer a view of the Corsican male that is the antithesis of both the stereotypical machismo of the bandit and outlaw with which Corsican men have been unfairly burdened for centuries and the more recent ideal of manhood embodied in the new chansons with their militant political associations.

Women's Songs: Laments and Lullabies

It is in the practice of extemporizing laments for the dead that women's improvisational skills have conventionally been deployed to greatest effect. These laments, known as *voceri* (sing. *voceru*), constitute one of the most substantial categories of traditional Corsican song, as reflected in the inordinate amount of space they fill in the numerous song collections published in the nineteenth and early twentieth centuries.[10] The majority of these anthologies feature the texts only. Many of the "songs" have, however, lived on in memory even though the ritual itself is no longer found in the living tradition, while others can be found in collections of recordings made in the middle decades of the twentieth century (although these are invariably cases of the lament being resung "after the event": I do not know of any recordings made in situ).

The lament tradition in Corsica, which clearly has its roots in ancient pre-Christian practices and has proved itself to be remarkably tenacious despite being severely at odds with Christian morals and ideals of appropriate behavior, shares many features with lament rituals found in other parts of the Mediterranean. Lamenting would take place at the home of the deceased, prior to the funeral: the body could not be removed from the house until the voceru had been sung. Sometimes the singing would be resumed as the funeral procession wound its way through the village to the church. The singer could be either a relative or close friend of the deceased or a professional *voceratrice,* a woman set apart in her village by her gift for this type of improvisation.

Within the wider category of voceri, a distinction is generally made between laments for those who died of natural causes and laments for those who died at the hand of violence. The voceru for a victim of violent death belongs to the world of the vendetta, which dominated village life in Corsica until the 1930s.[11] In stark contrast to the chjam' è rispondi with its excess of courtesy, the text of such a voceru is full of hatred: it is designed not to make peace but to inspire war. The singer heaps terrible threats and curses upon the family of the aggressor and in some cases positively goads the men of her own family to action, mocking them for their lack of courage and their hesitation in taking up arms and embracing their duty to avenge the death.[12] Thus while women might traditionally have occupied a less public world than men—witness the stereotype of the Mediterranean woman—these lament texts reveal that in terms of political influence they were far from silent or passive. The men, for their part, in rising to the challenge, were to some extent defending their individual honor against the women of the family to whose scorn they would otherwise be subjected. Indeed, it could be argued that the knowledge that the vendetta, with its demand for immediate and decisive retribution, might strike at any moment rendered a man's honor and masculinity particularly fragile. The fact that the vendetta concerns the honor of the whole extended family, past and present, and that any existing credit in the honor stakes might be completely annulled by failure to rise to a new challenge, identifies it as the area in which male honor is most under threat.[13] If we apply the proverbial honor and shame model to the vendetta, it reveals a dynamic that is far more complex than the assumptions underlying the original Peristiany volume (1966), where shame is essentially seen to appertain to women and honor to men and where the primary male concern is to safeguard the honor of the family as embodied in the behavior and reputation (in essentially sexual terms) of its female members. In the vendetta, the tables are almost turned as women show themselves to be as much concerned with honor as their menfolk and where it is the men who are most vulnerable to being shamed.

Lament singing in this context—where the lament is perhaps better viewed as incantation rather than song—clearly represents more than an expression of suffering or even a mechanism by which women are able to establish an acceptable public voice (Magrini 1998). In some cases, the singer would go so far as to name the relative who has been chosen to carry out the vendetta, thereby condemning him—with what might be seen as tantamount to a curse—to the life of an outlaw and ultimately to the same fate as the kinsman who is being mourned. The voceratrice in this case assumes a quasi-mediumistic role, which Carrington sees, together with the trancelike or "possessed" state into which the singer would often enter, as sharing something of the occult nature of the Corsican *mazzeri,* the "night-hunters of souls" who had the power to foresee death. Carrington refers to a voceratrice she herself encountered who described her profession in terms of "speaking for the dead" (Carrington 1984, 238).[14] Corsican women of my own acquaintance also referred in more general terms to women's proximity to "the boundaries between the worlds" in the context of their function as singers.

Lullabies share this mediumistic quality insofar as they can be seen to function as a type of charm aimed at ensuring the child's future prosperity. In the text, the mother or grandmother typically gives expression to her wishes for the child's future, envisaging a favorable marriage and a happy and prosperous life. Other (fortunately rarer) examples exhibit a darker character: in the "Nanna di Palleca," for example, a grandmother recounts the history of the child's ancestors who have either fallen victim to the vendetta or been lost in the rebellion against the French and looks forward to the child growing up to bear arms and to be a proud bandit (cf. De Zerbi and Raffaelli

1993, 64). Male children might thus be seen to be conditioned even from the cradle for the necessary enactment of honor, while the prospect of taking up arms as a bandit and taking to the maquis might be as much a rite of passage as marriage. Meanwhile, the proverbially symbiotic relationship between sons and mothers characteristic of the Mediterranean region as a whole and reinforced by Catholicism is given added pathos by the need for every mother to be prepared to sacrifice her son.

In my discussion so far, I have attempted to show how the different examples of male and female singing events under consideration (even if they are by no means the only types of singing in which Corsican men and women have traditionally engaged) offer insights into the functions of the "songs," and the motivations of those who sing them, which are in many ways startlingly at odds with the stereotypical images of macho, hot-blooded men and silent, passive, and disempowered women. Men have been described as singing paghjelle for the pure joy of singing together. Auerbach's discussion of "the free exercise of musical joy" in the Epirot villages of northwest Greece as "essentially a male privilege" while women's musical activity is prescribed by their relation to mourning and is limited, as they progress through their lives, ever more to an expression of grief (Auerbach 1987, 26) can be seen to be applicable to some extent to the Corsican scenario. Certainly the types of male singing discussed here function essentially as an expression of, or means of cultivating, personal well-being and collective harmony, playing an important role in terms of male "bonding." Through singing, and in particular paghjella singing, men both nurture and exploit a sense of togetherness, the interaction being prolonged for as long as possible in sessions that often continue well into the night. The collective nature of the enterprise is underlined by the fact that these encounters are dependent for their success on the amenability and commitment of each individual member of the group: everyone has to be in the right mood, open to the muse and integrated into the overall flow of both physical and emotional energy. By contrast, the voceru is often sited in a climate of intense and bitter conflict, replete with passionate outbursts of hatred and recrimination, where the "song" serves as a direct inspiration to action, affecting the course of individual lives in the most profound way. Through the deployment of what might be described as their lamenting obligations, women are thus able to play an active and indeed decisive part in the direction of local politics. It is, then, not difficult to imagine that women in traditional Corsican society often held the strings of the "real life" of the community (Gilmore 1987, 195) while their menfolk were off up the mountain singing paghjelle. Moreover, "in the spiritual sphere," in Carrington's analysis, women "rule without question," and it is on account of their privileged position in terms of their access to the other world that what Carrington terms "the autocratic behaviour of men to women" can be seen to conceal, not far beneath the surface, "a deep, instinctive distrust . . . akin to fear" (1984, 43–44).

This excursion into prototypical forms of male and female musical expression has of necessity been selective, but I hope it has served to set the genres discussed in their wider cultural and social contexts and in particular to throw light on differences in pretext that might not have been apparent from an initial glance that restricted itself to the musical opus alone. The question of pretext will continue to be significant in the next part of my discussion, where I examine the fate of these and other musical practices following the dissolution of the "old" way of life that engendered them.

Changes in Musical Practice in Twentieth-Century Corsica

From the earliest years of the twentieth century but even more particularly during the war and postwar years, Corsica was, despite its relative isolation, by no means spared the onslaught of the forces of "progress," which for societies at the periphery have been as likely to bring stagnation as they have regeneration. The island entered into a state of both economic and cultural decline from which it did not begin to emerge until the 1960s. The story is a familiar one of the depopulation of rural areas associated with rapid urbanization and increasing emigration, accompanied by profound changes in both lifestyle and outlook. Added to this, in Corsica's case, was a process of ever more systematic integration into the French state (Corsica having "belonged" to France since 1769), with the enforcement of compulsory full-time education in particular posing an increased threat to the Corsican language.

I do not propose to offer here a detailed exposition of the fate of traditional music in general during this period. Suffice it to say that, as the old way of life was abandoned, many types of song were deprived of their function and context and so shared the fate of the rituals and practices they had once accompanied. Within the broader picture, however, there are a range of diverse factors and details that each in their own way had a profound effect on musical practice, some of which merit elaboration. It will also be pertinent to refer specifically to the type of circumstance that altered the dynamics of customary musical practice from the point of view of the division of labor and balance of power between the sexes.

That the advent of television was hugely detrimental in ousting domestic "fireside" music making and storytelling and at the same time undermining "community" in favor of a "stay-at-home" culture is self-evident, although Carrington also reports that "wives rejoice in television as a means of keeping their husbands out of the bars" (1984, 285). Many of my Corsican informants, however, were equally quick to point to the impact of the car. One singer described to me how, in her childhood, people were always walking from one village to the next and the men would sing all the way. In another village, the women spoke of how the men would set off at night to sing serenades in a neighboring village and could be heard singing all the way along the road, forming what one speaker referred to as "a path of voices." The only occasion now when people make their way singing from one village to another is as part of the Holy Week processions, which serve in part to retrace the boundaries of the local community and to rekindle the once vital connections between neighboring settlements.

The toll of the two world wars (and later wars in the French colonies) on the male population of the island cannot be underestimated. The extent of the damage is reflected in the alarming number of polyphonic masses—unique to individual villages and traditionally sung by small exclusive male ensembles—that fell into disuse as a result of the loss of one or more of the singers, so bringing to an abrupt end a chain of oral transmission unbroken for generations. In some places, priests were quick to seize their opportunity to install women's choirs (for the most part singing modern French canticles), which represented less of a threat to their own authority than the independently minded male ensembles, who understandably had held their own ancestral traditions in greater esteem than the newfangled fashions brought over from the continent by "foreign" clerics. This trend also coincided to some extent with the "reforms" following Vatican II.

Some traditional genres continued to find expression through the now somewhat maligned folkloric groups, which thrived particularly in the 1950s and 1960s, with their lyrically interpreted, predictably harmonized, and instrumentally accompanied versions of popular songs. It is significant to note in retrospect that membership of these ensembles was typically open to both men and women. It is also pertinent to my later discussion of the rather different ethos of the groups that were to proliferate in the 1970s to note that A Mannella—usually referred to in a class apart as the most authentic of the folkloric singing ensembles, since they drew the greater part of their repertory from their own rural village and reproduced it in traditional, unadulterated style—gave as one of their reasons for also including newly composed, "lighter" chansons in their program the need to find material for the women members to sing. The laments that were their traditional domain were understandably deemed inappropriate as entertainment for Continental audiences.

Opera singers and the so-called *chanteurs de charme,* epitomized in the figure of Tino Rossi, also played a part in the continued "airing" and dissemination of the various types of monodic song, but at the same time they contributed to a significant transformation at the level of style and interpretation. The popular rendition of certain well-known examples of voceri, for example, does seem to have been heavily influenced by the style of the opera singers who immortalized them in early recordings. De Zerbi, in her collection *Cantu nustrale,* comments on the voceru "O Mattè di la surella": "The melody has become theatrical and emphatic due to the fact that it has been sung by opera singers. But other versions of the song also exist which are simpler and closer to the Corsican tradition" (De Zerbi 1981, 320). Women in particular, with lives focused more on the indoor world of the home, had ample opportunity to listen to these records, whose style they would naturally imitate when they themselves came to sing for a field recording, a circumstance noted by Laade during his fieldwork in the late 1950s. The records found their way into homes throughout the island, to the extent that, even in the remoter areas celebrated in the literature as the last strongholds of authentic Corsican culture, the new chansons and the lyrical singing style of the popular artists of the day were preferred by many people to their own village songs and in particular to the rural polyphonic style, which tended now to be shunned as "primitive" or "uncouth" (see Bithell, forthcoming). People were in general also less inclined to improvise or compose their own songs but were happy instead to reproduce the material that appeared on the early commercial discs. At the same time, even in the late 1950s, gender divisions in terms of repertory were beginning to break down as men adopted into their monodic repertories some of the laments and lullabies that had been popularized via records and journals and now increasingly functioned as "folk songs" (Laade 1981, 1:80). The male monopoly on singing in company was also to begin to give way. Laade (1981, 1:94) reports that, when he returned to the island in the early 1970s, he found that women were more easily persuaded to sing than they had been in the 1950s: singing was no longer seen as a male prerogative.

The paghjella and the chjam' è rispondi, being unsuitable material for inclusion in commercial recordings featuring solo artists and therefore escaping the process of popularization that threatened to emasculate other traditional genres, remained to all intents and purposes untainted by the changing fashions, even if they were seriously eclipsed by the more popular commercial repertory. Though their practice has undoubtedly declined, it is these two forms—the twin pièces de résistance of male musical expression—that can still be found in their natural habitat with their primary functions intact. I propose now to tease out at greater length the various circumstantial threads that might be seen to contribute to the continued tenacity of these genres— an exploration that will take me into geographical, psychological, and political, as well as social realms.[15]

At a broad level, the decline was particularly felt in the realm of women's songs, which, being more often tied to particular events or rituals, were affected either by the demise of the ritual practice itself or by a more general change in lifestyle and ethos. While the same is true of some of the men's song types, for example, the tribbiera (traditionally sung while threshing with oxen), the paghjella and the chjam' è rispondi have always been less restricted in terms of requiring a specific practical pretext for their performance: they do not need a death or a crop ripe for harvesting. Rather, as we have seen, they are associated with contexts of conviviality, and eating, drinking, and making merry have always been less subject to the vagaries of fashion. It is also significant that, while they might on occasion be sung around the family table, these songs are traditionally situated in men's territory, whether in the village bar or up in the mountains where they have their flocks. Their survival can therefore, I propose, further be attributed to the fact that aspects of the old way of life still continue in the men's world, particularly, if not only, in rural areas. In many cases, men have deliberately kept alive the contexts for singing that have always been important to them, choosing, for example, to shear by hand because bringing in a machine to do the work neither offers the same excuse to invite one's friends nor makes for an atmosphere that is conducive to singing.

To talk simply in terms of lifestyle at a tangible or practical level, however, is not enough. It would seem that women's mentality has developed differently from that of men: they have embraced modernity with perhaps fewer regrets, being only too glad to be relieved of both the relentless domestic drudgery and the oppressive moral codes that had previously dominated (if not blighted) women's lives.[16] Thus, while it is true that women and men have always inhabited different geographical planes or loci (in terms of indoor versus outdoor, village versus forest or mountain), it might be proposed that, from a certain perspective, they now also inhabit different temporal planes. The men, when they take off into the maquis to hunt, are metaphorically returning to the past, to an outdoor world that has suffered neglect but has essentially changed very little. The mountain fairs can similarly be seen as doors into a past age offering a refuge for practices and behavior that might otherwise no longer have a place in the modern world. It is the women with their continuing (if less grueling) domestic responsibilities who inhabit the world of modern conveniences, and women's traditional songs clearly do not belong in an "American" fitted kitchen in the way that men's songs still do belong in a clearing in the forest.

In the case of the paghjella, political dynamics also came into play. With the renewed impetus given to the move toward cultural revival by the nationalist movement in the 1970s, the old traditional songs came to play a vital part in the reclamation and statement of an unequivocally Corsican identity, and the paghjella in particular went through a process of "coming out" as it was adopted by the younger generation as a public statement of solidarity (see Bithell 1996 and forthcoming), to the point where, in Salini's words, "polyphony became synonymous with Corsican" (Salini 1996, 191). The rate at which the genre continued to spread, following this initial reappropriation, among singers who had grown up in the towns rather than in those remaining areas of the island's interior where they would naturally have been exposed to the paghjella tradition, suggests that the functions of this type of singing and the apparent metaphysical benefits derived from it (as discussed earlier) still find a strong resonance in the Corsican male psyche even in a more "modern" frame of reference.

Having sought to elucidate the various circumstances that together might explain the survival of at least some of the men's musical practices while conversely accounting for the decline in female musical activity that continued throughout the 1970s and into the 1980s, I turn now to a more detailed account of the manner in which the revival referred to above has continued to unfold during the past two decades. In particular, I will explore the part played by women in extending the boundaries of the polyphonic tradition and in forging a place for Corsican music in the new global soundscape.

The Female Comeback

Beyond the quasi-domestic spaces of the village street or superstore and the more egalitarian sphere of academia, male voices might still be seen to occupy a dominant position in the overall soundscape of public spaces. While many of the male groups have long since won their battle for airspace via local radio music slots, women still have some way to go to even out the balance. At village festivities, women work hard in the background—for example, preparing food and decorating the church—but they tend to maintain a comparatively low profile, certainly in any collective music making that might develop after dark. The fairs are amply populated by women and children during daylight hours, when all manner of tradesmen ply their wares and there might also be "rides" for the children or competitions of one sort or another for entertainment, but the night, when only the bars remain open for business, belongs to the men. When women are present, they are invariably quiet and restrained, while the men make most of the noise: my own tapes recorded at fairs feature almost exclusively male voices and other sounds produced by males—the clinking of glasses, occasional gunshots, the distant sound of engines revving.

The fact that paghjella singing in particular often takes place in contexts associated with the consumption of alcohol adds further to the exclusion of women, who are not expected to drink (or indeed sing) with such abandon as their male counterparts. Even so, there have always been exceptions in the form of independently minded women, "impassioned by song," who have resolutely claimed a place among the men: one contemporary singer talks of having "grown up with the lads" singing at the fairs. Hanging out with the men in decidedly dubious locations can certainly call into question one's motives and morals—or simply plain common sense. (In Malta I was told of how those few women who were wont to join in the singing at the Imnarja festival—and in particular in the *ghana spirtu pront*, the Maltese version of the chjam' è rispondi—would go in disguise in order to safeguard their reputation.) It can also, however, earn one a certain respect, not only for one's "courage," but also as a transference of the respect accorded to "the song" (or "singing") and, more particularly, "passion for the song." The fact remains, however, that women partaking in what are essentially men's songs are obliged to negotiate men's spaces and at the same time to compromise their own gender identity, which becomes of necessity ambiguous. In my own case, the fact that, as a foreigner, I was already outside the cultural norm combined with my "passion for the song" (reinforced by the distances I had traveled) to make it less problematic than might have been expected for me to move in men's spaces. I was also doubtless held to be pardonably naive as far as matters of honor were concerned.

The unease that men feel about women singing paghjelle nevertheless goes beyond questions of upholding custom and defending one's territory. Gilmore (1987, 15) has pointed to the lack of male initiation ceremonies in the Mediterranean as a whole and the resulting ambiguity as to what marks the passage of a boy at puberty from the female-dominated domestic world to adult male society. The fact that it is usual for Corsican males to become properly integrated into the paghjella-singing tradition at the time of their passage from adolescence to adulthood, as signified by the breaking of the voice (Catinchi 1999, 51), suggests elements of a male rite of passage that, together with the function of male bonding already discussed, makes any female intrusion understandably inappropriate or at least discomfiting.

In the context of the *riacquistu* (cultural revival or "reappropriation") of the 1970s and early 1980s (closely connected with the autonomist movement), a new public space presented itself as groups of young singers—with rare exceptions male—took to the stage, initially offering informal "performances" in the villages as part of their mission to redisseminate traditional material and later taking part in more formal large-scale events, which brought together a number of different groups to perform in support of political prisoners. In the climate of this period, when "cultural" activity was almost inextricably bound up with politics, the association of singing with militancy—essentially a male pursuit that might also be seen to contain elements of a male rite of passage—only added to the symbolic impediments to women's participation on the stage. I have described elsewhere (Bithell, forthcoming) the process whereby the seminal *groupe culturel*, Canta u Populu Corsu, progressed—in response to the rapidly deteriorating political situation of the mid-1970s—from a position of collecting and disseminating examples from the whole range of traditional musical genres (its first disc, *Canta u Populu Corsu: Eri, oghje, dumani*, being very close in conception to an anthology of field recordings) to a more overtly militant stance, which found expression in the group's subsequent discs (the second setting the scene with its unequivocal title *Libertà,* "Freedom") in a number of original songs, often referred to as *cantu indiatu* or *chansons engagées* with such titles as "A rivolta" (The Revolt), "Clandestinu" (Clandestine) or "Un soffiu di libertà" (A Breath of Freedom). Having from the outset conceived of themselves as "cultural militants," members of the group and others who followed in their wake came to be referred to increasingly in the press as *soldats-chanteurs* (soldier-singers). The typical style of the more militant male groups with their somewhat "macho" or at least heroic stance, arms folded or guitars held shieldlike across their chests, offered, and indeed continues to offer, a powerful role model for aspiring male singers but was understandably lacking in appeal to young women.[17]

A notable exception among the many male groups that proliferated in the 1970s was the duo E Duie Patrizie, "The Two Patrizias," Patrizia Poli and Patrizia Gattaceca, who were later to reform as Les Nouvelles Polyphonies Corses. The pair first met in 1975 (the year of Canta's first disc) through their Corsican-language teacher at the *lycée* in Bastia, Jacques Thiers, a writer and linguist of some stature. As well as using songs in his lessons—they offered accessible and interesting material while at the same time introducing an element of animation—Thiers also used to encourage his pupils to write their own poetry in the Corsican language. Recognizing and nurturing the complementary poetic and musical talents of Patrizia Gattaceca and Patrizia Poli, he was instrumental in launching them on their singing career as E Duie Patrizie, and they recorded their first disc, *Scuprendu l'alba corsa* (a collection of their own songs), in 1978. In the heady days of the riacquistu, they also functioned in the context of the *soirées de soutien* (concerts in support of political prisoners), sometimes appearing on stage together with Canta and later collaborating with the group I Chjami Aghjalesi on the disc *Esse*. As young women, however, they did not have the same emblematic appeal as the larger all-male groups, who projected a more potently militant image.

Nonetheless, E Duie Patrizie offered the first proof that, in our more liberated age, women can no longer be relied upon to automatically or subconsciously internalize the gender roles and expectations current in the society in which they are growing up, and throughout the late 1980s and early 1990s, Corsican women continued to lay claim to their right to sing in public, even to sing in polyphony as do their counterparts in other parts of the Mediterranean and the Balkans. Indeed, it is significant that my own initial introduction to Corsican polyphony took place in 1993 at the second Women's Voices Festival organized by the Cirque Divers in Liège, Belgium, which featured a fascinating four-day workshop in Corsican polyphonic singing led by Nicole Casalonga (of the association E Voce di U Cumune, whose activities are associated with the Casa Musicale in the village of Pigna) and a positively stunning evening performance by the all-female group Donnisulana. It was, in fact, this intriguing encounter and the myriad questions that arose in my mind as a result that catapulted me into my research in Corsica.

At that time, Donnisulana (the name translates roughly as "Island Women") was the only all-female performing group in Corsica. The ensemble E Voce di u Cumune and its alternative incarnation A Cumpagnia had, however, produced albums featuring polyphonic singing by both men and women, and the 1987 disc *Corsica: Chants polyphoniques,* directed by Marcel Pérès, had already enjoyed a certain success outside Corsica.[18] Other women occasionally played the part of what was seen by some as a token female voice in essentially male groups, having been included for the particular timbre of their voices. Meanwhile, Jacky Micaelli, Patrizia Poli, and Michèle Cesari were well on their way to successful careers as solo singers (see plate 2).[19] This development can be seen in the light of a wider assertion by contemporary women of their right to play a more active part in all areas of life, including those that were traditionally closed to them. It is also worthy of note that a number of the women who became active as singers in the late 1980s and early 1990s had spent a period of time "on the Continent" (or even further afield), developing a professional career and generally broadening their horizons while adapting to contexts where gender roles and expectations were often quite different and where public and professional life, certainly, had a more egalitarian face.[20] Hence the comment of one female singer, with respect to the appeal of polyphonic songs to Corsican women, that, not only are the songs "belles" (beautiful), but "it is also, perhaps, a way of occupying a public space." Curiously to some, no doubt, similar sentiments are expressed by director and composer Michel Raffaelli when talking about his motivation in helping to establish the group Donnisulana and in composing new polyphonic material for them. "It's my taste for justice," he explains, "my aversion to 'wastage' which account for my desire to open up to women access to roles from which they have been excluded" (De Zerbi and Diani 1992, 93). Raffaelli goes on to describe his work with Donnisulana as a way of vicariously restoring the voice of his own mother, whose right to speak had been taken away from her by the patriarchal system she entered at marriage.

Raffaelli's establishment, in the 1980s, of the Teatru di a Testa Mora (The Moor's Head Theater) on his permanent return to Corsica following a successful career on the Continent is an important landmark as far as the revaluation of traditional song in general is concerned. Prior to this, some singers had had the opportunity to "work on" their voices in association with the Teatru Paisanu, led by Dominique Tognotti, and also in the context of the musical-theatrical pieces, based on extended research into the island's traditional musical heritage, that emanated from the village of Pigna. Raffaelli's theater, which had its base in Bastia, inevitably attracted singers and so served as a springboard for his later musical projects, which resulted most notably in the disc *Canti corsi in tradizione* (1989). Motivated by his desire to make a record of singers—both male and female—who still sang, unaccompanied, in the traditional way, this disc represents an important and readily accessible document of a variety of genres of traditional song and in particular of monodic song, which had been largely neglected since the early years of the revival with its promotion of the polyphonic repertory.[21]

Raffaelli's work with the group Donnisulana also grew out of the activities of A Testa Mora. As director of the group, he put together a program consisting of both traditional songs (most, but not all, in polyphony) and his own original polyphonic compositions, later to be released on the disc *Per Agata* (1992). Donnisulana's debut appearance at the Festival de Musique Contemporaine in Lille in 1989 brought them to the attention of Iannis Xenakis. Xenakis immediately recognized in the voices of the Corsican women, who sang using the chest register rather than the head register, the more archaic quality now often referred to in terms of "peasant voices" that he had been looking for, and so it was that he engaged the ensemble to perform his *Hélène* at the Opéra Bastille (cf. De Zerbi and Diani 1992, 92–93).[22]

If, by the early 1980s, insular culture had become fused with politics to such an extent that traditional musical expression was for many virtually synonymous with a statement of nationalist sympathies, in the late 1980s and early 1990s a breath of new inspiration once again blew into Corsica in the form of "world music." In the more cosmopolitan climate opening up, the public space that offered itself most readily to women was the stage, for it was clearly easier to access than, for example, the bar, which remains more firmly a male stronghold. Moreover, concerts and other formal performances can be seen to fall into the category of extraordinary musical (and public) occasions,[23] which, not being tied to a long history of customary practice, offer greater flexibility for departures from the norm. The international stage in particular, which lacks the political ambiguity of the Corsican stage and positions the singer more explicitly in the realm of art and aesthetics, was to offer an important new platform for women's musical activity. Donnisulana, for example, went on to perform widely on the international circuit, their musical peregrinations soon taking them as far as Japan.

Of particular significance to the present account was the impact of the *Mystère des voix bulgares,* the name given to a series of discs compiled by Marcel Cellier in the late 1980s, which featured an impressive array of virtuoso Bulgarian singers and musicians belonging to various state ensembles that stunned "Western" audiences with their polyphonic singing. The *Mystère* phenomenon was freely acknowledged by a number of singers in Corsica as one of the most significant sources of their own inspiration or motivation— not only at a purely artistic level but also by alerting them to the idea that there might be an international market for traditionally derived musics. When the Bulgarian singers gave a concert in Ajaccio in the early 1990s, the stage presentation of the choir with its rigid choreography appeared to some Corsican singers distasteful—"every gesture dictated by a man," as one woman put it—but the musical product itself (as represented by the recordings) had already had a powerful and decidedly positive impact. The discs famously included material that, while drawing on the "folk" tradition and featuring village singers (now in the employ of the state ensembles) who sang in the characteristic "open-throated" style, had been professionally arranged or recomposed by approved composers such as Kutev. The effect that this had in Corsica was to suggest the possibility of generating new polyphonic material without losing a sense of continuity with traditional idioms. By legitimizing the practice of "arranging" traditional or neotraditional material for a performance context, the *Mystère* recordings opened the way for a creative as opposed to a purist or conservationist approach to "the musical heritage." Of further significance from the Corsican perspective is the fact that these recordings featured exclusively women's voices. (In Bulgaria, it is traditionally the women who sing while men play musical instruments.) This also had a profound impact insofar as it lent further validation to the practice of women singing polyphony in a culture where this had traditionally been a male domain.

It was partly as a result of the inspiration offered by the Bulgarian voices that Patrizia Poli and Patrizia Gattaceca (formerly E Duie Patrizie) decided in 1989 to form the group Les Nouvelles Polyphonies Corses. Patrizia Gattaceca refers to "this whole current, this polyphonic trend," which gave the duo the idea of creating their own polyphonic compositions.[24] Their first eponymous disc (1991) included both traditional and original polyphonic songs sung by mixed ensembles of male and female voices, overlaid in the studio with improvised instrumental lines contributed by an impressive lineup of international musicians. Distributed in thirteen countries, the disc was a spectacular success outside Corsica, its initial release leading to an invitation to the group to perform in the opening ceremony of the 1992 Winter Olympics in Albertville.[25] The song "Giramondu" (as sung at Albertville) was subsequently used in a Philips advertisement that appeared worldwide, while the success of the disc itself in the French Victoires de la Musique, where it was voted "best album of traditional music," further excited interest in Corsican polyphony, to the extent that it had soon sold 100,000 copies in France alone.[26]

It is perhaps in part because women singing polyphony have already stepped outside the traditional mold that Les Nouvelles Polyphonies Corses were able to allow themselves greater liberty to explore new directions and develop new modes of expression. In addition, the fact that women are not bound by such strong allegiance to the male-dominated nationalist movement and the associated identity of "cultural militant" means that they can more easily assume the role of artist and pursue their chosen craft for its own sake. The tradition now began to be seen as something that should naturally evolve, rather than remain "stuck" in the past. For Les Nouvelles Polyphonies, it was important to "sing polyphony as we feel it today."[27]

Les Nouvelles Polyphonies were thus the first Corsican ensemble to be propelled so dramatically into the global "world music" market, their remarkable trajectory preparing the ground for other Corsican groups, some of whom were still preoccupied with more insular concerns and in particular with their identity as cultural militants. This is not to argue that those who have courted a more cosmopolitan career have left their political concerns behind them. Success in terms of international tours and record sales is, they argue, a valid and meaningful way of promoting awareness of the island and its problems at an international level and is no less a proof of their commitment to the cause. Nor is this argument restricted to women alone: male groups have increasingly adopted a similar position as the role of "cultural militant" (seen by some to have become redundant with the passage of time) has undergone a transformation into that of "cultural ambassador."

The impact of the Bulgarian singers and their subsequent visit to Corsica seems to have seems to have coincided with a new wave of intense polyphonic activity among men as well as women, witnessed by the appearance in the years 1992–94 of a veritable rash of discs of Corsican polyphony by contemporary groups (including A Filetta, Voce di Corsica, Tavagna, Cinqui Sò, and Madricale, as well as Donnisulana and Les Nouvelles Polyphonies), most of which included new original compositions in addition to items from the traditional repertoire. As the singer Petru Guelfucci comments, "After the Bulgarian voices, I think there was a desire to go further . . . to discover other things."[28] Guelfucci's own group, Voce di Corsica, went on to produce one of the most acclaimed albums of Corsican polyphonic singing to have appeared in the past decade. With this disc, the group followed in the footsteps of Les Nouvelles Polyphonies by again going on to win the prize for "traditional music" in the 1995 Victoires de la Musique. Meanwhile, the extent to which the *Mystère* phenomenon served as a point of reference for polyphonic production in general is reflected in a press review of a concert by the group A Filetta that appeared in a 1992 issue of *L'Événement* under the title "L'Événement de la semaine: Le mystère des voix corses" (The Event of the Week: The Mystery of [the] Corsican Voices). It was the success of these and other groups who took Corsican polyphony out to the wider world that finally broke the back of the various stigmas that had attached themselves to paghjella singing in Corsica itself: "primitive" and "nationalist" associations finally became a thing of the past. At the same time, conventions relating to gender had also been successfully challenged.[29]

Changes were also taking place at a more grassroots level. One of the byproducts of the ardent engagement in "cultural" activity in the 1970s was the proliferation of a number of what are commonly referred to as *scole di cantu* or *écoles de chant* ("schools of song" or "singing schools"). A number of such "schools" are still in operation, most commonly taking the form of weekly classes or rehearsals, using a local church or meeting room as a temporary base. Some of the earliest were established by members of the group Canta u Populu Corsu in the main towns of Ajaccio and Bastia as a means of transmitting musical material to young singers growing up away from the villages, which in the past had represented a natural training ground. At the same time, they served to foster a sense of cultural identity. Some schools devoted themselves more or less exclusively to the previously neglected traditional polyphonic canon (both profane and sacred), while others with a more overtly political identity also taught the new *canzone indiate.*

Many of these scole, in keeping with the performance context out of which they had grown, attracted a predominantly or wholly male membership. In some cases, this was also predetermined by the fact that the main function of the "school" was to produce a group capable of singing the mass in polyphony (which traditionally requires an équipe composed exclusively of male voices). Indeed, the material being taught in the majority of schools—whether polyphonic songs or Canta-style chansons—itself belongs essentially to the male repertory. A significant few schools, however, have played an important part in helping to open the field of traditional song, and of polyphony in particular, to women. Certain of the women singers now active at a professional level, for example, first worked on the traditional repertory with Jean-Paul Poletti at his original school in Bastia (capital of Haute Corse).[30] (One such singer commented that, despite having grown up in Bastia, when she first heard "the village songs" she felt as though she already knew them: it was "as if we had been waiting for one another.") Others attended the continuing program of workshops and classes hosted by the Casa Musicale in the village of Pigna in the Balagne, where a number of them have also become involved in associated performance projects. A Filetta's classes in the village of Lumiu, also in the Balagne, led to the more recent formation of the all-female group Anghjula Dea, selected to represent Corsica at the 1997 Printemps de Bourges festival. The series of A Filetta's classes that I myself attended in 1994 and 1995 attracted more or less equal numbers of male and female singers, although the first class I witnessed was attended by nine women and only four men. Some of these same women also took the initiative of forming themselves into an ensemble to sing the mass for the patron saint's day of a village to which one of their number belongs. Some of their sons, who were also attending the school at the time, were initially outraged at the prospect, but the women stood their ground, saying, "If the men can't get it together, then we will do it!"

Some of the schools that operate in the form of extracurricular activities at the *collèges* and *lycées* also attract significant numbers of girls, some of whom are then motivated to take themselves off to the fairs in search of the "real thing." The fact remains, however, that female role models are still relatively thin on the ground, as are women singers who can teach the repertory. A similar position exists with respect to the *confréries,* the (male) lay brotherhoods who typically have responsibility for processions and funerals and have also in some cases preserved in their repertories unique and valuable musical material, often in relatively "archaic" styles and sung using distinctive methods of voice production. A number of these have been revived in recent years and offer the increasing numbers of adolescent boys that they attract the opportunity both to learn vocal repertory and to develop technique. As one woman singer pointed out, nothing parallel exists for girls and women.

Inevitably, perhaps, men's music continues to dominate the public domain in Corsica itself. Even though times have changed and the roles and identity of women have advanced significantly, women still report that they are inhibited from singing in public because they feel vulnerable to male criticism: it is not easy to break through this barrier, which almost has the force of a taboo.[31] From a certain perspective, public performance places women themselves in a quasi-militant role, in this case with respect to patriarchal as opposed to colonialist authority. One male singer claimed that it shocked him to hear women singing polyphony, expressing the opinion that women should not try to do what men do. "Why change things?" he objected, "It is wrong to step outside the norm." There is also a lingering sense that, for some men, women's public performance still smacks of brazenness. To a very small minority of younger men, such behavior on the part of women apparently remains offensive in the extreme; to the older generation, it tends to be mildly discomfiting simply on account of its unfamiliarity, although some can still recall cases of women joining in paghjella singing with male members of their own families and so find the prospect of women singing polyphony less difficult to countenance. A more generally liberal attitude notwithstanding, then, today's generation of women, even if they have long since dissociated themselves at a personal level from traditional concepts of what constitutes "honorable" behavior (in musical terms or otherwise), cannot fail to remain aware of the ways in which notions lingering in society at large continue to restrict or color their activities. Meanwhile, the fact also remains that the relatively scant attention paid to female artists by the media in Corsica in comparison with that accorded to some of the male groups is certainly disproportionate to their obvious talent, the quality of the "product," and their success at an international level.

But male disapproval or disinterest does not deter all women: from the perspective of one extremely active and successful woman singer, such protestations of handicap are "a false excuse." It would also be quite wrong to imply that male disapproval was de rigueur. As indicated above in my discussion of the scole di cantu, a number of male singers have been instrumental in encouraging and nurturing women singers. Most recently, Philippe-Jean Catinchi, in his *Polyphonies corses* (1999, 141), has spoken in glowing terms of the work of Corsica's female artists, declaring that "women have made a magisterial contribution to the revaluation of traditional song." Notwithstanding, the fact remains that, while today's generation of young men continue to behave as though it were the most natural thing in the world for men to sing—whether informally in public places or to go on to form a group—and freely appropriate public spaces (from bars to churches) for musical rehearsals and impromptu singing sessions, for women the act of singing in public, whether casually or professionally, still involves an element of "breaking out."[32] As one non-Corsican resident commented recently of the island, "girl-power has yet to manifest itself strongly and durably here in public." The international stage, however, has offered women the opportunity to "speak out" in a way that has not been possible within the confines of Corsica itself. As a woman artist commented, it was *un grand souffle* (a blast of fresh air) to be able to go outside Corsica and to do things that are appreciated at an international level. The broader perspective and opportunities offered by the international stage have also been important in offering motivation and inspiration, encouraging women performers to continue to develop their work.

When all is said and done, however, singing polyphony in the professional or semiprofessional context of a "group" clearly holds different meanings for the men and women performing today. For men, it still retains the symbolism of male collectivity and operates in part in continuity with past "tradition." In the case of women, it is apt to operate more as an individual statement. In terms of geography, too, the perspective is different: while Les Nouvelles Polyphonies Corses, for example, have always looked out beyond the confines of the island (and are not, in any case, expecting any great encouragement from critics on their home ground), many male groups have begun with a more insular point of reference, seeing the island itself as the arena in which to act out their musical evolution. An implication of this is that such groups are subject, initially at least, to the approbation of native audiences who are more likely to look for a style of musical expression that is representative of their idea of "Corsicanness." International audiences, by contrast, are free from any such prejudice regarding appropriate and traditional behavior, and more particularly from the authenticity controversies that occupy those within the culture. Instead, they evaluate the musical product primarily in aesthetic terms: it is judged on its own merits, quite divorced from its original cultural context, with individual "talent" being recognized and rewarded.

For men, polyphonic singing and improvised debate may still function as a part of everyday life—a spontaneous, unpremeditated act motivated by an inner impulse originating in the circumstance of shared time and experience. Groups such as Voce di Corsica, Tavagna, or Madricale might sing a program of prepared repertory, including some of their own arrangements and compositions, in a concert situation, but then afterward join in a different kind of singing around the bar—one imbued with a collective, almost instinctive spirit and involving an element of improvisation and continuing adaptation to others. Different sets of skills are involved in this type of singing activity, with more "traditional" behavior patterns coming into play: the emphasis shifts back from product to process. For women involved with the polyphonic repertory, such singing is more likely to retain the aura of an activity apart—self-conscious, planned, and formally worked on. It takes time for them to integrate, through opportunity and experience, a knowledge of the musical language and its parameters that will then enable them to "improvise" and to adapt to the variants of other singers. This is, however, also (if not more) the case with many of the younger generation of male singers, who now, initially at least, learn polyphonic songs as "repertory," relying heavily on recordings made by other groups. The recordings may offer them a model (often skillfully and accurately reproduced) but cannot truly teach them "the art of song."

Ultimately, perhaps the most significant advance as far as women singers are concerned is the way in which they have succeeded in transcending their traditional identification with lamenting and have found a way to sing both for the joy of singing and as an expression of a newfound sense of female togetherness and solidarity. With the help of their excursions into the polyphonic landscape, Corsican women have at last found a way to say, "I exist."

Notes

This chapter grew out of fieldwork carried out in Corsica from 1993 onward. An extended stay of fifteen months in 1994–95 was supported by the British Academy; grants towards a series of shorter visits were received from *Music and Letters* and from the University of Wales, Bangor. In addition to those mentioned by name in the text, together with those who have contributed anonymously to my research, I would like to thank Line Mariani for her continuing encouragement and ever welcome "feedback," and Midi Berry for updating me on recent CD releases and for sending me posthaste at the last minute one of the latest new publications. All translations of non-English sources in this chapter are my own.

1. Patrizia Gattaceca, personal communication.

2. The exclusive identification of polyphonic singing with men, as found in Corsica and Sardinia, occurs in some other parts of the wider Mediterranean region as well, but it is by no means symptomatic of the Mediterranean as a whole. In Bulgaria, by contrast, polyphonic singing is a strictly female activity, while the Prespa Albanians offer an example of a culture where both men and women sing polyphonic songs but in distinctive styles, which can be seen to reflect cultural ideologies regarding gender differences and notions of appropriate behavior (Sugarman 1997).

3. Laade (1981, 2:3) emphasizes the difference between the male and female song repertories in terms of tessitura and voice placement: men's songs are generally sung with a high tessitura and "forced" voice, while the women he recorded (in the late 1950s and early 1970s) used a middle tessitura and more normal vocal production.

4. Through such events women would, of course, have been familiar with much of the male canon of monodic song. Past (male) researchers making field recordings in singers' homes often had the experience of the women prompting their husbands and filling in textual lacunae. Otherwise, they remained a discreet presence, appearing to view singing, in these circumstances at least, as a male prerogative (Laade 1981, 2:72).

5. Extensive ethnographic documentation relating to the different genres of song, together with a survey of the relevant literature, can be found in Laade (1981). Examples of the different genres can be found on the discs *Musique corse de tradition orale* (1982) and *Corsica: Traditional Songs and Music* (1990).

6. Parigi's recent collection of paghjelle texts (1995) consists entirely of single stanzas.

7. Even when paghjelle are sung on stage, they are performed in a manner that contrasts sharply with the way in which the more contemporary chansons are performed. Two concerts by different groups stand out in my mind. In each case, the evening began with a short program of traditional polyphonic songs for which the singers grouped themselves in the typical horseshoe formation toward the back of a dimly lit stage where they almost appeared to be singing for themselves in a quasi-ritualistic gesture. For the remainder of the program, which consisted of their own chanson compositions, they moved to the front of the stage, where they adopted a linear formation in front of microphones. When groups such a A Filetta present programs consisting entirely of a cappella polyphonic songs, they adopt a position center stage but retain the horseshoe format, even when they are obliged to use microphones.

8. Parallel practices to the chjam' è rispondi are still to be found in many other oral cultures, both in the Mediterranean region and beyond, the nearest being Sardinia, where the individual poets in a *gara poetica* are often backed by a *concordu* choir, and Tuscany with its *ottava rima*.

9. Listening to old field recordings, I encountered the interesting example of an exchange between a man and a woman where the man sings his stanzas to the standard currente melody while the woman uses a very different, "female" melody type (such as would normally be used for a lament or a lullaby). More recently, on a visit to the island in the summer of 2002, I was intrigued to hear about an exchange between a Corsican researcher and the wife of one of the chjam' è rispondi singers. The wife, when asked, "But what did you women used to sing when you were together and the men were away?" had replied, "We used to improvise—we would joke about the men!" (Nicole Casalonga, personal communication).

10. Studies and collections of song texts devoted almost exclusively to the voceru include Fée ([1850] 1985), Ortoli ([1887] 1992) and Marcaggi ([1898] 1994 and 1926). Viale's *Canti Popolari Corsi* ([1855] 1984) contains twenty-eight songs, of which twenty-three are laments. Laade's *Die Struktur der korsischen Lamento-Melodik* (1962) is concerned exclusively with an analysis of lament melodies (although not all of the texts featured are laments).

11. As an illustration of the scale of the vendetta in past times, Marcaggi ([1898] 1994, 35) reports that in 1714 it was established that 28,000 murders had been committed during the preceding thirty-two years (at a time when the population of the island barely exceeded 200,000).

12. Di Bella makes the observation that, in neighboring Sardinia and Sicily, "the endless . . . vendettas invariably conceal at least one woman who ensures that men take revenge on a murder" (1992, 155).

13. My analysis here draws to some extent on Gilmore's more general discussion of the particularly precarious nature of male honor in the Mediterranean region as a whole (Gilmore 1987, 9–10).

14. Tolbert (1990) has written fascinatingly on the shamanistic aspects of Finnish-Karelian laments.

15. Some of the ideas included in this part of my discussion were first presented in a paper given at the European Seminar in Ethnomusicology meeting in Toulouse, 1995.

16. Carrington (1984, 285–86) has commented on the remarkable way in which Corsican women have liberated themselves in recent decades, entering into the modern world and assuming professional careers with exemplary competence.

17. In addition, the tradition whereby only men should sing in public continued to be evoked in some circles even when the material itself was distinctly nontraditional. (The earlier folkloric groups had at least been more democratic in this respect.)

18. A Cumpagnia's first disc, *Canti è strumenti antichi è d'oghji* (1978), featured a polyphonic song for three female voices inspired by the singing of the three then elderly sisters referred to earlier. This disc, together with the group's associated public performances, has been cited as representing the first overtly public presentation of what might be referred to as "women's polyphony."

19. It is common for Corsicans to be known by both the French and the Corsican version of their given name. Michèle therefore also appears as Mighela, Michel as Mighele, and so on.

20. One spoke of the experience of singing in a group in Paris, where men and women occupied the stage as equals. In Corsica, she explained, it doesn't work in the same way: you look around and yet again you realize that you're at the back of the stage without knowing how you got there.

21. Raffaelli has continued to pay attention to monodic song through his ongoing work with singer Michèle Cesari, which has resulted in the discs *U cantu prufondu* (1993), *Di li venti, a Rosula* (1997) and, most recently, *U cantu prufondu 2* (1999), each featuring Cesari's vocals with instrumental accompaniment by Raffaelli himself.

22. Some of the members of Donnisulana have subsequently worked with Marcel Pérès in Paris, together with members of A Cumpagnia (the two groups share some members in common), and also feature, as part of the ensemble Organum, on his recording of

Franciscan material, *Chant corse: Manuscrits franciscains, XVII–XVIIIe siècles.* The group as such has now disbanded, although individual former members continue to develop their careers both as solo singers and in other formations.

23. Auerbach (1987, 31), in her discussion of the musical possibilities open to women in northern Greece, quotes Friedl's observation : "Festival and therefore extraordinary public occasions are accompanied by a change in the permitted movements and activities of women" (1967, 100).

24. "Tout ce courant, cette tendance polyphonique" (Patrizia Gattaceca, interviewed by the author, 1994).

25. I have commented elsewhere (Bithell 1996) on the way in which the music of Les Nouvelles Polyphonies Corses has come to inhabit a symbolic space that is in some respects similar to that occupied by the Bulgarian voices. Just as the latter had offered a rich treasure-trove of material for use as backing music for British television documentaries (and even commercials), so Les Nouvelles Polyphonies' interpretation of the madrigale "Eramu in campu," with "New Age" sounding synthesized instrumentals added to the more traditional vocals, was used to back an illustration of a fourteenth-century diptych featured in the opening sequence of part 1 of the 1996 BBC 2 series *The History of British Art.*

26. Patrizia Gattaceca, personal communication.

27. Patrizia Poli, interviewed by the author, 1995.

28. Petru Guelfucci, interviewed by the author, 1995.

29. Having once set foot on the polyphonic path, women have not been content to restrict themselves to material from the profane repertory but have also embraced the sacred. Jacky Micaelli's disc *Corsica sacra,* which also features the voice of Marie-Ange Geronimi, is devoted entirely to items from the sacred repertory, while Les Nouvelles Polyphonies' second disc *In paradisu* (produced by John Cale) presented contemporary arrangements of semi-forgotten traditional mass settings from a region of northern Corsica (the vocal arrangements being credited to Poli and Gattaceca and the instrumental arrangements to Cale). New groups and reformations of earlier ensembles continue to appear. The Patrizias Poli and Gattaceca have most recently reincarnated as the group Soledonna, where they are joined by Lydia Poli: a performance by the group in the summer of 2001 in the convent of Morsiglia was heralded in the press as "Exceptional, because for the first time female voices will resound beneath the vaults. The trio will have the heavy task of effacing more than five centuries of male domination" (*Corse-Matin,* 10 August 2001). The group continues to compose their own "new polyphonies." Nicole Casalonga, Gigi Casabianca, and Joëlle Tomasini, under the name Madrigalesca, have recently joined together with four instrumentalists to work on a program of lament arrangements. A recent disc entitled *Corsica: Women's Polyphonies* by the ensemble Donni di L'Esiliu (Women of Exile) has put female artists even more firmly on the map—even if, somewhat confusingly, the group here presents a range of traditional pieces normally sung by men. In including items from the sacred canon, however, they follow the quasi-revolutionary trend noted above. A Festival of Polyphonic Song held in Cervione Cathedral in August 2001 featured another new group, Santavuglia, again composed entirely of young women.

30. Poletti has since moved to the southern town of Sartène where he is director of the Centre d'Art Polyphonique and the choir Granitu Maggiore.

31. The issue is perhaps not one of singing in public so much as singing for diver-

sion, as opposed to singing in the service of the community, as in lamenting, which fulfills a ritual need. See Auerbach's discussion (1987, 31) of the justification of women's performance of wedding songs and Saint John's Day songs, as well as laments, as "a necessary community service," such ritual songs being seen as "efficacious" rather than "recreational."

32. This impression is certainly reinforced by the repetition—in reports that appeared in the daily newspaper *Corse-Matin* in April 1995, concerning Canta's "comeback" disc, *Sintineddi*—of the notion that the inclusion of a lone female voice, that of Anna Rocchi singing the song "Più chè u sole," can be seen to bear witness to "une profonde volonté d'ouverture" [a profound willingness (or desire) to open up].

References

Auerbach, Susan. 1987. "From Singing to Lamenting: Women's Musical Role in a Greek Village." In *Women and Music in Cross-Cultural Perspective,* edited by Ellen Koskoff, 25–43. Greenwood Press.

Bithell, Caroline. 1996. "Polyphonic Voices: National Identity, World Music, and the Recording of Traditional Music in Corsica." *British Journal of Ethnomusicology* 5 : 39–66.

———. Forthcoming. "Shared Imaginations: Celtic and Corsican Encounters in the Soundscape of the Soul." In *Celticisms,* edited by Philip V. Bohlman and Martin Stokes. Lanham: Scarecrow Press.

Carrington, Dorothy. 1984. *Granite Island: A Portrait of Corsica.* London: Longmans, 1971. Reprint, London: Penguin.

Catinchi, Philippe-Jean. 1999. *Polyphonies corses.* Paris: Cité de la Musique—Actes Sud.

De Zerbi, Ghjermana. 1981 *Cantu nustrale.* Altone: Scola Corsa di Bastia and Accademia d'i Vagabondi.

De Zerbi, Ghjermana, and François Diani, eds. 1992 *Cantu corsu: Contours d'une expression populaire.* Ajaccio: Editions Cyrnos et Méditerranée.

De Zerbi, Ghjermana, and Mighele Raffaelli. 1993 *Antulugia di u cantu nustrale.* Book 1. Ajaccio: La Marge.

Di Bella, Maria Pia. 1992. "Name, Blood, and Miracles: The Claims to Renown in Traditional Sicily." In *Honour and Grace in Anthropology,* edited by John G. Peristiany and Julian Pitt-Rivers, 151–65. Cambridge: Cambridge University Press.

Fée, A. L. A. 1985. *Voceri, Chants Populaires de la Corse.* Paris and Strasbourg, 1850. Reprint, Paris: Librairie Benelli.

Friedl, Ernestine. 1967. "The Position of Women: Appearance and Reality." *Anthropological Quarterly* 40 (3): 97–108.

Galletti, Abbé Jean-Ange. 1863. *Histoire Illustrée de la Corse.* Paris.

Giacomo-Marcellesi, Mathée. 1982. Booklet to accompany *Musique corse de tradition orale.* Paris: Archives Sonores de la Phonothèque National.

Gilmore, David D., ed. 1987. *Honour and Shame and the Unity of the Mediterranean.* Washington, D.C.: American Anthropological Association.

Laade, Wolfgang. 1962. *Die Struktur der korsischen Lamento-Melodik.* Sammlung musikwissenschaftlicher Adhandlungen. Vol. 43. Baden-Baden.

————. 1981. *Das korsische Volkslied: Ethnographie und Geschichte, Gattungen und Stil.* 3 vols. Wiesbaden: Franz Steiner Verlag.

————. 1990. Booklet to accompany *Corsica: Traditional Songs and Music.* Music of Man Archive, Jecklin-Disco.

Magrini, Tullia. 1995. "Ballad and Gender: Reconsidering Narrative Singing in Northern Italy." *Ethnomusicology Online* 1. http://research.umbc.edu/eol/

————. 1998. "Women's 'Work of Pain' in Christian Mediterranean Europe." *Music and Anthropology* 3. http://www.muspe.unibo.it/period/MA/

Marcaggi, Jean-Baptiste. 1994. *Chants de la Mort et de la Vendetta.* Paris, 1898. Reprint, Nîmes: Lacour.

————. 1926. *Lamenti, voceri, chansons populaires de L'Ile de Corse.* Ajaccio.

Ortoli, Frederic. 1992. *Les Voceri de L'Ile de Corse.* Paris, 1887. Reprint, Petricaghju: Cismonte è Pumonti Edizione.

Parigi, Paulu Santu. 1995. *Paghjella.* Corte: Le Signet.

Peristiany, John G., ed. 1966. *Honour and Shame: The Values of Mediterranean Societies.* Chicago: University of Chicago Press.

Salini, Dominique. 1996. *Musiques traditionnelles de Corse.* Ajaccio: A Messagera—Squadra di u Finusellu.

Sugarman, Jane C. 1997. *Engendering Song: Singing and Subjectivity at Prespa Albanian Weddings.* Chicago: University of Chicago Press.

Tolbert, Elizabeth. 1990. "Magico-Religious Power and Gender in the Karelian Lament." In *Music, Gender, and Culture,* edited by Marcia Herndon and Susanne Ziegler, 41–56. Wilhelmshaven: Florian Noetzel Verlag.

Viale, Salvadore. 1984. *Canti Popolari Corsi.* Bastia, 1855. Reprint, Bologna: Forni.

Discography

A Cumpagnia. *Canti è strumenti antichi è d'oghji.* Ricordu LM24 RI 250, 1978.

A Filetta. *Ab eternu.* Saravah 591061, 1992.

Anghjula Déa. *Anghjula Déa.* Fa Dièse, 1997.

Canta u Populu Corsu. *Canta u Populu Corsu: Eri, oghje, dumani.* Ricordu LM 02, 1975.

————. *Libertà.* Ricordu LM 04, 1976.

————. *Sintineddi.* Albiana CDAL 001, 1995.

Canti corsi in tradizioni: Canti, nanne, lamenti, voceri, paghjelle a capella. Fonti Musicali fmd 158, 1989.

Cesari, Mighela, and Mighele Raffaelli. *U cantu prufondu.* Ricordu CDR 088, 1993.

————. *Di li venti, a Rosula.* Auvidis Chorus AC 6458, 1997.

————. *U cantu prufondu 2.* Harmonia Mundi MPJ 111012, 1999.

Cinqui Sò. *Chants polyphoniques corses.* 7 Productions WMD 242 040, 1992.

Corsica: Traditional Songs and Music. Field recordings by Wolfgang Laade. Music of Man Archive, Jecklin-Disco JD 650-2, 1990.

Donni di L'Esiliu. *Corsica: Polyphonies féminines / Women's Polyphonies*. Buda Records, 2000.

Donnisulana. *Per Agata*. Silex Y425019, 1992.

E Duie Patrizie. *Scuprendu l'alba corsa*. Ricordu LM17, 1978.

Ensemble Organum / Marcel Pérès. *Chant corse: Manuscrits franciscains, XVII–XVIIIe siècles*. Harmonia Mundi HMC 901495, 1994.

E Voce di u Cumune. *Corsica: Chants polyphoniques*. Harmonia Mundi HMC 901256, 1987.

I Chjami Aghjalesi. *Esse*. Ricordu LM 32, 1981.

Le Mystère des voix bulgares. Vol. 1, Nonesuch 79165, 1987; vol. 2, Nonesuch 79201, 1988; vol. 3: Polygram / Fortuna 846626, 1990.

Les Nouvelles Polyphonies Corses. *Les Nouvelles Polyphonies Corses*. Philips 848515-2, 1991.

———. *In paradisu*. Philips 532453-2, 1996.

Madricale. *Polyphonies corses*. Consul CM 88-19, 1992.

Micaelli, Jacky. *Corsica sacra*. Auvidis Ethnic B, 1996.

Musique corse de tradition orale. Field recordings by Félix Quilici. Archives Sonores de la Phonothèque National, Paris, APN82-1/3, 1982.

Tavagna. *A Cappella*. Silex Y225201, 1992.

Voce di Corsica. *Polyphonies*. Olivi Music OVI 45204-2, 1993.

2

Body and Voice:
The Construction of Gender in Flamenco

Joaquina Labajo

The first stereotyped images of flamenco were constructed by non-Spanish writers and male artists in the nineteenth century. The development of professional flamenco cannot be explained without acknowledging this active and influential foreign presence, which was the most imputable factor in the flowering of an exotic gendered language of gestures and attitudes. Today, as in old times, "pure" Spanish flamenco is in demand by the international show business market, requiring the ostentation of all its stereotypes. These are always guaranteed by a clear reference to its "traditional" commercialized legacy, despite their being "modernized" to a greater or lesser extent. However, we must also consider that flamenco in Spain is—and has been for a long time—a popular practice in daily life characterized by a multiplicity of forms. Consequently, outside the world of theater flamenco is always fused with other musical cultures and styles. Improvisations on daily problems and *aflamencamiento* (performance in the style of flamenco) of popular songs have been a common daily practice in many places throughout Spain.

A wide gap separates flamenco expressions in everyday life from those performed in a flamenco show. It is my aim to emphasize this gap by analyzing the two worlds of flamenco: on the one hand, the models that characterize professional flamenco shows and include a gendered distribution of roles, as well as stereotyped vocal and bodily expressions; on the other hand, a more complex reality in which women are at the center of social and musical performances, challenging the official tradition.

It is well known that since the mid–nineteenth century flamenco has generated an extensive legacy of references in literature, poetry, painting, photography, cinema, and even advertising. An overall look at this legacy confirms that, despite its heterogeneous character and the interval in time separating certain images and stories, a mythical aspect—created from a distance and filled with symbolic elements—is always present.

This myth seems to underlie the apparent rigidity characterizing the way in which the voice and gesture are used by men and women in flamenco performances, through which given stereotypes are constantly recreated. Both in the nineteenth-century *cafés cantantes* and in today's theaters and films, these stereotypes emphasize a precise element of flamenco's identity, the predominant presence of Gypsy artists from "Moorish Andalusia," which is linked to southern Spain and apparently related to a marked preference for men as regards singing and instrumental performance, and for women as regards dancing. Without any pretense about evaluating or attributing a greater or lesser role to Roma in the creation of flamenco (Mitchell 1994, 5), it is nonetheless clear that Roma have played an essential part in its development and evolution, and that they have been considered the most profound incarnation of this genre among both Gypsies and *payos* (non-Gypsies).

There are many myths about Gypsies that for many reasons the Rom community itself has helped to perpetuate. These include the ancestral character of Gypsies' "primitive" customs, their supernatural powers, their biblical origin, their pride and their love of freedom, and also their passionate love life, the product of their men's extreme virility and their women's exaggerated sensuality. Fictional stories about their magical powers, mystery, aristocratic extraction, and independence were used by Roma to construct strategies of resistance in Spanish society, to confront their exclusion to some degree, and to safeguard their dignity and cultural differences. Both dignity and culture were frequently threatened by the stamp of poverty characteristic of the Rom way of life and settlements, both inside and outside cities. For centuries the culture of Spanish Roma has been identified with these legends in both the oral tradition and literary texts.

While nowadays Roma want to distance themselves from these legends, many professional flamenco artists, on the contrary, express pride in being real Gypsies, connecting themselves to the legendary tradition and reinforcing the link between flamenco and Rom identity. In this context, it is possible to state that the Rom community has been locked into Gypsy myths in the same way that Andalusia and even Spanish society as a whole are locked into flamenco.

What we do know is that the word "flamenco" started to be used in Seville and Jerez around 1860, as a term designating a particular musical form related to urban taverns and cafés (Ortíz Nuevo 1990, 342; Steingress 1990, 135). Moreover, by that time, many gender icons that originated in the different cultures imported to the Iberian peninsula in previous centuries had already been well assimilated by Spanish society.

For this reason, the study of gender within the complex reality of flamenco is not easy. My aim is to demystify the images of flamenco—laden with exotic and romantic references—transmitted to us through the years, by confronting them with other social, political, religious, and economic realities and strategies of both the past and the present. From this perspective, I will try to analyze the most basic elements of staging, including role distribution and female and male corporal practice in singing, dancing, and instrumental performances.

The Actors Play Their Roles

"The Deep Song is a Man's Thing . . ."

"Veterano is a man's thing": with this motto and an *aflamencada* melody, one of the best-known brandy cellars in Jerez launched its advertising campaign on Spanish TV during the last decades of the Franco era. The association of simple and powerful images—flamenco, men, and the bull—was devised in order to reinforce the identity of the Andalusian sherry. Behind the superficial images of the advertisement, however, there are more subtle associations, evoking the closed circles of the *aficionados* (men fond of *corridas de toros*), connected to flamenco circles, gathered around a bottle of wine—very frequently the *manzanilla* of Mérimée's *Carmen*.

These stereotypes emphasize the manliness associated with the deep song. The bull is masculine, primitive, and strong, and its fate celebrates both rebelliousness and acceptance of pain. Thus, the choice in the sixties of the bull as a national emblem is inevitably connected with defending the masculinity of the equally emblematic deep song, confirmed by the apparent scarcity of women in the practice of *cante*. In fact, when one scans the lists of professional singers in the bibliography of Spanish flamenco, it seems that only one in four or five singers happens to be female. Nevertheless, comparing these data with those provided by current publications, it is possible to observe a slight increase (4 percent) in new entries of professional female singers. Although this kind of information is not always accurate and must be handled with great caution, the increasing percentage of professional singers of flamenco is significant. From the 1960s on, many authors have felt the need to provide explanations for the "traditionally" scarce female presence in the flamenco song. In 1967, José Monleón wrote: "At first glance, it appears that women had to remain at the margins of the process of development of the deep song. Perhaps women were able to express themselves only where conditions of life were less harsh" (1967, 35).[1] One can agree that the birth of the deep song was strongly related to the foundation of musical shows as well as to some specific relationships between Gypsies and *señoritos,* upper-class men of leisure, who requested private musical parties at which Rom singers performed. In such situations, women's participation in cante would not have been favored. Nevertheless, this does not completely account for the silence about women in written sources—broken only by a reference to a small group of famous female singers. Indeed, the present slight increase in the number of women in flamenco can be interpreted as an attempt to recover the history of women in cante, in response to reproaches regarding the machismo of flamenco circles, both from inside and outside the country in the 1960s.

At times the defense of masculinity is expressed in terms of preference for a particular kind of voice: "It is easy to observe that the deep song attains its full expression in the bass and baritone voices; women who have practiced a good 'cante' owe their success largely to their naturally thick, harsh and low voices, which gave them virility. This means that the deep song is only appropriate for men's performances. Or, as it is often stated by fans impressed with this marked virility: it is mostly for machos" (Cabalanda and Cabalanda 1988, 118). Once this archetype of the male voice was established, legends about the characteristic ways of life of singers reinforced it. Even today it is not unusual to hear many men confess that they have to *rajar* (rasp) their voices by smoking and drinking to make them hoarse and low-pitched, in order to prepare themselves to sing in a "pure" style (Pasqualino 1996, 92). In this way, the singers demonstrate that they live "like men," that is, they frequent men's bars and indulge in behavior restricted to men. Thus while the artist's social life is irrelevant to his audience during his performance, the type of voice he possesses can certainly codify a whole set of imaginary associations with a particular type of behavior and habits.

Female voices, on the other hand, are generally thought in Western culture "to be high and shrill or breathy while men's are low and quiet or harsh" (Dunn and Jones 1994, 3). Women's raucous and low-pitched voices in flamenco are distant from this ideal model, and one can speculate upon the moral meanings they might evoke as a consequence. As Sarah Webster Goodwin has stated, women "singers, like other female performers, have historically been associated with courtesans; and the women represented as singing in romantic poetry generally are sexually accessible by virtue not only of gender but also of lower social class and/or foreignness" (Goodwin 1994, 68). Spanish romantic literature confirms this observation: the respectability of women who sang in secret male places was threatened because of their association with the icon of medieval slave girls in Muslim Spain, perpetuated through history by other female characters performing for male amusement. These women did not always manage to keep their performances separate from real life in the minds of their male audience. Nonetheless, it is worth noticing that they broke away from the silent female condition in public life. In today's changing society, professional women in cante no longer fear what their voices might mean, since being a singer of flamenco does not involve any identification with a given lifestyle. Nowadays the low voice in flamenco has no negative connotations, and in fact has come to symbolize women's right of expression beyond conventional gender roles.

Furthermore, the image of male and female voices in flamenco has evolved over time: although loud and low female voices were already significant in Muslim Spanish culture, today's tradition of an "archetypically" low, broken male voice has existed for merely forty years. At the beginning of the twentieth century, the most popular male voices of the genre, Antonio Chacón, for example, were clearly linked to the refined image of the opera virtuoso. Moreover, homosexual relationships in flamenco circles, as well as male transvestism, were always present despite strong censorship. The famous singer Miguel de Molina, very well connected within these circles, explained in his memoirs: "In the 1930s, all the men who sang 'cuplés' tended to be popular by imitating female stars. By wearing feminine suits . . . they searched for the success of women singers" (1998, 85). Within intellectual circles presided over by García Lorca, clean and classically trained female voices, such as La Argentinita, were also in demand. Therefore, it should not be difficult to understand why during the first flamenco competition in 1922, when Manuel de Falla and García Lorca tried to prove their theories about the religious nature of the deep song, they both decided to close the door to professional popular singers who performed in taverns and cafés cantantes (Gallego Morell 1992, 32) and to promote others such as "El Tenazas de Morón," whose clear sonority was highly valued by Falla (Vaquero 1997, 1). Until the sixties, religious and political circles in Spain were seriously concerned about the messages embodied in flamenco voices, and their influence on morals and social practices. Since the deep song was conceived by the religious Falla as a popular practice worthy of representing Spanish nationalism, it could in no case be related to licentious behavior. This paradox led the composer to draw analogies between flamenco and the Byzantine liturgy or primitive Indian modulations, which were corroborated by Aziz Balouch thirty years later. Balouch, a cultural attaché for Pakistan, had visited Spain for the first time in the years prior to the Civil War. However, it was not until the fifties, during the Franco era, that he wrote a small book in which he criticized the usual consumption of wine by Spanish flamenco singers, and recommended that "the excesses of physical pleasures" should be avoided for the benefit of singing (Balouch 1955, 42).

For a long time, clearly, the need to remodel flamenco according to the requirements of Spanish nationalism conflicted with the parallel need to satisfy the foreign demand for deep song symbols. The seductive figure of the flamenco singer connected to an ambiguous nightlife could not appeal to many social groups in Spanish society. The diffusion of the radio among the middle-class exerted further influence on the genre's remodeling. As a new audience of housewives and maids was created, a new type of *cantaor* also appeared. With a clear "throat" voice that bore no traces of the traditional macho sound, this new type of singer—who in midcentury Spain represented the thrifty hard worker who never frequented "dens of iniquity"—attracted new popular audiences among Spanish women. Nevertheless, such singers were not looked on with favor in traditional flamenco circles, where a soothing tenor voice and courteous love practices were suspect. As a result, the cantaor's virility had to be reinforced in popular fiction, such as the film *Café de Chinitas* by Gonzalo Delgras (1960), in which the protagonist is called upon to defend his honor by fighting "like a man."

As the Spanish audience embraced the new figure of the cantaor, foreign fans of flamenco were always in search of another Carmen—as well as other Gypsy characters from Mérimée's and Borrow's novels—and frequenting, for example, the taverns and the Gypsy caves of Granada's Sacromonte (Starkie 1944). In the 1960s, the influence of foreign demand and Spain's tourist industry lead to a remodeling of flamenco according to a stereotyped view of the genre. The structure of the flamenco show widened considerably in the

1960s and 1970s, but the distribution of roles invariably followed a model that privileged male singers. At the same time, the Rom cantaor Antonio Mairena was reintroducing romantic theories about the Gypsy roots of flamenco, establishing its geographical cradle around Jerez and making the symbolic association of the authenticity of this Andalusian genre with the purity of the region's bulls (Molina and Mairena 1979, 25). The idea of distinguishing between what is "pure" and "impure" in the flamenco song would ground Mairena's influential theory, following Antonio Machado (1947, 17), on how to preserve the received legacy without tainting it—for example, in the case of a Gypsy woman's honor, as pointed out by Timothy Mitchell (1994, 206).

In conclusion, the evolution of voice models in flamenco during the twentieth century reveals a bias toward the association of the male voice with hypermale attributes. However, the final model is the outcome of a complex history and an evolving image of manhood. It is even possible to observe that the different voice models hide different images of virility, hierarchically organized according to the beliefs of the *peñas de aficionados* (fan clubs), which have controlled flamenco's paths into this century. All in all, the stereotyped image of the male flamenco singer cannot be considered a static ahistoric creation. For better than a century there have been changes both in the behavior of performers and in the social meaning of the deep song. These changes have also affected the concept of male gender as revealed in the history of flamenco.

"Près des remparts de Séville. . . . j'irai danser la séguidille et boire du manzanilla"

Bernard Leblon (1991, 41) has stated that a specific Gypsy dance style can definitely be identified in the sixteenth and seventeenth centuries. In contrast to the insignificant role attributed to women in cante by flamenco writers, all Gypsy women were traditionally considered skilled in dancing. For a long time, one of the main sources of income for women in the Gypsy community was the money that they received for dancing at country festivals and market fairs. However, in the eighteenth century before the birth of flamenco, some dances included in today's flamenco repertoire—such as *seguidillas* and *fandangos*—were danced in many places in the Iberian peninsula by men and women who were not necessarily Gypsies and did not belong exclusively to the lower or working social classes (Labajo 1997). Flamenco dance was thus nourished by some popular dances as well as by the forms imposed by the urban dance academies of Seville. These conventions included a legitimization of particular gender choices in relation to social or ethnic identity, implying the idea of "becoming you in what you are," as pointed out by Bourdieu (1992, 120). Even today some academic traditions born in the nineteenth century consider some movements or gestures "typically feminine": for example, those made from the waist up or with hands imitating doves. Given the existence of a female dance tradition, why have many women preferred to adapt virtuoso masculine techniques like heel tapping to their dances throughout more than a century?

Gender stereotypes in flamenco dance were not created in the villages or at Gypsy fiestas, nor did they originate at home or in the academies of the middle class. The flamenco legend was constructed in taverns, in the cafés cantantes, on stage, and in the workplaces, where the violins and tambourines—used by Gypsy men and women to organize domestic dance in other times—had already disappeared. In these venues a mystified solemnity under the control of men replaced the improvised expressions of old times, in which a relaxing atmosphere and the presence of children and old people protected and surrounded the performers. In the new setting, when a woman went up to the stage and began to dance she had to sell the image of her body to men's eyes. It has never been a very secure situation for a woman, as pointed out by Karin van Nieuwkerk (1998), who has argued within the context of female entertainment in Egypt that "beauty and being desirable mean money. Yet, it can also mean trouble." Thus, for women dancers, one of the most immediate solutions was to recreate the role played by the familial group, placing musicians at the back of the staged flamenco scene. This strategy enabled the dancer to feel confident, less restrained by the eyes upon her, and at the same time it reinforced the communication between artists and audience.

The dances performed during the nineteenth century in southern Spain were danced according to different styles, depending on geographical regions and local cultures. However, it is interesting to note how in books written by both travelers and local authors, the perceived dynamism of the Gypsy style is what captured attention. Théophile Gautier's observations of Spanish dancers in Les bals de l'Opera in 1834 were typical: "Their dance is more a dance of temperament than a dance following rules. It is possible to feel in every gesture all the force of southern blood. A similar dance performed by a blond-haired woman would be a great absurdity. How could it be possible that such a hot dance, so impetuous, with such stressed movements, with such free gestures, is not considered indecent, while a smaller deviation of a French woman dancer is already such a striking immodesty?" (1837, 33). Carmen, of course, is the most successful character modeled on this female stereotype. Prosper Mérimée's wicked, corrupt heroine was reduced by Bizet's librettists to a man eater. The opera's opening in Paris in 1875 launched Carmen as an image of both scandal and fascination. When the opinion of outsiders becomes part of an artistic expression, the outcome can be unpredictable for the evolution of later performances. Thus, in the film *Carmen* made in 1915 by Cecil B. De Mille, the star Geraldine Farrar reinforced the myths of Gypsy dance even more. Her jerky, improvised movements are unusual in the context of flamenco, but the image she transmits is clear: her "masculine" control of the scene and the brusque movements of her arms and legs emphasize her demonized femininity.

When in the 1930s the Gypsy dancer Carmen Amaya began to appear on the international scene, she knew very well that her Gypsy identity would allow her to develop dances and attitudes reserved traditionally to men. She used with no restriction all kinds of movements based on rapid motions of the legs and heel tapping, which she regarded as more attractive for the development of the artistic virtuosity of her show than those reserved to feminine roles. Her film *María de la O,* made in 1936, is an example of the construction of a Gypsy woman stereotype. The script is centered on the dynamic figure of Carmen Amaya. Director Francisco Elías deliberately contrasts Amaya's dance, full of passion and rage, with the trivial, academic *sevillanas* performed "from the waist up," in a "typically feminine" style by the other Gypsy women in front of the Alhambra palace. At the end of Amaya's dance, her manner is that of an athlete recovering from her exertions. In the film, her performance is watched by a North American painter, her unknown father. The entire scene is absurd. It is obviously a lie, although one perfectly fitting existing stereotypes, and therefore coherent with the distant and virtual image of Gypsy girls. Carmen is the protagonist in this context, as she is the only woman dancer in the Gypsy group representing in her performance "the truth of her race." The masculine model that Amaya chose for her dance was reinforced by her apparel (plate 3). She very often appeared in trousers, in order to show what she was capable of doing with her feet. However, English journals like the *Dancing Times* criticized Amaya's new look, on the grounds that she had broken away from Gypsy customs and offended the pride of the Gypsy race (Bois 1994, 182). However, to suggest that her attire or performance would be considered negatively by the Spanish Gypsy community seems too simplistic. The Gypsies have always differentiated strategies for earning a living from their internal behavioral rules. If we consider the relaxed humorous atmosphere at private family fiestas and compare it with the attitude of Roma dancing before an audience in a show, we must conclude that Gypsy people have never had difficulties in separating real life from their performances.

Moreover, when English flamenco fans criticized Amaya's clothes, they probably did not know the long tradition of transvestism in Spanish Muslim society, as pointed out by John Boswell 1998, 219). What is more, they had no idea that transvestism was common in the world of flamenco during the nineteenth century. Thus, recovering the masculine aspect in some of her dances had for Carmen Amaya two meanings we touched upon previously: on one hand, it related her art to that of the women in old photographs who used to wear masculine and rustic clothes (plate 4); on the other hand, it increased the possibility of her access to power in the dance world, protecting her female condition from potential sexual connotations.

The appropriation of virtuoso movements from the men's dance gave women dancers another way to present their bodies to strangers. The feminine virtue of moderation was not sufficient to protect their bodies from men's burning eyes; men were sometimes unable to tell the difference between what was and what was not for sale during a show. Carmen Amaya opened the way to the transgression of gender roles by showing that the *farrucas* and other dances reserved in the past exclusively to men could also be performed by women. Therefore, dance on stage began to be not only a practice full of sexual meanings, but also a display of athleticism performed according to compelling theatrical rules. Gypsy women thus established a more liberated style of dance, asserting in this way their power and authority and simultaneously evoking their oriental roots and Indian origin in order to satisfy the desire for exoticism of their masculine audience.[2]

The Guitar: A Discrete Witness of Power Relationships

If the recognition of women's role has been scarce as regards cante, it is almost nonexistent as regards playing the guitar. This omission is historically unjustified. Pictures and etchings, as well as oral memory and written documents, inform us of the presence of women guitarists in connection with flamenco singing (plate 5). Pineda Novo reports (1996, 64), for example, that in 1926, La Macarrona—a famous Gypsy dancer highly considered in the flamenco cafés—declared: "Today there [are] barely half a dozen Sevillian girls who play the guitar, when the guitar is so beautiful! Today in Seville the poet would not be able to write this couplet: *Don't play the guitar anymore / because it makes me jealous / seeing it always on your skirt*" (Pineda 1996, 64). By contrast, articles that appeared in the press in the last decades of the nineteenth century relate how the boom of flamenco in private parties among the Spanish bourgeoisie and aristocracy had led young ladies to replace their piano lessons, so typical of women's education in upper- and middle-class circles, with guitar lessons (Cobo 1997, 35–38).

The guitar in flamenco has now been removed from female hands for an entire century. The reasons for this, however, prompt no simple explanation. Guitar players began to use the orchestral style in the twentieth century to accompany dance in *tablaos* and theaters, in order to dramatize and enlarge their stage presence. Moreover, the transformation of flamenco into a theatrical show and an organized business favored the specialization and instrumental virtuosity of guitar players. This soon became a virtue in a man's hands and a defect in the hands of a woman, as is frequently the case in middle-class musical practices (Leppert 1984). Playing guitar, then, ceased to be conceived as a practice connected to personal entertainment and accompaniment to songs, as in former times, and became a profession geared toward the show. Women began to abandon the guitar entirely. The following description gives a precise idea of this new reality: "Juana La Macarrona went out to dance, while an extraordinary trio of guitarists created an energetic musical base: Manolo Caracol sang Alegrías and a dozen Gypsy women from Sacromonte clapped flamenco rhythms" (Molina Fajardo 1962, 137). In short, as I argue later, there are precise reasons for the exclusion of female guitar players: their presence reversed the established gender relationships that still support the symbolism of the "traditional" flamenco stage.

Apart from the specialized companies organized around a dance star, it is possible to state that for a long time the male singer has been the most respected figure within the flamenco group. Until the 1960s, he was the exclusive soloist performer on stage. However, his voice was usually supported by the music played by another man: the guitarist. Singer and guitarist thus established a dialogue based on mutual and attentive listening in which the guitarist acted as a sort of confidant: he depended on the initiatives taken by the flamenco singer and had to react accordingly. An evaluation of the guitarist in this classic role is based not solely on his skill and technique but also on his ability to support the cantaor's improvisations in an effective way. Both the singer and the guitarist are perfectly aware of the importance of their active cooperation (Frayssinet 1992, 26). The sort of "osmosis" established between the two men also tends to be reflected in their mutual position on stage suggesting a "face to face" relationship.

The strict relationship between singer and guitarist is realized when the two musicians are men. When a woman is singing, however, a major physical and emotional distance is set up between the two performers. Mutual confidence gives way to a merely professional relationship, and the guitarist shows no more than respect for the cantaora's discourse. The clear distance established between man and woman in flamenco performances also explains why a woman could never perform the role typical of the male guitar player: Gypsy women have never been regarded as confidants of men, or as capable of establishing and correcting the basis of a man's discourse.

The leading role of the cantaor is also exerted with regard to dance, in particular when the dance is performed by a woman. With her body a female dancer must express the emotions sung by the cantaor, and interpreted musically by the guitarist. She must interiorize their poetic and musical discourse and make it her own. The condition of dependence characteristic of female dancers, as well as their reaction against it, is well represented, for instance, in *Café de Chinitas*. Despite the rebellion of a *bailaora* who refuses to interpret the song of her unfaithful lover, a friend keeps insisting: "Rocío will dance the song El Rondeño sings to her. That is her fate!" This kind of underlying conflict between man and woman in the performance of flamenco has frequently been interpreted in romantic literature as part of the myth of the "Gypsy woman's pride" vis-à-vis men's behavioral rules.

The interactions of singer, dancer, and guitarist are clearly dependent on their being male or female. When a woman takes part in the performance as a dancer, the previously described relationship of intimacy between male singer and guitarist disappears. The guitarist acts now as a neutral element, detached from the conflict between male singer and female dancer but entirely at the disposal of the cantaor. His role on stage becomes secondary; he is essentially an instrument, an object. Other men, usually younger than the singer, may take part in the performance as dancers. Their gestures must strictly interpret the words of the cantaor, but once again, when the singer is a woman the situation changes. However, it is extremely unusual for a female singer to lead the performance and the dance. Indeed, a woman will never be allowed to induce a man of her own age, or an older one, to dance according to the feelings that she expresses in her singing. This would represent an inconceivable inversion of gender roles, and would be taken to mean "She does whatever she wants of him; he is no longer a man, but her puppet"—a comment that no Spanish man would like to hear about himself. Only when the cantaora is no longer young, when she has become a "sexless" symbol of matriarchal power (Koskoff 1989, 6), is it possible to see youths of both sexes dancing to her song.

When there is no singer on stage, the number of guitarists usually increases and the "guitar orchestra" becomes the ideal basis for male and female dancers, who can freely elaborate their discourse of gestures. In this case, a male dancer will reinforce the virile and independent aspects of his character, autonomously developing his control of the stage. The role of a woman dancer in this context is more complex: on the one hand she can express "her love of freedom" and "her firmness when facing the whims of men"; on the other hand she may appear unfortunate as "she has no one to sing to her."

Since the 1960s, the figure of the male guitarist has acquired a new and more important role in flamenco thanks to the fusion of Spanish music and jazz. He is no longer considered, as in the past, simply a support for the singer but has become a protagonist in his own right. He can establishe a new kind of dialogue with the cantaor, free from hierarchical distinctions, the two men claiming equal rank on stage. (This new relationship can provoke some rivalry, as it did between Camaron and Paco de Lucía, which led the singer to choose a more traditional guitarist for his performances.) Moreover, the guitarist may now claim a privilege traditionally reserved to the cantaor: that of carrying the show as a soloist, and of organizing the stage layout according to his own discourse, singing not with his vocal strings but with the strings of his guitar. Indeed, the increasing export of flamenco outside Spain has favored the role of guitarists as soloists. The cante, sung in Spanish with Andalusian-Gypsy accents and idioms, is not easily understandable outside Spain, while dance requires higher costs than instrumental music for live performance. Consequently, the new male guitarist as an independent protagonist on stage is in the best position to negotiate the future path of Spanish flamenco abroad, and to a dialogue with other musical styles in the world.

Locked into Gypsy Myths

To what extent can a present-day flamenco performance be considered a metaphor of reality? One of the most important concerns of those who have tried to control this musical genre has been that of making flamenco stereotypes credible beyond the space of the scene. They have been eager to preserve an art in which life and musical performance seemed to converge, as we can read in a story related by Fernanflor in 1904:

> The cantaora's profession was a dangerous one, surely, for an eighteen-year-old girl who appeared to be in the prime of her life. . . . people accustomed to wild living and debauched lifestyles eagerly tried to win her heart. No one could do it. . . . The Viscount listening to her felt a strange anxiety: that voice produced within his breast unknown passions, desires, bitterness and anxieties. . . . After the song, María de Alcor sat down with a group of women to chat. . . .

her comments must have been as sad as her songs, for the Viscount saw expressions of piety and even tears on the women's faces, which had been tanned by the misery and the sun. (Cobo 1997, 57–58).

Theories on flamenco based on Gypsy myths and legends have converted "bodies in pain" (Washabaugh 1996, 97) into the most acclaimed and convincing expression for a marginalized and repressed social group such as the Rom people. For instance, Antonio Mairena has associated the origin and "purity" of the expression of pain in the cante with the misery and suffering experienced by Roma. José Monleón, a supporter of Mairena's theory, also maintains that "without a specific and anguished set of experiences, 'cante' remains unexplainable" (1967, 26). Despite the apparent opposition between *gitanistas* and *andalucistas,* or "purists" and "modernists" (Labajo 1996), neither has ever wanted to question flamenco's links with pain and misery. Poets and writers have also encouraged these clichés, with the complicity of the artists themselves. In postwar Spanish cinematography, for example, one can find statements such as: "Flamenco is pain, it is a lament, it is born only in misery" (from the film *Café de Chinitas*).

This demand for the theatricalization of pain has found full response among the Gypsies. It is worth stressing that in their view the evaluation of the expression of pain strongly depends on gender issues. The performance of the characteristically painful leitmotif by men is highly esteemed because "a woman cries over any trifle but when a man weeps, one falls apart" (Pasqualino 1996, 83). Men's dramatic strength in *cante jondo* is appreciated because of their embodiment of profound feelings. However, it is important to remember that in the past the performance of these songs of lament was the prerogative of women rather than men, in Andalusia as well as in other regions of Spain and Europe (see Magrini 1998). There is general agreement about women's role in the expression of pain: "women lamenters are said to 'cry with words' as opposed to men, who merely 'cry with the eyes.' . . . It is the presence of textually and melodically stylized crying that characterizes the lament as intrinsically feminine" (Tolbert 1994, 180). Therefore, we should conclude that in the last century Andalusian men appropriated the feminine repertoire that had originated both in motherly singing and in songs from taverns and cafés. Their presence was established in competition with women who sang accompanied by their guitars. Hence these women were gradually marginalized in the public scene. The increasing expression of pain in the male deep song at the end of the nineteenth century was justified in different way, by the general misery of the southern people, for example, or by men's loneliness while in prisons, or by the trials suffered by the Gypsy people in the past.

Significantly, the social history of Roma and that of flamenco as a commercialized performance have neither followed the same path nor shared the same meanings. Even in the 1960s, when the recognition of the influence of Rom culture in this musical expression increased and huge amounts of money to promote it as a tourist attraction were raised—tourism being developed at that time as the country's main industry—only a minority of professional Gypsies took a long-term part in the world of commercialized shows. The rest of the Rom community—who had no access to social housing—settled in ghettos and slums around large cities, mainly in Barcelona and Madrid. The industry needed cheap manpower in Andalusia, and a large number of Rom families ended up at the lower-paid end of this type of work, with bad or no contracts at all. In those years, the regular presence of "Gypsy" women begging in the streets and offering to tell fortunes helped to reinforce the stereotype of their inability to enter the labor force. At the same time, Gypsy men, forced to develop strategies of mobility and alternative occupations in order to support their families, appeared to reinforce the old and worn stereotype of their being wandering spirits eager for freedom (San Román 1997, 163).

There is thus a great distance between the social reality of Spanish Gypsies and the myths that nourished flamenco and shaped its gender stereotypes. Furthermore, this distance is increasing because—while there are doubtless more professional Gypsies within the world of shows and while flamenco has become an international music language—the Rom community is threatened now more than ever, risking complete disintegration as a group.

Moreover, it must be emphasized that in the Gypsy world of the past musical expression and gender roles were actually different from the models typical of the commercial flamenco show. When women sang in private circles, humor and irony—and not only pain—could characterize a performance of flamenco and help to create social integration. At private Gypsy fiestas, the stereotypical behaviors characteristic of the flamenco show disappeared, and the atmosphere could be relaxed and humorous. Gender roles could be inverted. Women did not have to have a young body or a low voice to participate in musical performance, and their aflamencamientos, the adjustments of any popular song to a particular or daily meaning, were warmly received by the whole family group as well as by non-Gypsy families.[3] These attitudes are confirmed by the conversations and recordings of old amateur performers, women who abandoned the world of the theater after marriage. They are highly in demand today as representatives of an interesting, marginalized expression, and indeed have made a "new" flamenco available. At present such practices are very limited because many families live in small flats where big gatherings are not possible. What is more, the influence of the world of theater throughout the past century has favored a redistribution of gender roles in many family fiestas.

The loss of opportunities and places to meet among Gypsies has been partly replaced by religious celebrations that take place within the net of the "Philadelphia" Christian Church, which offers the community more chances to develop inner bonds of solidarity. The religious flamenco performance introduces a hierarchically established separation by sex: the choir is located in the lead part at the right of the minister, men and instruments in the first line, and female voices behind them. The rest of the singers' community is also divided into two groups: men on the right, women on the left. Women are represented here as mothers, daughters, or wives, who are all called "little sisters" by the minister. Bodies are objects of moral censure. Consequently, dance—the only expression in the flamenco show in which women were always accepted—disappears. Women's contribution is limited to vocal participation in a big female choir directed and supported by three or four men who play guitars, organ, and drums. The voice becomes the main means of expression for women, although the control of their voices is in the hands of male guitarists. Pain and dramatic expression are not suitable for religious music: the main element of the ritual is the sacral happiness represented by the women's voices and reinforcing the unity of the group.

The Spanish authorities displayed a dual political morality toward flamenco that was closely related to two opposing strategies. One consisted of exporting a commercial image, in accordance with romantic foreign references, full of machismo, mystery, pain, sacrifice, and the "primitive customs" of a "static" tradition. The other directed sharp criticism against flamenco images as a threat for the Spanish domestic economy vis-à-vis the new model of an industrial hard worker who should not spend money on taverns and shows. Thus, flamenco and wine were considered good if offered to foreigners but unsuitable for the domestic customs of Spanish citizens.

The power of stereotypes is proved also by anecdotes about flamenco dancers or singers. For example, when in 1945 a journalist in Buenos Aires offered a cigarette to Carmen Amaya, she replied: "I can dance anything you want but smoking is for men." It is well known that at the time the bailaora smoked two packets of cigarettes a day. Similarly, although she was a Gypsy from Barcelona, in her tours outside Spain she needed to stress that she had been born in the Gypsy caves of Granada's Sacromonte "where," she assured her audiences, "from the age of four I was already applauded by Englishmen" (Bois 1994, 103, 110). In this way she tried to project her good reputation and "purity" to foreign audiences.

These half-lies with which flamenco performers tried to make real life closer to stereotypes were not always clearly perceived by foreign scholars, who frequently preferred to believe that their mythical hypotheses were well founded on readily evident practices and expressions. The puns and out-of-place topics with which Pitt-Rivers constructed his theory of honor and social class in Andalusia (1966) disclose how an "anthropology of birds of passage" can stereotype an entire society. It can be argued that many of his appraisals might easily form part of the plot of a flamenco scene. The stereotypes about Andalusian women and men were constructed by the Oxford group in the dramatic times between the 1950s and the 1960s, the difficult age in which the modernization of Spanish industry disarticulated the traditional work and familiar social structure of the peasants.[4]

In the same years, the basic characters and myths of professional flamenco were definitively established. Nevertheless, as I have tried to argue in this chapter, Spanish flamenco can be observed from two different perspectives: one that is the image endorsed by men devoted to domestic or foreign tourism, full of stereotyped roles and well known today throughout the world; and a more complex performance in which women exert an active role as regards social and musical expressions, both in the Rom community and in mainstream Spanish society. The large presence of women as flamenco professionals, amateurs, or consumers has tended to destabilize the gender relations established within the official tradition, a fact that has hardly been recognized so far.

In order to gain and maintain the control of these expressions men have tried to exercise their power on various fronts: in the domestic sphere, rich in abstruse aesthetic and "machistas" theories defended by the secrecy of the peñas de aficionados; at the national level led by sociopolitical objectives; and in the more sophisticated international domain, in which private business tied to flamenco expression has united foreigners as well as natives in a single triumphant strategy.

Today the mystifying idea of "respecting the tradition" leads one to forget a part of flamenco history, and to ignore the real and multifaceted roles of both men and women in the past and present world of the deep song.

Notes

1. Unless otherwise noted, all translations in this chapter from non-English sources are my own.

2. As a consequence of women's protagonism and activity in dance, in this century men have tried constantly to work out new types of movements and representations in order to rival the dynamic and impressive female repertoire. For instance, today some of these men are looking for new hypermale roles: sometimes men do not simply walk on the stage but take long strides; they do not only play the bullfighter but act as bulls. Moreover, sometimes they do not only woo and despise the love of women but even the love of other men. Finally, the representation of Gypsy pain is no longer sufficient, and now even Christ's suffering is represented.

3. In her interviews, Herminia Arredondo (Arredondo Pérez 1999, 166) has collected the stories of several women from the Peña Flamenca Femenina de Huelva that document the widely spread domestic practice of flamenco: "I began to sing Spanish songs at the age of four years . . . , and I have always liked flamenco. . . . Here in Huelva it is very weird for a family not to have at least one member who sings. . . . My mother is very witty and invents things but she has a good rhythm and my father also dances very well" (Mati Hidalgo, member of Cuadro de Cante, Peña Flamenca Femenina de Huelva).

4. It should be no surprise that the Spanish ethnologist Julio Caro Baroja, who was invited to participate in the Oxford group in 1959, should want to distance himself from its members. In the preface to the Spanish version of *Honour and Shame* published in 1968, he wrote some ironic comments about how the Mediterranean beaches, transformed into a famous tourist attraction, could become perfect platforms for the development of a "mango-tree anthropology" (Caro Baroja 1968, 6).

References

Arredondo Pérez, Herminia. 1999. "Mujeres y flamenco: La Peña flamenca femenina de Huelva." In *Actas del IV Congreso de la Sociedad Ibérica de Etnomusicología*, edited by C. Sanchez Equiza, 161–70. Navarra: SIbE.

Balouch, Aziz. 1955. *Cante jondo: Su origen y su evolución*. Madrid: Ensayos.

Bois, Mario. 1994. *Carmen Amaya o la danza del fuego*. Madrid: Espasa Calpe.

Boswell, John. 1998. *Cristianismo, tolerancia social, y homosexualidad*. Barcelona: Biblioteca Atajos. Originally published as *Christianity, Social Tolerance, and Homosexuality* (Chicago: University of Chicago Press, 1980).

Bourdieu, Pierre. 1992. "Los ritos como actos de institución." In *Honor y gracia*, edited by John G. Peristiany, 111–24. Madrid: Alianza Universidad.

Cabalanda, Carlos, and Pedro Cabalanda. 1988. *Andalucía, su comunismo y su cante jondo*. Cadiz: Universidad de Cadiz.

Caro Baroja, Julio. 1968. "Prefacio." In *El concepto del honor en la sociedad mediterránea*, edited by John G. Peristiany. Barcelona: Labor.

Cobo, Eugenio. 1997. *El flamenco en los escritores de la Restauración, 1876–1890*. Cornellà de LLobregat [Barcelona]: Aquí.

Delgado, Luis. 1997. *El sentir flamenco de Ginesa Ortega*. http://www.musicspain.com/artmay97.htm#art_voi_02/

Delgras, Gonzalo. 1960. *Café de Chinitas*. Film produced by Estela Films S.A. and distributed by Floralva Exc., Spain (b/w).

De Mille, Cecil B. 1915. *Carmen*. Film produced by Bruce Higham and Douglas Schwalbe and distributed by Video Artist International (color tinted).

Dunn, Leslie C., and Nancy A. Jones. 1994. *Embodied Voices. Representing Female Vocality in Western Culture*. Cambridge: Cambridge University Press.

Elías, Francisco. 1938. *María de la O*. Film produced by UFISA-ULARGUI and distributed by Polygram (b/w).

Frayssinet, Corinne. 1992. "Le flamenco à la rencontre d'un 'art naturel.'" *Tsiganes* 92 (1): 11–35.

Gallego Morell, Antonio. 1992. *I consurso de cante jondo, 1922–1991*. Granada: Archivo Manuel de Falla.

Gautier, Théophile. 1837. "Les Danseurs espagnols." *La charte de 1830*, April 18.

Goodwin, Sarah Webster. 1994. "Wordsworth and Romantic Voice: The Poet's Song and the Prostitute's Cry." In *Embodied Voices: Representing Female Vocality in Western Culture*, edited by Leslie C. Dunn and Nancy A. Jones, 65–79. Cambridge: Cambridge University Press.

Koskoff, Ellen. 1989. *Women and Music in Cross-Cultural Perspective*. Urbana: University of Illinois Press.

Labajo, Joaquina. 1996. "Música y tradición: Anotaciones sobre la mecánica de los procesos de cambio en las sociedades urbanas." *Boletín de la Real Academia de Bellas Artes de San Fernando* 83:255–69.

———. 1997. "How Musicological and Ethnomusicological Is Spanish Flamenco?" *TRANS Iberia* 1. Special edition of *Transcultural Music Review*. http://www2.uji.es/trans/TRANSIberia1/

Leblon, Bernard. 1991. *El cante flamenco*. Madrid: Cinterco.

Leppert, Richard. 1984. *The Sight of Sound: Music, Representation, and the History of the Body*. Berkeley and Los Angeles: University of California Press.

Machado Álvarez, Antonio. 1947. *Cantes flamencos*. Madrid: Espasa Calpe.

Magrini, Tullia. 1998. "Women's 'Work of Pain' in Christian Mediterranean Europe." *Music and Anthropology* 3. http://www.muspe.unibo.it/period/MA/

Mitchell, Timothy. 1994. *Flamenco Deep Song*. Yale: Yale University Press.

Molina, Miguel de. 1998. *Botín de guerra*. Barcelona: Planeta.

Molina, Ricardo, and Antonio Mairena. 1879. *Mundo y formas del cante flamenco*. Seville: Librería Al-Andalus.

Molina Fajardo, Eduardo. 1962. *Manuel de Falla y el cante jondo*. Granada: Universidad de Granada.

Monleón, José. 1967. *Lo que sabemos del flamenco*. Madrid: Gregorio del Toro.

Nieuwkerk, Karin van. 1998. "'An Hour for God and an Hour for the Heart': Islam, Gender, and Female Entertainment in Egypt." *Music and Anthropology* 3. http://www.muspe.unibo.it/period/MA/

Ortíz Nuevo, José Luis. 1990. *¿Se sabe algo? Viaje al conocimiento del arte flamenco según testimonios de la prensa sevillana del XIX* . Seville: Ediciones El Carro de la Nieve.

Pasqualino, Caterina. 1996. "La voix, le souffle, une séance de chant flamenco chez les Gitans de Jerez de la Frontera." *Tsiganes* 94 (2): 83–104.

Pineda Novo, Daniel. 1996. *Juana, La Macarrona, y el baile en los cafés cantantes.* Cornellà de LLobregat [Barcelona]: Aquí.

Pitt-Rivers, Julian. 1966. "Honour and Social Status." In *The Values of Mediterranean Society,* edited by John G. Perestiany, 19–78. Chicago: University of Chicago Press.

San Román, Teresa. 1997. *La diferencia inquietante: Viejas y nuevas estrategias culturales de los gitanos.* Madrid: Siglo XXI.

Starkie, Walter. 1944. *Don Gypsy.* Barcelona: Ediciones Pallas.

Steingress, Gerhard. 1990. "La aportación de Schuchardt a la investigación del flamenco: Un resumen 109 años después." In *Los cantes flamencos,* edited by Gerhard Steingress, 131–55. Seville: Fundación Machado. Originally published in 1881 as *Die Cantos Flamencos.*

Tolbert, Elizabeth. 1994. "The Voice of Lament: Female Vocality and Performative Efficacy in the Finnish-Karelian Itkuvirsi." In *Embodied Voices: Representing Female Vocality in Western Culture,* edited by Leslie C. Dunn and Nancy A. Jones, 179–94. Cambridge: Cambridge University Press.

Vaquero, Pedro. 1997. "Las grabaciones del concurso (colección Manuel de Falla) y la colección Federico García Lorca." In *I concurso de cante jondo,* CD and booklet. Sonifolk S.A. 20106.

Washabaugh, William. 1996. *Flamenco, Politics, and Popular Culture.* Oxford and Washington: Berg.

3

Those "Other Women":
Dance and Femininity among Prespa Albanians

Jane C. Sugarman

In the early 1990s, I returned to Toronto to visit members of the
Prespa Albanian community, whose wedding singing I had researched several years earlier (see Sugarman 1997). At three
large community events I attended, I was surprised by a shift I
detected in the style of the community's dancing. In past years,
Prespa events had been dominated by stately line dances, often
led by older individuals and executed in clearly demarcated male
and female styles. Now much of each evening was devoted to a
more Near Eastern style of solo dancing, and young women in
their teens and twenties were emerging as the most enthusiastic
dancers on the floor. Their movements had a sensuality and the-
atricality that was eschewed in the older line dances, and their
presence attracted the onlooker's attention in a new and provocative way.

This solo dancing, which Prespare call *çoçek,* was not completely new to me. Living in Macedonia a decade earlier, I had
learned a catchy new line dance, popular in both Skopje and the
Prespa villages, that was danced to songs and instrumental tunes

played in a syncopated 4/4 meter. The tunes themselves originated mostly among Rom wedding bands in eastern Macedonia, particularly the father-son clarinet and saxophone players Ilmi Jašarov and Ferus Mustafov. Both these and other tunes in 9/8 played by the same bands were labeled čoček (the Macedonian equivalent of Albanian çoçek).[1] What I was witnessing in Toronto was the arrival of çoçek tunes in 4/4 among immigrant Prespa communities in North America, who danced to them both the catchy line dance and the new solo dance.

Gradually I began to inquire as to why solo çoçek was so popular: why had it become the Prespa fad dance of the nineties? Most women didn't have a ready answer. The most common reasons offered had to do with contacts that community members had had with Turks and Turkey, with which the dancing was readily associated. One young woman, however, had an altogether different response. Raising her hands in the air and moving her torso back and forth, she intoned, "Move your body!" in imitation of ads with model Cindy Crawford that were then playing on MTV.

Notions of femininity and sexuality have always deeply informed Prespa women's music and dance, as they have the performance forms of women in communities throughout southeastern Europe. On the one hand, women seen as holding a "respectable" place in society have generally sung and danced in such a way as to mask their sexuality in order to convey their modesty and propriety. On the other hand, women who have functioned as professional entertainers have often presented themselves as eroticized objects of male—or even female—desire. What young Prespa women are accomplishing through their style of çoçek dancing is a fusion of those two feminine images in the body of a single performer. Like the young woman who alluded to Cindy Crawford, I see their adoption of this dance primarily as an attempt to constitute for themselves a new, more sexualized notion of femininity that is consistent with the ideals of the Western urban societies in which they now live.

Line Dances and Gender

At the time I began my research in Prespa villages in the early 1980s, most of the dancing that took place at community events was performed in the courtyard of the host family's home by integrated lines of men and women.[2] This dancing was executed to songs and instrumental music provided by professional bands of evgjitë, or Albanian-speaking Roma. At times, however, both women and men performed what I will call "dance songs": dances executed to unaccompanied singing. Women customarily performed their dance songs at weddings, either during evening gatherings or when the groom's party went to the bride's home to "take" her as the family's bride. Men performed theirs much more infrequently: perhaps once or twice during a day of dancing or to cap off a night of singing. Interviews with Presparë confirm that men formerly had a large repertoire of such dance songs. Their comments also suggest that, until the late nineteenth or early twentieth century, much if not all Prespa dancing was performed to the accompaniment of singing rather than instruments.[3] In short, song and dance have a long and intimate association among Prespa Albanians. During the period in which I have carried out research in North America, since the mid-1980s, Prespa women have continued to perform dance songs at gatherings held in private homes, but I have yet to see a men's dance song performed overseas. Since the mid-1980s, most dancing at events both in Prespa villages and in immigrant communities has taken place in a large indoor hall, where guests perform line dances to amplified music.

Prespa women refer to their dance songs as *këngë pe më këmbë* (lit., "songs sung on one's feet"), and they contrast these with their repertoire of songs that are sung while seated, *këngë pe më mbythë* (lit., "songs sung on one's behind"). Men refer to their dance songs as *këngë me valle* (lit., "song with dance"). Despite these differences in terminology, the women's and men's genres are structured in the same way. One person serves as the leader of a dance line that moves counterclockwise in a semicircle. The leader also sings the first of two solo lines of an accompanying song. A second individual dances next to the leader, singing a second solo line that interweaves with the first. The remaining people in the line, generally about four to six individuals, follow the two lead dancers and simultaneously sing a drone on the syllable *e*.[4]

Today, when most line dances are performed to instrumental music, one can still gain an insight into their typical configurations by viewing them as extensions of dance-song formations. Elsewhere in the central Balkans, it is common for all the dancers in a line to perform essentially the same movements, even though the leader of the line might embellish some figures more than the other dancers. But in the area in and around southern Albania, two alternative configurations are much more common. In the first, the leader of the dance line breaks off to turn in place or, in the case of men's dances, performs virtuosic solo movements such as squats or leaps, supported by the second person in line. Probably the most well known dance of this sort is the Greek dance *tsamiko,* whose name derives from the Albanian-speaking Çam people who formerly lived along the Greek-Albanian border. In the second configuration, the first two dancers split off from the rest of the line and perform a duet, while the remaining dancers continue the basic dance step or simply stop to watch the two soloists. The Prespa men's dance *devolliçe*, which ends with a duet in triple time, is among the best known of such dances. Each of these configurations grants a special role in the dance to the first two persons in line: those who would also be the vocal soloists in dance-songs.[5]

Elsewhere (see Sugarman 1989, 1997) I have analyzed in detail the differences between Prespa women's and men's song performances, and the ways that these differences have functioned to construct notions of gendered identity. Presparë perform their older line dances in parallel ways, in a manner inherited from the dance-song repertoire. The contrast between men's and women's dancing is particularly noticeable in the dancing of the leader of a line. As with singing, individuals take turns leading line dances at a social occasion as a gesture of respect for the family hosting the event. It is thus the dance's leader to whom the view of onlookers is specifically drawn. Although dancing is thought to be a "happy" activity, it is most important in this older style of dance to project one's dignity and grace rather than feelings of joyous abandon.

Most dances that women participate in are moderate to fast in tempo and executed in a strict meter. Women generally take smaller steps than men and dance standing closer together. In the course of a dance, they vary their footwork and their posture only slightly, and they often look downward as they do when they sing. The most characteristic features of women's dancing are a rigid and erect torso and limbs held close to the body. When a woman takes a step, she keeps her knees close together; and when she lifts her arms, she holds her elbows close to her sides. When she executes a slight knee bend, her body rises and falls as a unit. Once, when I was watching a video of a wedding with a Prespa family, a younger man commented that the dancing of one older woman had been criticized by other women because she bobbed up and down so much that her breasts jiggled. By moving her body as a unit and carefully controlling the movements of her limbs, a woman assures that the attention of onlookers will not be drawn to the more "private" and sexual parts of her body. Through her subdued manner, she presents herself both as sexually proper and socially deferential, and she demonstrates her self-control by deflecting attention from her personal emotional state through a downward or blank gaze.

In contrast, the preferred men's dances are those that are performed slowly and in an elastic meter. A common sight at dance events is a man standing at the head of a dance line, gesturing emphatically to the musicians to "play more slowly!" One of the slowest Prespa dances is the first part of devolliçe, the only dance associated exclusively with a single gender. Even in dances that are performed by both genders, male dance leaders will often set a slower and more sinuous tempo for their performance. A slower tempo serves as an invitation to a man to display through his dancing his emotional involvement in the occasion, and hence to draw attention to himself as an individual personality in a way that would be unbecoming for a woman.

Male dancers frequently vary their footwork or the style of their movements considerably as they dance, adding to the personal and spontaneous quality of their performances. In contrast to the stiffer, more circumscribed movements of women, they move their bodies more freely, often bending over as they lift their legs or moving their shoulders forward and back. When they step, they stretch the upper leg away from the torso, and when they raise an arm, they arch the whole arm away from the body. In slower dances, the first man or men in line may execute full squats rather than steps. In faster dances, men may leap high in the air or subdivide the basic dance step with rapid hops or skips. A blatant physicality is thus an express component of men's performances, although it is a physicality that stresses strength and agility rather than sensuality. In short, whereas women highlight modesty, propriety, and grace in their dancing, men emphasize their *fuqi*: their physical strength, mental acuity, and sexual potency. Whereas a woman's demeanor deflects attention from her individuality, a man's projects it.

Similar gendered contrasts may be identified in women's and men's dance styles throughout the large region where Albanians and/or Macedonians live. Community members often describe such differences using terms that translate as "light" and "heavy" (Alb. *lehtë* and *rëndë*; Mac. *lesno* and *teško*). In place of the word lehtë (light), Prespare refer to women's dancing as *shtruar* (calm, smooth). This same word is used to describe both the slower and softer of women's song performances and a particularly reserved and demure bodily demeanor (e.g., she sat very shtruar). Through this term, women's song and dance styles are recognized as counterparts to the modest and deferential demeanor that is expected of women in all social situations. Slow, elastic men's dances such as devolliçe, in contrast, are referred to as rëndë (heavy), a word that connotes both seriousness and importance, thus alluding to the greater emotional depth that is seen to characterize men's performances. These usages are akin to the American slang word "heavy" or the "heavy" in "heavy metal" music, and also to the frequently gendered designations, found in several world areas, of "classical" versus "light classical" music.[6]

Solo Dance in the Ottoman Period

I have just analyzed Prespa dance as if it were a closed system, in which women and men have mutually constructed notions of gendered identity through their own and each other's dancing. But at least since Ottoman times, the line dancing of villagers such as Presparë has also contrasted strongly with styles of solo dance that have been common primarily in the towns. I characterize this dance as "solo" not because it is danced by a single individual, but because each person dances individually without holding another dancer's hand or waist. For most of the Ottoman period, solo dance seems to have been the domain of two types of individuals: slaves, primarily women, who performed only within their own household; and hired entertainers, who might be either women or young boys, and who sometimes performed in public venues. A number of terms were used for these professional entertainers, including *rakkas, köçek,* and *çengi* (the first two primarily for males, the last for either gender). What the various types of solo dance had in common was an emphasis not on footwork, as in line dances, but on delicate arm and hand movements, which sometimes involved manipulation of a kerchief or the playing of wooden or metal clappers (*çalpara* or *çampara*). To these were often added a shimmying of the shoulders or breasts and various movements of the torso, abdomen, head, and eyes. Depending on the context of performance, dancers might also incorporate more virtuosic or theatrical elements: backbends, twirling, manipulation of objects such as plates and swords, and routines in which performers of a single gender mimed heterosexual amorous encounters. Gradually the various forms of this dance developed into both cabaret "belly dancing" and types of social dancing such as the Turkish *çiftetelli* (in 4/4; cf. Greek *tsifteteli*) and *karşilama* (in 9/8), and related Balkan forms whose names derive from the word köçek: *kyuchek* (among Bulgarians), *čoček* (among Serbs and Macedonians), and *çoçek* or *çyçek* (among Albanians).

Primary sources on Ottoman solo dance, whether in what is now Turkey or in southeastern Europe, consist primarily of pictorial representations by Ottoman or European artists and accounts by European travelers or longtime residents of the empire. To these may be added a few descriptions by Ottoman subjects, such as the writings of Evliya Çelebi (Evliya 1846), and some early-twentieth-century writings by residents of the new Balkan nation-states. The picture that emerges from these various sources is far from clear, and the Orientalist tone of some writers, including those from the region, makes interpretation all the more challenging. What follows is an attempt to piece together a cautious account of solo dance that allows for variation both over time and between locales. In my descriptions, I will follow a convention among recent writers of designating boy dancers as köçeks and women dancers as çengis (see, for example, Sevengil 1985, And 1976, and Popescu-Judetz 1982).

For most of the Ottoman period, it would seem that the dancers who performed in public spaces were the köçeks. Several sixteenth-century miniatures show a single male dancer or small group of dancers performing at the court of the sultan, in the courtyard of elite homes, or in procession with court musicians and other entertainers (see And 1976 for many such depictions). Their distinctive style of dress linked them clearly to the feminine: a long, wide skirt; a tight jacket, often with a peplum; and long hair worn either loose or tied up on the head and held, perhaps by a skullcap. They accompanied their movements with a pair of wooden çalpara held in each hand. Similar dancing could be seen in the homes of the elite, presented by the household's female slaves:

> Her fair maids were ranged below the Sofa, to the number of twenty, and put me in mind of the pictures of the ancient nymphs. I did not think all nature could have furnished such a scene of beauty. She made them a sign to play and dance. Four of them immediately began to play some soft airs on instruments, between a lute and guitar, which they accompanied with their voices, while the others danced by turns. This dance was very different from what I had se[e]n before. Nothing could be more artful, or more proper to raise *certain Ideas*. The tunes so soft!—The motions so languishing!—accompanied with pauses and dying eyes; half-falling back and then recovering themselves in so artful a manner, that I am very positive, the coldest and most rigid prude upon earth, could not have looked upon them without thinking of *something not to be spoken of.* (Lady Wortley Montague, writing in 1717; see Montague 1994, 90)

The performance of music and dance was considered important as a feminine accomplishment, and slaves were at times given formal training in both (see Davis 1986, 158–62).[7]

Already by the seventeenth century, some boy performers were organized into professional companies, or *kols*. In his detailed description of Ottoman life dating from the seventeenth century, Evliya Çelebi (Evliya 1846, 240–41) mentions twelve companies of boy dancers and mimics who performed in Istanbul, each numbering between one hundred and three thousand. They would then be hired out in small groups that performed set choreographies:

> The rest danc't 4, 6, sometimes 8 in a company. It consists most in
> wriggling the body . . . , slipping their steps round gently; setting and
> turning. Never is there arming, or any figure, or handling. . . . They
> alwayes come before the person (where they dance) running . . . ;
> then they fall either into a semi-circle or whole round, and so con-
> tinue falling out of one tune and humour into another, till at last with
> a merry wherry of their musick, they turn round (as the Dervises) a
> long time, and so stopping they bow, and away run to their musick,
> which are always hard by. (And 1976, 139–40, quoting *Dr. Covel's
> Diary* from the 1670s)

Companies of köçeks were a major attraction at the many wine taverns (*mey-
hanes*) found in the Galata district of Istanbul. According to both Evliya
and subsequent European writers, they were generally not ethnic Turks but
members of various minority ethnicities such as Greeks, Armenians, Jews, or
Roma.[8]

Although they may have existed earlier, the first mention of a kol of
female çengis dates from the eighteenth century (see And 1976, 143–44;
Davis 1986, 160). The account describes a company of twelve dancers who
performed lengthy choreographies in four sections, accompanied by women
musicians playing violin, small kettledrums (*çifte nağara*), and two frame
drums (*daire*). A single miniature from the same period provides some idea
of the çengi's attire (see And 1976, 57). It depicts a solo dancer wearing
an ankle-length gown of transparent silk with long, loose sleeves; loose red
pants that are visible beneath the gown; and cloth slippers. Over the gown a
long brocade coat with a low, scooped neckline and cutaway sleeves is but-
toned across the upper torso and belted at the waist, and then opens to reveal the dancer's legs. On her head is a small turbaned headdress with large
plumes on either side, and in each hand she carries wooden çalpara.

In place of slaves, troupes of çengis might be hired to perform in elite
homes for the entertainment of women guests, as in this description of a large
gathering in Istanbul in the 1720s:

> The troupe was composed of ten women slaves who performed differ-
> ent concerts, during which a band of dancers, not less richly but more
> indecorously dressed, came to execute different ballets sufficiently
> agreeable because of the figures and variety of the steps. The dancers
> were of the best troupe, for they ordinarily performed in private
> houses: soon a new band of twelve women, dressed as men, arrived,
> without doubt to add to this tableau the appearance of the sex the

festivities lacked. These feigned men commenced then a sort of joust, in order to contend for and secure the fruits which the other slaves came to throw into the pool. A little boat conducted by female boat-men, equally disguised as men, gave the foreigners the pleasure of a promenade on the water, after which, rowed to the sultan, they prayed leave of her with the ceremonies of usage. (Davis 1986, 160–61)

As this instance illustrates, female troupes often included dancers dressed as men, sometimes referred to as *tavşans*, who pantomimed flirtatious encounters with those dressed as women. Not all women's performances were for other women, however; a few accounts suggest that concubines and slaves also danced for their masters.[9]

By the nineteenth and early twentieth centuries, women entertainers had moved into more public and less elite settings. European writers provide several descriptions of women dancers performing with wedding musicians for both male and female spectators. While, to my knowledge, no earlier account suggests the ethnicity of women performers, these later descriptions are invariably of Roma. The following account is significant in that the observer was a man:

> Another girl was brought in, also gaudily dressed, and the two began to dance, all the assisting crowd clapping their hands in unison. More wine was brought, and two glasses were handed to the girls, who gulped them down, and began to dance more furiously than ever. The dance was a variety of the usual Turkish *danse du ventre*—more than usually lascivious. After a time, when the movements were at their height, the two *cheia* [young Rom girls] threw themselves on their knees in front of me, and continued to dance with the upper part of their bodies and arms and fingers, at the same time thrusting their faces nearer and nearer mine, and using their black eyes with great effect. I then did what was expected of me: I took pieces of money, and licking them, stuck them on the foreheads of the girls, who immediately got up, and handed the money to the pipe-player as soon as it showed signs of becoming loose. (Gilliat-Smith 1910–11, 79; see Garnett 1891, 359, for another account of Rom women dancers)

Descriptions linking women dancers to male wedding musicians suggest that the earlier kol system, in which male and female dancers performed in separate, single-gender companies, was giving way to, or being augmented by, mixed-gender performance ensembles, principally of Roma, that may well have been family-based.

European observers invariably found the movements of solo dance, particularly those that emphasized the torso or abdomen, to be overtly sexual, and frequently described them as "lascivious" and "wanton." But were they regarded as such by members of Ottoman society? It is clear from Ottoman sources that audiences regarded dancers of either gender, at least when performing for men, as objects of beauty and desire. In earlier centuries, elite men were known to squander large sums of money upon boy dancers, and to address verses of love poetry to them:

> *Rakkas,* is this state [of ecstasy] in your dance?
> Is your lover's sin on your neck [i.e., your responsibility]?
> I haven't had enough reunion evenings with you like the fasting day's
>   night [a reference to nighttime social gatherings during Ramadan]
> Ey silver-bodied one, is [this state] in your morning's embrace?
>
> (Sevengil 1985, 86)

In the early nineteenth century, an Ottoman gentleman named Enderunlı Fazıl Bey compiled two books about köçeks that highlight such erotic associations (And 1976, 141). The first, the *Defter-i Aşk* (Book of Love), is a collection of love verses dedicated to a single köçek, Çingene (Gypsy) Ismail, who lived in the eighteenth century; while the second, the *Çenginame* (Book of Dancing Boys), describes famous dancers of the early nineteenth century. Both European commentators (see, for example, those quoted in Brandl 1994, 233) and twentieth-century Turkish writers (Sevengil 1985, 83–86; And 1976, 143) have characterized either the köçeks or the sentiments shown them by Ottoman men as homosexual. Within Ottoman constructions of sexuality, however, a man might feel erotic attraction to both women and young men without being seen to be something that would translate as "homosexual," and being an object of male desire as a young man did not preclude marriage at a later date. In 1857, in the wake of the Tanzimat reforms, the köçeks were outlawed by the Ottoman government. The ban was ostensibly part of a crackdown on the Janissaries, the empire's most elite troops (And 1976, 141). But occurring at a time when the government was seeking more and more to model the empire upon European societies, it is possible that it was in part an attempt to impose European notions of morality on Ottoman society.[10]

It seems likely that the ban on köçek performances encouraged the development of a class of women dancers who performed for male audiences other than their masters. This situation, together with the increased presence of Western visitors to Turkey, may in turn have prompted them to develop the more eroticized and flamboyant style of performance that is implied in later writings. The display of feminine beauty, grace, and delicacy was always a part of the women's style of performance, and flirtatiousness and sensuality must surely have been emphasized in earlier performances presented for the men of a household. But some Turkish writers have alluded to a homoerotic component in performances for women as well. Sevengil's description of çengis, written in the 1920s, focuses largely on their same-sex orientation, claiming that they had sexual relations with each other and were the objects of longing on the part of their women patrons (Sevengil 1985, 87–90). Neither he, however, nor later writers who have passed on his commentary (e.g., And 1976, 143) provide citations for this information. Nevertheless, some corroborating evidence exists for related types of performers. Oldenburg (1990), researching present-day women entertainers (*tawa'if*) in northern India, found that they were organized into women-led companies reminiscent of the Ottoman kols. Of the women whom she interviewed, a few said that they considered their only possibilities for love relationships to exist with other women in the group.[11]

Descriptions of solo dance in the Ottoman Balkans closely resemble those from Turkey proper. In the early nineteenth century, the series of European travelers who made their way to Janina (Gk. Ioannina) to visit the courts of the renegade Albanian ruler Ali Pasha and his sons reported styles of music and dance much like those found in the Ottoman court or in elite homes of Istanbul (see Brandl 1994 for an overview of this literature). In a tour of Ali's palace, for example, Hobhouse was shown the place where his favorite women danced for him:

> it is to this retreat that the Vizier withdraws during the heats
> of the summer, with the most favored ladies of his harem, and in-
> dulges in the enjoyment of whatever accomplishments these fair
> ones can display for his gratification. Our attendant pointed out to
> us, in a recess, the sofa on which Ali was accustomed to sit, whilst,
> on the marble floor of the saloon, his females danced before him
> to the music of the Albanian lute. (Hobhouse Broughton 1817,
> 1:69–70)

A few years later, Thomas Hughes encountered köçeks, as well as a small *mehter,* at an entertainment held in the home of a prominent Christian at which Ali was present:

the rooms were brilliantly lighted up, and the clang of cymbals,
drums, and Turkish instruments of music, denoted the presence of
a potentate. We stopped for a short time in a large ante-room, where
the vizier's band was playing to a troop of dancing boys, dressed in
the most effeminate manner, with flowing petticoats of crimson silk,
and silver-clasped zones around the waist: they were revolving in one
giddy and interminable circle, twisting their pliant bodies into the
most contorted figures, and using the most lascivious gestures,
throwing about their arms and heads like infuriated Bacchanals,
and sometimes bending back their bodies till their long hair actually
swept the ground. (Hughes 1820, 2:48)

Consistent with the mid-nineteenth-century ban on köçeks, however, all
the descriptions dating later than Ali Pasha's time are of women performers,
most of them Roma.[12] Brandl (1994, 234–37; 1996, 9), noting the presence
of Jewish musicians in Ali's court, has suggested that new economic opportunities provided to non-Muslims by the Tanzimat reforms, which began
in the 1830s, might gradually have led non-Rom musicians in the empire to
abandon that profession in favor of more lucrative ones. Roma were nevertheless excluded from such opportunities. It is thus perhaps first in the post-
Tanzimat period that Roma became the preeminent performers of popular
music and dance in both Turkey and the Ottoman Balkans.

One of the most complete descriptions of the çengis who came to the
fore after Ali's time is that of Ekrem Bey Vlora, a member of the Muslim Albanian landowning class. Here he describes a performance at a men's gathering held in the home of an elite gentleman in Berat (see also plate 6):

Four Rom beauties honor[ed] us today: Shahe, Mini i Vogël ("Little
Mini"), Hysnie, and Dife. The first represented the falling, and the
fourth the rising, star in the sky of beauty, art, and love. All were
radiant in multicolored, gold-covered velvet and silk clothing. . . .

The[y] entered the room in a row, greeted [the guests], and sat
down, with tambourine (def) in hand, in front of the musicians.
Then they stood up to sing and dance, accompanying themselves
with the def and keeping the beat of the music. At other times they
exchanged the def for çampara.

. . . The çingis do not cultivate [line dances]: they dance dyshe.
This is a very specific figure-dance, similar to the minuet performed
in pairs, in which the steps and posture are constantly varied and in
which, when danced in an artful manner by pretty young girls, grace

is not lacking. Even more difficult is the "Aliko-Lamçe," known for
the name of its originator, which is danced by two or, more often,
by a single dancer. The çingis are also masters of the Oriental belly
dance (*Bauchtanz*), within which they incorporate several feats. So,
for example, Shahe placed a full glass of water on her head and then
isolated all the various parts of her body in trembling movements
without spilling even one drop of water. Dife, prompted by this,
threw a jatagan on the floor and, following the beat of the music,
bent over completely backwards until she could grab the blade with
her teeth and pick up the weapon from the floor.

Each round of applause, and even each favorable nod of the
head, produced a storm of lovely fairies, who fell back [into the lap
of their] admirer; so that he, depending on his financial capabilities,
would place a larger or smaller amount of change on their forehead
or cheek. Not seldom I have seen someone moisten with spit a heavy
gold piece that didn't wish to stick, even though this might be seen
as ungallant. (Vlora 1911, 72–73)[13]

A similar account from 1903 is offered by the Serbian ethnographer Tihomir
Đorđević describing musical life in formerly Ottoman territories that were
annexed by Serbia in 1878. Although his account is in the present tense, it
would seem to refer back to the final days of Ottoman rule:[14]

In conclusion, I must also mention the Rom dancers čočeke or čengije, who cultivate dancing for pay in the guesthouses and private
homes of the new regions. . . . One or two Rom women dance, bending and turning with the greatest elegance and lightness and keeping
the beat with castanets attached to their fingers. These are the čengije
or čočeci. While they dance, one or two Rom men play the violin
and a Rom woman plays the drum. From time to time they also sing
some Turkish song or one composed in the Oriental spirit. Both the
music and the song intoxicate and transport the listener with the Oriental magic of their particular charms. The beauty of many a čoček,
their dexterous dance, their gracious pliancy, the agility of their individual limbs, their ingratiating Oriental music, the charming song
and its ambience commonly engender an uncommonly delightful,
unforgettable impression. (Đorđević 1903, 48)

Performances by Rom çengis at the women's portions of weddings have also
been noted for western Macedonia (Džimrevski 1985, 34–35; see also Has-

luck 1938, 2:25–29, for descriptions of Rom dance of various types in Albania). When çengis performed for women's gatherings, they often participated as part of a small women's ensemble that included singers, dancers, and musicians playing daire (frame drum) and, less commonly, violin (Hasluck 1938, 2:24; Janković and Janković 1939, 95; Džimrevski 1985, 37). In instances where they performed for men's gatherings or for integrated events, however, they were often brought to the event by a larger ensemble (Alb. *aheng,* Mac. *čalgija*) of male musicians who sang and played violin, clarinet, daire, any of several types of lute, and perhaps *kanun* (Vlora 1911, 71; Hasluck 1938; Çaushi 1974). In Albanian areas, these male musicians might be Roma or Albanian, or an ensemble might be of mixed ethnicity (Çaushi 1974).

Despite their popularity and appeal, two factors surrounding the performances of çengis or çoçeks seem to have led to deeply ambivalent attitudes toward them on the part of the local population. First was the fact that, unlike community performers who sang or danced at rural celebrations, the çengis and their accompanists solicited monetary payment for their services. Furthermore, such payments could be excessive. Like the earlier male köçeks, whose designation they seem to have inherited, female dancers became the preoccupation, and at times the ruin, of their male admirers. Ekrem Bey includes in his account the lyrics of a love song written in honor of the çengi Shahe from Berat (Vlora 1911, 87–88):

Mbi balluke tende	[Above the bangs of your hair
Po kendonte zogu,—	The sparrow sang.
Na sevdaje Shahes,	For love of Shahe
çeli borziloku!	The basil bloomed!
Mbi balluke tende	Above the bangs of your hair
Po kendon bilbili—	The nightingale sang.
Na sevdaje Shahes,	For love of Shahe
çeli trendafili!	The roses bloomed!
Vetullat e tua	Your eyebrows
Si kalem meqtepi.	Are [as fine as] a feather quill.
Qjo sevdaje Shahes,—	This love for Shahe
mua s'eç me ndezi!	Has extinguished me in flames!]

Ekrem Bey and others also describe lavish tipping following çengi performances (Vlora 1911, 73; Hasluck 1938, 2:27–28). Hasluck notes that, in the early part of the century, "vast sums were squandered by the young and foolish on dancing girls," and that evening entertainments could develop into a contest between rival admirers (1938, 2:28–29). The gentleman who ruins himself for love of a Rom çengi is in fact the theme of one of the classics of Balkan literature: the play *Koštana,* by Serbian playwright Bora Stanković, which recounts life in turn-of-the-century Vranje. In reaction to this syndrome, the Albanian government banned çengi performances in public venues in the late 1920s, although the ban was lifted several years later.[15]

A second factor was the reputation for sexual immorality that dogged the çengis. Ekrem Bey labeled the dancers whom he witnessed "courtesans" (*kurtisane*), and suggested that they feigned romantic sentiments toward their male clients (Vlora 1911, 73). Hasluck, in her extensive report on Roma in Albania, noted that "courtesans" were common among sedentary Rom women, explaining that only through relations with them could young Albanian men gain the degree of sexual experience that was expected of them before marriage. While some were "kept" by individual men, others were "at everyone's beck and call" (Hasluck 1938, 3:115–16). Berzatnik (1930, 68), who encountered former dancers in Albania at the time of the ban on çengis, accused Rom women and girls of "selling their love," although he implied that it was the ban itself that had left them without an adequate livelihood. What is important here is not the "truth" of such statements, but the fact that çengis were consistently associated with prostitution. Even if not actual prostitutes, çengis could be interpreted as "selling their bodies" simply because they performed for men for pay in a way that drew specific attention to their bodies.[16] Their identity as Roma was yet another factor contributing to their poor reputation, leading to a highly ironic situation for them: having taken up the role of entertainer in part because it was one of the few economic niches available to them as a marginal social group, they were then further marginalized by the profession itself. Their perceived indecency could then be ascribed by non-Roma to the moral character of their ethnic group, rather than to the particular social and economic conditions and gender arrangements that prevailed within late Ottoman society.

By the turn of the twentieth century, when nationalist movements heated up throughout southeastern Europe, the immorality associated with çengis could also be called upon by Christian groups to symbolize the decadence of Muslim society in general. As one example, a Serbian publication from 1910 on "Macedonia and the Macedonians" (Ivanić 1910) features a series of illustrations contrasting Macedonian Christian Slavs with their Muslim Albanian neighbors. In one plate (p. 177), a Macedonian woman and child are pictured bringing a saint's day meal to Macedonian men lying chained in an Ottoman prison. This is contrasted with several plates showing Albanian men carousing raucously in a tavern (p. 163 and facing p. 192), or clustering around a dancing girl performing in the streets (pp. 103, 131). In a provocative misrepresentation of the characteristic çengi attire, one of the dancers appears dressed only in balloon pants and a short vest, her breasts otherwise bared to her male onlookers (see plate 7). Such depictions reveal not only the stance of disapprobation adopted by commentators wishing to align themselves with more European and "Christian" notions of morality, but also a fascination with the sensual, the exotic, and the "Oriental" that is equally evident in the more sympathetic commentaries of both Balkan and Turkish writers of this period (as, for example, Đorđević 1903 and Sevengil 1985).

As accounts from the early twentieth century attest, women entertainers were gradually emerging from the realm of elite private gatherings and entering the public realm of taverns (meanas) and "coffee houses" (kaf[e]anas, which were more often restaurants or nightclubs). Džimrevski (1985, 34–35) mentions dancers known as zejbeks who performed in the meanas in the town of Tetovo in western Macedonia; and provides a detailed description of the women, known as čočeks, who appeared regularly in the kafeanas of Skopje during the 1920s:

> In the group of [ensemble leader] Redžep Said three to four women took part, professional dancers called čočeks. Of the dancers the one who was considered the most outstanding and unusually talented in her dancing was Roza, who had spent several years in Arabia, and afterwards came to Skopje as a specialist in Oriental čoček dances. Another dancer by the name of Stela [Ashkenazi] distinguished herself with her outstanding voice and interpretation of Turkish folk songs. The dancers, that is, the čočeks, often used metal finger cymbals or wooden spoons in their dancing, depending on the character of the dance, with which they realized the rhythmic basis of the dance. For the audiences at the kafeanas, the dancing of the čočeks represented a true balletic-artistic accomplishment. Since there were no čočeks in Skopje, more often such groups came from Solun. The čočeks named Roza, Ida, Lala, and Pepina were of Jewish descent and at the kafeanas, in addition to dances, also performed Jewish folk songs. For a certain time the čalgija of Redžep Said played in Beograd at the kafeana "Dardaneli." (Džimrevski 1985, 36)

The photos accompanying his description show the women not in the older Ottoman style of dress, but rather sporting fashionable "bobbed" haircuts and wearing Western dresses in a sort of "flapper" style. Both their image and their seeming emphasis on professionalism suggest an attempt to fend off the scandalous reputation of women performers by assimilating their role to that of the European cabaret or *café chantant* singer.[17]

The most extensive descriptions from the early twentieth century of dance in Macedonia are those of Ljubica and Danica Janković. In their seven-volume collection, one finds glimmers not only of the types of performance mentioned above, but of a richer and more varied situation for dance. On the one hand are dances that would seem to descend from much earlier performances by köçeks and çengis, such as a type of pantomime dance performed by Muslims in the town of Debar:

> Čiček is a Muslim dance in which two men or two women participate. In the first part each of them holds a stretched kerchief at its two ends; the kerchief is not used at all in the second half. The dance portrays a chase. The motions of the hands indicate the desire of the hunter to catch the other dancer. The hunted dancer defends himself with his hands. During the whole time they look each other in the eye without blinking. In the end the hunted one is caught. (According to one Debar man, the dancers must kiss at the end, but the two dancers who showed the dance to us were ashamed and so they didn't perform this final action.) Even though people of the same gender participate, the dance expresses an erotic moment. (Janković and Janković 1939, 97–98)

One brief passage also includes what seems to be the first mention of a specific type of Rom dancing known as čoček:

> the Gostivar Gypsies . . . also cherish their čoček dances, which involve movement of the abdomen, shoulder blades, and hips as well as a movement of the head from right to left as if it were being transferred from shoulder to shoulder. (136)

On the other hand are many descriptions of the social dances of Christian and Muslim urban families, many of which were performed either solo or, without holding hands, in pairs or larger configurations. One of the most evocative descriptions is of Muslim women's dancing at weddings in Tetovo:

> The typical form of old Muslim women's dances is the solo dance. The Muslim woman performs, in various rhythms, very elegant and expressive movements. Her bearing in this is calm, but not dead.

Gentle bending at the waist and adroit movement of the arms which are raised out to the side at shoulder height while the elbows are pressed against the waist—give their dance a special charm.

In addition to solo dancing, Turkish women also nurture dancing in groups, maintaining in this the basic characteristics of solo dancing. Earlier, Turkish women never joined hands in dance. Now, sometimes they join hands only by the little finger while their arms remain raised to shoulder height out to the side. Then they dance very harmoniously, together and tastefully, in a calm tempo.

Besides a beauty of movement, Turkish women also display a very developed sense of rhythm, which is sometimes quite complex. (95) [18]

In contrast with the more flamboyant performances of çengis, here the dancers' emphasis seems to have been on an erect posture, a bending at the waist rather than pelvic or abdominal movements, and small movements of the arms and hands. In other words, here was a type of solo social dance, deriving from the dance of the Ottoman elite, which was probably very similar in ethos to the dignified line dancing of Prespa women.

What has been the legacy of köçeks and çengis since the early twentieth century? Because of the early ban against them, there is little community memory within former Ottoman areas of the köçeks. Nevertheless, And (1976) notes performances of boy dancers as well as young women at rural weddings in Turkey, each carrying on aspects of the older performance forms. And Hunt (1996, 56–57) has documented a carnival dance in northern Greece performed by Rom boys in female dress who are known as kechekides. Like their predecessors, they perform to their own singing and playing of finger cymbals, accompanied on lyra (vertical fiddle) and frame drums.

The çengis, however, are present as a shadowy memory in many types of female performance. In Turkey, aside from rural performers, the most direct descendants are the Rom "belly dancers" who perform in Istanbul nightclubs both in tourist areas and in the Rom quarter Sulukule.[19] And (1976, 133–34) also implies that pantomime dances such as those performed by köçeks and çengis developed in the early twentieth century into forms of stage performance, such as Kanto, in which a woman singer used facial expressions and hand gestures to enact the lyrics of her song. In southeastern Europe, such techniques are still very much a part of the performances of Rom and non-Rom women "folk" singers in kafanas and stage shows, who may also execute dance movements during instrumental interludes. Since the socialist period, folkloric troupes in Yugoslavia have regularly performed choreographic suites drawn from the çengi repertoire, although under Tito they were given ethnic ascriptions in line with the country's pluralistic cultural policies. "Turkish" suites might feature dancers who balance trays or other props on their heads, while the celebrated "South Serbian" choreography features women dressed in short vests and balloon pants dancing with frame drum in hand. Within Muslim communities, the legacy of çengis is even more immediate. Particularly in western Kosova (Serb. Kosovo), Rom women known as çengis have frequently been hired to sing and play daire for dancing at the women's portion of Albanian weddings and other celebrations (see chap. 12, this volume).[20] And as of the late 1980s, there was evidently at least one female Rom dancer, known as a çoçek, who performed for Muslim men's social occasions in Skopje.[21]

As the descriptions of the Janković sisters suggest, the solo dance of the Ottoman period also lives on throughout the region in forms of social dance, which have themselves at times become the basis of folkloric choreographies. Perhaps closest to their description of Muslim women's dance is *kcim,* performed by young Albanian women in Kosova and western Macedonia (see Reineck 1985). This is solo dance at its most dignified and proper, danced with downcast eyes and with an emphasis on side-to-side arm movements and delicate undulations of the hands, but without any articulation of the torso. In the socialist period a choreographed version of kcim, known as *shota,* was developed by the national folkloric troupe "Kolo" from Serbia to represent Kosova Albanian dance. Unlike the village form, it is performed by a male-female couple in an upbeat, flirtatious manner and features much broader arm movements. Aspects of this choreography have since been adopted by Albanian troupes as well. Rom women, at their own community occasions, perform what they call čoček, a dance that features a distinctive up-and-down movement of the pelvis in addition to shimmying and arm movements. In recent decades, Rom troupes in the former Yugoslavia have presented choreographed versions of this dance on television and at large festivals, capitalizing on its exotic appeal to non-Roma.[22] In Turkey, women executing solo dance at a wedding or other large event often incorporate shimmying, as well as movements of the hips and abdomen, that they have seen in nightclub belly dance performances, bringing their style of dance closer to the older professional forms. In short, the solo dance of the Ottoman period has gradually developed into a great variety of closely related forms danced by virtually all ethnic groups in former Ottoman territories. In recent years, several of these forms have contributed to the emergence of a new type of çoçek dancing among Albanians.

Çoçek and the Sensualization of Prespa Dance

In recent years, the influence of Ottoman solo dance has become apparent in the otherwise stately dancing of the Prespa community. Among overseas families, dancing has emerged as the expressive form of choice for most younger individuals, while singing is becoming increasingly the domain of older members of the community. There are many reasons for this apparent shift in emphasis, but one crucial factor is a desire on the part of younger Presparë to redefine themselves in ways that are more congruent with urban life both in the former Yugoslavia and in North America. The community's local song and dance repertoires, with their narrowly defined constructions of femininity and masculinity, evoke images of personal and group identity that younger Presparë find constricting, and they imply power relations with which many community members are increasingly uncomfortable: not only the precedence granted in many domains to men over women, but also that granted to older adults over younger ones. In response, younger Presparë are creating new forms of music and dance that combine an assertion of Albanian and Muslim identity with greater generational autonomy and new sense of a more "sexualized" gendered identity (cf. Abu-Lughod 1990, 49).

One recent innovation has been the formation by younger men of amplified bands that play music for listening and dancing in the style of older Rom ensembles. These bands provide a setting for musical experimentation that is not overseen by the community's elders, and members are able to carve out a musical role at events that is distinct from that of the older generation. One home gathering that I attended in the mid-1980s in fact threatened to turn into an intergenerational showdown when a band made up of four young men intermittently interrupted the older men's singing at points throughout the evening. The primary venue for their playing, however, is not home gatherings but large dance events held in a banquet hall, where they perform on an elevated stage.

Younger women have been far less successful in developing a new musical role at such events. The greatest restriction upon them as singers has been that they must avoid any style of performance that would summon up the historic image of the kafana singer. At gatherings held in a home, they must be careful to avoid any mannerisms such as gesturing with their hands, making eye contact with those around them, or using their facial expression to illustrate the sentiments conveyed in their song: all techniques associated with professional entertainers. Until the early 1990s, women also refrained altogether from singing at events held in a banquet hall, even simply singing unaccompanied songs with other women into a microphone. At that time, however, one young woman from Kosova who had married into the community did begin to perform as a solo singer with her husband's band. To do so she risked her honor and that of her household; it was only after two or three years that the gossip died down and she was able to feel that her new role as a singer had been accepted.[23]

Rather than singing, most younger Prespa women are experimenting with new images of femininity through their dancing, primarily by drawing upon, modifying, and combining two older types of solo dance: shota, in emulation of the way it is danced in Kosova, and a slower type of solo dance that they call çoçek. With its links to the old performance form of Rom women, çoçek would have no place at a Prespa event were it to be danced as a solo form. Younger Presparë therefore mitigate its performative associations by dancing it as a line dance, as is also the case with shota. Fifteen years ago in Prespa, I saw each of these dances performed occasionally as a line dance: shota to the tune of an upbeat song from Kosova called "Shota mashalla," and çoçek to a slow, Turkish-style clarinet improvisation. In recent years, dancers at overseas events have gradually combined them into a single form that can be danced in a range of tempos. In this new form, groups of younger women, as well as mixed couples who might be married or simply relatives, begin a simple line dance in duple time. The leader, or the first couple, then breaks off and begins a series of soloistic movements that combine the broad arm waving of shota with the subtle torso and hip movements, kerchief manipulation, and delicate hand gestures of çoçek. The new dance is thus consistent with the standard configurations for older Prespa dancing: a line dance with an active solo dancer or couple at its head.

Each of these borrowed dances carries a range of associations for Presparë. As with virtually any folkloric form from Kosova, shota is an important symbol of Albanian patriotism. When danced by a male-female couple, it also suggests an Albanian society that is modernizing away from the gender segregation of the old order. Çoçek implies the worldly sophistication of the old Ottoman urban elite, but simultaneously elements of licentiousness and exoticism: if not associated directly with the professional çoçek dancer of the past, then with the current Rom dancers familiar to Presparë through folkloric presentations. Its successful incorporation into a line-dance format therefore requires particularly careful negotiation on the part of the individual dancer. At events that I attended in Toronto in the mid-1980s, the outer limit of acceptability was defined by the daughters of the local oxha, or Muslim religious leader, who was not Albanian but Bosnian. Rather than dancing çoçek as do the local Albanians, the oxha's daughters incorporated into their dancing movements of the torso, hips, and arms derived from contemporary

Turkish belly dance. Prespa women who are somewhat older generally emphasize small arm and hand gestures and interactions with their partner using a kerchief: both types of movement that seem to have been part of the older dancing of elite urban women. Those in their teens and twenties, however, may add small hip and torso movements, sinuous movements of the arms and shoulders, or coquettish facial expressions: movements that clearly evoke the çengi performances of an earlier era.

What younger Prespa women are accomplishing through their experiments with çoçek is a merging of two types of dance that were formerly regarded as utterly opposed: the demure line dancing of villagers and the more provocative solo dancing of urban entertainers. Although their performances are often cautious, the playfulness and sensuality of their movements, their overt interaction with their partners, and the degree to which their dancing becomes the focus of attention for others present signal a major departure from the community's older dance style. In the mid to late 1980s, only married women participated as leaders of this dance, and my interpretation was that it was not deemed appropriate for a woman not yet married to depict herself as being in touch with the sensuality of her body. Women also performed the more sensuous movements of this dance only when dancing with other women. By the early 1990s, however, this new type of dancing had become the most popular style for young unmarried women as well, who also perform it with each other rather than with young men. By dancing in this manner, they suggest at the very least an awareness of their sexuality, if not firsthand experience with it, that would have been disturbing to past generations of Prespa parents, but that is now ruefully acknowledged as a factor to be reckoned with, given the societies in which young people are being raised.

Aside from the implications of its movement repertoire, the new dance style signals a major transformation in courtship practices within the community, and thus in who it is that young women "perform" for at a community event. In earlier periods, when dancing took place at segregated gatherings, unmarried girls were on display for older generations of women who were actively scrutinizing them as potential brides for their sons. They were thus very much objects of a "female gaze," although emphatically not a sexual one, and so it was essential that they emphasize both their sexual propriety and their deference to their older audience. Today it is often a young man who initiates his family's inquiry into a prospective bride by spotting an attractive young woman at a large, integrated social event. As they float across the dance floor, young women are thus offering themselves to the gaze of the men of their own generation. By dancing with another woman, they are able to display their grace and sensuality to all the young men present, while avoiding the gossip that would result if they danced with a particular young man.

The body that a young woman displays on the dance floor is also a somewhat new one. At a women's gathering in Toronto in the early 1990s, a Prespa grandmother took me aside and explained to me that a young woman's dancing was formerly taken as evidence that she was physically fit enough to be considered an appropriate bride. For past generations, an eligible young woman was expected to be reasonably slender-waisted (*bel-ollë*) but also to be sturdily built so that she could carry out an array of physically demanding household chores. Such a female ideal was so widespread that it is still firmly entrenched in the Albanian language. As in most dialects, Presparë use the adjective *e shëndoshë* to mean both "healthy" and physically plump, whereas a woman who is very thin is *e dobët,* literally "weak." At present, however, young Prespa women both in Macedonia and in North America are increasingly cultivating an ultrathin body as their physical ideal, one that is typified by the fashion models, soap opera stars, and winners of beauty pageants that they have encountered through the Western media. Rather than clothe their bodies in modest dresses with long skirts and sleeves and high necklines, as did previous generations of Prespa women, many young dancers also flout community standards by wearing dresses that highlight their new physiques through low necklines, tight bodices, and short skirts, again patterned after Western media images. As young women emulate quintessential Western "objects of the gaze," they present a body at dance events that is sexualized in a manner consistent with the moves that it performs.

When asked about their interest in çoçek, Prespa women in North America refer most often to Turkish culture. Some attribute it to Turkish families from Macedonia, and specifically from Prespa, who have moved to their towns in recent years and begun to interact and intermarry with their families. Conversations with older women, however, reveal that çoçek is new even for these Turkish villagers, who in the past generally performed line dances like their Albanian neighbors. Other women have emphasized the long-term links that most Albanians in Macedonia retain with relatives who migrated to Turkish towns in the decades following World War II. As these relatives come to Prespa homes for lengthy visits, or as Prespa families visit their relatives in Turkey, Prespari—like Albanians throughout Macedonia—have gradually been exposed to the style of solo dancing cultivated in Turkey. Regardless of this injection of Turkish influence, the use of the term çoçek signals to me that the fad for the dance among Albanians began in Macedonia itself, drawing on elements of older urban social dance, memories of the performances of local çoçeks, and the staged presentations of Rom folkloric troupes. But the Turkish ascription suggests one important dimension to the dance's current popularity: it represents a local form of urban culture through which newly urban Albanians may affirm their distinctive identity as Muslims and reassert the enduring ties that their communities retain with Turkey and its Ottoman heritage.

This aspect of çoçek dancing became more apparent to me in the summer of 1999, when I spent three weeks in the city of Skopje. Owing to its legacy as a regional capital in the Ottoman period and its large, multiethnic Muslim population, including the largest Rom population in Europe, Skopje remains a center of Turkish culture in Macedonia. Although most young Albanians there speak Albanian as their first language, many are also fluent in Turkish, and are as well-versed in the current pop music hits of Turkey as they are in those of the United States. In addition to circumcision and wedding celebrations, the principal venues for Albanian dancing in Skopje are no longer kafanas catering to male-only audiences, but youth "discos" or "dance clubs" featuring a mix of live and recorded music, where women are admitted free of charge to assure an integrated clientele. As in a Western dance club, alcohol is served and the lights are kept low except for colored strobe lights that flash on and off throughout the evening. In addition to Western and Turkish pop hits, the evening's fare includes local line dances, danced in integrated lines, and medleys of çoçek tunes, during which young couples or clusters of younger women crowd onto the dance floor. Here çoçek is danced purely as a solo dance, and most young women dance it in a virtuosic manner that is closer to present-day Turkish style. At the club that I frequented, I saw women from age twelve up through their forties whirling, shimmying, and undulating through complex individual renditions of the dance that were the result of long hours of practice and refinement. One evening a prize was awarded for the best female çoçek dancer of the night.

The Albanian music at such clubs is no longer provided by Rom ensembles but by Albanian singers and bands from Macedonia or Kosova, a few of which include Rom members. In response to the fad for çoçek, these performers (and their songwriters) have created a whole new repertoire of dance songs with a pronounced Turkish or Rom flavor. Many of the lyrics refer specifically to the dance's movements. Sung from the viewpoint of a male spectator, they exhort young women to "dance with me, dance" (*luj me mua luj*), "dance with your hands, dance with your arms" (*luj me duar, luj me krah*), "move your body for me" (*lujma lujma belin-o*), or "shake your body, beautiful" (*dridhe moj shtatin bukuri*), at times sounding suspiciously like Cindy Crawford. Among the cassettes of such music that I bought in the open market is, in fact, one entitled *With a Beautiful Body Like an Actress,* which sports on the cover a photo of Cindy twirling in a torso-hugging dress.[24]

Danced with a partner or small group of friends to tunes in a duple meter, incorporating arm movements and displacements of the torso that draw attention to the body and that suggest movements of sexual pleasure, çoçek very much resembles types of club dancing that are popular among youth throughout North America, Europe, and beyond. By dancing it, young Presparë and other Albanians in and from the former Yugoslavia can participate in the creation of a distinctive youth culture that has clear affinities with its Western counterpart and yet affirms their specific identity as Balkan Muslims. In this respect, it may be compared to other types of contemporary dance cultures, including Algerian *raï* or the "remix" dancing of South Asians in North America, whose musical styles—like the new çoçek tunes—juxtapose local musical features with ones drawn from Western pop idioms.

Those "Other Women"

Let me now draw some more general lessons from this examination of Prespa women's dancing. Over the past two decades, scholars such as myself have researched a great variety of women's music and dance genres within a broad world area that includes not only the countries of the Mediterranean but also much of Europe, the Middle East, and Asia, as well as communities with origins in those areas living in the Americas and elsewhere. In our scholarly attempts to analyze and generalize about women's cultural forms in this area, we have tended to focus on single genres in isolation, rather than recognizing that contrasting ones—performative and participatory, professional and amateur, urban and rural—have often existed side by side within any given locale, each deriving meaning from its juxtaposition with the other. Often these performance forms have in fact been instrumental in constituting distinct categories of women who have thereby been associated with distinctive personal attributes and assigned to distinctive roles or strata within society. Women such as those in the Prespa community, whose music and dance styles have been premised upon a display of modesty and propriety, have felt compelled to structure their performances in such a way as to distinguish themselves not only from the men of their community, but also from those "other women"—be they professional entertainers, courtesans, prostitutes, or ritual specialists—who have lived and performed in their midst. Here I am thinking of performers such as *ghawazi* in Egypt, *sheykhat* (also *sheikhat* or *shikhat*) in North Africa, *tawa'if, načni*s, and *devadasi* in India, *geisha*s in Japan, *taledhek* in Java, European courtesans of past centuries, and even showgirls and "exotic dancers" in American cities: women whose performances have occupied a space outside the societal codes that have governed the familial realm.

During the past century or so, as gender roles and notions of sexuality in these regions have changed in conjunction with the adoption of modernist ideologies, many of these performance-related professions have declined or disappeared. Often the genres once associated with them have been adopted by "respectable" women, and even men, who have elevated them to elite forms of expression. In the process, the newly reconstituted forms have in some cases been stripped of overtly erotic elements, while in other cases those elements have infused older forms with a new sensuality. In India, the Hindustani song genres of *thumri* and *ghazal,* which originated among tawa'if singer-dancers, are now presented by both men and women as dignified concert genres. This is true also for the Karnatak style of dance now known as Bharata Natyam, which was once the domain of devadasi, or temple dancers.[25] Women throughout southeastern Europe and the Middle East who have turned to the movements of cabaret dancers to transform their social dancing represent another version of this process, as do middle-class North American and western European women who cultivate some of the same styles of "Eastern" dance. The classic dichotomy of virgin and whore that is fused in the performances of American pop divas such as Madonna is yet another example. In each of these instances, cultural forms have been instrumental in a larger process through which women within societies that have historically been patriarchal have been renegotiating their sense of themselves as women: often not by dismantling forms originating in patriarchal contexts, but rather by combining and juxtaposing them so as to convey a greater range of what women have come to regard as desirable "feminine" qualities. As Abu-Lughod (1990) has noted for young Egyptian Bedouin women, the construction of new, more "sexualized" forms of femininity by women in these world areas, even when undertaken as a rebellion against notions of proper demeanor held by prior generations, may unwittingly pull women into a new set of patriarchal structures: those characterizing the hypersexualized feminine identities that have developed within "advanced capitalist" societies.

For those of us who observe such processes from a scholarly perspective, it is easy to respond with enthusiasm to the resourcefulness and "agency" that women display in the many new performance forms that they are creating. But we must be cautious about assuming that these new forms, simply because they are new and perhaps closer to Western models, are contributing to a genuine improvement in the overall situation of women within their society. We must also not lose sight of the individuals of any gender who, because of their position as members of an ethnic or religious minority, a marginal class or caste, or what Butler (1993, 138) has referred to as the "sexual minorities," have gradually been edged out of forms of music and dance in which they were once preeminent by women of a more privileged and respectable status. Ultimately our task as scholars is not to celebrate feminine inventiveness per se but to be alert to the processes that are unfolding before our eyes, be aware of the factors that are propelling them, and be willing to delve into fragmentary and often convoluted histories in order to illuminate them.

Notes

This article is derived from earlier versions given at the annual meeting of the Society for Ethnomusicology in 1992, the Feminist Theory and Music II conference at the Eastman School of Music in 1993, and the Department of Music of the University of Illinois in 1995. Fieldwork in Toronto and Chicago in 1993 was funded by a Faculty Development Award from SUNY Stony Brook, while archival research during 1997 on the history of Ottoman solo dance was sponsored by a Summer Stipend from the National Endowment for the Humanities. Fieldwork in Macedonia in the summer of 1999 was aided by a grant for East European Studies from the American Council of Learned Societies. My special thanks go to Sonia Seeman, Zev Feldman, Bob Leibman, Steve Kotansky, and Joe Graziosi for providing me with references to and translations of materials on the history of dance in Turkey and southeastern Europe. Unless specifically indicated, all translations are my own.

1. I discuss the derivation of Balkan terms for this genre and its variations below. Çoçek tunes in duple time are played with a 3-3-2 drumming pattern (cf. Arabic *malfuf*); in 9/8, the pulses are grouped 2-2-2-3 (cf. Turkish *aksak*).

2. Presparë are southern Albanian Muslims whose home villages are located to the north and east of Lake Prespa, which is located in southern Macedonia. I conducted research in their home villages between 1980 and 1982, and among immigrant families in the United States and Canada between 1985 and 1988 (see Sugarman 1997). I then made return trips to Canada in 1993, 1994, and 1996.

3. This was true of many districts of southern Albania until much more recently. See Kruta 1973 for information on dance songs in the Skrapar region.

4. In most southern Albanian communities, the two vocal soloists dance a duet while those droning stand in a circle around or to one side of them. Prespare are somewhat unusual in that they perform their dance songs in a line.

5. Most Çam families were forcibly relocated from Greece to Albania after World War II. Devolliçe is also known across the border in the Korçë and Devoll districts of Albania, as well as among Slavic families who once lived in the Kastoria region of northern Greece.

6. For a complementary analysis to mine, see Jane Cowan's classic study of Greek dance (Cowan 1990).

7. According to Davis (1986, 99–118), women slaves (*cariye*) might be either war captives, from areas such as the Balkans, Russia, or Italy, or girls from the Caucasus, where a slave trade had existed even prior to the founding of the Ottoman Empire. By the nineteenth century, virtually all slaves were Circassian or Georgian. They were purchased by families as servants of the head of the household or of his wife, and usually some became the master's concubine (*odalık*). Those who were particularly accomplished might later be chosen by an elite man as his bride. It is possible that elite women themselves were trained in solo dance, as they were in music. Those slaves who married elite men may also have continued this practice even in their new position. As yet, however, I have located no evidence of this, perhaps because they would never have allowed themselves to be seen dancing by anyone other than a family member (158–59). Friend (1996) describes such a situation among elite Iranian women.

8. According to Evliya Çelebi (1846, 247–49), the taverns in Istanbul were owned by Greeks, Armenians, and Jews: non-Muslims who were permitted to operate a type of business that is forbidden to Muslims. This may also explain the predominance of non-Muslims among köçeks.

9. See, for example, Davis 1986, 117. Although distant geographically, a vivid depiction of the relationship between a master and a female concubine/dancer can be seen in the Tunisian film *The Silences of the Palace*.

10. Speaking of Ottoman society in the period before the mid–nineteenth century, Kandiyoti writes of "glimpses of a more fluid world where rank, ethnicity, and sexualities could map out a complex social landscape, one in which palace boys who had liaisons with powerful patrons could themselves become respected patriarchs surrounded by their wives and children" (1998, 280). She goes on to compare these "complex gender regimes" of earlier eras with the norm of the monogamous, heterosexual couple that was embraced by the urban middle classes during the latter part of the nineteenth century. I thank Sonia Seeman for her translation of the Ottoman verse.

11. Oldenburg's study suggests several possible avenues of inquiry into the history of çengis. She found that women sometimes became tawa'if because they were sold into the trade by their families or were running away from an oppressive family situation. Similar circumstances seem to have surrounded the entry of young Caucasian girls into the Ottoman slave trade; either they or their parents often saw it as a way to escape a cruel life at home or to attain a higher station in society as a slave in an elite home (Davis 1986). Such evidence suggests that the profession of entertainer provided one of the few ways that a woman whose ties to her family had been broken through poverty or mistreatment could support herself.

12. In Albanian areas, these performers have generally been described more specifically as *evgjitë* or *jevgj*: settled Roma who speak Albanian as their first language rather than Romani (Hasluck 1938; Çaushi 1974).

13. By this period çampara were probably metal finger-cymbals rather than the

wooden clappers of earlier eras. The term dyshe refers to a type of dance duet, related to solo dance, that was and is also performed by southern Albanian women.

14. In an article from 1910, just seven years later, Đorđević lamented, "With the freeing of Serbia from the Turks and with the Serbianization of the towns, Turkish music faded away in the towns. The čočeks and the captivating Eastern songs and music to which they danced, have today completely disappeared" (Đorđević 1910, 77).

15. I am indebted to Stephen Kotansky for bringing *Koštana* to my attention. Berzatnik (1930, 40) gives as a reason for the ban that the money being spent was frequently coming from government officials who were raiding the public coffers; according to Hasluck (1938, 2:29), the ban was rescinded in 1934 in favor of taxing the establishments that featured çengis. For an incisive analysis of the present-day atmosphere at Serbian kafanas, see Port 1998.

16. In the early 1980s, I worked extensively with a group of Muslim male dancers in Skopje who were famous for performing "heavy" men's line dances and who were often invited to dance at local weddings. When I asked one of the dancers if they were ever paid for their performances, he was deeply offended. "And sell my body like a Gypsy?!" was his response. His is the only evidence I have for any sort of community recollection of male dancers in Albanian areas of the Balkans.

17. In the description of Skopje čočeks, one is reminded of the famous Greek Jewish singer of the early twentieth century, Roza Eskenazi. For similar sorts of negotiation by women performers in Egypt during this period, see Danielson 1991 and Nieuwkerk 1995.

18. As Christians, the Janković sisters may have used the word "Turkish" here simply to mean Muslim. But since they were generally very precise in their ethnic designations, it is likely that they used it to refer to women from families that spoke Turkish at home; such families were often ethnic Albanians. My translations of their writings are reworkings of ones provided me by Bob Leibman.

19. For the musical repertoire of Sulukule, see *Sulukule: Rom Music of Istanbul* (Traditional Crossroads CD 4289). The excellent notes to this CD discuss çoçek and its antecedents from the perspective of the Turkish Rom community (Seeman 1998).

20. Although Kosovo is the internationally recognized form of the name, it is also the Slavic form. I prefer to use the Albanian name, Kosova, in accordance with the wishes of the majority population.

21. Sonia Seeman, personal communication. Seeman, who conducted research with Rom instrumentalists in Skopje in the 1980s, was told by one musician that the Rom singers who performed in kafanas through the 1950s used to sit on the laps of male customers and disrobe as part of their performance, and that they also often worked as prostitutes. It would seem that, in local Muslim parlance in Kosova and northern Macedonia, a woman who sings and dances in a kafana came to be called a çoçek, whereas a woman wedding singer who performs with frame drum is a çengi.

22. For discussion of čoček as danced by Skopje Roma, see Carol Silverman's chapter in this volume (chap. 4) and Dunin 1971, 1973, and 1977. There is a short segment of a young Rom girl from Skopje dancing čoček in the video *The Romany Trail,* from the *Beats of the Heart* series from BBC television. A particularly subdued performance of shota is included in the *JVC Video Anthology of World Music and Dance,* as performed by an amateur folklore group from the town of Zhur in western Kosova. Evidence for the develop-

ment of various types of social dance similar to the entertainment forms leads inevitably to a reexamination of the style in which some south Albanian women perform their dance songs, in which the two lead singers dance holding hands while waving a kerchief in their free hand. This type of dance is essentially dyshe supplemented by a droning chorus. Hoerburger 1994 puzzles through many of the connections between types of solo and pair dancing in southeastern Europe, but without relating them to the dancing of köçeks and çengis.

23. Her unusual situation may have come about because of the precedent set by the many women who now sing professionally in Kosova. Another innovation that I have already written about (Sugarman 1997, 334–36) is that of a man and woman singing a polyphonic song together at a home event. This remains an unusual type of performance, however, and women maintain their traditional modest demeanor in this type of singing.

24. These fragments of lyrics come from songs recorded, respectively, by the Aliu Brothers, "Luj me mua luj"; Ramadan Krasniqi, "Kënaqu sonte"; Ramize Caka and Sala Bekteshi, "E majra e lalës"; and both Gjyle Çollaku and the Mustafa Sisters, "Hidhe moj hidhe vash' shaminë." *Trupin të bukur si artiste* (With a Beautiful Body Like an Actress) features a performer identified only as Gazi (not the well-known Rom singer Gazmend Rama).

25. For information on north Indian tawa'if and their performance genres, see Post 1987; Manuel 1986, 1987, and 1988–89; Oldenburg 1990; Ollikkala 1997; and Qureshi 2001. The transformation of the *sadir* dance of the devadasi into Bharata Natyam is described in Srinivasan 1985 and Allen 1997.

References

Abu-Lughod, Lila. 1990. "The Romance of Resistance: Tracing Transformations of Power through Bedouin Women." *American Ethnologist* 17:41–55.

Allen, Matthew Harp. 1997. "Rewriting the Script for South Indian Dance." *The Drama Review* 41 (3): 63–100.

And, Metin. 1976. *A Pictorial History of Turkish Dancing*. Ankara: Dost Yayınları.

Berzatnik, Hugo Adolf. 1930. *Europas Vergessenes Land*. Vienna: L. W. Seidel & Son.

Brandl, Rudolf M. 1994. "Der Hof Ali Pasas in Jannina und seine Ausstrahlung." In *Höfische Kultur in Südost Europa*, edited by Reinhard Lauer and Hans Georg Majer, 205–45. Bericht der Kolloquien der Südosteuropa Kommission, 1988 bis 1990. Göttingen: Vandenhoeck & Ruprecht.

———. 1996. "The 'Yiftoi' and the Music of Greece: Role and Function." *The World of Music* 38 (1): 7–32.

Butler, Judith. 1993. *Bodies That Matter: On the Discursive Limits of "Sex."* New York: Routledge.

Çaushi, Abedin. 1974. "Martesa në qytetin e Elbasanit" (The wedding in the town of Elbasan). *Etnografia shqiptare* (Tiranë) 5: 231–56.

Cowan, Jane K. 1990. *Dance and the Body Politic in Northern Greece*. Princeton: Princeton University Press.

Danielson, Virginia. 1991. "Artists and Entrepreneurs: Female Singers in Cairo during the 1920s." In *Women in Middle Eastern History: Shifting Boundaries in Sex and Gender*, edited by Nikki R. Keddie and Beth Baron, 292–309. New Haven: Yale University Press.

Davis, Fanny. 1986. *The Ottoman Lady: A Social History from 1718 to 1918.* New York: Greenwood Press.

Đorđević, Tihomir. 1903. "Die Zigeuner in Serbien. I. Teil." *Mitteilungen zur Zigeunerkunde* (Budapest) 2:1–80.

———. 1910. "Cigani i muzika u Srbiji" (Roma and music in Serbia). *Bosanska Vila* (Sarajevo) 25 (3–6): 75–81.

Dunin, Elsie [Ivancich]. 1971. "Gypsy Wedding: Dance and Customs." *Makedonski Folklor* 4 (7/8): 317–25.

———. 1973. "Čoček as a Ritual Dance among Gypsy Women." *Makedonski Folklor* 6 (12): 193–98.

———. 1977. "The Newest Changes in Rom Dance (Serbia and Macedonia)." *Journal of the Association of Graduate Dance Ethnologists* (UCLA) 1:12–17.

Džimrevski, Borivoje. 1985. *Čalgiskata tradicija vo Makedonija* (The Čalgija tradition in Macedonia). Skopje: Makedonska Kniga.

Evliya, Efendi [Çelebi]. 1846. *Narrative of Travels in Europe, Asia, and Africa, in the Seventeenth Century.* Vol. 1, part 2. London: Parbury, Allen & Co. Reprint, New York: Johnson Reprint Company, 1968.

Friend, Robyn. 1996. "Persian Classical Dance: An Exquisite Art." *Habibi* 15:6–8.

Garnett, Lucy M. J. 1891. *The Women of Turkey and their Folk-Lore.* Volume 2, *The Jewish and Moslem Women.* London: David Nutt.

Gilliat-Smith, Bernard. 1910–11. "The Fate of Kasim Pasha." *Journal of the Gypsy Lore Society,* n.s., 4:79–80.

Hasluck, Margaret. 1938. "The Gypsies of Albania." *Journal of the Gypsy Lore Society,* 3d series, 17 (2): 49–61; 17 (3): 18–30; 17 (4): 110–22.

Hobhouse Broughton, J. C. 1817. *A Journey through Albania and Other Provinces of Turkey in Europe and Asia, to Constantinople, during the Years 1809 and 1810.* 2 vols. Philadelphia: M. Carey & Son. (The section on Albania was reprinted in 1971 by the Arno Press as *A Journey through Albania.*)

Hoerburger, Felix. 1994. *Valle popullore: Tanz und Tanzmusik der Albaner im Kosovo und in Makedonien.* Edited by Thomas Emmerig in cooperation with Adelheid Feilcke-Tiemann and Bruno Reuer. Frankfurt am Main: Peter Lang.

Hughes, T[homas] S[mart]. 1820. *Travels in Sicily, Greece, and Albania.* 2 vols. London.

Hunt, Yvonne. 1996. *Traditional Dance in Greek Culture.* Athens: Center for Asia Minor Studies.

Ivanić, Ivan. 1910. *Makedonija i Makedonci.* Novi Sad: Knjižara "Natošević."

Janković, Ljubica S., and Danica S. Janković. 1939. *Narodne igre* (National dances). Vol. 3. Beograd: Štamparija Drag. Gregorica.

Kandiyoti, Deniz. 1998. "Afterword: Some Awkward Questions on Women and Modernity in Turkey." In *Remaking Women: Feminism and Modernity in the Middle East,* edited by Lila Abu-Lughod, 270–87. Princeton: Princeton University Press.

Kruta, Beniamin. 1973. "Polifonia e Skraparit dhe disa çështje tipologjike të saj" (The polyphony of the Skrapar region and several of its typological characteristics). *Studime Filologjike* (Tiranë) 27 (2): 209–36; 27 (4): 131–51.

Manuel, Peter. 1986. "The Evolution of Modern *Thumri*." *Ethnomusicology* 30 (3): 470–90.

———. 1987. "Courtesans and Hindustani Music." *Asian Review* 7 (1): 12–17.

———. 1988–89. "A Historical Survey of the Urdu Ghazal-Song in India." *Asian Music* 20 (1): 93–113.

Montagu, Lady Mary Wortley. 1994. *The Turkish Embassy Letters,* edited by Malcolm Jack. London: Virago Press.

Nieuwkerk, Karin van. *"A Trade Like Any Other": Female Singers and Dancers in Egypt.* Austin: University of Texas Press, 1995.

Oldenburg, Veena Talwar. 1990. "Lifestyle as Resistance: The Case of the Courtesans of Lucknow, India." *Feminist Studies* 16 (2): 259–87.

Ollikkala, Robert Charles. 1997. "Begum Akhtar: From Court to Concert Hall." Ph.D. dissertation, University of Illinois at Urbana-Champaign.

Popescu-Judetz, Eugenia. 1982. "Köçek and Çengi in Turkish Culture." *Dance Studies* (Centre for Dance Studies, Jersey) 6: 46–69.

Port, Mattijs van de. 1998. "Kafana." Chapter 5 of *Gypsies, Wars, and Other Instances of the Wild: Civilisation and Its Discontents in a Serbian Town.* Amsterdam: Amsterdam University Press.

Post, Jennifer. 1987. "Professional Women in Indian Music: The Death of the Courtesan Tradition." In *Women and Music in Cross-Cultural Perspective,* edited by Ellen Koskoff, 97–109. Westport, Conn.: Greenwood Press.

Qureshi, Regula Burckhardt. 2001. "In Search of Begum Akhtar: Patriarchy, Poetry, and Twentieth-Century Indian Music." *World of Music* 43 (1): 97–137.

Reineck, Janet. 1985. "Wedding Dances from Kosovo, Yugoslavia: A Structural and Contextual Analysis." M.A. thesis, University of California at Los Angeles.

Seeman, Sonia. 1998. Notes to *Sulukule: Rom Music of Istanbul.* Traditional Crossroads, CD 4289.

Sevengil, Refik Ahmet. 1985. *Istanbul Nasıl Egleniyordu?* Istanbul: Iletisim Yayınları. First published in 1927.

Srinivasan, Amrit. 1985. "Reform and Revival: The Devadasi and Her Dance." *Economic and Political Weekly* (New Delhi) 20 (44): 1869–76.

Sugarman, Jane C. 1989. "The Nightingale and the Partridge: Singing and Gender among Prespa Albanians." *Ethnomusicology* 33 (2): 191–215.

———. 1997. *Engendering Song: Singing and Subjectivity at Prespa Albanian Weddings.* Chicago: University of Chicago Press.

Vlora, Ekrem Bey. 1911. *Aus Berat und vom Tomor.* Sarajevo: Daniel A. Kajon.

4

The Gender of the Profession: Music, Dance, and Reputation among Balkan Muslim Rom Women

Carol Silverman

In the long history of discrimination against Roma, music has perhaps been the only legitimate niche in which they have been perceived to excel by the majority non-Rom population.[1] All over Europe, Rom men are known as expert musicians, yet little has been written about women's participation in Rom musical arts. Considering the emerging literature on gender and music in the Mediterranean region (Sugarman 1997; Magrini 1998; Nieuwkerk 1995, 1998; Kapchan 1996), it behooves us to re-examine analytical models with specific historically nuanced case studies.

This article explores female musical performances among Muslim Balkan Roma in Macedonia and Bulgaria, focusing on both professional and nonprofessional contexts in terms of performers, events, space, instrumentation, repertoire, reputation, and commercial viability.[2] I concretize one strategy of performance through the commentary of international singing star Esma Redžepova from Macedonia. Though atypical, Esma's life illuminates how and why she resisted norms. Esma's success was grounded in a number of paradoxes: she succeeded in part because of the marketing ability of her non-Rom mentor and husband; her image drew on stereotypes of Rom women as exotic, nubile, emotional, and musical; and finally, she bridged the ambivalent Rom attitude of requiring, aestheticizing, and respecting female musical performances in nonprofessional realms while stigmatizing them in professional settings. A wider political economic framework juxtaposes Rom prominence in music and dance with low political, economic, and social status. Professional music has been an important medium of exchange between Roma and non-Roma, and the association of women with sexuality becomes symbolic capital to negotiate in the marketplace.

A Historical Approach to Female Performance: Instruments and Singing

Whereas instrumental music is primarily a male domain for all ethnic groups in the Balkans, the frame drum (*def, daire*) has been associated with Balkan Muslim Rom female performers for at least a hundred years, and probably longer (Vukanović 1962, 52; Pettan 1996b; Dunin 1971, 1973).[3] Like female frame drum players in the Middle East, those in the Balkans were regarded by non-Rom patrons as marginal but powerful: "As outsiders, their subversive power, self-assertion and independence threatened the status quo and led them to be stigmatized" (Doubleday 1999, 121). Picken similarly notes that frame drumming was suspect not only because of the instrument itself but because of its association with Rom women: "Not only is it a women's instrument, it is also an instrument of women of ill-repute" (1975, 144). Rom women were coded as dangerous because of their imputed sexuality and freedom; Roma in general continue to be the quintessential "other" to European society (Trumpener 1992).

Among Balkan Muslim Roma, two daires often accompanied women's singing. Other female instruments were violin, *ud* (short-necked plucked fretless lute), *kanun* (plucked zither), and *tarabuka* (hourglass shaped hand drum).[4] Vukanović writes:

> In several regions of Yugoslavia . . . (where there has been . . . a considerable number of Moslems) . . . the music in harems and other women's apartments were chiefly performed by female musicians, for the most part Gypsy women. They were the principal protagonists of the oriental harem music, playing the tambourine and singing. This kind of music disappeared gradually, in some parts of Yugoslavia at the beginning of the nineteenth century. . . . Nevertheless, in some

towns where the oriental way of living has been partly maintained,
this activity is still being practiced on various occasions of social and
family entertainments." (1964, 52)

Until the 1950s, professional female Rom musicians were hired for
women's celebrations by patrons from various ethnic groups. The performers knew the varied repertoires of these client groups and sang in their lan-
guage(s). Rom professional musicians were, like their male counterparts,
multimusical, and multilingual. Seeman, for example, writes that during the
pre–World War II period in Skopje, Macedonia, all-female *čalgija* ensembles
consisted of violin, daire, and sometimes ud, with the women accompanying
their own singing. Čalgija ensembles played Ottoman-derived vocal and instrumental music in a heterophonic style based on the *makam* (Turkish melodic modal) system, emphasizing innovation and improvisation. Female
performers were usually relatives of male musicians (Seeman 1990, 19).

Nonprofessional Rom women also sang and played daire at their own
family and community events. The few song texts that have been collected for
these celebratory events are not, unfortunately, identified as to the sex of the
performers, but we can surmise that many of the songs dealt with typical
pan-Balkan ritual themes such as family life, love, and blessings for the fertility of the land and people (Petrovski 1993; Jakoski 1981; Marushiakova
and Popov 1994; 1995). In Yugoslavia and Bulgaria, Rom women and girls
were sometimes hired by Slavic villagers to sing ritual songs in the local Slavic
languages on the occasion of Saint Lazarus' Day, falling eight days before
Easter. They were also hired during the summer drought months to sing *do-
dole* (Serbian) or *peperuda* (Bulgarian), magical songs to induce rain (Peičeva,
Dimov, and Krusteva 1997). Popov believes that this role of Roma was a late-
nineteenth-century innovation that peaked in the 1920s and 1930s; it was
instituted to continue the waning practice among the majority Slavs (Popov
1993, 28–29). From the point of view of Roma, it may have been a welcome
income-producing activity.

In the early 1990s (before the wars in Yugoslavia), the practice of daire
playing seemed to be most alive in Kosovo, much less so in Macedonia, and
virtually gone in Bulgaria. During a five-month period in 1990 in Šuto Orizari, Macedonia, I heard only one woman play the daire and sing on the
women's "bath day" of a wedding. She was quite elderly and used the daire to
accompany a ribald song jokingly instructing the bride in sexual matters.
Many women in Šutka, however, remarked that professional daire players and
singers could still be found in Kosovo. The Bulgarian situation can in part be
explained by the prohibitions of the socialist government against Muslim

music and other displays of Muslim identity (Silverman 1989, 1996a). But why did female ensembles decline throughout the Balkans? Since the 1970s, indoor unamplified ensembles have been replaced by amplified male wedding bands composed of Western instruments such as saxophone, clarinet, guitar, bass, synthesizer, and drum set. These amplified ensembles became a symbol of high status and were associated with the introduction of electricity, Western values, and modernity. In the Balkans, Roma are musical innovators open to eclectic styles and textures (Silverman 1996a). Seeman (1990) and Dunin (1985) chronicle the change from unamplified čalgija ensembles to electrified outdoor dance bands in Skopje during the 1970s. Similarly, in Bulgaria I witnessed the fascination with amplification take hold. Whereas male performers were able to make the transition from unamplified to amplified music, which was played outdoors and in public places (such as banquet halls), women were not because of the social constraints on female public performance. Pettan describes an interesting case study from Kosovo, whereby male homosexuals who played frame drums in female contexts transferred the women's repertoire to amplified bands, creating the genre called *talava* (Pettan 1996b and chap. 12 in this volume). In the past thirty years, then, the introduction of amplified music, which is performed primarily by men, is directly related to the decline in female daire and singing ensembles. Other reasons for their decline, such as the relaxation of sexual segregation, are discussed below.

Sexual Segregation: Historical Implications

In speaking with older Rom women, I consistently heard that sexual segregation was the norm for celebratory events until the 1970s (Dunin 1971, 1973). This was also true for Christians and for non-Rom Muslims of the Balkans (Rice 1982; Sugarman 1997). In comparison to Christians, Balkan Muslim women were expected to adhere to more stringent norms of modesty and honor. Esma Redžepova, speaking of her childhood in the 1950s, remembered clearly, "Women used to be in a separate room, men separate, and they used to celebrate segregated at weddings." During the women-only bathing-the-bride ritual at Esma's wedding in 1968, there was a female orchestra composed of one violin and two daires (Teodosievski and Redžepova 1984,108). Some women conceived of space as two events happening simultaneously: a women's party and a men's party. An older woman remembered the 1950s as follows: "During the Saturday celebration of the wedding at the bride's house, there would be a professional female orchestra—two violins, a daire (frame drum) player, and the singer, usually the daire player." Esma similarly recalled, "Among us, for example, there was one female violinist, and there were two female daire players—my sister at one time played the daire and the tarabuka and sang at weddings. But this was only for women, not for men. It wasn't shameful because they sang for women, they were, in fact, very popular."

The spatial segregation during celebrations was often described in terms of the "inside" women's world and the "outside" men's world. This concept of space is shared with non-Rom Muslims of the region (Sugarman 1997). In the henna ceremony, for example, Esma recalls that "the women were inside, the men were outside with the *zurle* [double reed aerophone] and *tapan* [two-headed drum]." Pettan reminds us not to take the words "outside" and "inside" too literally. In the Balkans many courtyards have high walls; thus a women's courtyard performance is outside but not as public as the street. The courtyard is sharply distinguished from the street, where men perform (see Pettan 1996a, 316, and chap. 12 in this volume). Henna celebrations in Šuto Orizari, Macedonia, for example, take place either "inside" the house or "inside the courtyard" of the bride. Women from the groom's family dance through the streets with trays of henna and clothing, accompanied by hired male zurla and tapan players. When they reach the house of the bride, they are either led inside or they make the courtyard area women's space. Here they enact the required rituals; if men are present, they look on from the periphery.[5]

Note that I am deliberately avoiding the term "domestic" to define female space. Rosaldo's classic article (1974), which explains female subordination as a result of the domestic/public split, claims that women are identified with the domestic sphere (defined as the sphere of mothers and children) and men with the public, leading to hierarchy. This argument has been challenged by many scholars for many reasons, for example, the slippage between domestic and private (MacCormack and Strathern 1980; Ortner 1996). The domestic, rather than being marginal and excluded from political power, is the site of important decision making regarding family budgets, marriage choices for children, and evaluating other people's reputations.[6] The opposition domestic/public obscures rather than illuminates because the domestic arena is not always private and subordinate but is often part of community life. For Roma, there are many publics. First, there is the public sphere of the larger society, which is dominated by non-Roma but in which Roma must work. Second, there is the sphere of the Rom public, which I term the Rom community. Third, there is the sphere of the extended family, and fourth there is the sphere of the residential family. When I speak of the family and community, I mean the sphere of local public life that is visible to other Roma, be they kin or neighbors. The non-Rom public is irrelevant here, and as a rule, non-Roma do not have access to these local settings.

These nesting public spheres are not prohibited terrain for Rom women. Both historical references and my ethnographic observations point to a great deal of movement of Rom women into public arenas, primarily for economic activities such as music, dance, seasonal agricultural work, and middleman selling at markets. Pettan observes a greater freedom of movement of Rom women, in comparison to other non-Rom Muslims of Kosovo: "Similarly to non-Gypsy ethnic groups and musicians in Kosovo, Gypsy men are oriented towards the public domain while Gypsy women primarily towards the private domain. Their private domain, is however, extended in comparison to most non-Gypsy women" (Pettan 1996a, 316).[7]

In the 1930s, the freedom of movement of Rom women was noted by Catherine Brown, a British traveler:

> One of the most striking features of these gypsy women is their great freedom and independence of bearing as compared with other Mohamedan women in Macedonia. Although among orthodox Mohamedans one may occasionally see on feast days groups of men strolling about the village together, tinkling gently and rather half-heartedly on small stringed instruments, no women are ever to be seen with them, the women's festivities being invariably quite separate and confined to the harem. Here [among the Roma] men and women joined freely together in whole-hearted enjoyment. The whole scene resembled an enormous ballet. (Brown 1933, 307)[8]

Unlike upper-class non-Rom Muslims, Rom women have historically worked outside the home with men among non-Rom women and men. Economic imperatives loosened sexual segregation, although as we shall see, ideals regarding appropriate female behavior remained conservative. In the realm of dance, çengis, female professionals, are documented as far back as the seventeenth century. In the Ottoman Empire, çengis, who were often but not exclusively Roma, performed sensual solo dances with torso movements for men in aristocratic, courtly, and military as well as tavern settings (see chap. 3 in this volume). The occupation of professional dancer waned during the twentieth century, but Seeman reported that in the 1980s there was one professional Rom dancer in Skopje, Macedonia, who was hired for men's celebrations.[9] Clearly, contemporary professional "Oriental Dance" and belly dancing in Turkey and the Balkans have roots in çengi dancing. Although there is little historical information about professional Rom dancers in Macedonia,[10] there is quite a bit about nonprofessional women's dancing, to which I now turn.

Female Dancing, 1970s–1990s

Dunin's research in Macedonia shows the significant participation of non-professional Rom women in all community dance realms; she describes women looking "very comfortable and confident of their movements probably due to the frequency of dancing, which occurs almost every week" (1971, 323–24; 1973; see also Dunin 1977, 1985, 1998). Indeed, my own research in the 1990s confirms the occurrence of numerous dance events and the presence of females as regular nonprofessional participants. From June to September in Šuto Orizari, Macedonia, on any weekend evening one can find from five to ten weddings on the streets. The outdoor dance portions of the weddings are regularly viewed by scores of uninvited onlookers, and there are times when uninvited people may dance. More than a few dance-crazy Šutka teenagers would regularly make the rounds looking for the best music for dancing!

It is not surprising to find so much music and dance in Šutka, for it is possibly the largest Rom settlement in Europe (40,000 people, with very few non-Roma), and music and dance are the community's expressive focus (Silverman 1996b). In smaller neighborhoods, Rom weddings are less numerous but can be found practically every summer weekend.[11] Besides weddings, dance events include circumcisions, housewarmings, soldier-send-off celebrations, and calendrical celebrations such as saints' days, the most important of which is the spring holiday of Erdelezi (see Dunin 1997). In the North American diaspora, events also include New Year's Eve and graduation and birthday parties.

While men have a virtual monopoly on instrumental music, dance is perhaps the most important women's performance art. Participants structure events through dance, which enacts some of the most important rituals in the wedding (Sugarman 1997). In Macedonia, for example, Saturday, the bride's day of the wedding, is initiated by the most important elder female family member (usually the bride's mother) leading the first dance line with a decorated object, for example, a sieve. The sieve symbolically links the fertility of the land (wheat and flour) to the fertility of the family through the bride, and the mother's leading the dance indicates respect both for the elder generation and for her role in ritual management. The dances go on for hours, and one by one, kin groups are called up, in order of closeness to the sponsoring family, to lead the dance. As each family, often led by a woman, goes up to the front of the dance line, someone requests a tune from the musicians. Males, not females, of the family usually tip the musicians.

Close kin women are expected, even obliged, to dance for hours at weddings, sometimes for three or four days in a row, no matter how hot and how tired they are (see plate 8). The only excuse not to dance is illness or mourning. Women who do not dance well or who are mentally or physically disabled also dance and even lead dance lines. Because women have so many obligations, such as ritual enactments, food preparation, and dancing, men end up taking care of children during celebrations, something that rarely happens outside of rituals. Male dancing is more optional than female dancing. There are some moments where male dancing is required: males, too, must dance at celebrations when their families are called up to lead the dance line. The males of the bride's family must solemnly dance with her just before she is transferred to the groom's family. Men dance for entertainment too, and some men dance a great deal, but they are not obliged to dance. A typical wedding dance line, whether located in the Balkans or in the diaspora has a ratio of approximately three women for every man. Men often dance together, put a great deal of energy into the dance for a short while, and then sit down. In the diaspora, I have noticed groups of young men who always dance together; they look for each other at celebrations and try out complicated steps. Whenever their favorite melody is played, these boys will appear. Women and girls also tend to dance with their relatives and friends; they too join the dance line in pairs or groups, never alone. But unlike men, women and girls are on the dance floor for practically the whole event.

As noted above, in the post-1970s era of amplified music, professional singing and playing of instruments have become male domains. Dancing, however, remains participatory, and women and children of both sexes and all ages take part. On the dance floor, one finds both children learning by immersion and imitation and elders who often know older styles and step patterns. The dance line now serves as a meeting place for young people, as gender mixing is permitted. Since dating is not practiced and arranged marriages are still the ideal (although they are declining in actual numbers), youths of the opposite sex look each other over in the dance line and exchange glances. Young men and women sometimes dance next to each other (as long as friends or relatives are close by watching) and conversations are initiated.

There are three forms of dance: line, processional, and solo. Processional dancing is used to travel from one place to another, such as dancing through the streets to pick up the bride at her house. Line dances are part of the Balkan constellation of regional dances.[12] In contemporary communities, elder

Rom women as well as men are often called upon to lead the slow, heavy, older line dances, which young people do not know. As early as 1967, Dunin noted that line dances were sexually integrated (1985, 112). This resonates with my point above that sexual segregation has not been very strict for certain expressive genres. Especially when comparing Roma to other Muslims of the Balkans, one notices the more relaxed attitude toward segregation among Roma.

Čoček

The most characteristic Rom dance form is the solo dance known as *čoček* or *čuček* in Macedonia and Kosovo and *kjuček* in Bulgaria.[13] An improvised dance, utilizing hand movements, contractions of the abdomen, shoulder shakes, movement of isolated body parts (such as hips and head), and small footwork patterns, *čoček* is clearly an heir to the dances of the Ottoman çengis, but its subtlety and restraint distinguish it from contemporary belly dancing. I conceive of solo *čoček* dancing as a continuum, with subtlety and a covered body (as found at Rom community events) on one end and belly dancing and exposed skin on the other end. Čočeks are found in 2/4 (sometimes counted 3-3-2) ; 7/8 (3-2-2); or 9/8 (2-2-2-3); *čoček* may also take the form of a 4/4 čifteteli: ♩ ♫ ♫ ♩ | ♩ ♩ ♩ or ♪ ♩ ♪ ♩ ♩ .

Solo *čoček* and line dances are typically combined at Rom dance events. Čoček is danced in the middle of the dance floor near the front of the line; simultaneously, the line snakes around. For example, on the bride's day of a wedding, the bride's close female kin will dance *čoček* in the center as groups of relatives are called up to lead the dance line. A few female members of the beckoned relatives (rarely men) will join the bride's women in the center to dance *čoček*. The style changes as new tunes are played and new family members are summoned. Even though women may ostensibly be doing the same dance for hours, its texture migrates from fast and bouncy to slow and heavy through varying combinations of emotions. While ritual contexts of *čoček* are obligatory, dancing *čoček* for entertainment is also common, for example, during the less structured parts of dance events.

A good *čoček* dancer has the admiration of the entire community and her family will show off her talents.[14] At a wedding in Šutka in 1990, the father of an excellent teenage dancer was very angry at her because she was nowhere to be found when the family was called up to lead the dance line. His family's display of competence depended partly on his talented daughter. It is clear that *čoček* is currently coded as a valuable female genre. Women and girls squarely take center stage as excellent dancers. People crowd around them to watch much more readily than men and boys. Esma remarked, "That was the most beautiful, to show dignity. A mother-in-law might say to another mother-in-law, 'my daughter-in-law raises her hand [to dance] as if she could take everyone's life!' This would show how delicately she danced; this was the realization of Rom tradition." Girls are coached by family members to dance well, while boys are not. At home, taped music is played as experienced dancers demonstrate moves and technique. Talented young girls are especially encouraged to develop their skills. At dance events, mothers "put up" their daughters to dance on tables. Dance talent, is, in fact, an asset for marriage.

In the 1970s, line and processional dancing were sexually integrated, while solo čoček dancing was segregated. Dunin remarks that "whenever the dancing began during segregated parties, the curtains or drapes were secured so that no one could look indoors. If a child playfully pulled the curtains from outside, he was sent scurrying for fear of being punished." Dunin continues "this dance was meant to be performed by women for women and not in mixed situations" (Dunin 1973, 195). As I will discuss, one reason for the segregation of čoček is the importance placed upon women's sexual modesty in front of men.

By the 1990s, however, owing to Westernization and the relaxation of gender divisions in many areas of life čoček could be found in mixed company. In banquet halls, on the street at weddings, and at home parties, women began to dance in the presence of men; of course, women also continued to dance in sexually segregated events such as henna parties. Let me be specific in describing a typical mixed audience for čoček dancers. At a wedding in Šutka in 1990, a mother put her sixteen-year-old daughter on a table to dance, while she, her sister, her husband, the dancer's sister, and the dancer's brother all danced in front of her (on the ground), encouraging her with shouts of appreciation and even with monetary tips. Similarly, female relatives of good dancers often stop dancing and instead clap for the talented performer. In spatial terms, the closest audience for female čoček dancers is composed of relatives. Strangers, however, do watch from afar. Ironically, it is precisely for strangers that the girl's talent needs to be shown. The physical proximity of relatives is not only a permeable wall—a shield of protection against charges of sexual immorality, but also a transparent screen through which to view female bodily displays.

Aside from in-group Rom events, where else might čoček be performed? First, čoček as a solo dance form has been adopted by non-Rom Macedonians, Bulgarians, and Albanians as a social dance, often with sexual connotations (see chap. 3 in this volume; van de Port 1998, 1999). Whereas in the 1970s čoček was played among Macedonians and Bulgarians only at the end of weddings, when males became drunk, now it is a widely popular dance form all over the Balkans and is related to folk-pop fusions such as *čalga* in Bulgaria and *muzica orientala* in Romania. Second, in the 1960s, Yugoslav Roma formed amateur ensembles and incorporated čoček into their performance repertoires for festivals. In Bulgaria, no amateur Rom ensembles existed until 1989 because the socialist government prohibited all religious and ethnic displays, especially by Muslims. One of the first public Bulgarian concerts to be labeled with the words *Tsiganska muzika* (Gypsy music) took place in downtown Sofia in 1990. The audience, all Roma, was visibly excited to be able to hear Rom music in a public hall. The dancing in the concert, however, was not the subtle kjuček, which Roma do at their in-group events, but rather belly dancing with bare midriffs and gross bodily contortions. I learned that the dancers were not Roma but Bulgarian women. In more recent years, belly dancers (some non-Roma, some Roma) have started appearing with bands at Bulgarian Rom music festivals, creating a virtual craze.[15] Similarly, in Yugoslavia, New Year's Eve television programs in the 1980s and 1990s regularly featured Rom musicians with a bevy of writhing, scantily clad belly dancers. When watching these programs with my Rom friends they remarked how those belly dancers had virtually nothing in common with Rom čoček dancers, plus, they gave Rom women a bad name.[16] Esma commented in her interview

> In recent times, you know that in Macedonia there has appeared,
> for example with Ferus Musfafov [a Rom musician], a Macedonian
> woman [she isn't Rom] who does belly dance—and they show this as
> if it were Rom. This isn't Rom, it is Turkish. That is Ferus's mistake.
> He makes a profit—money—from this. My generation knows this is
> Turkish or Arabic. A Rom woman would never be undressed to show
> her belly button and those things. Women used to be in a separate
> room, men separate, and they used to celebrate segregated at wed-
> dings. At our weddings our women used to be dressed in beautiful
> *dimija* [wide Muslim pants], beautiful shoes—nothing could you see
> bare—nothing at all bare—beautiful vests, underdresses, handker-
> chiefs at their hands, blouses with handmade lace. When they got
> up to dance, two-by-two (a daughter-in-law from one family with
> a daughter-in-law from another, or a daughter and a daughter), all
> of the elders sitting inside would cheer whomever danced better.
> Among us, we didn't do any mixed (*mešano*) dances—we only

danced čoček. You dance čoček with your stomach, you don't dance [with your hips] in a circle, you don't dance it with moans; we didn't have any of the new things with which people now deceive people. That is the tradition of the Roma.

While it is beyond the purview of this chapter to analyze why non-Roma enact dance stereotypes of Roma,[17] we may legitimately inquire why Rom-sponsored events and media products engage in the hypersexualization of the female body. One answer lies in the commercial success of these belly dance performances. A cursory glance at videos and cassettes of Rom music produced in Macedonia and Bulgaria in the 1990s reveals that the majority of them feature partially nude belly dancers in graphic cover designs and performances.[18] Even Esma Redžepova, despite her objections to belly dancing, has produced videos with veiled writhing dancers, although no flesh was shown. In Bulgaria, the belly-dancing craze is embedded in ethnic and political displays of the postsocialist period. First, it is a youth phenomenon; the 1995 Stara Zagora festival, for example, was attended by a few thousand Roma, most under thirty years of age. Second, it is tied to the cultural and political mobilization of Roma in a society that actively discriminates against them. Rom music festivals often feature speeches by politicians and are sponsored by political organizations. Perhaps professional belly dancing is more popular in Bulgaria than in Macedonia because only 50 percent of Bulgarian Roma are Muslims, and those 50 percent are less religious than Macedonian Rom Muslims. Most important, Bulgarian Roma are closer geographically and musically to Turkey, and they readily adopt Turkish stylistic features.

Roma engage in self-stereotypification (or mimesis of other's projections of them) in part because of market considerations. Female performances sell precisely because they fit the image non-Roma have of Rom women—sexually alluring, promiscuous, provocative, and musically talented. The historical information about Ottoman çengis can be interpreted from this angle: çengis were selling not only their musicality but also their perceived (and often actual) sexuality. "Self-orientalizing" moves, however, need to be seen within the webs of power in which they are located (Ong 1997, 195). Roma have throughout history had to rely on outside patrons and the trade in outsider-created images for work. For certain groups of Roma, the market in female stereotypic images encompassed not only music, but also fortune-telling.[19] Some observers have criticized Roma for "cashing in" on outsider stereotypes. This position ignores the tremendous power inequalities between Roma and the non-Rom world of promoters and media producers. In truth,

Roma have historically had few choices about their work and their images and even today lack access to image-creating mechanisms (Hancock 1997).

Modesty, Sexuality, and Reputation

Condemnations of belly dancing and the ideal separation of the sexes are both grounded in an ideology of female modesty and decorum shared by all Balkan groups regardless of religion, but appearing most strongly among Muslims. Do the rituals themselves require segregation (along with the music embedded in them), or do the music and dance propel segregation? On the one hand, we may notice that nonmusical rituals, such as decorating the wedding sieve, and nonmusical socializing, such as drinking coffee with neighbors, are often segregated activites. In both the public and private realms, women still socialize primarily with other women according to age hierarchies. Rituals dramatize and amplify these daily divisions. On the other hand, there is something marked about women singing and dancing: the embodied nature of dance and music highlight its association with female sexuality.

The literature on honor and shame in the Mediterranean region is useful here but must be criticized for reducing complex and variable systems to a rigid dichotomy. Various authors have shown that the supposed pan-Mediterranean concept means different things to different cultural groups (see the introduction to this volume). For Balkan Roma, the moral system of Romanes (doing things in the Rom way) contrasts *pativ, also pačiv or pakiv* (Romani, "respect") with *ladž* (Romani, "shame"). In the south Slavic languages, Roma speak of these concepts as *čest* (honesty) and *sram* (shame). A bride who is a virgin is *čestna* (honest, pure). A belly dancer *nema sram* (has no shame).[20] A family's reputation is expressed by offering hospitality to guests, respecting elders, and caring for family members in gender-specific ways. A man works and provides for his family; women work too, but they also cook, clean, and take care of children, and serve and defer to men in public. In public, women are expected to adjust to men, as they are nominally "heads of households."

These are the ideals of Romanes, but they are contradicted by realms of female power and influence. The female role in income-producing activities, in budget decisions, in marriage decisions, in information networks, and in ritual management all mitigate her subordination. In the realm of sexuality, however, women must conform most to ideal behavior precisely because sexuality poses the greatest danger of ladž or sram. Women are scrutinized by other women as to their bodily appearance and deportment. Speech patterns, clothing (especially hem lines and bodices), makeup, eye contact, socializing patterns, company kept, time spent outdoors—all are noted and evaluated for violations of modesty. The most highly charged symbol of the proper deportment of female sexuality is the test for the virginity of the bride, still performed today in many Muslim Rom families in the Balkans and in the diaspora.[21]

The association of women with sexuality bears directly on the stigma of the female professional musician, for it is both the commercial relationship with a paying audience and the display of the body to strange males that threaten female modesty. Dancing professionally is regarded by Roma as far more immoral than singing professionally. Yuri Yunakov, a Bulgarian Muslim Rom musician remarked that he would never let his daughter (who is a very talented dancer) become a professional dancer, as it was a degrading profession. His wife agreed. Dancing for money involves performing for strange men, selling one's sexuality and thereby devaluing it. Dancing nonprofessionally also has its dangers, although they are mitigated by the high value on dance as a female art form. Now, in an era of more relaxed sexual segregation, females dancing čoček are surrounded by the permeable wall of their relatives.

The common social structural argument explaining the potency of female sexuality argues that in patrilocal societies such as that of Roma, the possibility of a woman having a child with a man who isn't her husband or a girl having a child out of wedlock disrupts the patriarchal system and poses a problem of affiliation of the child. Other views argue that it is the female body itself that is inherently sexual, in contrast to the "productive" body of men (Nieuwkerk 1995, 154). A third view interprets Islam as conceiving of women as more sexual than men, thus needing to be constrained (Mernissi 1975). These views are somewhat relevant for Roma, but they are insufficient explanations. Roma talk constantly about the problems of a child who isn't rightfully attached to an extended family; out of wedlock children and children conceived in adulterous relationships are pitied and their mothers are rebuked. But a woman's deviant sexual behavior has no solution—it is part of her intrinsic moral character. Roma seem to view sexuality as inherent to females, but not in contrast to the "productive bodies" of males. True, males have to worry less about public scrutiny of sexuality, but on the other hand, Roma also view females as productive bodies. In fact women are often viewed as more productive than men. Most Roma agree that women hold the family together emotionally and culturally (e.g., their role in ritual), and in addition, many families survive on women's incomes.

The intersection of sexuality, marginality, and the marketplace is the site all professional performers inhabit, but women face a double stigma. Structurally, Rom women are to Rom society what Rom men are to non-Roma. For non-Roma, Roma represent sexuality and marginality, the "other" in our midst. Male professional performers are desired and needed by non-Roma but suspected of deviance, danger, and sexual allure (Trumpener 1992; van de Port 1999). To non-Roma, female Rom professionals are coded as doubly dangerous: first as Roma, second as women. For Roma, on the other hand, female Rom professionals are dangerous for different reasons: first, because they embody sexuality, they can disrupt the social system from their positions as insiders; second, the selling of their performances in the marketplace foregrounds the paradox of economic necessity versus ideal modesty (Okely 1975). This highlights the structural subordination of Roma vis-à-vis non-Roma: Roma have had to rely on patrons to construct their images, and often they perform their patrons' stereotypes (van de Port 1999).

Female Professional Singing: Esma Redžepova

Like the stigma of professional dance, the stigma of professional singing derives from the publicly displayed female body. Roma regard most professional singers as loose and lacking decorum, an attitude echoed by non-Rom audiences. For example, I often heard Rom women discuss the degrading ways in which professional singers accept monetary tips. Like the çengis of the Ottoman era, women often receive tips in a tactile fashion, as drunk and sweaty male patrons paste bills to their foreheads and other body parts. Indeed, tipping as a display of humiliation may also be foisted upon male Roma.[22]

It is not surprising, then, that among Balkan Muslim Roma there are very few female professional vocalists in comparison with males.[23] Those women who defy convention are subject to ridicule and charges of immorality. Salif Ali, a Bulgarian Rom drummer explained that it was totally unacceptable for his daughter to become a singer. When the rare set of parents do agree to a daughter's singing professionally, her career often ends with her marriage.[24] One way to circumvent public disapproval, however, is to marry a musician. This mitigates the professional's immodesty because one's husband (or father or brother) serves as the protector of his wife's honor. Indeed, the majority of female vocalists today perform with family members.[25]

Esma Redžepova's early life sheds some light upon how a woman might defy conventions and become a well-known singer. Esma has toured all over the world, has given thousands of concerts, and is featured on hundreds of recordings. Born in 1945, Esma performed in elementary school productions, where her talent was noticed by a Radio Skopje editor, who invited her to sing for an amateur program called "The Microphone Is Yours." She feared her parents' wrath if they found out that she had sung over the radio. She writes: "A Gypsy girl, beautiful, who also sang—that would have been really dangerous. The family decided that I, like all other girls, should marry early, and have children, and obey my husband without question, and work" (Teodosievski and Redžepova 1984, 89).

Esma remembers, "I was a girl at the time, I wasn't yet married. . . . According to our tradition it was a shame to sing publicly." Singing was a sensitive topic in the Redžepova household because of the disgrace Esma's sister had brought on the family:

> For Ibrahim, my father, himself a wonderful singer, really hated singing! Or at least singing in public. For him singing in public meant singing in low grade restaurants (*kafanas*), it meant drinking and carousing. And he had every reason to think that way. My sister Sajka, a pretty talented girl, had brought disgrace on the family and become a singer in a kafana. Ibrahim couldn't get over it: his lovely Sajka singing to drunks who smashed glasses for kicks. For him, Sajka was "dead." . . . I believe that had she kept on and had more luck, she would have become a great singer. . . . How beautifully she sang! I listened to her in wonder. My father and mother cursed her. If only Sajka had someone to lead her, to show her the way. But the kafana "ate her up.". . . I remembered Sajka's fate, because something similar awaited me too. And it also helped me to understand why my parents would so bitterly resent me even thinking of becoming a singer. (Teodosievski and Redžepova 1984, 90–91)

Despite their parents' disapproval, Esma's brothers supported her first steps toward a singing career: "My brothers . . . never mentioned in front of my parents where and when they had seen me in town. . . . My brothers would say to our parents: 'Why do you worry so much about Esma, she is not Sajka! She has a will of her own and if she decides to sing she will sing! But she will be a real singer, an artist!'" (Teodosievski and Redžepova 1984, 91) Similarly, Esma's teacher told her father: "Don't spoil your daughter's chances, Ibrahim! She is a great talent. Singing does not necessarily mean singing in a kafana" (93).

When she was thirteen years old, Esma was brought to the attention of Stevo Teodosievski, a non-Roma Orthodox Slav Macedonian accordionist and folk music arranger who worked for Radio Skopje. He was struck by her talent and sparkle, and remarked, "You have some talent, but you really will have to work." Stevo wanted to take her on as a pupil and train her, but Esma's parents said no. "My father said, 'What? A singer? No. No, she's ready for marriage; people are already asking, saying she'll be married in a year or two. Why should singing break up my family?'"[26] Her parents strongly opposed her singing career. They said: "She will not sing. She will listen to her mother and father." But Stevo managed to make an arrangement with them that he would make her into an artist, not a café singer, if they would postpone marriage until she was eighteen years old. "When Stevo promised him faithfully that he would help me to become a good and famous singer—not a singer in any old nightclub—when my father had reassured himself that Stevo's intentions were honest, that he would look after me, he finally agreed" (Teodosievski and Redžepova 1984, 95).

In the early 1960s under the banner "Esma—Ensemble Teodosievski," Esma and Stevo launched a successful career characterized by daring innovations. Esma was the first Balkan Rom musician (male or female) to achieve commercial success in the non-Rom world; she was the first Rom singer to perform commercially in the Rom language for non-Roma; she was the first female Rom artist to record in Yugoslavia; and she was the first Macedonian woman (Roma or non-Roma) to perform on television. According to Esma, her success is due to her teacher, Stevo, who became her husband in 1968. She claims, "What I am singing is not what I am singing but what Stevo taught me. He was wise, about twenty years ahead of his time; he taught me how to understand music. . . . Whatever he promised to me came true."

Humility aside, Esma herself wrote many of her songs, choreographed her performances, and provided the talent. On the other hand, it is true that Stevo planned Esma's career very carefully. One early strategy was not to allow Esma to perform at kafanas and weddings, but only at concerts and for radio and television recordings. In effect, Stevo created a new category of female concert artist that didn't have the same degree of stigma as the café or wedding singer.[27] Today, Esma is very proud of the fact that she has not engaged in restaurant work and she only sings at friends' weddings for free.

Stevo was very conscious about creating a specific Rom niche for Esma in the commercial world. Even before meeting Esma, he was promoting Rom music at Radio Skopje. In 1956, he taught two Macedonian singers songs in Romani and had them dress up in dimija. They flopped because they were so bland; the stylistic fit was obviously wrong. Stevo remarked "At that time it would have been impossible for a Rom woman to perform, owing to the racism." Esma, then eleven years old, remembers thinking, "I can do better than that—why don't I sing?"

Esma's singing in the Rom language was a statement of pride in her heritage. "I was the first Roma to sing Rom songs in the Rom language. It was actually historical, that Yugoslavia was the first place to broadcast Rom songs on radio. It was kind of a shame to sing in Romani in my time; many singers hid the fact that they were Roma. When I came out singing my own songs in Romani, a lot came out after me." As Esma explained in her interview, "many singers passed [as other ethnic groups] because there was an embargo on Rom singers. There was discrimination against them as performers. I took a risk when I said I was Roma and I want to sing in my own language." She continued, "Our Rom women were afraid at the time to say they were Roma— they said they were Turkish, Macedonian, Albanian, anything but Roma. . . . They were afraid of being Roma. After the cleansings of World War II, the Roma were afraid for their lives and at no time would admit they were Roma." Stevo commented, "Esma was the first leader with the flag! All the other people looked at her to see if she was accepted. Esma agreed: "And after me, they could say they were Roma. It was no longer a shame, the stamp was made." As Stevo told it: "On her first record . . . it was written 'Gypsy music.' It was very clear! For the first time 'Gypsy music' was written on a label." Esma concluded with pride: "I opened the way for Roma. In the first place, to admit that they are Roma, and not to be ashamed they are Roma."

But Esma and Stevo's achievement was not a foregone conclusion. They endured the racism of Macedonian institutions and the gossip of the public. Stevo's colleagues said cruelly, "Stevo why have you brought this Gyspy to disgrace us" (Teodosievski and Redžepova 1984, 95). In the beginning of her career, Esma was deliberately denied opportunities: "They took from her the song she knew and did best and gave it to another girl" (38). The atmosphere became so stifling that in the early 1960s Stevo and Esma moved to Belgrade, the capital of Yugoslavia, where they would have more musical opportunities. As Esma explained in her interview: "People knew me too well, they were talking too much about us in Skopje, and we had to get out of that environment." Stevo expanded: "They chased me out of Macedonia because of Esma (we had to move to Belgrade)—'Why do you play that Rom music?—let it go—you are not Roma.' People can corroborate my story. I was a member of the Communist Party through Radio Skopje—they objected. They threw me out. . . . The secretary of the Party said, 'Why do you bother with Esma?

Vaska Ilieva, Anka Gieva—they are Macedonians, Esma isn't!' From then I had nothing to do with the Party—it didn't interest me any more."

Stevo's genius was to create a recognizable image and trademark staging for Esma, which evoked historical stereotypes of Roma women as sensual and fiery but kept the pageant tasteful. Esma was the first Rom performer to appear in dimija for non-Rom audiences. "I was the only one, with Teodosievski's help, to jump up publicly on stage and wear dimija (and I wear them to this day). I am not ashamed to wear them and I am not ashamed to say I am Roma." Dimija, which emphasize even the slightest hip movement, linked Esma specifically to Roma, to other Muslims of the Balkans, and to tradition. Her dimija, however, were fashioned in the most modern of fabrics and colors, and Esma further innovated with accessories and headpieces. Some of her headwear evoked Turkish themes, and one musical number featured a veil.

Another trademark feature introduced by Stevo was that all the performers stood up, giving them unprecedented freedom of movement on stage. And most daring, Esma danced during musical interludes:

> I am a traditional woman—growing up among the women gathered
> inside. I adopted all the old ways. Stevo told me when I was young,
> "You will dance exactly how you danced inside with the women at
> a wedding." I answered, "But that is shameful." He said, "It is not
> shameful—it is your tradition—it is your national dance. Others
> dance differently, but you are dressed in dimija, it is not a shame,
> you have something to dance about! You aren't bare, you don't dance
> [with your hips] in a circle, you dance with your stomach." And he
> persuaded me that I don't need to feel ashamed of that—I have to
> show my culture—it is our national dance. I have accepted [em-
> braced] exactly what Stevo taught me. After I got on the stage
> and danced, it was easier for other Rom women and girls.

Indeed, Esma's performances legitimated Rom music and dance as a female art form.

Stevo staged Esma's performances as miniature dramatic scenes in which she enacted the text. Her voice showcased emotional qualities of the text (often using cries and yelps) amplified by hand gestures. Similar to Ottoman çengis and to generations of male musicians, she masterfully played to audience sentiment. Stevo also introduced the tarabuka to concert performances; associated with Muslims, the tarabuka had never before been used on a concert stage. Furthermore, Stevo engaged young Rom boys to dramatically play the tarabuka while they danced, building up to a climactic pace, which sig-naled Esma's entrance.

India represented an important international tie in Esma's career. In the early 1970s, Roma in Macedonia were beginning to develop a sense of their historical ties to India as part of a larger politicization process and a move-ment to define their identity.[28] Roma began naming their children Hindu names and musicians started using Indian themes in their čočeks. Ensemble Teodosievski made its first (uninvited) trip to India in 1969, followed by two invited trips in 1976 and 1983. In 1976, Stevo and Esma were crowned "King and Queen of Rom Music" at the First World Festival of Rom Songs and Music in Chandigarh. This link between Rom identity politics and music helped to facilitate Esma's acceptance among Roma.

While Esma's career soared among the non-Rom public, Esma's relation-ship to Rom audiences was more ambivalent. Her parents had to defend her reputation: "At that time it was the easiest thing to offend my girlish pride, my purity. Especially as we Skopje Roma were very sensitive about such things. Some busybody would go up to my father . . . and tell him there was 'something going on' between me and Stevo, always together on trips, in ho-tels. 'Poor Ibrahim' they would say and my father would wish the ground could swallow him" (Teodosievski and Redžepova 1984, 96). But for Roma, Stevo's Macedonian ethnicity was even more problematic than the alleged in-decent relationship. According to Esma's cousin Sani Rifati, Roma at first re-jected Esma not so much because she was a professional singer, but because she spent time with and later married a non-Rom man.[29] At that time it was virtually impossible for Roma and Macedonians to intermarry; neither group desired it. Esma remarked during her interview: "We were the first mixed marriage . . . ! That was a big deal! Can you imagine how many people were at our wedding? Ten to fifteen thousand people came to see if it were true that the two of us were getting married, and if he would take me to Belgrade."

Eventually, after marriage and international stardom, Esma was accepted and respected by her own community. Although not representative of Rom women, Esma created with Stevo an unprecedented niche for Rom singers, both male and female. Moreover, she raised female arts to a level of respect-ability by tailoring images of sexuality to the framework of the elite concert stage. By achieving success among non-Roma first, she legitimated her role among Roma as a professional. Today Esma is a living legend for many Roma.

The current constellation of Rom female performers, including both pro-fessionals such as Esma and belly dancers and nonprofessionals such as female family members, points to the convergence of a specific set of historical, economic, political, social, and aesthetic factors. Within Rom communities, female musicality and dance, although tinged with sexuality, are valued, prized, and encouraged to flower in appropriate settings. Female musicianship is related to income and to other female realms of competence, such as ritual knowledge and the economic management of family budgets (Silverman 1996b). Moreover, female artistry as an occupation has a long history, as witnessed by Ottoman çengis and early-twentieth-century frame drum players and singers.

In spite of the economic necessity propelling professionals and in spite of their demand by non-Roma and Roma alike, female singers and dancers are still criticized as immoral. Sexuality is necessary, but dangerous. The position of female Rom performers to Roma structurally mirrors the position of Rom male performers to non-Roma: they are marginal, sexual, and dangerous, yet for their patrons the artistry and musicality they embody bring out the "soul" of a celebration. Okely makes a parallel point about British Rom fortune-tellers, who mingle freely with non-Roma for work but are expected to preserve modesty and reputation (1975).

Thus fortune-tellers, dancers, and musicians have been stereotyped by non-Roma as quintessential images of Rom women. The marginal position of Roma, their lack of control of image making, and their role as service workers all contribute to the trafficking of their arts in the realm of the market. Females have a significant role in this market, as their talents, images, and bodies are a saleable commodity. Stereotypes of Rom women are rarely designed by women themselves, but rather rely on patron fantasies, which may then be mimetically performed back. While those who control female images are usually non-Roma like Stevo Teodosievski, sometimes they are male Rom entrepreneurs. Some Roma capitalize on stereotypes to attract the huge buying audience of Roma, illustrated by the belly dance craze among Bulgarian Roma. In short, Roma often use the same strategies to sell to Roma that they have used to sell to non-Roma. Women, however, are not passive in this process. Although they are rarely in charge of the institutions that manage their performances, Rom women have managed to carve out new domains of performance, as Esma's case shows. They tailor their talents and sexuality to varying contexts. The nexus between in-group ideals of female modesty and the economic and aesthetic requirements of the marketplace has created a space for a variety of female performers. These women, like Esma, strategize to maximize both their commercial success and their reputation. Few succeed, but each woman's life charts a creative path.

Notes

Field research for this chapter took place in Šuto Orizari (known as Šutka), a Rom neighborhood of Skopje, Macedonia (1990, 1994); in Bulgaria (1980–94); and in Macedonian Rom communities in New York, Toronto, and Melbourne (1989–99). Interviews with Esma Redžepova and members of her ensemble occurred 1996–2001. Balkan fieldwork was supported by the International Research and Exchanges Board; writing and fieldwork in the United States were supported by the University of Oregon a through a Summer Faculty Research Award and a Research Grant from the Center for the Study of Women in Society. Unless otherwise noted, all translations from non-English sources are my own.

1. Linguistic evidence reveals that Roma migrated westward from northwest India and reached the Balkans by the fourteenth century. Facing hatred and discrimination in virtually every European region, Roma have endured genocide in the Nazi period and as-similation attempts by the Austro-Hungarian Empire and the socialist states. Since the 1989 revolutions, there has been a rise in physical violence and discrimination against Roma (Fraser 1992; Hancock 1987, 1997; Silverman 1995). Balkan Roma have been indispensable suppliers of services to non-Roma, such as music for celebrations, fortune-telling, metalworking, horse dealing, woodworking, and seasonal agricultural work. A primarily instrumental male professional niche requires Roma to know expertly the co-territorial musical repertoire and interact with it in a creative manner (see Silverman 1996a and 1999; Rice 1982; Pettan 1996a,b,c, and chap. 12 this volume).

2. I do not discuss musical style in this chapter (see Silverman 1996a and 1999). Although there are some cultural and historical differences among Macedonian and Bulgarian Muslim Rom groups (Silverman 1996a), broad similarities allow me to generalize about gender patterns. In Bulgaria 50 percent and in Macedonia approximately 80 percent of Roma are Muslim; most do not observe Islam strictly.

3. Note Middle Eastern and non-Rom Muslim Balkan parallels, although Doubleday's posited connection between the frame drum and the sacred does not appear to apply (Doubleday 1999).

4. Rom men also played and still play these instruments, as well as other instruments (Rice 1982; Silverman 1999). The daire has been associated with urban music in Macedonia, Albania, Kosovo, and Epirus (Greece); in village contexts, it is more exclusively a women's instrument (Jane Sugarman, personal communication).

5. In North America, henna ceremonies take place in urban apartments in a room designated for women. At a 1996 New York ceremony that took place in a three-room apartment, approximately twenty-five women occupied the living room and the few men were relegated to the kitchen.

6. See Silverman 1996b and 2000 for a discussion of female power in family life.

7. Pettan further explains that while the above is true for sedentary Roma, nomadic Rom women are even more exposed in the public realm, through fortune-telling, selling herbal medicines, and begging (Pettan 1996a, 316). See also Okely 1975, Stewart 1997, and Sutherland 1986.

8. Brown is most likely comparing Rom women to Albanian or Turkish women in Skopje. Brown continues: "It is striking that among the gypsies even quite old women remain slim and agile, and there seemed nothing incongruous in a middle-aged woman's taking part in this rather coquettish performance" (Brown 1933, 308).

9. Sonia Seeman, personal communication.

10. Note the photograph of Jewish Macedonian professional dancers in a pre–World War II Skopje nightclub in Džimrevski's book on čalgija music (1985). In the 1960s, Dunin observed Rom girls dancing professionally at Serbian fairs and cafés (1973, 193; 1977, 12).

11. In the postsocialist period, the number and size of celebrations have declined owing to economic constraints.

12. There is a substantial literature on Balkan line dances (see, e.g., Dunin and Višinski 1995). Many line dances have been adopted from non-Rom cultures but may be danced in a distinct Rom style. A few line dances may have originated with Roma and spread to other ethnic groups, such as *kuperlika,* which is an urban Muslim dance first described by the Janković sisters in 1939 (see Dunin 1995, 127). This line dance (sometimes known as *oro*) in 2/4 or 7/8 is now danced by both men and women of varied ethnic groups in integrated lines all over Macedonia and the Macedonian diaspora and is associated with contemporary electrified music (see chap. 3, this volume).

13. The word čoček comes from *köçek,* a professional boy dancer of the Ottoman period who was, like a çengi, often Rom (see chap. 3, this volume).

14. In New York City, women evaluated dancers while visiting and having coffee together.

15. At the 1995 Rom Music Festival in Stara Zagora, many bands appeared with a belly dancer (*kjučekinja*); the band Džipsi Aver brought five dancers. At the Balkanromfest in 1996 in Sofia, the belly dancer with Džipsi Aver won first prize for dancing.

16. Kapchan points out that in Morocco professional dancers and singers (*shikhat* or *sheikhat*) both use the media and are used by the media. They make videos to sell on the one hand, and on the other hand, government television stations use regional shikha performances to display images of folkloric diversity (Kapchan 1996, 206). Similarly, Yugoslav television used belly dancers and Rom music to promote the discourse of cultural diversity under the Titoist banner of "brotherhood and unity."

17. See van de Port 1998 and 1999 for a discussion of Serbian enactments of "Gypsy behavior." See chapter 3 of this volume, for Sugarman's discussion of čoček (çoçek) among Albanian women.

18. Videos sometimes feature fantasy scenarios, for example, Rom clarinetist Ferus Mustafov dressed in a doctor's uniform playing to his bedridden female patients, who at the sound of his music shed their hospital sheets and emerge as belly dancers.

19. See Okely 1975 and Sutherland 1986.

20. Note that the word *marime* (polluted, socially ostracized) is not found among Muslim Balkan Roma, although the concept has some moral weight.

21. The bridal sheet is examined for virginal blood, and if the "news is good," the sheet is sent to the bride's mother and displayed for the guests.

22. Stephen Kotansky videotaped a particularly humiliating tipping sequence in Mac-

edonia in which a Rom zurla player was made to accept a great number of bills into his mouth. Also see van de Port 1999, 302–4.

23. A cursory review of Rom music festivals in Macedonia and Bulgaria reveals fewer female singers than males. This situation seems to be true for non-Rom Balkan Muslims and for Roma from other areas of Europe. Sugarman reports, "Until recently, no south Albanian women from Macedonia had ever performed at an event as a professional singer (1997, 369). On the 1999 Gypsy Caravan Tour, out of thirty Rom musicians, only one was a woman, and she was a wife of a participant. Gitanos seem to be an exception to this pattern. The 1999 CD Gypsy Queens (Network 32843) is a recent attempt to highlight the contribution of women to Rom music.

24. This ideology exists among non-Roma of the Balkans as well. I heard a number of stories from Orthodox Bulgarian women whose parents, mothers-in-law, or husbands prohibited them from joining professional ensembles because it was shameful.

25. These include Lisa Angelova and Zlatka Činčirova from Bulgaria, who performed with their fathers, and Ramiza Dalipova and Esma Redžepova from Macedonia, who performed with their husbands. Similarly, most Bulgarian non-Rom wedding singers, such as Maria Karafezieva, Ruska Kalčeva, Binka Dobreva, and Pepa Papazova, were in bands with their husbands. In the Hungarian Rom group Kalyi Jag, the only female participant, Agnes Kunstler, was the wife of another participant, Jozsef Balogh. Sugarman also reports that the few female Prespa Albanian singers were in bands with their husbands (1997, 342). For Middle Eastern parallels, see Nieuwkerk 1995, 68 and 128.

26. Esma resisted her parents' attempts to marry her off in her teens. When her mother mentioned marriage, Esma replied "I tell you, I'll hang myself in the little square in front of the school, on the monument. . . . I don't know if my mother really believed my threats, but anyway, they didn't manage to marry me off at the age thirteen!" She also had to fight off taunts from relatives. Her sister-in-law Veba often scolded her: "'Ha! You want to be singer, do you? Well you'll wash windows and scrub floors as a married woman.' 'Hey, I will not, you know. I don't want to be a servant I want to be an artist.' 'You can want all you want when your parents marry you off. They've already had offers'" (Teodosievski and Redžepova 1984, 92).

27. Karin van Nieuwkerk claims in Egypt there is a hierarchy with nightclub entertainers at the bottom, wedding entertainers a little higher, and concert entertainers at the top (1995, 122–32).

28. The first International Rom Congress was held in London in 1971.

29. Sani Rifati, personal communication.

References

Brown, Catherine. 1933. "Gypsy Wedding at Skoplje." *Folk-Lore* 48:305–9.

Doubleday, Veronica. 1999. "The Frame Drum in the Middle East: Women, Musical Instruments, and Power." *Ethnomusicology* 43 (1): 101–34.

Dunin, Elsie. 1971. "Gypsy Wedding: Dance and Customs." *Makedonski Folklor* 4 (7/8): 317–26.

———. 1973. "Čoček as a Ritual Dance among Gypsy Women." *Makedonski Folklor* 4 (12): 193–97.

————. 1977. "The Newest Changes in Romani Dance (Serbia and Macedonia)." *Journal of the Association of Graduate Dance Ethnologists* (University of California, Los Angeles) 1:12–17.

————. 1985. "Dance Change in the Context of the Gypsy St. George's Day, Skopje, Yugoslavia, 1967–1977." In *Papers from the Fourth and Fifth Annual Meetings, Gypsy Lore Society, North American Chapter,* edited by Joanne Grumet, 110–20. New York: Gypsy Lore Society.

————. 1998. *Gypsy St. George's Day—Coming of Summer: Romski Gjurjuvden, Romano Gjurgjovdani—Erdelezi, Skopje, Macedonia, 1967–1997.* Skopje: Zdruzenie na Ljuboteli na Romaniska Folklorna Umetnost Romano Ilo.

Dunin, Elsie, and Stanimir Višinski. 1995. *Dances in Macedonia: Performance, Genre, Tanec.* Skopje: Okmomvri.

Džimrevski, Borovoje. 1985. *Čalgiskata Tradicija vo Makedonija.* Skopje: Makedonska Kniga.

Fraser, Angus. 1992. *The Gypsies.* Oxford: Blackwell.

Kapchan, Deborah. 1996. *Gender on the Market: Moroccan Women and the Revoicing of Tradition.* Austin: University of Texas Press.

Hancock, Ian. 1987. *The Pariah Syndrome.* Ann Arbor: Karoma.

————. 1997. "The Struggle for the Control of Identity." *Transitions* 4 (4): 36–44.

Hasluck, Margaret. 1938. "The Gypsies of Albania." *Journal of the Gypsy Lore Society,* ser. 3, 17:20–30.

Jakoski, Voislav. 1981. "Pesnite na Gjurgjovden na Romite vo Skopje." *Etnološki Pregled* 17:293–302.

MacCormack, Carol, and Marilyn Strathern. 1980. *Nature, Culture, and Gender.* Cambridge: Cambridge University Press.

Magrini, Tullia. 1998 "Women's 'Work of Pain' in Christian Mediterranean Europe." *Music and Anthropology* 3. http://www.muspe.unibo.it/period/MA/

Marushiakova, Elena, and Veselin Popov. 1994. *Studii Romani.* Vol. 1. Sofia: Club '90.

————. 1995. *Studii Romani.* Vol. 2. Sofia: Club '90.

Mernissi, Fatima. 1975. *Beyond the Veil: Male-Female Dynamics in a Modern Muslim Society.* Cambridge: Schenkman.

Nieuwkerk, Karin van. 1995. *"A Trade Like Any Other": Female Singers and Dancers in Egypt.* Austin: University of Texas Press.

————. 1998. "'An Hour for God and an Hour for the Heart': Islam, Gender and Female Entertainment in Egypt." *Music and Anthropology* 3. http://www.muspe.unibo.it/period/MA/

Ortner, Sherry. 1996. *Making Gender: The Politics and Erotics of Culture.* Boston: Beacon.

Okely, Judith. 1975. "Gypsy Women: Models in Conflict." In *Perceiving Women,* edited by Shirley Ardener, 55–86. London: Malaby.

Ong, Aihwa. 1997. "Chinese Modernities: Narratives of Nation and of Capitalism." In *Ungrounded Empires: The Cultural Politics of Modern Chinese Transnationalism,* edited by Aihwa Ong and Donald Nonini, 171–202.

Peičeva, Lozanka, Vencislav Dimov, and Svetla Krusteva. 1997. *Romska Muzika: Priturka kum Učebnicite po Muzika za 5–8 Klas.* Sofia: Papagal.

Petrovski, Trajan. 1981. "Običajot Vasilica Kaj Skopskite Romi," *Etnološki Pregled* 17: 317–23.

———. 1993. *Kalendarski Običai kaj Romite vo Skopje i Okolina.* Skopje: Feniks.

Pettan, Svanibor. 1996a. "Gypsies, Music, and Politics in the Balkans: A Case Study from Kosovo." *World of Music* 38 (1): 33–62.

———. 1996b. "Female to Male—Male to Female: Third Gender in the Musical Life of the Gypsies in Kosovo." *Narodna Umjetnost* 33 (2): 311–24.

———. 1996c. "Selling Music: Rom Musicians and the Music Market in Kosovo." In *Echoes of Diversity: Traditional Music of Ethnic Groups—Minorities,* edited by Ursula Hemetek, 233–45. Vienna: Bohlau.

Picken, Laurence. 1975. *Folk Musical Instruments of Turkey.* New York: Oxford University Press.

Popov, Veselin. 1993. "The Gypsies and Traditional Bulgarian Culture." *Journal of the Gypsy Lore Society,* ser. 5, 3 (1): 21–33.

Rice, Timothy. 1982. "The Surla and Tapan Tradition in Yugoslav Macedonia." *Galpin Society Journal* 35:122–37.

Rosaldo, Michelle. 1974. "Woman, Culture, and Society: A Theoretical Overview." In *Woman, Culture, and Society,* 17–42. Stanford: Stanford University Press.

Seeman, Sonia Tamar. 1990. "Continuity and Transformation in the Macedonian Genre of Čalgija: Past Perfect and Present Imperfective." M.A. thesis, University of Washington.

Silverman, Carol. 1989. "Reconstructing Folklore: Media and Cultural Policy in Eastern Europe." *Communication* 11 (2): 141–60.

———. 1995. "Persecution and Politicization: Roma (Gypsies) of Eastern Europe." *Cultural Survival* 19 (2): 43–49.

———. 1996a. "Music and Marginality: The Roma (Gypsies) of Bulgaria and Macedonia." In *Retuning Culture: Musical Change in Eastern Europe,* edited by Mark Slobin, 231–53. Durham, N.C.: Duke University Press.

———. 1996b. "Music and Power: Gender and Performance among Roma (Gypsies) of Skopje, Macedonia." *World of Music* 38 (1): 63–76.

———. 1999. Romani (Gypsy) Music. In *Garland Encyclopedia of World Music,* Europe volume, edited by Timothy Rice, James Porter, and C. Goertzen, 270–93. New York: Garland.

———. 2000. "Macedonian and Bulgarian Muslim Romani Women: Power, Politics, and Creativity in Ritual." *Roma Rights: Newsletter of the European Roma Rights Center,* April 2000, no. 1.

Stewart, Michael. 1997. *The Time of the Gypsies.* Boulder: Westview.

Sugarman, Jane. 1997. *Engendering Song: Singing and Subjectivity at Prespa Albanian Weddings.* Chicago: University of Chicago Press.

Sutherland, Anne. 1986. "Gypsy Women, Gypsy Men: Paradoxes and Cultural Resources." In *Papers from the Sixth and Seventh Annual Meetings, Gypsy Lore Society, North American Chapter,* edited by Joanne Grumet, 104–12. New York: Gypsy Lore Society.

Teodosievski, Stevo, and Esma Redžepova. 1984. *On the Wings of Song.* Kočani: Dom Kulture Beli Mugri.

Trumpener, Katie. 1992. "The Time of the Gypsies: A 'People without History' in the Narratives of the West." *Critical Inquiry* 18:843–84.

Van de Port, Mattijs. 1998. *Gypsies, Wars, and Other Instances of the Wild: Civilisation and Its Discontents in a Serbian Town*. Amsterdam: Amsterdam University Press.

———. 1999. "The Articulation of the Soul: Gyspy Musicians and the Serbian Other." *Popular Music* 18 (3): 291–308.

Vukanović, Tatomir. 1962. "Musical Culture among the Gypsies of Yugoslavia." *Journal of the Gypsy Lore Society*, ser. 3, 41:41–61.

Plate 1. Chjam' è rispondi singers at a *tundera* (sheepshearing), Santa Lucia di Mercuriu, June 1995. Photograph by Caroline Bithell.

Plate 2. Jacky Micaelli in concert at the Settembrinu festival in Tavagna, September 1994. Photograph by Caroline Bithell.

Plate 3. (*above left*) The bailaora Carmen Amaya in the 1930s.

Plate 4. (*above*) The bailaora Salud Rodriguez, "La Niña del Ciego," late nineteenth century.

Plate 5. (*left*) The cantaora Ana Amaya Molina, Blas Vega Archive, late nineteenth century.

Plate 6. The çengi Mini i Vogël from Berat, who strikes an Orientalist pose for the camera. From Ekrem Bey Vlora, *Aus Berat und vom Tomor: Tagebuchblätter* (Sarajevo: Daniel A. Kajon, 1911), fig. 14.

Plate 7. Artist's rendering of a çengi, labeled "Young woman's dance to singing among the southern Albanians." From Ivan Ivanić, *Macedonija i Macedonci: Opis Zemlje i Naroda* (Novi Sad: Knjižara "Natošević," 1910), 2:131.

Plate 8. (*above*) Female relatives of the bride dance čoček during the henna ceremony, Šuto Orizari, Skopje, 1990. Photograph by Carol Silverman.

Plate 9. (*below*) Gypsy dancer before the start of the procession, Riace, September 1999. Photograph by Goffredo Plastino.

Plate 10. Gypsy dancer during the procession, Riace, September 1999. Photograph by Goffredo Plastino.

Plate 11. Dancer at the head of the procession, Gioiosa Ionica, August 1986. Photograph by Goffredo Plastino.

Plate 12. Rebetiko singer Sotiria Bellou. From the singer's personal archive.

Plate 13. Meddahat orchestra during a wedding in Oran. Photograph by Marie Virolle.

Plate 14. A shikha with her berrah and her gellali during a wedding in Sfisef. Photograph by Marie Virolle.

Plate 15. (*above*) A shikha incites nashaṭ. Photograph by Deborah Kapchan.
Plate 16. (*below*) A gesture of nashaṭ. Photograph by Deborah Kapchan.

Plate 17. (*above*) Ethnic Albanian women sing to the spun copper pan accompaniment, Gllogovc/Glogovac, 1987. Photograph by Svanibor Pettan.

Plate 18. (*left*) Tonë Bikaj with lahutë, Tuzi, 1960. Photograph by Marijana Gušić.

Plate 19. Performing the talava, Prizren, 1990. Photograph by Svanibor Pettan.

5

Come into Play: Dance, Music, and Gender in Three Calabrian Festivals

Goffredo Plastino

The Shy Dancer

In 1896, folklorist Giovanni Battista Marzano described the basic peculiarity of Calabrian *tarantella* as follows: "The dance style of the Calabrian people reflects their respect for women and their concern with the latter's honor. The dance style of the Calabrian people is not like the one that gentlemen used to dance. In folk dancing, not only can a man and a woman not dance jointly in an embrace, but they must also keep a distance between themselves, not even offering their hands to each other" (Plastino 1997, 53).[1] With just a few words, Marzano fixes the gender rules of this Calabrian dance: A man and a woman cannot touch each other. A woman's honor must be guaranteed by the man who dances with her. The "people" have these rules and observe them carefully; by contrast, the "gentlemen" have different rules: Marzano refers here to the dances performed at the court balls (waltz, polka, and mazurka), which had become widespread in Calabria at the end of the nineteenth century.[2]

Marzano seems to have written a list of precise rules, a catalog of good intentions, rather than a description from life. Meanwhile, peasants and shepherds continued to get close to and touch one other while dancing, even hitting each other's buttocks. They would gaze at each other purposely, challenging each other to resistance and seduction. Many would also dance the waltz, polka, and mazurka with great enjoyment.[3] The way in which Calabrian people danced tarantella had already been described in a number of books in the nineteenth century; yet the model whereby women are kept under strict control by men has been amplified and underlined to such an extent that it has become a commonplace. Thus, in 1935, an anonymous author could write about Calabrian tarantella: "The shy dancer assumes different and poised poses, at times raising her skirt slightly or putting her hands on her hips, and at other times imitating male poses in a more poised and graceful way" ("Tarantella calabrese" 1990, 117).

On many pages and through many years, the "shy" and "poised" Calabrian female dancer has come down to us as consistent as she was in the past.[4] This is yet another portrayal—like many others—of Mediterranean women as rather passive and silent, kept under control by men, and concerned with maintaining an immaculate reputation. Anthropologists and ethnomusicologists have recently underlined how this gender description of the Mediterranean woman is a stereotype that cannot explain the complexity of female behavior in the contemporary Mediterranean world (Magrini 1998). As far as Calabria is concerned, a number of studies show how women seem subordinated, marginal, and segregated only at a superficial glance (Minicuci 1989, 381). In this chapter, I do not intend simply to reverse the stereotype that subordinates the Calabrian woman to male approval during the dance. On the contrary, my aim is to identify—through the analysis of some specific performances—discrepancies and convergences with the stereotype in the behavior of Calabrian women.

To date, the time and space set aside for dance and music in Calabria are mostly those of the festival. A festival is an event that involves the collective community in which it takes place, revealing the rules of social organization and cultural patterns. Music has an important role in a festival, and it often constitutes its climax. Behavior related to musical performance and dance can be shown at its height in festivals (Lortat-Jacob 1994, 11–12). In Calabrian festivals, the participants both play and listen to the others playing, and both dance and watch the others dancing. Men and women set out on long journeys to listen to a good player, or to dance more often and for much longer than they normally can during the rest of the year (Plastino 1993).

For this reason, festivals provide the best opportunity to investigate not only gender roles in dance, but whether a large number of rules and expectations still actually govern those roles. In short, a festival is the ideal arena to understand whether it is still possible to meet the "shy" dancer or to find out if this character has indeed disappeared. By now it could well be that this undoubtedly charming character is like an old photograph: yellowed by age, the image shows us a moment in the past as revealed through the eyes that seized it. Similarly, the fixedness of sociocultural rules may depend on the eyes that observe them. Thus, gender relationships in Calabria (and in other Mediterranean contexts) may be more complex than the way in which they have been represented to us.[5]

Polsi

The festival of the Madonna della Montagna (Our Lady of the Mountain) is one of the most famous in Calabria. It takes place every year between 31 August and 2 September in Polsi, in the very heart of the massif of Aspromonte, in the municipal land of San Luca. The believers reach the sanctuary (built after the year 1100) in the early days of August. The church and its enclosed monastery are situated in an evocative setting at the bottom of a gorge surrounded by high mountains. The roads that have been cut through the massif to connect Polsi to nearby villages (San Luca, on the Ionic slope, and Gambarie on the Tirrenic slope) are—even in our time—hard to travel.[6]

There are differences between the festivals of the past (in the form they took until the sixties) and today's festivals, and such differences have partially influenced musical and dance performances. Isolated in the heart of the massif, until a few years ago Polsi could be reached only on foot. Thousands of people visited the sanctuary from the villages near Aspromonte and from other places in the Calabrian inland. Walking, it took pilgrims hours or even days. Word of the Madonna's miracles had made the festival an important date for Calabrian believers, who would make preparations well in advance for the difficult journey ahead.[7] During their pilgrimage, they danced along long stretches of the road. Women in particular might make the vow to dance along the entire route if they wanted to ask for a favor or to give thanks. Writer Corrado Alvaro, an alert observer of the behavior of Calabrian women and men, wrote: "Girls thus dance along the entire route, and will be dancing night and day for the hours that they have specified in their vow, until they will collapse on the ground or need to lean on a wall while their feet are still moving" (Alvaro 1931, 91).[8] Those who attended the festival remained by the sanctuary for a few days. But besides a few little buildings near the church, there was no other type of lodging, and people had to camp in the valley under the trees or in proximity to the brook that flows down the gorge. During the most important days, there could be more than ten thousand people in Polsi.

The festival of the Our Lady of the Mountain was essentially a festival of music and sound.[9] Many musicians would be present: bagpipers, diatonic accordion players, guitarists, and tambourine players.[10] Musical events in the festival were mainly of two types: religious and profane. The former comprised the religious chants sung by women during the pilgrimage as well as at their arrival in Polsi, in the church, and during the short procession on 2 September (see Teti 1980b). The nonreligious musical performances—for example, love songs accompanied by the guitar, accordion, or bagpipe, and especially dances (tarantelle)—took place elsewhere. These performances could be carried out anywhere but in a church. Because of the great flow of people in the area, singing, playing, and dancing would feature in many places in the valley. All participants would dance intensely, particularly at nighttime. Tarantelle were interrupted only during the procession. Everyone in Polsi wished to dance. This was the occasion on which one could show one's skill and endurance; indeed, the women from a village near Aspromonte were appreciated for these two qualities: "Young girls from Cardeto, original in their red bodices laced up around their breasts, can be said to be the queens of the dance. They have cast-iron legs, and dance all night long to the dismay of even the strongest among the peasants" (Alvaro 1912, 61).[11]

The contemporary festival is very different. The walking pilgrimage has almost disappeared. Only a few pilgrims now walk to Polsi: nobody dances on the way.[12] People drive to the sanctuary, mainly by truck, though the roads are suitable for motor vehicles only for short stretches. The trip by truck is dangerous but is said by the new pilgrims to be protected by the Madonna, and the journey is accompanied by the sound of religious chants and tarantelle played by portable amplifiers.[13] The use of vehicles has made the old custom of a stop at the sanctuary almost fade out. Most people now prefer to go back home for a few hours once they have reached the church and completed their thanksgiving prayers. Just a few hundred people stay overnight during the entire length of the festival, and most of the believers attend the festival only on the day of the procession.

Fewer and fewer musicians are staying in Polsi for a long time.[14] Even if the religious chant does not seem to have changed remarkably over the past forty years, all participants noted nostalgically that in Polsi people dance less than they used to in the past. Indeed, during the day there are only a limited number of opportunities to listen or dance tarantella. At night, however, in the large square in front of the sanctuary or near the huts, which function as bars or *trattorie* (eating houses) during the festival, people can dance in a way similar to what was characteristic in the past. Today Polsi is still a place where one can see the Calabrian tarantella being danced according to traditional rules.[15]

In order to dance tarantella, one must still make a *rota* (wheel): a circle of people, made by the diatonic accordion and tambourine players and by the dancers and the other people watching, who are sometimes invited to take part. The diameter of the circle can measure between eight or ten meters to more than twenty meters, according to the number of participants. It can be increased during the dance if many other people get closer to attend the event. Once the role of *mastru a ballu* (dance master) has been assigned, tarantella can start. In Polsi, a tarantella can last up to one hour and sometimes even longer. The dance master—always a man—brings one person at a time into the circle: tarantella is always danced in pairs. The dance master is in charge of leading in whoever wishes to dance, identifying dancers in the circle of bystanders. But with a joking invitation, he can also drag into the center someone who looks, and who may indeed be, unwilling to dance. In general, in order to invite an onlooker to dance, the dance master only needs to touch one's shoulder, or to take one by the hand or by the arm. When he wants to dismiss the person with whom he is dancing he uses verbal forms of farewell, for instance, *fora u primu* (get out, first one), or *grazie u primu* (thank you, first one). Refusing to dance is usually considered more or less seriously as an unkind act.

In this way, the dance master and other dancers alternate in the circle formed in tarantella, in conformity to a standard pattern, which can be represented as follows:

1. the master dances alone for a short time;
2. the master chooses the first dancer and dances with this partner;
3. dancing, the master chooses the second dancer;
4. the master brings in the second dancer, who dances with the first one; the master then stops and chooses another dancer;
5. the master returns, dismisses the first dancer, and dances with the second one;
6. the master calls the third dancer, who dances with the second one, and then the master stops and chooses another dancer.

And on it goes. The pattern will be performed again and again until the dance master deems that no other combinations can be made: at that time, he can vary the entries in the circle, or repeat them—or the tarantella can be brought to an end.

The dance master has a double responsibility. He must operate without disappointing anyone who wants to participate. Concurrently, he must be careful not to let men and women who have had, or could have, conflicts meet in the dance. His role is therefore very delicate: not only must he be a very good dancer, but he must also observe the crowd carefully, especially when he is not familiar with those whom he invites to participate.

According to tarantella rules, a dancing pair should consist of a man and a woman, although pairs consisting of two men can be seen more frequently than female pairs. In Polsi, a man and a woman almost never touch each other during tarantella. They may take each other by the hand and walk together along a part of the circle's perimeter. Although their bodies are more or less distant, during the performance a complex relationship is enacted, with allusions, gestures, and looks that show a multiplicity of bonds. During the dance, courtship between a man and a woman is almost always involved: whether real or represented, it is nonetheless intense. The woman tends to stay at the center of the circle while the man goes around her. She always turns her face toward his; eyes may meet, but much depends on the intention of both dancers. Looking at one another can be as "dangerous" a moment as it can be a moment of appreciation and mutual satisfaction. The movements of a woman's arms and trunk have limited width: she only moves the lower part of her arms while the upper arms remain still; she also keeps her trunk still. If a man dances with a woman, he moves his arms little, preferring hand gestures; he makes wider movements with his trunk bowed forward and sometimes swinging. The space that a man covers while dancing is wider than that covered by a woman. Generally a woman's steps are not as wide as those of a man.[16]

The rules determining a "correct" tarantella performance seem to be respected in most performances in Polsi, assigning a "subordinate" role to women. Women dancers appear subject to a corporal censorship that limits their movements. Furthermore, a man dancing with a woman limits his gestures so that they are more moderate than when he is dancing with another man. When men dance in pairs, their movements can enact a challenge, nowadays symbolic but once real.[17] Subtly but nevertheless significantly, rules are not strictly respected during the performance. The role of the dance master is not always as determining and "authoritative" as it might appear. Tarantella is not always performed outdoors: when it is performed in the little trattorie, there is no dance master and the alternation of dancers is free. Furthermore, the woman's passivity in this dance is often more of a wish than reality. By changing her movements (for instance, amplifying a particular gesture, and moving toward a man in a narrower space), a woman elaborates a personal and recognizable style (like Cardeto girls used to in the past), concurrently "forcing" the rules to adapt them to her bodily needs. Moreover, the allusive game of seduction enables the expression of the eroticism implicit in dancing. This is a type of eroticism that in theory is controlled by community norms but that women in particular sometimes like to show. A woman must not necessarily be the one who is seduced while dancing: she can also seduce. That is why in Polsi during a night tarantella, when the darkness covers the players and dancers, along with shouts of happiness and encouragement, one can also hear exclamations like "Madonna, forgive us because we are sinning."

Riace

The festival of Saints Cosimo and Damiano is celebrated in Riace, a village on the Ionic coast, annually on 25 and 26 September.[18] Like many villages in Calabria, Riace is a "double village": it also has a subhamlet on the Ionic coast. The original Riace, a little center of approximately twelve hundred inhabitants, dates back to the Basilian period and is situated inland some seven kilometers from the coast. The festival does not involve the new hamlet: it takes place in the old center near the sanctuary on the road to the sea, two kilometers from the village. During the days of the festival, this road is busy, and on its two sides there are stalls in which all kinds of goods are on display (food, clothes, shoes, books, tape cassettes and CDs, farm tools, furnishing objects, etc.).

A few days before the festival, groups of Gypsies from the various communities living in Calabria, especially those of Sambiase and Nicastro, in the province of Catanzaro, reach Riace. The day of Saints Cosimo and Damiano is in fact, in accordance with an old custom, the feast of Gypsies. Gypsies, who reach the village by car, old trucks, and on foot, meet near the sanctuary, away from built-up areas, where they camp for several nights.

The dance and musical culture of the Gypsies in Calabria does not differ substantially from its traditional Calabrian counterpart. In particular, the tarantella and use of musical instruments (mostly diatonic accordions, tambourines, and Jew's harps) do not diverge in their form and style—with the exception in some cases of a preference for "virtuoso" performances characterized by a particularly complex rhythmic acceleration and melodic ornamentation.[19]

Some dances are performed in the outskirts near the sanctuary on the night before the procession. Gypsy players with diatonic accordions, tambourines, and sometimes a triangle, joined by friends and acquaintances, move toward the wooden and tin huts, where they eat and drink. After having asked the owners for permission, they play tarantelle, which are danced mostly by men. Other tarantelle are played and danced during the same night in the open space around which the Gypsies' cars and other vehicles are parked. These dances are set according to the rules followed in Polsi: the musicians place themselves on a segment of the circumference of the dancing circle, which is in theory, but not always, completed by the onlookers. Inside the circle, the dancers—with a slight prevalence of men—alternate. The relationship of the male and female dancers is like that observed in Polsi: the man who has the role of dance master constantly introduces men and women into the circle, almost continuously making men dance with women. The women's behavior during this night dance seems to be less subject to the rules than it is the case in traditional tarantella.

On the first day of the festival (25 September), the dance assumes different features and seems to be set according to different gender rules. Before the statues of Cosimo and Damiano are carried out into the square before the church, the Gypsies meet in another little square that lies a few hundred meters away and start to dance together. None of Riace's inhabitants, pilgrims, or onlookers joins them. The separation between the Gypsies and the *calabresi* (Calabrian people) is emphasized by the exclusiveness of space and action. The ethnic separation is maintained subsequently. The Gypsies' tarantella is performed according to rules frequently followed in other circumstances: what must be noted in this case is the greater, at times exclusive, participation of women. The diatonic accordionists and tambourine players accompany the dance of the women, who sometimes dance alone and sometimes together with between two and five other women (plate 9). Their men (husbands, sons, relatives, and friends) merely watch and comment aloud. When the saints' statues are carried out of the church, the crowd gathered in the opposite square acclaims their arrival, and then turns and flows into a narrow street that leads to the Gypsies' square before moving onto the road that slopes down to the sanctuary. At this stage the Gypsies stop dancing and gather together ahead of the procession, so far from the statues that, in fact, they can hardly see the saints at all. As the crowd flows by, they begin another dance—the processional for which the Riace festival is famous all over Calabria.[20]

Accompanied by diatonic accordion and tambourine players, the Gypsy women start dancing a tarantella that ends only when the statues enter the sanctuary approximately two hours later. The space in which the processional dance takes place is not exactly determined, and tends to be defined largely by wherever the dancers happen to be. In fact, the dancing women stay within a compact group that slowly walks to the sanctuary. In order to dance, it is necessary to create the space of the dance by putting into effect a series of strategies and evaluations. The dancers are preceded by some of their menfolk, who control how the group moves in order to avoid problems with the Calabrians. Thus, these men physically signal the dividing line between the space of the Gypsies and that of the Riace community. The women dance and push their way through the crowd in the procession and the people who are standing in front of stalls as they shop. The space in which they dance is achieved by dancing and pushing (violently) the people around the dancing group. This sometimes also causes violent verbal reactions from those who are suddenly thrust aside: the Gypsies are often the object of vicious insults. Thus the women proceed through dance, at times moving forward in little steps and at other times keeping to a particular spot if the crowd is too dense. They lay themselves out in rows of three, four, or five. Not everyone dances for the whole route, and the heat and stress of working one's way through so many people makes it necessary to rest now and again. Women often dance alone (plate 10), although all the female dancers (up to a maximum of fifteen) may also dance together along short stretches of the route.

The musicians always remain behind the group of women, closer to the statues of the saints. The women constantly urge them to play, as they cannot stand interruptions in the musical performance. They express their appreciation of music with cries and phrases that underline the skill of the players.[21] At times, as the procession moves along, the musicians become separated from the dancers. The dancing will then pause for a short time until the men can move forward again and the music can be clearly heard. If the performance is interrupted while the women are near a stall where cassettes and CDs of Calabrian traditional music are on sale, the owners will play a tarantella as loudly as they can on portable speakers, to the acclamatory cries of the women, who dance to the piece until the return of their own players.

During the dance, the women often hold hands, sometimes taking each other by the arm. But more often they dance without touching each other, although keeping very close. Bodily interactions depend also on the denseness of the crowd as they cross it. No group position remains the same: every dancer can change her position, stopping or getting closer to the others. Sometimes a woman gets moved far from the group and performs some dance step alone.

While dancing, the women start singing chants for the saints or strophes of nonreligious songs. The steps and movements of the traditional dance alternate occasionally with nontraditional forms. For example, at the rhythm of tarantella, the women may start to jump on the spot with their feet joined and their arms up. In this case, they introduce into the processional context an expression typical of a dancing style usually performed by young people in discos. If the musical performance is interrupted or the crowd becomes too dense and hampers movement, the dance also stops. Women take advantage of this break to rest in the shadow of the stalls; they cool themselves with a drink, at times throwing water upon themselves (this behavior is strongly objected to by the other people who visit the sanctuary), or they start talking and laughing in low voices. They want to show that they are "another" group in the context of the procession; they are visible to but somehow separate from everybody else.

The processional dance finally reaches the sanctuary. In front of the little church there is large esplanade, where the dancers can arrange themselves in a wider space. While the saints are approaching, the women separate and establish new relationships with the men. The women dance in groups of three or five around the musicians who have joined those playing in the procession. Some male dancers also join the women, who nevertheless continue to keep the situation under control. These groups break up and rejoin rapidly, because of the continuous flow of people in the square. Other women join those who have participated in the procession. While the dance goes on, the statues of the saints reach the square and are carried slowly through the crowd into the sanctuary. When the saints have entered the sanctuary, the dancers and the believers shout acclamations and applaud. The dance continues for a few more minutes, but in a situation of confusion in which the previous relationships between dancers and players have been interrupted. The dance would probably go on longer, but the ecclesiastical authorities—through loudspeakers outside the church—command silence, forbidding the dancers to continue their dance. Rapidly the dancers and musicians leave the square, where the mass, broadcast at top volume over the loudspeakers, begins. The contrast of sound is striking.

On the second festival day (26 September), the statues are carried in a procession from the sanctuary back to the village. The Gypsies, however, have already left, departing from the camp on the previous afternoon or night, on foot and by cars and trucks. During the second procession, nobody dances or performs tarantelle. The festival, at least as far as the dance and the music are concerned, is over, and this is what the Gypsies appear to refer to when they say smilingly: "We are the feast."

Gioiosa Ionica

On the last Sunday of August, the festival of Saint Rocco is celebrated annually in Gioiosa Ionica, another village on the Ionic coast. Gioiosa Ionica is also a "double" settlement, with a recent hamlet on the seaside about seven kilometers from the center. Gioiosa Ionica, home to approximately seven thousand inhabitants, is a village of ancient origins. The architectural structure is still mostly medieval in the upper quarters of the village, while the quarters lower on the slope date to the seventeenth or eighteenth century.

In Gioiosa Ionica, as in many other Calabrian villages, the celebrations in honor of Saint Rocco begin on 16 August.[22] They end with a long processional dance, the festival's most important event, which draws many tourists, as well as thousands of people from nearby villages. The dance lasts about twelve hours (it starts at 8:00 A.M.) and is accompanied by hundreds of snare drum, bass drum, and cymbal players, the majority of whom are locals (Plastino 1989). The dancers are also from Gioiosa Ionica, but for some years young people from nearby villages and many boys and girls on holiday on the coast have also taken part in the dance.

The current form of the festival dates back only to the 1970s. Up until that time, both the procession and the dance lasted approximately four to five hours (Nadile 1994; Plastino 1989, 139–41). The procession, preceding the statue of the saint, started off from the church of Saint Rocco in the center of the medieval village, where it returned after a circular route through the newer quarters. The dance was accompanied by bagpipe, diatonic accordion, *lira,* and tambourine players, but mostly by snare and bass drum players.[23] The processional dance was considered a display of faith, a form of devotional behavior through which it was possible to ask the saint for a miracle or thank him for his intercession. When the musicians were passing by, the dancers would perform the religious dance, whose movements did not differ from those of Polsi's tarantella, for a few minutes. Men and women danced moving forward with the players along a stretch of the route, stopping when they thought that the vow had been fulfilled.[24] Dancing for fun was also allowed. Groups of ten or fifteen people performed tarantella, at times forming a circle that moved forward following (or surrounding) the musicians. Although it was allowed, this different type of dance, during which the body movements of men and women were freer, was not deemed an essential element of the procession—at least from a religious point of view.

The choreutic and musical organization of the festival remained substantially unchanged until the 1970s, when new social and cultural trends began to be felt in Gioiosa Ionica. In 1970, for example, the priest, while following the statue, abandoned the procession to protest against the bare-shouldered young women and shirtless boys who were dancing tarantella; strong opposition to the mafia system began to be voiced, and its rules were openly discussed and denounced; traditional cultural behavior was contested in the name of values that celebrated the feelings and lifestyle of the young. The explicit and implicit clash with their forefathers' tradition expressed at the cultural, political, and social levels also involved the religious domain. The feast of Saint Rocco, a fundamental moment in the identity of Gioiosa Ionica's inhabitants, was deeply modified by this process of change.

At present, young people are once again "reappropriating" the feast, adapting the organizational and performative rules of both the music and the dance. The number of musicians has increased sharply; most young people now prefer to play snare and bass drums or cymbals. As time goes by, this will result in the marginalization of other musical instruments. Drums now provide the dominant rhythm of tarantella, and the beat has become quite uniform in order to accommodate a larger number of players. The loudness of the feast has grown remarkably and is now one of the most appreciated elements in musical performance. What nevertheless does not seems to have changed is the rule that forbids women to play drums (Plastino 1989, 141–51).

As well as involving more people, both the feast and the procession take up more time and space. From a length of approximately five hours before 1970, they now last about twelve hours. A few days ahead of time, the players and the dancers decide when the statue must enter the church. The increase in the procession's length demands that particular strategies must be followed carefully by everyone. Although it is not possible to determine the direction of the feast, the dancers and musicians know when they must stop performing and slowly move forward. The precise alternation of these two moments punctuates the journey of the saint, who closes up the procession, allowing the players and dancers to control the duration of the dance, which the local church would like to be shorter.[25] The old route, within the historic center of the village, has also been extended to include more recently built quarters. This influences the length of the feast even more noticeably. The number of people who dance or play is by now in the region of thousands. The old procession no longer exists.

The celebration of Saint Rocco's Day starts on the night before the procession. The players meet up in agreed-upon places in the village and then move to the square in front of the saint's church. Inside the church, women sing religious chants or recite the rosary. Sometimes the players enter the church playing tarantella. Boys and girls keep flowing into the square, and before midnight everyone starts to dance. This night dance already presents all the features of the processional dance. Anyone can dance in any style. Some dancers perform the harder steps of traditional tarantella; others dance according to the (simplified, and often invented) style elaborated by the professional folk groups of Calabria.[26] Many dance to the rhythm of tarantella but with the gestures and movements typical of disco dance.

On the next morning, well before eight o'clock, the square is almost filled with players and dancers. As soon as the mass ends, tarantella begins, and the crowd walks through a narrow street to the left of the church. The space where the dance takes place is compact: dancers and players are side by side and often compete over the possibility of performing. The dancers may join groups as big as twenty people, but they can also dance in pairs or alone. What or how one dances is unimportant; what matters is dancing per se. Groups break up and form continuously. Sometimes it is possible to see older people tracing the steps of the old dance as some among the youngsters imitate them. However, this religious dance has now become marginal and is less frequently performed and followed. When space allows, dancers might position themselves in a circle. They do not wish, however, to create the space of traditional tarantella, which cannot be enacted in the absence of a dance master, especially as other dancers and players may also come to modify the situation.

Dancers and musicians will take a short break (coinciding with another mass) near a church close to the saint's church: it will have taken them approximately two hours to cover the short stretch of road. The dancers relax and prepare for the second, longer procession, which will continue without a break until about eight that evening.

The women's behavior during the processional dance seems to be uncensured. Young girls in particular express a body language that is far from any traditional rule. Their bodies are shown, admired, and touched. They thus display themselves both to men and other women, especially when—to beat the heat—they poor large quantities of water on themselves. Their physical interactions with men are explicit; indeed, physical contact is demanded with satisfaction. The traditional rules regulating interpersonal relations, and relations between the sexes, are abolished. Unthinkable, and even formally forbidden, contacts are displayed. A girl may be carried about or "dance" while sitting on a man's shoulders. Many hug their partners while they are dancing or moving. Various girls gain recognition for their personal style as they "go through" the processional dance, moving from one place in the procession to another, and setting up or reestablishing the dance with other girls or boys. Girls move in pairs or groups, signaling new ways of establishing relationships. Some perform traditional gestures, for example, lifting a red scarf held by both hands. However, these gestures are part of a totally new bodily attitude that can be performed in different circumstances—when the girl dances alone or with friends, or while pushing through the crowd or moving to another place in the procession (plate 11). While the basic steps and forms of the dance are often those of traditional or "modern" tarantella, the girls nonetheless freely introduce variations to them. Furthermore, the women's relationship with men in the dance is not based on respect for impossible-to-determine hierarchical roles. Nobody can tell anyone how, where, and how long for one should dance. Many young women and men dance alone and are indifferent to the people who surround them as they concentrate on moving their bodies to the beat of drums.

The processional dance is performed anywhere, and all places can be suitable for music and dance. Thus the entire space of the procession coincides with the space of the dance in which the old gender relationships are redefined or abolished. For these reasons, the time of the (simultaneously old and new) feast is very much appreciated by boys and girls from Gioiosa Ionica, the nearby villages, and other places, and it must be protracted for as long as possible. In Gioiosa Ionica dancers seem to want to seize time, or at least to expand it.

After eight hours, having alternated rest with dance, players and dancers return from the street to the square they left that morning. The square slowly fills with people. Many boys and girls wait for the end of the rite while lying on the pavement and smiling in their partner's arms. Dancing becomes increasingly impossible as the crowd grows. Approximately one hour before the end, the statue of Saint Rocco enters the square, welcomed by shouts and the rhythm of tarantella. With difficulty, the statue is turned around until its back faces the portal, where it is kept for a number of minutes. The last offers and requests of grace are made to the saint in a remarkably sonorous if chaotic atmosphere. A few children are raised above the crowd, passed from hand to hand, undressed under the statue, put close to the saint, re-dressed, and returned, in tears, to their parents. The sound increases until the statue is finally carried into the church. The musicians then stop playing, and the dancers—tired but with joyful expressions on their faces—leave in groups or alone. The feast—the real one—is now over.

Dance to Another Tune

Studies of the female condition in Calabria, and particularly of the condition of younger Calabrian women (Minicuci 1987; Siebert 1997), reveal that there is a rather clear difference between the role and mentality of female teenagers and girls and those of their mothers and of previous generations. The acceptance of traditional models of female dignity still appears to be binding for elderly women and indeed is felt to be a basic element of their identity (even if carried out with difficulty and at times even with unexpressed anguish). In contrast, young Calabrian women have little respect for "tradition."

Calabria has lived, still lives, its shift into modernity (and postmodernity) without having experienced real cultural, social, and economic development. The transition is happening through the readjustment of traditional culture whose rules are nevertheless valid in certain circumstances. The roles that women are supposed to play in Calabrian society (subordination to men, a clearly separate female domain, and economic inferiority) does not seem to have altered from the way it was in the past. While these accepted roles provide social groups with a degree of tranquility (in the declared continuity of behavior), it is also a source of dissidence and strong tension among them.

On one hand, the young Calabrian woman is driven to play a role determined for her in the past and still shared by most men and women; on the other hand, she can hardly resist the attraction of different patterns of behavior that are influencing areas even as depressed as Calabria. She seems to live in a precarious balance between a role typical of the past that she experiences as anachronistic but cannot shake off completely (as it is still dominant in Calabrian society) and a "new" role that she cannot yet fully enter into. Girls thus find new forms of expression in order to be both "respectful" of a past that is not felt as binding and independent in a modernity that has not yet been fully reached.

Tarantella dance reflects and expresses the complex condition of women in Calabria. As Judith Lynne Hanna wrote, "When moving images created by dancers violated expected male and female roles and their conventional expressions, the novel signs onstage charge the atmosphere and stimulate performers and observers to confront the possibility of altered lifestyles. As a medium of gender education, dance can both reflect and influence society, transmit or transform a cultural heritage" (Hanna 1992, 227).

Besides women's presumed subordination to the role of men (as players, dance masters, and censors of any possible unorthodox behavior by women), these three different ways of performing tarantella show how women can in fact determine the centrality of their role. As a result of the "explosion" of the traditional rules of tarantella, where no censorship on the body can be made, women have been put in a condition of total autonomy. These three tarantelle thus represent three ways of being a woman in contemporary Calabria. This woman is part of a traditional heritage that is still fundamentally significant for the society; she determines her autonomous space inside the tradition; and ultimately she readjusts traditional behavior without giving it up entirely.

The stereotype of the traditional dance—in which Calabrian women are simply subordinated to a rigid system of rules that strictly regulate their bodily behavior—therefore does not appear to be confirmed. On the contrary, women seem to have gained the opportunity to control the dance in any (more or less favorable) situation, and to be its leading, and at times only, characters. They also appear to possess a greater number of opportunities to express themselves in tarantella than do their male counterparts.

In the three feasts considered in this chapter, women are almost completely excluded from musical performance. Although they can sing religious chants in the church, and during the procession and the dance, they rarely play a musical instrument.[27] Instrumental music is, then, a male domain, in accordance with rules that are well known and observed in other Mediterranean areas (Auerbach 1987; Reinhard 1990; Ziegler 1990). But although the fact that women are not allowed to play one or more instruments can be interpreted as an exclusion and a clear separation of male and female roles, this is an advantage as far as the dance is concerned. During the dance, those who play are at the disposal of those who dance. In Riace and in Gioiosa Ionica, female dancers behave much more independently than the musicians. Indeed, in Riace, musicians may even be replaced by a recording, while in Gioiosa Ionica they are not allowed to interrupt their performance. By contrast, women can stop dancing anytime they so desire. The weak role, thus, falls to those who play.

The control of a woman's "honor" during the dance is more of a declaration than an actual demand. In Polsi, where dance rules are more binding, the female dancers manage to express their corporeity by modifying traditional movements to their advantage. Even in the past, by demonstrating their superiority in dance and having the greatest resistance to fatigue, they declared that they knew how to administrate their bodies according to their own wishes and not those of men. In Riace, in an almost completely female dance, censorship can only be self-censorship; men limit themselves to watching the dance from afar, and to accompanying it; when they do dance, they are barely tolerated. In Riace, the intense, uninterrupted joy of the dance is revealed by the women's facial expressions, whereas in Polsi that satisfaction must be achieved through confrontation with a man.

In Gioiosa Ionica, the possibility of controlling women seems to have vanished. This has irritated religious authorities who have witnessed the growing independence of local girls. While some have intervened in the name of honor and lamented the betrayal of tradition, their complaints have been in vain.[28] The dance of Gioiosa Ionica is the dance of contemporary Calabria. It is a votive and processional dance (many young women and men declare that they dance as a sign of their faith, invoking Saint Rocco in their cries); it is a tarantella performed to a traditional rhythm and often characterized by traditional steps. It is concurrently a completely new dance: anyone can participate; dancers, together with musicians, determine its length; and bodily expression is free. In Gioiosa Ionica, the dancers let themselves behave in a joyfully erotic fashion along the processional route without being subjected to general disapproval.

Hence the "shy" dancer no longer exists. Perhaps she only danced through the pages of some writers. In her place instead we find a Calabrian woman who lives in a complex society, who is subjected to contrasting urges and wishes, but who is able to determine wider spaces of freedom for herself (Siebert 1997, 354–55). In everyday life, as in tarantella, she is dancing to another tune.

Notes

1. Unless otherwise noted, translations from non-English sources in this chapter are my own. Calabria is the furthest region in the Italian peninsula. It is known as a seaside land (for the length of its coasts), but it is also a region of mountains and hills (for more than 90 percent of its territory). Placed in the middle of the Mediterranean, Calabria was both a transit and a stopping place for many ethnic groups and peoples. The Arabs, the Normans, the Spanish, the French, the Greeks, and the Albanians lived and still live in this region, whose cultural contrasts—as evident as its natural contrasts—constitute one of the reasons for its appeal. For an overall view of the physical and cultural features of this region, see Gambi 1978; on Calabrian traditional music, see Magrini 1986 and Plastino 1990, 1995b.

2. On the diffusion of the waltz in Western countries at the end of nineteenth century, see Hess 1989.

3. For some historical and literary sources on dance in Calabria in the nineteenth and twentieth centuries, see Plastino 1994a, 21–68; 1997, passim. A typology of Calabrian traditional dances has not yet been written, in contrast to the case of nearby Sicily (see Bonanzinga 1999).

4. For example: "The female character, less noble than its male counterpart, usually stays at the center of the 'rota' (wheel), a position of prestige and respect. Physical touch

among dancers is not allowed, while hand touch is usually the only type of contact permitted" (Castagna 1988, 12).

5. In the following pages I refer exclusively to a dance performed during religious feasts that is called *tarantella* (pl. *tarantelle*). Undoubtedly tarantella is the most famous dance among Calabrian people; its musical features are different according to places and instruments. Especially in the past, many other types of dance were performed in Calabria. (see "La Pecorara o 'A pasturara" 1990; Plastino 1995a, 111–16; 1997, passim).

6. On the history of Polsi, see *S. Maria di Polsi* 1990.

7. Among her miracles, the Madonna is still praised in religious chants for having restored the son of the prince of Roccella to life after he was brought to the sanctuary in a coffin (Plastino 1993).

8. Corrado Alvaro (1895–1956), one of the most important twentieth-century authors of Italian literature, was born in San Luca. Both his birthplace and the feast of Polsi, which he attended several times, were the subject of much of his work (e.g., Alvaro 1912).

9. On the Polsi soundscape, see Plastino 1994a, 19–68; Leydi 1986.

10. On Calabrian musical instruments see Ricci and Tucci 1988.

11. On recordings of tarantelle played and sung by Cardeto women see Lomax and Carpitella 1999.

12. Some families still reached Polsi on foot or dancing as late as the end of the 1970s: see Lombardi Satriani and Meligrana 1983, 33.

13. In Calabria there is a vast market for tape cassettes, LPs, and (more recently) CDs of traditional music and religious chants. These products are generally distributed in the region, although some were also sold abroad, mostly in the United States. No detailed study has yet been carried out on this important, possibly growing phenomenon. For some observations see Leydi 1986 and Plastino 1995b, 49, 51–52.

14. In particular, bagpipe players have disappeared almost completely, although the number of diatonic accordion and tambourine players is constantly increasing.

15. It appears that the collective criteria—which had determined the good reputation of Cardeto women—for evaluating a female dancer's ability have now disappeared.

16. For a labanotation of some tarantelle, see Carbone 1988. For descriptions of female and male behavior in tarantella, see Castagna 1988 and Staro 1988. However, these two analyses are based on direct or indirect observation of a limited number of dances, presenting a rather static view of what is in actual fact a complex reality. For recordings of tarantelle in Polsi, see Ricci and Tucci 1991 and Plastino 1993.

17. The dance between men is often called *scherma* (fencing), as it includes the gestures of a challenge with the knife, represented by the joined forefinger and middle finger of the right hand (see Castagna 1988, 11).

18. According to hagiography, the two saints were brothers: one was a doctor and the other a chemist. In popular devotions they are known as "the doctors' saints" and thought capable of healing diseases. See Giallombardo 1998.

19. The most important collection of recordings of musical performances by Calabrian Gypsies is "Canti e balli zingaroti" (Gypsies' songs and dances), ALA Records CA 141 (no date of release). However, this is a hard to find tape cassette with no distribution outside Calabria. See note 13 above.

20. See Teti 1980a. Also elsewhere the processional dance seems to be the essential feature of the feast of Saints Cosimo and Damiano. For an analysis of the dance (accompanied by a brass band) during the feast of the doctors' saints in Sferracavallo (Palermo, Sicily) see Giallombardo 1998.

21. For another example of gender role separation in a Mediterranean Gypsy group during a public performance, see Ziegler 1990.

22. Saint Rocco, a French saint (of noble origin) who lived in the fourteenth century, by miracle healed himself, according to hagiography, from the plague that infected him.

23. The lira is a small three-string, bowed instrument played in all the area surrounding Gioiosa Ionica (see Plastino 1994b).

24. People who were ill and could not take part in the procession would dance on the balcony or at home when the players were passing by (see Plastino 1989, 141).

25. As regards the length of the procession (as well as the behavior of young people during the dance), there were, and are, intense disagreements between the ecclesiastical authority and the players and dancers. A few years ago, the statue of the saint was suddenly brought back to the church a few hours after departure over roads that were not part of the usual processional route. Most of the participants in the procession were far from the statue and could not take part. This event provoked strong tension in the village and was not repeated. In general the local church has expressed clear opposition to the feast of Saint Rocco in its present form, especially as regards the processional dance, but without any real effect (see Nadile 1994).

26. Detailed descriptions of the dance of Calabrian professional folk groups (many of which have no relationship with Calabrian traditional dance) are in Squillace 1982. These groups constitute the only way for many young Calabrian people to become acquainted with more or less traditional forms of this dance.

27. Women are allowed to play the tambourine, and some women play the diatonic accordion. The latter are nevertheless an exception.

28. This is well known in the Mediterranean area; see Nieuwkerk 1998.

References

Alvaro, Corrado. 1912. *Polsi nell'arte, nella leggenda, nella storia.* Gerace: Tipografia D. Serafino.

———. 1931. *Calabria.* Firenze: Nemi.

Auerbach, Susan. 1987. "From Singing to Lamentig: Women's Musical Role in a Greek Village." In *Women and Music in Cross-Cultural Perspective,* edited by Ellen Koskoff, 25–43. Urbana: University of Illinois Press.

Bonanzinga, Sergio. 1999. "Tipologia e analisi dei fatti coreutici." *Archivio Antropologico Mediterraneo* 2 (1/2): 77–105.

Carbone, Donata. 1988. "Rota e viddanedda: Un'altra descrizione." In *Danza tradizionale in Calabria,* edited by Ettore Castagna, 59–82. Catanzaro: Abramo.

Castagna, Ettore. 1988. "Scherma, rota, mastru i ballu: Osservazioni sulla tarantella reggina." In *Danza tradizionale in Calabria,* edited by Ettore Castagna, 9–26. Catanzaro: Abramo.

Gambi, Lucio. 1978. *Calabria.* Turin: UTET.

Giallombardo, Fatima. 1998. "Oblazioni virili e gemelli divini." *Archivio Antropologico Mediterraneo* 1 (0): 61–91.

Hanna, Judith Lynne. 1992. "Tradition, Challenge, and the Backlash: Gender Education through Dance." In *Gender in Performance: The Presentation of Difference in the Performing Arts,* edited by Laurence Senelick, 223–38. Hanover: University Press of New England.

Hess, Remi. 1989. *La valse.* Paris: Éditions A. M. Métailié. Published in Italian as *Il valzer: Rivoluzione della coppia in Europa* (Turin: Einaudi, 1993).

"La Pecorara o 'A pasturara." 1990. In *Danze popolari italiane,* 119–20. 1935. Reprint, Firenze: Edizioni Taranta.

Leydi, Roberto. 1986. "Il pellegrinaggio alla Madonna della Montagna di Polsi, Aspromonte, Calabria, 31 agosto–2 settembre." In *La musique et le rite sacré et profane,* edited by M. Honegger and C. Meyer, 1:49–68. Strasbourg: Associations des Publications près les Universités de Strasbourg.

Lomax, Alan, and Diego Carpitella. 1999. *Calabria.* CD and booklet. Recordings by Alan Lomax and Diego Carpitella. Edited by Goffredo Plastino. Rounder Records 11661-1803-2.

Lombardi Satriani, Luigi Maria, and Mariano Meligrana. 1983. "Emigrazione simbolica: Il pellegrinaggio a Polsi." In *Un villaggio nella memoria,* edited by Luigi Maria Lombardi Satriani, and Mariano Meligrana, 31–37. Rome: Casa del Libro.

Lortat-Jacob, Bernard. 1994. *Musiques en fête: Maroc, Sardaigne, Roumanie.* Nanterre: Société d'Ethnologie.

Magrini, Tullia. 1986. *Canti d'amore e di sdegno.* Milan: Franco Angeli.

———. 1998. "Women's 'Work of Pain' in Christian Mediterranean Europe". *Music and Anthropology* 3. http://www.muspe.unibo.it/period/MA/

Minicuci, Maria. 1987. "Essere e apparire: Note sulla condizione femminile nella realtà e nella rappresentazione di una comunità calabrese." *Quaderni del Circolo Semiologico Siciliano* 26/27: 343–53.

———. 1989. *Qui e altrove: Famiglie di Calabria e di Argentina.* Milan: Franco Angeli.

Nadile, Vincenzo. 1994. *Il culto di S. Rocco a Gioiosa Ionica, 1593–1993.* Bovalino: Diaco.

Nieuwkerk, Karin van. 1998. "'An Hour for God and an Hour for the Heart': Islam, Gender, and Female Entertainment in Egypt." *Music and Anthropology* 3. http://www.muspe.unibo.it/period/MA/

Plastino, Goffredo. 1989. "I tamburi di San Rocco." *Culture Musicali* 12–14:139–58.

———. 1990. "La poesia senza canto: Le ricerche sulla musica tradizionale in Calabria." In *L'acqua di Gangà II: Note sulla poesia e la musica tradizionale in Calabria,* edited by Vito Teti and Goffredo Plastino, 275–404. Vibo Valentia: Qualecultura/Jaca Books.

———. 1993. *Calabre: Musiques de fêtes.* CD with booklet. Maison des Cultures du Monde W 260051.

———. 1994a. *Risonanze: Letteratura e musica in Calabria.* Soveria Mannelli: Rubbettino.

———. 1994b. *Lira: Uno strumento musicale tradizionale calabrese.* Vibo Valentia: Monteleone.

————. 1995a. *I suoni, la memoria, i segni.* Soveria Mannelli: Rubbettino.

————. 1995b. "Etnomusicologia in Calabria." *Il Corriere Calabrese* 1:7–54.

————. 1997. *Suoni di carta: Un'antologia sulla musica tradizionale calabrese, 1571–1957.* Lamezia Terme: A.M.A.

Reinhard, Ursula. 1990; "The Veils Are Lifted: Music of Turkish Women." In *Music, Gender, and Culture,* edited by Marcia Herndon and Susanne Ziegler, 101–13. Wilhelmshaven: Florian Noetzel Verlag.

Ricci, Antonello, and Roberta Tucci. 1988. "Folk Musical Instruments in Calabria." *Galpin Society Journal* 41:37–58.

————. 1991. *Folk Music of Calabria, Italy.* CD with booklet. Musicaphon BM 55 803.

S. Maria di Polsi: Storia e pietà popolare. 1990. Reggio Calabria: Laruffa.

Siebert, Renate. 1997. *È femmina però è bella: Tre generazioni di donne al Sud.* Turin: Rosenberg and Sellier.

Squillace, Consolato. 1982. *Calabria: Canti—danze—suoni.* Firenze: Editrice La Ginestra.

Staro, Placida. 1988. "Rota: Regola e improvvisazione tra realtà e rappresentazione." In *Danza tradizionale in Calabria,* edited by Ettore Castagna, 27–55. Catanzaro: Abramo.

"Tarantella calabrese." 1990. In *Danze popolari italiane,* 115–19. 1935. Reprint, Firenze: Edizioni Taranta.

Teti, Vito. 1980a. *Religione e salute: SS Cosma e Damiano.* Film produced by RAI Radiotelevione Italiana–Sede Regionale per la Calabria, Italy (color tinted).

————. 1980b. *Il viaggio religioso: Polsi.* Film produced by RAI Radiotelevione Italiana–Sede Regionale per la Calabria, Italy (color tinted).

Ziegler, Susanne. 1990. "Gender-Specific Traditional Wedding Music in Southwestern Turkey." In *Music, Gender, and Culture,* edited by Marcia Herndon and Susanne Ziegler, 85–99. Wilhelmshaven: Florian Noetzel Verlag.

6

~~~~~

The Female Dervish and
Other Shady Ladies of the Rebetika

Gail Holst-Warhaft

The period in which the *rebetika* developed and flourished in Greece corresponds roughly with the burgeoning of other urban popular musical styles such as flamenco, tango, and the urban blues of the United States.[1] The rebetika share a number of characteristics with these types of music, including the fact that they are genres in which male musicians, singers, and dancers play a role that is viewed, by the outsider at least, as stereotypically macho. Viewed from the inside, or with a more subtle gaze, the traditional roles of men and women in all these popular musical genres may be more ambivalent than they at first appear; they may even subvert the very stereotypes they project.[2] In the case of the rebetika, both the role of real women in the performance of the music and the image of women projected in lyrics of the songs varies from the early Asia Minor– or Smyrna-style songs through those of the Piraeus period to the broadly popular bouzouki music of the 1960s. Despite its tough milieu and the predominance of men as performers and songwriters, even the rebetika of the 1930s, dominated by Markos Vamvakaris and the Piraeus Quartet, cannot be neatly characterized as macho. One of the charms of rebetika is their humor; despite the posture of the dress, the male exclusiveness of the dance, and the strident tone of the bouzouki, there is an element of self-parody in the tough pose, a wink that undercuts the swagger. The songs suggest a camaraderie among members of a subgroup that is largely male but not entirely so. Women who sang re-betika, especially in the early period of the *café-aman* seem to have kept themselves aloof from the world they sang about. Others, who were prepared to flout the norms of Greek society, could enter the rebetika world either as singers or as fans of the music, even of the *arghilé,* or hookah. We find enough references in the song lyrics to the type of woman who shared this male world to suggest that, though she may have been an anomaly, she was an accepted part of the rebetika scene and that her daring made her an object of admira-tion.[3] Women who mixed with socially marginalized *rebetes,* either as artists or fans, may even have enjoyed a degree of freedom available nowhere else in Greek society.

Greek Gender Studies

Over the past decades, ethnographic studies of gender in Greece and other Mediterranean countries have revealed a more subtle picture of the relation-ships between men and women in these societies than had previously been recognized. Scholars like Ernestine Friedl (1967), Jill Dubisch (1986), Anna Caraveli (1986) Loring Danforth (1982, 1989), Michael Herzfeld (1981, 1993), Jane Cowan (1990), Nadia Seremetakis (1991), and Laurie Hart (1992) have called into question the classic "honor and shame" dichotomy formulated by Pitt-Rivers (1961) and perpetuated in Greece by such observ-ers as Campbell (1964), du Boulay (1974) and Peristiany (1966). Neverthe-less, the analysis of gender roles has been largely based on village life, where the relationships between the sexes are, or were until recently, more conser-vative and tradition-bound than in the cities. The urban life of Greece has, for reasons that undoubtedly include its fluid complexity, received less attention from ethnographers. Renée Hirschon's insightful studies of Asia Mi-nor refugees are an exception (1981, 1983, 1989), but her focus has been a refugee community unusually contained and isolated from the larger urban milieu. It has been left largely to literature and to literary studies rather than ethnography to explore the relationship between women and men in urban Greek life.[4] Studies of Greek popular music, including the rebetika, have, with few exceptions, ignored the question of gender relations among musi-cians or within the circles who frequented the hashish dens and other haunts of the *manges*.[5] Nor have the gender roles projected in the lyrics of the songs been considered. Yet it seems to me that the rebetika, like the other musical forms with which they invite comparison, offer us a unique means to explore questions of gender, both in terms of the relations between men and women in the circles of musicians and their audience and in the stylized representations of women found in the song lyrics composed by men.

The Taste for the Forbidden

The lyrics of popular songs may be a poor guide to reality, but they are probably a fair guide to the fantasy life of a generation. Popular songs have been successful to the extent that they have inspired or reflected the mood and dreams of a particular population. That may be less true today in a world in which mass culture has become global culture, but for styles such as the rebetika or the tango, music clearly played a role in confirming the identity of a new urban class.[6] Whether or not they began in the subculture of a disreputable group like the manges of Piraeus, the new musical styles all had a flavor of the forbidden about them, especially forbidden to women. In the rebetika, songs about the underworld, about smoking hashish, prison, and shady or exotic women, were popular with a much broader audience than the members of the small subculture depicted in such songs. No doubt the taste for the illicit, the sensual, or the uninhibited that swept Europe in the nineteenth century spread to the urban centers of the late Ottoman Empire. As Jerrold Seigel demonstrates (1986), the "bohemian" events were staged in order that the bourgeoisie could vicariously participate in libertine or exotic lives. In Spain, William Washabaugh notes a similar opposition between the figure of the Gitano and the well-to-do customers of the *cafés cantantes* who came to watch and listen to flamenco (1998, 12). Before the recording industry was established in Greece, songs of low life were already part of the repertoire of the Asia Minor musicians who performed in the Greek communities of Istanbul, Smyrna, and the musical cafés of Athens.

After commercial recordings popularized the bouzouki in the early nineteen-thirties, the bouzouki clubs and taverns of Athens were patronized by a mixed audience that included middle-class men and women. Like their counterparts in Madrid or Buenos Aires, the Athenian bourgeois audience came to listen to songs that described a world they knew very little about, presented to them, in many cases, by artists who had very little in common with them. The audience may have come to sample the exotic at a safe distance, but what of the performers, especially the women singers? Were they, in fact, beyond the pale of respectable society? Did they view themselves as outsiders? And what of the shady women depicted in the lyrics? Were they real or simply invented to satisfy a taste for the bohemian and forbidden?

Asia Minor Origins

We may argue about origins and precise chronology, but we can broadly agree that the rebetika were popular with a fairly large audience of Greeks, most of whom were urban and not wealthy, from the early decades of the twentieth century until the early 1960s and that they were revived in the 1970s, becoming popular with a quite different audience, one with no direct ties to the generation or milieu that created them. Songs that contain some of the characteristics of the mature style appeared, with or without the designation "rebetiko," in the towns of the late Ottoman Empire, particularly in Smyrna (modern Izmir) and Istanbul, many of them recorded in Greek and Turkish versions. Soon after, they were recorded by Greek musicians in the United States and in Athens. The Turko-Greek War, the destruction of Smyrna's Christian quarters by fire in 1922, and the ensuing peace settlement that imposed an exchange of populations on the two countries, caused a massive influx of refugees from Asia Minor into mainland Greece. This forced emigration dramatically changed what had been a traditionally agricultural country with a relatively homogeneous population into one with a poor urban population comprised largely of immigrants with quite different customs and traditions from the local population. Despite their poverty, most refugees had come from a more sophisticated and ethnically diverse urban milieu than the one they found themselves in. Within a few years of their arrival, many of the refugees had achieved some success. Others remained for years in the shantytowns that grew up on the fringes of Athens and Piraeus. Musicians who came from Istanbul and Smyrna were more skilled than local Greek musicians and could perform in a broader variety of styles. They soon moved out of the slums of Piraeus and began to dominate the Athens music scene as singers, instrumentalists, and musical directors of the new recording studios established in the 1930s.

The Asia Minor music the refugees brought with them was already familiar to some Athenians. It was a mixture of instrumental music based on the classical Ottoman tradition, of popular songs from Istanbul and Smyrna, of regional Greek folk songs and European-style café music. Refugee musicians performed in both the so-called cafés-aman, named for the vocal improvisations known as *amanedhes* (sing. *amanes*), which were a standard part of the repertoire in such establishments, and in the *cafés-chantants,* where European light songs dominated. Songs about hashish smoking and other disreputable aspects of life in the back streets of Istanbul, Smyrna, and Piraeus also seem to have been a popular part of the musical café repertoire. The typical ensemble that performed the café-aman songs consisted of a violin, a *santouri* (hammered dulcimer), and an *outi* (Arab-style lute), guitar, or other plucked instrument. The singer, who was as often a woman as a man, was as skilled at improvisation as the musicians she performed with.

It is not surprising that the amanes, usually based, like its Turkish equivalent the *gazel,* on a melancholic or nostalgic quatrain, should have been popular in the aftermath of a catastrophe that marked the end of a long and rich Greek presence in Asia Minor. In such vocal improvisations, the singer not only demonstrated musicianship, but created a mood of nostalgia and longing. The style of performance was emotional, and the despairing lyrics were interspersed with exclamations of *aman!* (mercy!). In the Ottoman tradition, where the art of instrumental and vocal improvisation was highly developed, the audience may have listened to such pieces as much for their musical display as for their emotional content. In Greece there seems to have been, from the beginning, a perception that the amanes was a type of stylized lament, one that represented the oriental and feminine side of the Greek character.[7]

In the years following the Turko-Greek War, when immigrants formed a sizable part of the Greek population, the café-aman singers, male and female, were popular with a broad audience. The well-known rebetiko performer and songwriter Vassilis Tsitsanis claimed that in the early 1930s, when he was growing up in the provincial town of Trikala, Roza Eskenazi was the most famous Greek woman singer.[8] When Tsitsanis first saw her perform in Athens in 1934, she was singing with two of the outstanding Asia Minor musicians of the day, the violinist Dimitrios Semsis, also known as "Salonikios," and Agapios Tomboulis. Since Eskenazi is one of the women on whom Kostas Ferris based his portrait of female performers in the movie *Rebetiko,* it is worth noting that this singer, a Greek Jew born in Istanbul and raised in Thessaloniki, Komotini, and Athens, was already a successful recording and performing artist by the time Tsitsanis heard her. In her autobiography (1982), she admits that her mother tried to dissuade her from a life as a singer and dancer, but she persisted, finding work in a theater in Athens, where she was discovered by the director of Columbia Records, Panayiotis Tountas. Tountas was a composer and mandolin player, a refugee from Smyrna; together with Semsis, he taught Roza to sing Greek folk songs in addition to the Asia Minor repertoire she knew. Eskenazi's friend and sometimes rival Rita Abadzi, whose family came as refugees from Smyrna to Athens when Rita was eight years old, also enjoyed a successful career as a singer, first performing Asia Minor–style music and Greek folk songs, and later, like Eskenazi, recording rebetika with bouzouki players. Neither Roza Eskenazi nor Rita Abadzi seems to have suffered, during their careers, from discrimination because they were women, nor does Eskenazi describe her fellow musicians with anything but affection and admiration. On the other hand, Angeliki Maroniti, a refugee from Smyrna who came from a family of musicians and had sung in the musical cafés of Smyrna with her father from a young age, was forbidden by her husband, the well-known rebetiko musician Vangelis Papazoglou, from pursuing her career as a performer in Greece.[9] In the early 1930s, however, Papazoglou allowed his wife to record six amanedhes, together with a daring rebetiko song of his own composition. To record was, apparently, a very different thing from appearing on the stage.

At least during the years of their greatest popularity in the 1930s, both Roza Eskenazi and Rita Abadzi worked principally with musicians who had begun their careers in the cosmopolitan cities of Asia Minor. The café-aman singers were as well known for their performance of Greek folk songs as they were for their amanedhes and rebetika. They included songs about the Piraeus underworld in their repertoire, but they saved their emotional fire for the amanedhes and performed the underworld songs with a light touch that detached them from the shady milieu of the lyrics. In a radio interview she gave in 1972, Eskenazi spoke of the bouzouki players she worked with, mentioning the fact that they smoked hashish but distancing herself from their behavior (Eskenazi 1982, 71–72). The singers of the café-aman style may have had an advantage over their Greek contemporaries in that they were outsiders.[10] Photographs of Eskenazi, Abadzi, and Marika Papagika at the height of their popularity show them fashionably dressed, their hair bobbed, and their eyebrows plucked to slim black scimitars.[11] Confidently poised at the center of an ensemble of male musicians, they appear sure of their stardom. On their recordings, this self-confidence is reinforced by the mutual display of admiration exchanged with their musicians in the form of spoken interjections that are a trademark of the style.

The musical clubs of Athens where Asia Minor musicians performed and the recording studios established in the 1930s may have offered women performers a rare degree of freedom in their interactions with men. How much this interaction and public visibility transgressed mainland Greek norms can be inferred from the reaction of Papazoglou to his wife's singing career. But women singers who were willing to flout the conventions of Greek society were in demand not only in the musical cafés of Athens but in the less respectable postwar bouzouki clubs. How were women like Sotiria Bellou,

Marika Ninou, and Stella Haskil, who sang rebetika with the postwar ensembles of bouzouki players, judged by the Greek men and women who listened to them? Did they enjoy the same respect as male performers? Did their popularity encourage at least some urban Greek women to follow their example?

The Singular Sotiria Bellou

One of the most remarkable performers of rebetika was the singer Sotiria Bellou (plate 12). Nothing about her life or personality conformed to Greek norms of female behavior. She was born in 1921 in Chalkis and in 1940 traveled alone to Athens after the failure of her marriage, determined to find work as a musician. Bellou's own role model was the well-known Greek popular singer and cabaret artist Sophia Vembo, noted for her performances of tangos. Bellou survived the German occupation and the civil war by selling cigarettes and occasionally singing to her own guitar accompaniment in taverns. During those years, she also played an active role in the Resistance. During the civil war, she fought in pitched battles on the side of the left. She was arrested, jailed, and beaten during those years, but eventually found work in a tavern. Bellou had a strong sense of her own worth. Even when she worked as an itinerant singer in a tavern, she knew she was something more than a cheap entertainer: "I went to the tavern nearly every day and played and sang for whatever money the people at the tables gave me. In the meantime they saw that I was no cheap woman. I was decent. And I was also very beautiful." [12]

Singing at the tavern, Bellou was discovered by the playwright Kimon Kapetanakis, who introduced her to Vassilis Tsitsanis. Tsitsanis was so impressed with her voice that he immediately wrote two songs for her. Tsitsanis's interest in her and the success of the recordings they made together launched Bellou's career as a rebetiko singer. By then, the bouzouki players had moved from Piraeus to respectable taverns in Athens. The audience they performed for were no longer the lower-class manges. Bellou describes the audience at the famous club "Jimmy the Fat's" where she began performing with Tsitsanis in 1948 as "quiet" and "aristocratic." She was the only woman singer performing there with a group of male bouzouki players and singers that included Zacharias Kasimatis, Spyros Peristeris, Stelios Kiromitis, and Kostas Roukounas. Soon after she began singing at the club, a group of men entered and asked her to perform the royalist song "Son of the Eagle." When she refused, they attacked her. She fought back, but not one of the male musicians came to her aid. Badly beaten and angry she left "Jimmy the Fat's," apparently holding no grudge against Tsitsanis or the male musicians. She soon found work with Markos Vamvakaris at another bouzouki club. Markos and his brother Argyris were performing with the guitarist Karipis and with Lili Nikolesco. At their club, Bellou was "discovered" again, this time by the composer Manos Hadzidakis. Together with the Vamvakaris brothers, Bellou performed for an audience of intellectuals and artists gathered in the Art Theater of Athens to hear Hadzidakis present the rebetika as a neglected treasure of Greek culture.[13] In the decade that followed the concert, when bouzouki music was at the height of its popularity, Bellou worked at various rebetika clubs, playing guitar and singing. Sometimes she was the only woman on the platform; at others she was joined by a second or third woman singer. She performed with the most successful bouzouki players and songwriters of her day, including Ioannis Papaioannou and Manolis Hiotis. She made a comeback as a recording artist in the 1960s and spent the seventies and eighties working with Tsitsanis again until his death.

Bellou was an exceptional woman in many respects. For one thing she was a remarkable singer; for another she was openly gay. Neither her gender nor her sexual preferences seem to have stood in the way of her career. Her own account of her successful life as a woman performing rebetika (Bellou 1995) is supported by the evidence of contemporary photographs that show her in mannish attire, sitting at ease and smiling among her male companions. Nevertheless, it is interesting that when the Asia Minor–style of popular song gave way to the Piraeus-based rebetika, the first woman singer to appear on the platform alongside Tsitsanis and his all-male band of bouzouki players was not only gay but had a deep, almost masculine voice.

The mature period of bouzouki-based rebetika began with the Piraeus Quartet, consisting of Markos Vamvakaris, Stratos Payioumdzis, Anestis Delias, and Yiorgos Batis. The group was soon supplemented by other male musicians, but it was the gravely voice of Vamvakaris and the strident sound of the bouzouki that gave the new style of the 1930s its bite. Unlike the professionally trained refugee singers, Payioumdzis among them, Vamvakaris's voice had the "authentic" sound of the underworld mangas. It was popular because it matched the mood of the songs Vamvakaris wrote, and the instrument he played. It was more than a decade after the new style had established itself that Bellou was "discovered," but her initiation into the rebetika world and her enduring popularity undoubtedly owed much to the fact that her voice had the "metal" admired in a rebetiko singer, an unsentimental toughness that suited the new style. That Bellou, together with Vamvakaris and his ensemble, was singled out by the gay composer Manos Hadzidakis and presented to the public as an artistic treasure is not without significance.

Rebetika and the Homoerotic

The songs and dances of the rebetika flourished within the almost exclusively male communities of the hashish den, the merchant navy, the prisons, and the dockyards. This all-male world was immediately attractive to bourgeois Greek homosexual artists like the painter Yiannis Tsarouchis and the composer Manos Hadzidakis, but it also became, like the Argentine tango and the Andalusian flamenco, popular with a broader middle-class audience. Ilias Petropoulos, who helped to popularize the rebetika with his book *Rebetika traghoudia* (1968) and who belonged to a small circle of sophisticated Greek and foreign aficionados of the music, was also interested in the gay underworld of Greece and compiled a dictionary of homosexual slang. Petropoulos was fascinated by the marginal and exotic. He spent some time in prison, where he collected information about the criminal underworld. He compiled glossaries of the *mangika* argot and the *kaliarda,* an argot spoken by Greek homosexuals that is similarly sprinkled with words borrowed from Turkish, Italian, and French. He also observed that men dancing a *tsifteteli* together would often hold their testicles and perform a crude mimicry of women belly dancers.[14] This playful gender reversal in the dance should not be read, necessarily, as indicative of a homoerotic relationship between the dancers. Maria Papapavlou observed that men dancing flamenco in a *juergas* after the women had left would frequently dance the *buleria* together making provocative sexual movements, while men who watched them called out: "Take a look at them, the faggots!" (in Washabaugh 1998, 45–46). Sometimes a participant would bring along a wig to make the spectacle more amusing. The shouting about homosexuality and the ribald laughter continued until the men tired and went home to their wives. Undoubtedly homosexual activity existed in rebetika circles, but as in flamenco clubs, it was neither the norm nor the ideal. Rather, the male dancer, secure in his masculinity, could afford to play the homosexual and provoke laughter. To the bourgeois, European-educated Greek artists and intellectuals as well as to a select group of foreign fans, there was an enviable "Zorba" quality to the genre: a glimpse of a world where men could dance for themselves or with other men, confident in their own virility.

The dances of the rebetika may also be substantially different from those associated with the other popular musical forms of the period in that the male body neither dominates the female, as in the tango, nor is displayed in its full patriarchal ascendancy, as in flamenco (Washabaugh 1998, 40). Neither the tsifteteli, with its playfully eroticism, nor the comradely *hasapiko,* danced by two or three men with their arms around each other's shoulders and depending, for its successful execution, on a certain amount of rehearsal, could be described as emblematic of male pride. Only the solo male dance at the center of the genre, the *zebekiko,* had the passionate intensity of flamenco, but the degree of its male posturing varied from period to period and from milieu to milieu. Within the closed world of the hashish dens and underworld haunts of Piraeus, it was danced when the dancer had smoked or drunk enough to get high. It was an introverted dance whose inward-circling, uncertain steps expressed the dancer's altered mood. The zebekiko was not apparently danced for an audience, and yet it was observed by other men, men who seldom looked directly at the dancer. It carved out a territory within which the dancer was free to interpret the music as he wished and which was violated by another man at the risk of serious bodily harm. If fights broke out over the zebekiko, it was partly because, as the rebetika became more popular, the dancer paid a high price to have the floor to himself. To pay the bouzouki player a large sum for the pleasure of entering into a personal relationship with the music was, like the later smashing of plates, part of the conspicuous display of extravagance that characterizes Greek male behavior in many contexts.[15] But to be admired, the dancer had to maintain at least the fiction of solitary introspection. To the extent that the dance was seen as a genuine expression of a man's pain, it was admired. The rebetes had no tolerance for the *fighouradzis* (poseur), either in the dance or among the knife-carrying manges.[16]

The writer Kostas Taktsis describes how during the war years the zebekiko came to be enjoyed by a much broader audience than it had been before (Holst 1977, 202–9). In his opinion, the harsh economic and social conditions of the German occupation acted as a leveler, turning the entire society into something akin to the prewar urban underworld. Houses were transformed into the hashish dens of Piraeus: "The zebekiko found space to develop and did so rapidly. Suddenly it was no longer the dance of the underworld, but of a large number of Greeks, mostly in the urban centers. Many of the songs we first heard immediately after the war had been written during the occupation, and they were different from the pre-war, heavier 'hashish' rebetika" (204).

Taktsis goes on to say that while the waltzes, tangos, and foxtrots that had been popular before the war continued to be heard, they were recognized as being "all honey and milk," whereas the zebekika (he uses the term metonymically for the rebetika as a genre) spoke about reality. Although they were not overtly political, they were understood as corresponding to "the *spirit* of the resistance" (Holst 1977, 205). The partisans fighting the Germans in the mountains may have had their own patriotic songs, but in the underground taverns of the Greek cities, the ordinary people sang the zebekika. In the period following the war and the civil war, according to Taktsis, the tango was all the rage again and the rebetika's popularity began to wane, but with the championing of the rebetika by Hadzidakis, the fashion for the once-despised bouzouki music spread even to the haute bourgeoisie, who began flocking to the bouzouki taverns, paying increasingly high prices to hear bouzouki players, and breaking plates at the feet of showy dancers. The end result, according to Taktsis, was that a brilliantly successful robbery took place under the noses of the ordinary Greeks. What had been stolen was "the right of the people at least to bewail their fate" (208).

What Taktsis has to say about the zebekiko suggests that war transformed the rebetika. Not only did they emerge from a shady and almost exclusively male milieu to become broadly popular, but they acquired a certain national character.[17] By the time the rebetika had become urban, rather than underground, they had acquired a classless and genderless ability to express the sorrows of everyday Greek life. The nonchalant lurch of the zebekiko dancer was, in this period, a gesture against authority, one that, in the right company, could be admired not for being macho but almost for its opposite: for the dancer's willingness to weep silently in public.

Rebetisses

There were always women who penetrated the world of the manges, and others who lived on its margins. Even in the hashish dens, some women joined their male companions in smoking an arghilé. Indeed, there is a recurrent female type in the songs who hangs out with the rebetes, the type called variously a *mangissa, hasiklou, meraklou, alaniara,* or *derbederissa.* But did this gender-bending or gender-defiant woman exist, or is she a fiction? And if so, why is she there, in the lyrics of this predominantly masculine music?

One of the earliest manifestations of the female rebetis occurs in a song called "Elli." First recorded in Istanbul around 1915 (Orfeon Records), the song describes a beautiful, black-haired young woman who denies her family for her lover, Lefteri. Elli wants "sugar and hashish flour / to make sweets to send to Lefteri." The refrain of the song is lighthearted and humorous:

> Elli, Elli, the young soldier doesn't want you
> Unless you change your mind and give him a kiss.[18]

But in the final stanzas Elli's behavior is condemned in conventional Greek terms:

> On Christmas Day the bells were ringing,
>   the bells were ringing,
> And the Christians all in church and Elli with the Turks
>   and Elli with the Turks.[19]

In a version of the same song recorded in the United States by the Greek Record Company in 1920, Elli's behavior is condemned more strongly:

> Elli should be killed, should be guillotined,
>   guillotined
> Because she left her husband and children,
>   all her children.[20]

Another Greek version of the song made four or five years later again suggests Elli be killed, this time with a dagger, because she left her husband for a Turkish commissar. Recordings of the song continued to be made both in Greece and in the United States. One American version by Victor (1925–30) set the song firmly in streets of Smyrna:

> When Elli walked in the lanes of Smyrna,
>   the lanes of Smyrna;
> The Turks thought Ramadan had come,
>   Ramadan had come.[21]

The song, based perhaps on a true story, conforms to a type that concerns a desirable woman of dubious morals. Another song of the period, "Eleni," describes the behavior of a Greek girl living in Istanbul who frequents the cafés and smokes the hookah with her boyfriend. In the song, her brother begs her to return to their grieving mother but she refuses, whereupon he shoots her. At the funeral, Eleni's brother is overcome with remorse and kills himself.[22]

   A variant of the fallen, but still desirable woman is the Turkish or Asia Minor Greek woman referred to in the lyrics of the songs as *hanoum, hanoumi, hanoumissa,* or *hanoumaki.* The word *hanoum,* with or without its Greek diminutive endings, is simply the Turkish word for a woman, but in the rebetika, it has exotic associations with the harem. Such orientalized women may consort with the rebetes and even smoke arghilé with them. One of the first appearances of this character is in a song recorded simultaneously in Smyrna,

Istanbul, and probably in Athens with the title "To neo hanoumaki."[23] The Istanbul version of the song contains a stanza not found in the Smyrna version in which the relationship of Greek to Turk is raised again. Following the opening stanzas, where the "hanoumaki" is addressed as being "tender as a pigeon" and "plump as a red mullet," she responds:

> I'm a Turkish girl
> And you a Christian boy.
> Such love doesn't match,
> A Turkish girl with a Greek boy
> To have love and sorrow.[24]

The man's reaction is surprising:

> So I've a good mind to change my faith,
> To enter the harem and carry you off.[25]

The theme of the flirtatious but unattainable or hardhearted woman remained popular in the rebetika. An early rebetiko song of this type, recorded in 1929 by Marika Papagika is "Fonias tha yino" (I'll Become a Murderer), where the speaker says he's prepared to become a murderer in order to have the "wicked sorceress" he has fallen in love with. However not all the hanoumaki songs present the woman as unattainable. In the well-known rebetiko song "Ta hanoumakia," the young women of the title apparently serve the customers in a hashish den near Piraeus:

> On the beach near Pasalimani you had your hashish den
> And I'd come there every day to drive away my pain.
> One morning I found them there, sitting on the sand.
> Two lovely hanoumakia, the poor things really stoned.
>
> Come here you dervish, sit here with us,
> And you'll hear a love song from our hearts.
> Take your baglama and entertain us awhile,
> Light up your joint and smoke with us.
>
> Fill me a waterpipe and let me get high,
> And then, hanoumakia, I'll take my baglama.
> I'll fill you a pipe with hashish that's Isfahani
> At Uncle Yianni's hashish den in Pasalimani.[26]

In this song, the hanoumakia address the rebetis on equal terms, aiding and abetting him in his smoking and sharing in his musical performance. Did women regularly serve male customers in the hashish dens? And were they refugees or local girls? Whatever the truth, by referring to the man in the song as "dervish" (a common label for a rebetis who smoked dope and was cool) and the young women as "hanoumakia," the song places the hashish den and its customers in an exotic oriental framework. The women of the song inhabit a milieu that may have been known to a singer like Rita Abadzi, who recorded it in the 1930s, but that world is sufficiently removed from her own life to allow her to perform it as a colorful tableau of low life.

Two songs that belong to a similar oriental fantasy type are Yiorgos Batis's "O boufedzis" (The Buffet Man) and Anestis Delias's "Mes tis Polis to hamam" (In the Baths of Constantinople). In the first, the protagonist wants to be a *boufedzis,* the man who sets up the smoking equipment on the buffet or sideboard of a hashish den, so that the "hanoumisses" will come in to smoke waterpipes:

> And when I enter the hashish den I see three delights:
> Three pretty girls sharing a pipe.
>
> One holds an arghilé, the other tamps it down,
> The third and youngest of the girls wants to have a smoke.
>
> One plays the baglama, the other the bouzouki,
> The third and youngest is stoned out of her mind.[27]

In Delias's well-known tsifteteli of 1935, "In the Baths of Constantinople," the pasha's harem is swimming in the baths when he orders his guards to bring them to him so they can play baglamas and dance for him while he smokes hashish in his hookah. The lighthearted fantasy of such a song is far removed from the reality of the world of the rebetes. By the 1930s, heroin had appeared on the streets of Piraeus and was soon being used by both men and women.[28] According to the accounts of musician friends, Delias, who died of an overdose of heroin in 1944, was deliberately turned on to hard drugs by a woman. In the early 1930s, both Roza Eskenazi and Marika Politissa recorded a song by Panayiotis Toundas about a woman addicted to cocaine. In this case the woman complains about the man who turned her on to the drug and ruined her life. Although such songs, when performed by the café-aman singers, were popular vignettes of the low life of Athens and

Piraeus, they were based, to a greater or lesser degree, on the seedier reality of the underworld.

Roza Eskenazi and Rita Abadzi both recorded another song of about the type of woman described in "Ta hanoumakia." In the song "Mes tou Zambikou" (At Zambikos's), a woman named Irini goes to a hashish den owned by Zambikos to try smoking a hookah. "Load up the pipe," says an admiring customer, "for the black-eyed girl to smoke":

> At Zambikos's hashish den, mercy on us,
> Rini's smoking a hubble-bubble.
> The manges are playing baglamas
> While Rini, my dear, is chasing out the blues.
>
> Here's to you, Irini, you're really hip.
> You've turned into a dope-head too![29]

In this song the woman is not referred to as a hanoumaki but as a meraklou, i.e. a woman who's a bon vivant, a connoisseur and devotee of good living, usually drinking. She is also referred to as a *hasiklou,* the feminine form of a *hasiklis,* or hashish smoker. The meraklou is another female rebetika character who is accepted and admired by the manges as one of their own. Abadzi also recorded a song called "Nea meraklou" (Young Bon Vivant), written by K. Tzovenos in the voice of a young woman, who hangs out all night in bars drinking to chase away her blues. She wants to love a mangas, but she begs her "dervish" boyfriend to quit smoking hashish:

> Hi there, my mangas dervish,
> Don't smoke hashish any more.
> Sit and drink some beer with me
> And afterward we'll talk things over.[30]

The young woman of the song proudly refers to herself as a meraklou. She makes it clear she is no puritan but an independent woman and an admirer of the hip mangas. On the other hand, she wants her lover to keep her company in a bar rather than getting stoned in the shadier world of the hashish den. The meraklou reappears in a number of songs that have to do with drinking and enjoying life. The hasiklou, on the other hand, may or may not be admired for her smoking habits. She may be told by her lover to quit smoking, as in the Papazoglou song "Marika hasiklou," recorded by Roukounas in

1934, in which the protagonist complains that the girl he wants to marry hangs out in the hashish dens smoking with the manges. A similar sentiment is expressed in the song "Kapnoulou mou omorfi" (My Beautiful Smoker), written by Bayiaderas (Dimitris Gogos) and recorded by him in 1935. Again the mangas protagonist complains that the girl he loves hangs out with other men, especially when stoned, and that she frequents the hashish den because she loves "the baglama, the bouzoukis, and the waterpipe."[31] A woman is sometimes blamed for turning the manges on to hashish, as in an early Asia Minor–style song called "The Widow and the Hashish," where the widow is blamed for the protagonist's ruin. Markos Vamvakaris also wrote a song about a woman who was responsible for turning the manges on. The protagonist of his song "Mortissa hasiklou" (Dope-head Dropout) recorded for Columbia in 1933 or 1934, is described as being "born in the hashish dens" and selling hashish to the manges, but she is praised for bringing comfort to them and getting rid of their blues.

The songs of Markos Vamvakaris are frequently about the women who hang out with the manges, smoke dope, and are unfaithful to their men. Depending on the song, they may be praised or cursed for their behavior, taken lightly or rejected. In two songs in which he refers to the women as *gomenes* (the term may mean "girlfriends" or "tarts," according to the context), the women are not only hanging out with the manges, but even, in one, cross-dressing to do so:

> And the broads have put on men's caps,
> They walk the streets in search of a smoke.
> You see that girl who's wearing a cap
> And walking like a mangas for everyone to see.
>
> And the broads have put on men's clothes
> And they're running off to smoke with the manges.
> You see, mangas friend, hip broads
> With their flirting, tricks, and silly whims.[32]

The picture Markos paints of the freewheeling girls of Piraeus is playful and affectionate. These sassy girls obviously have a sense of humor. If they've put on mangas clothes, it is not in an attempt to usurp their men friends' territory but to join them. Like the leather jackets and boots of the bikers' girls, the gear is worn as much to flirt in as to ride in.

Unlike the Asia Minor–style singers, Vamvakaris and the early rebetes did in fact live their lives in Piraeus, mixing with characters from the underworld, smoking hashish and worse. The world described in the songs may be stylized, but it is based on personal experience rather than hearsay. Women are present in this subgroup; they are portrayed listening to bouzouki music alongside their male friends and smoking hashish. Such women occupy a very different position from that of the women musicians who sang about the underworld at arm's length. They must always have lived on the extreme margins of Greek society, in a milieu where questions of propriety no longer applied. What is interesting is that there is, in many of these songs about the marginal woman of the mangas world, more than a sneaking admiration for her disdain for societal norms. Even Papazoglou, who put an end to his wife's singing career, allowed her to record his song "Dervisena" (Dervish Woman), in which the protagonist proudly claims to be a meraklou who smokes hashish and is in love with a dervish:

> I'm a wildcat, a goodtime girl, and I like to smoke hashish.
> That's why I got a nickname: they call me the dervish lover.
>
> I'll be a dervish lover until the day I die.
> And if I lose this dervish, I'll find another one.
>
> Wherever I am, whatever I do they call me the dervish woman.
> But I don't shed a tear for what dumb people say.
>
> Me, I like the dervishes because they have such fun;
> They're mighty cool dudes and troublemakers too.[33]

Rebetisses of the Postwar Period

The closing of the hashish dens, the persecution of musicians, and the censorship of songs under the Metaxas dictatorship (1936–41) did little to dampen the public enthusiasm for the rebetika. As the Piraeus-style rebetika became more broadly popular during the forties and fifties and new stars emerged, like Tsitsanis and Yiannis Papaioannou, the figure of the exotic, liberated, bohemian woman surfaced again in a significant number of songs.

Beginning in 1929 and reaching the peak of his career in the postwar period, Vassilis Tsitsanis recorded more than three hundred songs, the majority about male-female relationships. Among his earliest songs are oriental fantasies that recall Artemis's "In the Baths of Constantinople." They include the 1940 "Maghissa tis Arapias" (Enchantress of Arabia), "Arapines" (Arab

Girls) and "Maritsa sto haremi" (Maritsa in the Harem), both recorded in 1946. The Arab girls, described as "black lovers" with "bodies made like snakes," are paired not with the sound of the bouzouki and the bubble of the hookah, but with the more European delights of "whiskey and guitars." Scattered throughout Tsitsanis's recording career are a dozen more such songs that must have appealed to an audience who enjoyed escapist fantasy. Of the less exotic women who appear in Tsitsanis's songs, some are heartbreakers, others have their hearts broken by men. "Dhe me stefanonesai" (You Won't Marry Me) is written in the voice of a woman ready to sell herself in despair. The woman of "To omorfopedho" (The Handsome Fellow) is prepared to put up with her lover's infidelities because he is such a good-looking mangas. If one can generalize about the portrayal of women in the lyrics of Tsitsanis, the most influential and prolific of the postwar rebetika composers, it is that they are desirable but generally unfaithful heartbreakers. There are occasional appearances of the independent women of the Piraeus rebetika, as in the song "Trexe manga na rotisis," or "Run and Ask, Mangas," also known as "The Woman Dervish." The female dervish of the song, recorded by Tsitsanis in 1947 with Stella Haskil and Markos Vamvakaris, has all the flair of the prewar manges girls, but she's still a heartbreaker:

> Mangas, run and ask them to tell you who I am.
> I'm a great woman, a real swinger.
> Who plays men like dice through my hands.
>
> Love doesn't move me, a good time's enough.
> Every evening I keep on drinking
> While brave lads kill each other over me.
>
> Stop asking me how I can be all yours.
> I don't care for words, I made it clear;
> I was born in the taverns and cabarets.[34]

There's a dashing charm to this "dervish," especially when the song is performed by a woman like Stella Haskil or Sotiria Bellou. She knows her own worth and makes no promises. Unlike the girls of Tsitsanis's oriental fantasies, the dervish is a convincing femme fatale.

"Woman Satrap" (the word "satrap" has come to mean a domestic tyrant) is the title of another Tsitsanis song, recorded a year later than "Woman Dervish." The lady in question has abandoned the protagonist, who watches her go past in a carriage, embracing another man. Again, despite the woman's behavior, there is a playful tone to the song and the woman is clearly the one in charge of her own destiny. Tsitsanis's contemporary Yannis Papaioannou also wrote a song about a "female satrap" (*enas satrapis thilikos*). The boot is on the other foot in this song, with the melancholy "satrap" asking the bouzouki player to play something sweet to ease her broken heart. She also wants a lot of wine to drink before she finds her man. When she does, she says, she'll have it out with him "like a wild beast / and one of us will die." This is another song of the tough lady sort that Sotiria Bellou obviously enjoyed and rerecorded for Lyra in the 1960s.

The free-spirited woman who hangs out with the rebetika musicians may appear in fewer postwar songs than in prewar songs, but her presence is enough to suggest the perennial popularity of the fictive streetwise lady. Rebetika composers like Tsitsanis always wrote with a particular voice in mind. When performed by women like Marika Ninou, Stella Haskil, Sotiria Bellou, and Ioanna Yiorgakopoulou, such songs took on a convincing authenticity. As women musicians in a mostly male world, these singers were themselves an unusual phenomenon in Greek life. Unlike the performers in the prewar cafés-aman, where the women singers had a history of being accepted as a necessary component of the musical ensemble, the women singers of the rebetika club were introduced into what had been an exclusively male musical style. The postwar bouzouki clubs were not family entertainment; they were nightclubs that only warmed up after midnight. Even in the 1960s, the audience was more male than female, and there was still a certain raciness attached to going "to the bouzoukis." As a woman, to be a performer in a bouzouki club required some disdain for the norms of Greek gender relations. It is interesting to speculate whether the singers themselves may have provided a model for the songs about daring or unusual women.

Women in a Man's World?

From what might be called the "proto-rebetika" of the Asia Minor songs to the popular "laiko-rebetika" of the postwar period, there is only a brief interval during the 1930s when the music becomes exclusively male. On the other hand, it is this very period when bouzouki music, performed by a handful of musicians, becomes dominant that defines rebetika for many Greek fans of the genre. When the Piraeus Quartet first performed songs about the hashish-smoking mangas culture, rebetika acquired a Greek flavor, as distinct from an Asia Minor character. Intellectual Greeks like Hadzidakis or Taktsis who were attracted to the music, admired it for its directness, its lack of sentimentality. There is no doubt that the world described in songs, if not always lived by the first generation of bouzouki-playing musicians, was a man's world.

Women who were attracted to the rebetika had to be content with a position on the margins. Some penetrated the inner sanctum of manges as girl-friends and fellow smokers and, at least by the evidence of the song lyrics, some were admired as free spirits. By the 1940s and 1950s, when bouzouki clubs were popular in Athens, and women singers joined men on the platform, the situation had changed. For one thing, the cafés-aman ensembles had disappeared. There was no longer a division between the professional musicians who sang a wide repertoire of songs and the bouzouki-playing clubs where only rebetika were performed. Bouzouki music was now the established popular music of Athens. It may have taken an exceptional woman like Bellou to set the precedent, but women singers in bouzouki clubs soon began to occupy a position more like their Asia Minor forebears. They were successful recording artists with their own independent careers. It may also be that the rebetika, that most male of Greek popular musical genres, was never quite as exclusive as it appeared. Both the song texts and the stories of the women singers who performed them present us not with the stereotypes of male-female interaction we see in the movie *Rebetiko*, but with a more subtle picture of the rebetika milieu. Even in the Piraeus hashish dens, there were always girls, it seems, ready to put on their boyfriends' caps and light up an arghilé with them. And under the sobriquet "meraklou," "hanoumaki," or "derbederissa," the women of the rebetika left their dashing and charming presence behind them.

Notes

1. Throughout this chapter, unless otherwise noted, translations of non-English sources are my own. For comparisons of rebetika with flamenco and tango, see Steingress 1998. In the same volume (Washabaugh 1998) see Holst-Warhaft (111–26), and Washabaugh's introduction (1–26). For comparison with urban blues see Holst 1975 and Papadimitriou 1975.

2. Jeffrey Tobin (1998), for example, has argued that the tango, generally thought of as a dance exemplifying the Argentine macho stereotype, is in fact, a homoerotic display in which men watch men dancing and the woman is simply a body, an object displayed, a "symptom of the tango-dancing man."

3. Admiration for daring women is not confined to the rebetika but occurs in Greek folk song, particularly in the historical ballads and in the laments from Mani that deal with revenge. See Holst-Warhaft 1992, 77–88.

4. In the confines of this study it is impossible to provide a large bibliography of literary sources, but Karen Van Dyck's *Cassandra and the Censors* (1998) is an excellent guide to the writings of some Greek women who call preconceived notions of gender relations in modern Greek life into question.

5. Shand 1998 and Holst-Warhaft 1998 and forthcoming are exceptions.

6. Steingress (1998, 160) describes this as a "romanticizing role," and this is true, I think, for the rebetika.

7. One of the earliest Greek commentators on the amanes was the musicologist Phaidros (1881). In his monograph he traced the origins of the amanes to the ancient Egyptian lament for Linos mentioned by Herodotus. Phaidros uses the occasion to denigrate the Ottoman Turkish modal system of *makamlar* and to claim the genre of amanes as being essentially Greek. Later Greek writers and critics commenting on the amanes were divided between those who saw it as a legitimate Greek form and those who regarded it as oriental and foreign to Greek sensibility. The controversy about the "Greekness" of the amanes and of the music performed in the cafés-aman is discussed at length in Hatzipantazis 1986 and in Gauntlett 1989. Nikos Kazantzakis stood on the fence, hearing the amanes as both feminine and oriental but as an expression of the emotional side of the Greek character. In his *Taxidhevontas: Italia, Aigiptos, Sina, Ierousalim, Kipros, O Morias,* he describes how the small businessmen and officers he encountered, "so logical and selfish, break into melancholy eastern *amanedhes,* into a sudden longing; they reveal a psyche completely different from their sober, everyday one. A great treasure, a deep longing" (Kazantzakis 1965, 324–30). In a forthcoming paper I discuss the Greek associations of amanes with lament and hence with a traditionally female genre.

8. See his introduction to Roza's autobiography as told to Kostas Hadzidoulis (Eskenazi 1982, 7).

9. This is according to the cover notes by Kounadis, Papaioannou, and Sotiropoulos (1982).

10. As a Jew, Eskenazi was an outsider in more than one respect. It is worth noting that some of the most successful performers of Asia Minor–style songs in the United States during the 1930s and 1940s were also Jews and Armenians. They included Amalia and Diamando Baka and Victoria Hazan. It is also worth considering that the first woman to make a gramophone recording in Turkey was probably an Orthodox Christian named Eftalia (Aksoy 1998) and that her successful career as a café singer and recording star, an example soon followed by Muslim women, may have been possible because of her status as a non-Muslim.

11. Marika Papagika was born on the island of Kos and emigrated to the United States around 1918. She immediately began making recordings of Asia Minor–style music, Greek folk songs, and rebetika with her cymbalum-player husband, Kostas. By the time the couple opened a café-aman in Manhattan in the 1925, it was simply called, in recognition of her fame, "Marika's."

12. Unless otherwise noted, my account is from Bellou 1995. The pages are not numbered.

13. Bellou 1995. Excerpts from the text of Hadizidakis's speech on that occasion were published in "Elliniki Dhimiourghia" (*Greek Arts*, March 1949) and appear in Holst 1977.

14. This practice was still common when I first went to hear rebetika in the 1960s.

15. It is customary, in most parts of Greece, for a man to pay musicians for the right of his *parea,* or group, to dance. This is understood and respected by other groups. The zebekiko dancer is exceptional in that he pays to dance alone.

16. Two songs by Anestis Delias, "The koutsavakis" and "Figouradzis" illustrate the rebetis's disdain for the poseur. The lyrics of "The koutsavakis," recorded in 1935, go as follows:

> Hey mangas, if you're going to carry a knife
> You'd better have the guts, faker, to pull it.
>
> That stuff doesn't wash with me, so hide your blade
> Or I'll get high, poseur, and come to your shack.
>
> I told you to sit tight, because I'll beat you up,
> I'll come with my gun, poseur, and I'll call your bluff.
>
> Go somewhere else, poseur, and strut your stuff
> Because I've been smoking, faker, and I'm mighty high.
>
> [Re manga to maheri sou yia na to kousoumaris
> Prepei na ehis ti psihi, figouradzi, kardhia na to vgalis.
>
> Se mena den pernan afta kai kripse to spathi sou
> Yiati mastouris tha yino, figouradzi, kai tha'rtho sto tsardhi sou.
>
> Allou na pas, figouradzi. Na kanis ti figoura
> Yiati ki ego foumarisa, figouradzi, ki eho trelli mastoura.
>
> Sto 'pa na katsis fronima, yiati tha se tsakiso
> Tha'rtho me to koubouri mou, figouradzi, kai tha se kseftiliso.]

17. I have heard this confirmed by a number of intellectual observers including the composer Mikis Theodorakis.

18. Elli, Elli, fantaros den se thelei / Ektos an metaniosis ki ena fili tou dhoseis.

19. Animera Christouyenna, ktipousan i kambanes / Ki i Christiani stin ekklisia ki i Elli mes ts'ayadhes.

20. I Elli thelei skotoma, thelei karmaniola / Yiat'afise ton andra tis kai ta pedhia tis ola.

21. Vre i n'Elli, ade, eparpatise stis Smyrnis ta sokakia / Ki i Tourki, ade, enomisane pos einai Ramazania.

22. The song is performed by Mariza Koch on the record *Ta paralia.*

23. This recording history is according to the discography of rebetika in Smyrna-Constantinople before 1922 prepared by Kounadis and Papaioannou and published in the periodical *Mousiki* 41 (1981): 34.

24. Eimai Tourkopoula kori / Kai si Christiano agori. / Den tairiazei tetia agapi / Tourkopoula me Romio. / Na'hi agapi kai kaymo.

25. Etsi mou'rhetai tin pisti mou n'allaxo / Na bo mesa sto haremi na s'arpaxo.

26. The source for the lyrics is the 1991 CD produced by Martin Schwartz. The song is attributed to Manolis Chrisafakis:

Stis thalassas tin amoudhia eihes to tekedhaki
Ki erhomouna kathe proi ki espaga dalgadhaki.
Dhio hanoumakia emorfa, mastouria ta kaymena
Ena proi ta trakara stin ammo kathismena.

Plisiase dervisi mou kai kathise konda mas
Ki akou tragoudhia tou sevda vgalmen'ap'ti kardhia mas.
Par'to baglamadhaki sou ligo na mas goustaris.
Anaps'to tsigarliki sou mazi mas na foumaris.

Yemisate mou arghilé na pio, na mastouriaso
Ki'epeita, hanoumakia mou, ton baglama na piaso.
Tha sou patisoum'arghilé me toubeki spahani
Stou Barba Yianni ton teke,mes sto Pasalimani.

27. The source for this song is the Falireas Brothers' LP *Yiorgos Batis:*

Kai otan baino sto teke vlepo tria merakia
Treis kopeles emorfes na pinoun tsiboukakia.

I mia vastai ton argile ki'alli ton patai
I triti i mikroteri yirevi na foumari.

I mia paizi to baglama, i alli to bouzouki
I triti i mikroteri trelli sto mastourlouki.

28. This information comes from Panayiotis Kounadis's cover notes to the Falireas Brothers' 1988 recording of Delias.

29. The source for this song is the recording *Ta apagorevmena rebetika* (The banned rebetika), vol. 1 (Regal 034-410, 121). The lyrics are reproduced in Aulin and Vejleskov 1991, 60:

Mes stou Zambikou ton teke, vr'aman aman
Foumarei i Rina, arghilé
Pezoun i manges baglamadhes
Spai i Rini, kale mou, tous sevdadhes.

Yia sou, Irini, meraklou, vr'aman aman,
Pou mou'gines kai hasiklou.

30. From *Ta apagorevmena rebetika*, vol. 3, no. 641:

Yia sou manga mou dervisi
Mi foumaris pia hasisi.
Katse bira na ta pioume
Ki istera yia na ta poume.

31. The source for the lyrics for "Kapnoulou mou omorfi" and "Nea meraklou" is Aulin and Vejleskov 1991, 103, 62.

32. From the recording *Markos Vamvakaris, 1932–40*, vol. 3 (EMI 062-1702021):

Kai i gomenes foresane trayaskes
Kai stous dromous trigirnoun kai kanoun tsarkes.
Vlepis gomerna trayaska na forai
Kai san mangitissa averta perpatai.

Kai i gomenes andrikia kousoumaroun
Kai me manges trehoune na foumaroun
Vlepis manga mou dervisika koritsia
Me nazakia, me kolpakia kai kapritsia.

33.   Eim'alaniara meraklou, foumaro to hasisi
Yi'afto mou vgalan t'onoma, pos agapo dervisi.

Ego dervisi th'agapo, oste pou na pethano
Ki an tone haso ki allone dervisi the na paro.

Opou statho ki opou vretho, dervisena me lene
Ma kai yia ton koutokosmo ta matia mou den klaine.

M'aresoun i dervisidhes yiat'einai meraklidhes
Einai poli yiavasidhes kai ligo belalidhes.

34.   Trekse manga na rotisis na sou poun pia imai ego.
Imai ego yineka fina, derbederissa
Pou tous andres san ta zaria tous beglerissa.

Den me singinoun agapes, ftani na kaloperno.
Kathe vradhi na travao to potiri mou
Kai na svazonde levendes yia hatiri mou.

Pos tha yino ego diki sou, papse na to sizitas.
Dhe goustaro tis paroles sou ksigithika
Stis tavernes kai sta kabare yenithika.

References

Aksoy, Bülent. 1998. *Kadiköylü: Deniz Kizi Eftalyia.* Book accompanying the CD. Istanbul: Kalan.

Anastasiou, Theofilos, ed. 1995. *"Pedhaki me psihi kai zilemeni": 329 traghoudhia tou Vasili Tsitsani.* (A kid with heart, an enviable kid: 329 songs by Vassilis Tsitsanis). Trikala: Cultural Organization of the Demos of Trikkala.

Aulin, Suzanne, and Peter Vejleskov. 1991. *Hasiklidhika rebetika* (Rebetika hashish songs). Copenhagen: Museum Tusculanum Press, University of Copenhagen.

Bellou, Sotiria. 1995. *Greatest Greek Singers: The Rebetika of Sotiria Bellou.* Booklet accompanying Lyra CD. Athens: General Publishing Company.

Butterworth, Katharine, and Sara Schneider. 1975. *Rebetika: Songs from the Old Greek Underworld.* New York: Komboloi.

Campbell, John K. 1964. *Honour, Family, and Patronage.* Oxford: Oxford University Press.

Caraveli, Anna. 1986. "The Bitter Wounding: The Lament as Social Protest in Rural Greece." In *Gender and Power in Rural Greece,* edited by Jill Dubisch, 169–94. Princeton: Princeton University Press.

Cowan, Jane. 1990. *Dance and the Body Politic in Northern Greece.* Princeton: Princeton University Press.

Danforth, Loring. 1982. *The Death Rituals of Rural Greece.* Princeton: Princeton: Princeton University Press.

————. 1989. *Firewalking and Religious Healing: The Anastenaria of Greece and the American Firewalking Movement.* Princeton: Princeton University Press.

Dubisch, Jill, ed. 1986. *Gender and Power in Rural Greece.* Princeton: Princeton University Press.

Du Boulay, Juliet. 1974. *Portrait of a Greek Mountain Village.* Oxford: Clarendon Press.

Eskenazi, Roza. 1982. *Afta pou thimamai* (What I remember). Athens: Kaktos.

Friedl, Ernestine. 1967. "The Position of Women: Appearance and Reality." *Anthropological Quarterly* 40 (3): 97–108.

Gauntlett, Stathis. 1989. "Orpheus in the Criminal Underworld: Myth in and about Rebetika." *Mantatophoros* 34:7–48.

Hart, Laurie Kane. 1992. *Time, Religion, and Social Experience in Rural Greece.* Lanham, Md.: Rowman and Littlefield.

Hatzipantazis, Theodoros. 1986. *Tis Asiatidhos Mousis erastai.* Athens.

Herzfeld, Michael. 1981. "Performative Categories and Symbols of Passage in Rural Greece." *Journal of American Folklore* 94 (371): 44–57.

————. 1993. "In Defiance of Destiny: The Management of Time and Gender at a Cretan Funeral." *American Ethnologist* 20 (2): 241–55.

Hirschon, Renée. 1981. "Essential Objects and the Sacred: Interior and Exterior Space in an Urban Locality." In *Women and Space,* edited by Shirley Ardener, 72–88. London: Croom Helm.

————. 1983. "Women, the Aged, and Religious Activity: Oppositions and Complementarity in an Urban Locality." *Journal of Modern Greek Studies* 1 (1): 113–30.

————. 1989. *Heirs of the Greek Catastrophe: The Social Life of Asia Minor Refugees in Piraeus.* Oxford: Clarendon.

Holst[-Warhaft], Gail. 1975. *Road to Rembetika.* Athens: Anglo-Hellenic (Denise Harvey).

————. 1977. *Dromos yia to rebetiko.* Greek edition of Holst 1975, with a new appendix of articles about rebetika. Athens: Denise Harvey.

————. 1992. *Dangerous Voices: Women's Laments and Greek Literature.* London: Routledge.

————. 1998. "Rebetika: The Double-Descended Deep Songs of Greece." In *The Passion of Music and Dance: Body, Gender, and Sexuality,* edited by William Washabaugh, 111–26. Oxford: Berg.

————. Forthcoming. "From Gazel to Amanes: The Nationalizing of the Amanes." In *Proceedings of the 1998 Conference "The Influence of Asia Minor Hellenism on the Development of Modern Greek Song,"* edited by Panayiotis Kounadis.

Kazantzakis, Nikos. 1965. *Taxidhevontas: Italia, Aigiptos, Sina, Ierousalim, Kipros, o Morias* (Traveling: Italy, Egypt, China, Jerusalem, Cyprus, the Peloponnese). Athens: Eleni Kazantzakis.

Kounadis, Panayiotis. 1981. "To Smyrneiko Minore." *Mousiki* 48:33–39.

————. 1988. *Anestis Delias, 1912–1944.* LP cover notes. Athens: Falireas Brothers.

Kounadis, Panayiotis, and Spyros Papaioannou. 1981. "I Diskografia tou rebetikou sti Smyrni-Poli prin apo to 1922." *Mousiki* 41:28–34, 42:24–27, 43:20–22, 44:20–25.

Kounadis, Panayiotis, Spyros Papaioannou, and Panayiotis Sotiropoulos. 1982. *Vangelis Papazoglou.* Cover notes for LP. Athens: Falireas Brothers.

Papadimitriou, Sakis. 1975. "Rebetika and Blues." In *Rebetika: Songs from the Old Greek Underworld,* edited by Katharine Butterworth and Sara Schneider, 34–37. New York: Komboloi.

Peristiany, John G. 1966. "Honor and Shame in a Cypriot Highland Village." In *Honour and Shame: The Values of Mediterranean Society,* edited by John G. Peristiany, 171–90. Chicago: University of Chicago Press.

Petropoulos, Ilias. 1968. *Rebetika traghoudia.* Athens.

———. 1971. *Kaliarda.* Athens: Digamma.

Phaidros, Yorgos. 1881. *Pragmateia peri tou Smyrneikou mane i tou par'arhaious manero* (Treatise on the Smyrneic manes known to the ancients as maneros). Smyrna.

Pitt-Rivers, Julian. 1961. *The People of the Sierra.* Chicago: University of Chicago Press.

Schwartz, Martin. 1991. *Greek Oriental Rebetika: Songs and Dances in the Asia Minor Styles. The Golden Years: 1911–1937.* Booklet accompanying CD. El Cerrito, Calif.: Arhoolie-Folklyric.

Seigel, Jerrold. 1986. *Bohemian Paris: Culture, Politics, and the Boundaries of Bourgeois Life, 1820–1930.* New York: Viking.

Shand, Angela. 1998. "The Tsifteteli Sermon: Identity, Theology, and Gender in Rebetika." In *The Passion of Music and Dance: Body, Gender, and Sexuality,* edited by William Washabaugh, 127–32. Oxford: Berg.

Seremetakis, Nadia. 1991. *The Last Word: Women, Death, and Divination in Inner Mani.* Chicago: University of Chicago Press.

Steingress, Gerhard. 1998. "Social Theory and the Comparative History of Flamenco, Tango, and Rebetika." In *The Passion of Music and Dance: Body, Gender, and Sexuality,* edited by William Washabaugh, 151–71. Oxford: Berg.

Taktsis, Kostas. 1977. "Zeibekiko, 1964: Ena Dokimio." In *Dromos yia to rebetiko,* edited by Gail Holst, 202–9. Athens: Denise Harvey.

Tobin, Jeffrey. 1998. "Tango and the Scandal of Homosexual Desire." In *The Passion of Music and Dance: Body, Gender, and Sexuality,* edited by William Washabaugh, 79–102. Oxford: Berg.

Tsitsanis, Vassilis. 1979. *H zoi mou, to ergo mou* (My life, my work). An autobiography as told to Kostas Hadzidoulis. Athens: Nefeli.

Vamvakaris, Markos. 1978. *Aftoviografia* (Autobiography). Edited by Angeliki Kail. Athens: Papazisi.

Van Dyck, Karen. 1998. *Cassandra and the Censors: Greek Poetry Since 1967.* Ithaca, N.Y.: Cornell University Press.

Washabaugh, William, ed. 1998. *The Passion of Music and Dance: Body, Gender, and Sexuality.* Oxford: Berg.

7

Archivists of Memory: Written Folksong Collections of Twentieth-Century Sephardi Women

Edwin Seroussi

In a previous study (Seroussi 1998), I tackled the peculiar circumstances of the survival of the "secular" Judeo-Spanish folksong among Sephardi Jewish women within the framework of a traditional, religious society. Strategies to preserve these songs of mundane content and feminine concern were the subject of that early incursion into gender relations within a Jewish musical tradition.

Gender-oriented studies in Judaic studies, in the sense of observing the role of women in Jewish societies, have proliferated since the late 1980s (e.g., Sacks 1989, 1995), especially studies concerned with the religious sphere of Jewish women's life (e.g., Sered 1995, 1996; Weissler 1995). In this venue of inquiry, the presence or absence of women's voices in the synagogue, already being discussed in the nineteenth century (see Jacobs 1855), has been one of the few musically related subjects treated in the literature (e.g., Grossman and Haut 1992; Heskes 1992; Koskoff 1987a; Schreiber 1984–85). While ethnomusicology has offered in recent years several models for the study of gender in music cultures of the world (Koskoff 1987b; Robertson 1987;

Tolbert 1990), studies of Jewish music have been in general resistant to it, uncritically accepting a paradigmatic dichotomy between the musical spheres of men and women (for a critique, see Lamphere 1993). Such a dichotomy, rooted on the female segregation imposed by religious Jewish law (*halakhah*) is reflected in their separate repertoires, spaces, and social contexts of musical performance (Shiloah 1992, 178–80). Moreover, studies of Jewish music rarely mention the major role of professional Jewish women singers in several Muslim countries during the early twentieth century, Lila Sfax and Habiba Msika in Tunisia, for example (cf. Jones 1987, 73–74).

In light of data from recent ethnographies of Jewish music traditions carried out in Israel and elsewhere in the past three decades, a revision of such a strict binary model is an imperative. Thus, Loeb reports of the remote Jewish community of Habban in eastern Yemen: "It was religiously inappropriate for men to hear or observe women's song and dance. This attitude reinforced gender segregation at festive events such as weddings and circumcisions. But despite claims to strict observance, I found little evidence to support the notion that people closely adhered to this norm in practice" (Loeb 1996, 264).

Illiteracy is one of the stereotypes frequently associated with women in traditional Jewish societies. This perception is part of a common view in the literature that links literacy with men and illiteracy with women. However, the very concept of literacy in this model can be contested. Most Jewish men were indeed trained, since their early childhood, in the reading of prayer books and the Torah (Pentateuch), but much of that reading was of a mechanical, performative nature. Men relied heavily, as women did, on the intelligentsia of the community, the rabbis and scholars, for the reading and perusal of most other sacred texts. Moreover, writing was not as widespread among Jewish men as reading.

Clearly, the validity of this stereotyped view is limited on historical grounds too. Throughout Jewish history before the period of emancipation in Europe during the eighteenth century, which in Jewish historiography marks the "official" beginning of widespread literacy among Jewish men and women, one finds several exceptions to the schematic representation of Jewish women as illiterate. In medieval Spain (Cohen 1980), sixteenth-century Italy (Harrán 1996), seventeenth-century Germany (Bortniker 1972, 414–15), and eighteenth-century Morocco (Chetrit 1980, 1993), one finds women who were instructed in both reading and writing. Some Jewish women even taught sacred texts and wrote sacred poetry. Although these cases are, to be sure, remarkable exceptions, their very existence calls for a more cautious approach.

The proficiency of women in the Sephardi and oriental communities in reading and writing is inevitably linked to the deep processes of social change affecting these communities since the second half of the nineteenth century. An important role in the access of women to formal secular education was the establishment of the vocational schools belonging to the French-based Alliance Israélite Universelle movement in the Jewish communities of North Africa and the Middle East (Rodrigue 1993). The first Alliance school opened in Tetuán, Morocco, in 1862. A primary objective of the leaders and teachers of these schools was to eradicate the old custom of child marriages by keeping the girls in school as long as possible, and to provide them skills that would enable them both to challenge and to improve their traditional role as housekeepers and as mothers of very large families (Laskier 1983, 118ff.).

One consequence of this access of women to writing skills was its application to the collection of folksong texts. This is a rather neglected subject, because the collection of Sephardi folksongs collected mostly from Sephardi women is almost exclusively associated with Sephardi and Spanish scholars (all of them men), for example, Abraham Danon (1896), Manuel Manrique de Lara (Katz 1979), Alberto Hemsi (1995), Leon Algazi (1959), Isaac Levy (1959–73), Moshe Attias (1956, 1972), and many others. Their scholarly interests motivated most of their collections, published during their lives or posthumously. These interests derived from ideological motivations to "museonize" the musical tradition, keeping it as a museum piece, removed from any specific social context; to substantiate historical theses, for example, of the antiquity of the Sephardi folksong tradition; and to promote the interests of the Sephardi patrimony vis-à-vis the cultural capitals of other Jewish traditions.

Writing was recruited by twentieth-century Sephardi women to supplement oral tradition. In contrast to the scholarly and patrimonial concerns that drove men to collect these song traditions, the intentions of the women collectors were twofold: one may be defined as functional, to assist memory, while the second can be described as archival, to preserve the songs for future generations of women singers. This second intention is rooted, in my opinion, in a new social reality in which members of an older generation of transmitters were doubtful that their heirs would invest in the preservation of the cultural capital that in their eyes ensured the identity of their group.

This chapter therefore documents a modern strategy of Sephardi women to preserve their traditional lore within new social circumstances, that is, their codification of folksong texts previously transmitted orally (see, e.g., Weich-Shahak 1984, 1989, 1992, 1997, 1998). Judith Cohen, who has treated extensively the diverse roles of women in the transmission and performance of folksongs in the Sephardi realm, was among the first scholars to notice the phenomenon of the notebooks: "The idea that women are illiterate or disinterested in the written word is belied by the notebooks treasured by many Judeo-Spanish families, full of long ballad texts painstakingly copied out by their mothers, aunts and grandmothers" (1995, 191–92; see also Cohen 1997, 1998).

These manuscript notebooks are a rather neglected chapter in the study of the transmission of the Sephardi, and, as far as I know, of all Jewish song. A notable exception from the eastern Jewish world is the song notebooks of the Jewish women from Kerala in India. These women had access to systematic education since at least the nineteenth century and probably even before. Their notebooks preserve folksongs in Malayalam, the language of Kerala, and have been studied only recently (Johnson 2000).

We shall focus here on the archival aspect of the notebooks written by Sephardi women. Three issues arise from our discussion. The first concerns the relation of this phenomenon with the specific historical and social contexts that followed the introduction of secular education of European content to the Spanish-speaking Jewish communities of north Morocco in the second half of the nineteenth century (especially Tangier and Tetuán). Unlike their sisters from north Morocco, Sephardi women from the former Ottoman Empire (Turkey, Greece, Bulgaria, the island of Rhodes, Palestine, and so on) perpetuated older patterns in the transmission of their folksongs and had access to writing only later on. Second, the archivists are not always folk singers themselves, although they are clearly aware of the "value" of the tradition and have easy access to family members or neighbors who are singers. Third, some of these individual "archival" projects represent a major tool for modern scholarship.

A unique case of a Sephardi woman archivist in the early twentieth century reflects the extent of the exposure of Sephardi women from north Morocco to modern higher education. Zarita Nahón was a graduate student of Romance philology at Columbia University in the 1920s. In 1929, her teacher, the anthropologist Franz Boas, urged her to document her tradition of Judeo-Spanish *romances* (ballads). After consulting with the dean of *romancero* research in Madrid, Don Ramón Menéndez Pidal, she returned home in order to collect the folksongs of Tangier (Nahón 1977, [7]). Her familiarity with female society in Tangier was instrumental in her ethnographic endeavor: "As a member of the same Jewish community, Miss Nahón was able to avail herself of friendship and family ties to approach the best female singers of that period" (22).[1] Her manuscript collection was published in 1977, about half a century after its compilation.

Other unpublished manuscript collections by women from the Jewish community of Tetuán are known in the scholarly literature (probably many were lost or are still forgotten in the closets of Sephardi families throughout the world!). One is the comprehensive collection of Luna Benaim de Boaknín (1870–1959), gathered between 1919 and 1950. It is now located at the Departamento de Estudios Sefardíes of the Instituto de Filología, Consejo Superior de Investigaciones Científicas, in Madrid. Mrs. Perla Boaknín de Benitah, Luna Benaim's daughter, gave another version of her mother's compilation to Dr. Oro Anahory-Librowicz in 1986. In 1988, Anahory-Librowicz published the romances included in this manuscript, which includes texts written in no less than eight different hands. The daughter of Mrs. Benaim tells how this manuscript was compiled: "My mother would sing them to us, and we would write them down. We were always with the family. As you know, winter evenings in Tetuán were long and sad. We would hear all the Ramadan melodies, and that would be greatly impressive as we were little. To make us forget all that, my mother would then tell us—Come on, let's go singing" (Anahory-Librowicz 1988, 42).[2] Analysis reveals that several texts in this manuscript were copied from printed sources, a phenomenon found in many notebooks of this kind, as we shall see. Pondering the goal of Mrs. Benaim's collection, Anahory-Librowicz says that "maybe she also wanted to transmit the traditional songs to her children in a period in which their popularity was in decline. This, however, is less evident, in view of the great number of modern commercial and peninsular songs" (44).[3]

A second manuscript found and published by Anahory-Librowicz (1982, 1988) is the small Esther Benchimol notebook kept by M. José Benchimol of Tetuán. The circumstances of this compilation are extremely interesting, for they show the correlation between social changes and the transmission of traditional songs among the Jews in north Morocco:

> It contains twenty-three *romances* and six modern songs, carefully transcribed by her students at the instigation of their teacher, Mrs. Esther Benchimol de Benezri (1901–1986). . . . Mrs. Benchimol taught Spanish at the Alliance Israélite Universelle school in her native city. She must have appreciated the beauty of traditional poetry in a period in which this was not yet developed. She also asked some of her young primary school students to collect and transcribe old Sephardi songs next to their mothers and grandmothers. (Anahory-Librowicz 1988, 108)[4]

One can see from this report that the transcription of songs developed as a response to the loss of prestige of traditional Jewish culture in Tetuán. The efforts of Jewish educators to recover such prestige in the face of the fast advances of modern French and Spanish cultures led to "heritage" projects such as the one carried out by Mrs. Benchimol.

Several manuscripts, including notebooks and loose handwritten folios, are found at the Jacob Michael Collection of Jewish Music, in the Jewish National and University Library in Jerusalem (JMB 2336), all brought by my colleague Dr. Susana Weich-Shahak of the Jewish Music Research Centre during her extensive fieldwork among Sephardi Jews in Israel. Among these materials, the most impressive is the notebook by Azibuena Barujel (n.d.) that was prepared, as stated on its title page, as a present for the her daughters. This peculiar collection, dating probably from the 1960s, is a compilation of songs, the majority of which are ballads, copied from printed sources, especially from Arcadio de Larrea Palacín's well-known collection of romances from Tetuán (Larrea Palacín 1952). The novelty of this manuscript is not, then, in its content, but rather on the phenomenon it represents. This collection, which also includes modern Spanish and French songs, is actually a recycling of mediated, scholarly sources that are used as a source of "tradition."[5]

A Contemporary Sephardi Song Archivist

To the story and work of Emily Sene, a major Sephardi female archivist of folksongs, the rest of this chapter is dedicated. My acquaintance with Emily is typical of the contemporary global network of Sephardi song "fans," in which research, mere curiosity, and performance intermingle. In 1995, Nikos Tzannis, a musician from Saloniki with whom I collaborated in the preparation of a commercial CD, handed me a poor photocopy of a partial notebook of Sephardi songs written in Latin characters. Nikos had long been interested in the preservation and modern performance and recording of Sephardi music, but he could not provide me with any information about this source or about its origin. However, the title page included a seal with a name and an address: "Emily & Isaac Sene, 3718 W 173 St., Torrance, California." The title page also indicated that the songs had been collected between 1955 and 1979.

During my sabbatical at UCLA in the academic year 1998–99, I tried to locate the Senes in the Los Angeles area. Assuming that the individuals involved in the preparation of this manuscript were already of advanced age in 1979 (when, according to its title page, the collection was sealed), I was rather skeptical of my chances. However, a quick search in the electronic directory of Los Angeles showed that my doubts were unfounded: the address of Isaac and Emily Sene was still registered with the current telephone number. I called immediately and the voice of an old lady with a strong foreign accent quickly responded: it was the voice of Emily Sene, eighty-nine years old. Emily could not believe my story about the copy of her notebook in my hands: "I never gave this collection to anybody," she said, and besides, why should "a young person from Israel" be interested "in this stuff." We set up, after some negotiations (for security reasons, citizens in Los Angeles do not readily invite strangers to their homes), an appointment at her house in Torrance. This first meeting led to two interviews, to the photocopying of her complete manuscript, and eventually, to the transfer of her collection of reel-to-reel tapes (stored in suitcases in her garage, on the verge of being disposed of by her family!) to the Ethnomusicology Archive at UCLA.[6]

My interest in Emily's work is not, of course, circumscribed by her collection of songs, but looks to broader concerns, such as the meaning of the collection in the framework of modern Sephardi culture. Emily's story is quite unlike that of other archivists of Sephardi memory, scholars and amateurs alike. This uniqueness is clearly reflected both in the format and in the content of her precious collection.

Emily was born in Edirne, Trakia (at the crossroads of Turkey, Greece, and Bulgaria), in 1911. Her family left Edirne for Istanbul at the outset of World War I. As many Turkish Jews did, Emily and her family eventually abandoned the hardships of the young Republic of Turkey and moved to Havana, Cuba, in 1925. Cuba was one of the Latin American safe havens for Sephardi immigrants, especially after a drastic cutback on the number of visas to the United States in 1924. Certainly the language factor was also an incentive for the Spanish-speaking Sephardi Jews to settle in Latin American countries.

Fourteen-year-old Emily was a good dancer. She was, in her words, "light" and therefore coached young Sephardi Jews in Cuba toward their appearance in the monthly dance meeting in the Jewish social club, an event that was intended to promote Jewish identity and to avoid mixed marriages. The dances were set to the music of commercial records, including records of Cuban music.

Isaac Sene, Emily's future husband and her main source of information on the Sephardi song, was a gifted ʿud player and singer who attended these dance parties in Havana. He met Emily through his brother, Salvador, who arrived in Cuba on the same boat as Emily. She "picked up" Isaac because he was extremely shy, and she liked this aspect of his character. After two or three dance parties, he asked her to marry him. However, soon afterward, Isaac succeeded in leaving Cuba and entering the United States. He lived with Emily's brothers, who were already there, and began the process to bring

Emily over as well, despite the opposition of her future mother-in-law to their intended match. In 1928, Emily finally received her U.S. immigration papers, and in the same year she married Isaac in New York. They settled on Orchard Street, on the Lower East Side, where they lived in utmost poverty. Despite their situation, Isaac refused to take money for playing music and singing for Turkish, Arabic, and Greek audiences. In 1942, the Senes left New York and moved to Los Angeles looking for a better life. In Los Angeles their economic and social situation improved vastly. In later years, however, Isaac's health began to deteriorate slowly. He died in 1989 at the age of eighty-four.

The Collection Project: Motivations, Techniques, and Responses

Emily bought her first tape recorder in the mid-1950s in order to preserve the Sephardi songs she loved so much. She too suffered poor health, and the idea of collecting grew first from her desire to keep herself occupied: "I was all the day at home very sick. My husband did not let me do anything in the house. I said to myself, I do not want to be handicapped and I liked the songs very much and I started to do this [collecting the songs]." There were two stages in the recording process. The first stage included the rerecording of old commercial 78-rpm records, particularly those by the Sephardi singer Haim Effendi. Owing to her interest in these records, Emily became well known in Los Angeles and in Miami among Sephardi Jews from Turkey who had old records at their homes: "Yo las tomava de casa en casa. Todos los turkinos que tenian me las dieron a mi" [I used to collect (records) from house to house. All the Turks that had (records) gave them to me]. She recalled many of her donors, whose names she had taken care to write on the cases of the tapes: Ashkenazi from Miami, Alazraki from Miami, Dr. Benvenisti, Lili Kapuya, Jeanny Begenchi, Elisa Halfon, Sarina Hasson, Nissim Baralia, Sam Maya, Marco Levy, and her own sister, Jeannie Peres.

The second stage of Emily's collection included the field recording of her husband's songs because "she liked them." The urgency of this task was became apparent as Isaac's health started to fail. Isaac did not want Emily to record him, so she used to hide the tape recorder under the table. When I arrived once at Emily's house, she was listening, as she frequently did, to her late husband's voice on a very poor-quality cassette tape. Listening to Isaac's voice was her way to keep his memory alive.

Emily became an archivist perhaps in part to compensate for her own inability to sing. She testifies that she was a "lousy" singer, although she knew all the lyrics of the songs by heart. The neatness and accuracy of her collection shows an unusually "scholarly" approach by a nonscholar. For example, she designed her own thesaurus in order to keep standard spellings throughout the collection. She also recorded some comments pertaining to the instrumental sections of the songs, such as *taxim* (instrumental interlude in free rhythm, cf. song 102); *gazel* (vocalized improvisation, cf. song. 102); *muzik* (instrumental interlude; cf. songs 106, 107, 108, etc.); and *meam* (the Turkish musical term *meyan,* the middle section of a composition, apparently employed here with a meaning similar to *muzik,* cf. songs 46, 47, etc.).

Emily's awareness of the importance of her collection was also reflected in her care in the process of notation. She transcribed from her reel-to-reel tapes and was "copying day and night." She had problems transcribing the songs because the quality of the 78-rpm recordings was poor, their copies were even worse, and the manner of singing of Haim Effendi, the main source of the songs, was hard to decipher. Once she spent "several nights transcribing the song 'Ocho y ocho dieciseis' by Haim Effendi." Whenever she had difficulties deciphering a text, she used to consult with Sephardi singers and song consumers in Los Angeles and Miami. As she puts it: "In Redondo Beach [where the Turkish Jews met to sing] I used to go from person to person and ask: 'Do you know this song?'"

Emily's manuscript collection, well hidden in a closet between her sheets and blankets, reflects the story of her and her husband's life in Turkey, Cuba, and the United States. It is a systematic compilation of a very specific Sephardi song repertoire defined by the interests and tastes of a particular generation of Sephardi Jews . For this reason, the Sene collection is dominated by songs that differ from the "traditional" ones found in the works of scholars. This is a new repertoire that was dictated by the commercial discography of the Sephardi song, which set up the agenda for performers like Isaac Sene. He sung mostly the popular songs of Haim Effendi, not the old Sephardi folksongs, such as the romances. In turn, a "taste public" that demanded modern musical styles and new literary contexts also dictated the content of this discography.

Performance Contexts and Venues

In our conversations, Emily mentioned two contexts for performance of the songs she collected and for Isaac's public appearances: life-cycle events (weddings and bar mitzvahs) and *pasatiempos* (pastimes) of the *pareas* (groups) that gathered to sing together in Redondo Beach, as well as in Miami Beach, where Isaac Sene joined his family and performed for senior citizens during summer vacations. The Redondo Beach pasatiempos were held in the open air on Sundays, when one to two hundred Turkish Jews used to meet whenever they heard that Isaac Sene was coming to perform. Capitalizing on the success of this social activity, Emily organized a formal club in Ladera Park in Redondo Beach, in a space "provided by the government." In these gatherings they sang *canticas* (songs) in Judeo-Spanish, Greek, Turkish, French, and Arabic (see Weich-Shahak 1984, 30–32, and 1997, 17ff., for a similar phenomenon in Israel).

Emily remembered some of the musicians who participated in the Redondo Beach pasatiempos or played with Isaac at weddings and bar mitzvahs. Not all of them were Jewish, a clear reminder of the multicultural Ottoman Empire. Although Emily struggled a bit to recall exact names, she mentioned among the musicians who joined Isaac Sene, Tio Selam/Selomo, who studied violin with Isaac; Nahman/Nathan/Nat Samarel, a Jewish 'ud player from Turkey who lived in Las Vegas; Hayk, a renowned Armenian violinist (Emily recalled that in weddings "the Armenian took money, but Isaac asked all the money to be given to the Sephardi community"); Andreas, a great Greek player of European flute; Garbiz, a very famous Armenian 'ud player from Los Angeles and New York; Sara Palti, a Turkish Jewish singer, who according to Emily was "still alive in the Home of the Elderly in New York"; and Bat Sheva, another good singer from New York.

Repertoire

Emily transcribed 159 songs, numbering all but the last two.[7] Two of the songs appear twice; therefore there are 157 titles in the collection. All the songs except one are in Judeo-Spanish or in modern Spanish with traces of Judeo-Spanish pronunciation. The exception is song 153, the Hebrew religious hymn "Mehulal shem Adonay," which also appears in Judeo-Spanish translation; song 95 is a Judeo-Spanish version of the Hebrew prayer "Avinu malkenu," (Our Father, Our King). The repertoire relies heavily, as is clear from Emily's comments above, on the rich discographical output of the famous Sephardi singer Haim Effendi. Emily's exposure to Effendi started at her mother's home in Istanbul, where she first heard his records . According to Emily, Effendi was a great *cantador* (singer) who used to "go all over the Sephardi diaspora, including Cuba."[8] Effendi was the most recorded Sephardi singer before World War II. He recorded scores of songs for two different labels in Turkey: Orfeon/Orfeos and Odeon. His earliest recording dates back to 1907.[9] Effendi's repertoire included, besides Judeo-Spanish folk and popular songs, Jewish liturgical music and Turkish songs. His extensive repertoire of Judeo-Spanish songs, many of which were composed in the early twentieth century (some are attributed to him), had the greatest impact among the Sephardi masses during the first three decades of the twentieth century. Many songs by Effendi remained in the memory of Sephardi informants interviewed from the 1950s on. When modern research on the Sephardi folksong was launched in the 1950s by collectors like Isaac Levy, the songs by Effendi, delivered orally, where already part of the "tradition" (Seroussi 1995).

A second layer of the repertoire collected by Emily comprises songs by Sephardi singers from the former Ottoman Empire who established themselves and recorded in the United States: Jack Mayesh from Los Angeles, Victoria Hazan from New York, and Isaac Angel. Isaac Sene accompanied or had contacts with all these singers. According to Emily, Isaac met Victoria Hazan in Miami and used to accompany her there.

Many of the songs by all these Sephardi artists are actually Judeo-Spanish cover versions of popular Turkish songs composed in the first three decades of the twentieth century. Mayesh, for example, adopted Judeo-Spanish lyrics to Turkish tunes in songs such as "Missirlu," "Un día yo bezí," and others (Sene collection, songs, 53ff.). "Seda amarilla" and other songs (nos. 49–51) performed and recorded by Victoria Hazan and Isaac Angel are also covers of Turkish songs. Isaac Sene also "turned Turkish songs into Spanish." Emily remembered one titled "Eyer karalik."

The Sene collection is also remarkable for what it does not include. This repertoire clearly shows the difference in the agendas of scholars and the Sephardi people, a phenomenon noticed by Hassán (1987) in relation to the modern Sephardi folksongs in north Morocco. Notably, Emily's compilation includes hardly any romances, the Sephardi ballads of medieval Iberian origin that have so preoccupied modern scholarship on the Judeo-Spanish folksong. Among the few romances in the Sene collection there is a fairly complete version of "Delgadina" (no. 159). Another traditional song in the Sene collection is number 144, "O! ke mueve mezes" (Oh! These Nine Months), a *copla de parida,* or song for the mother of a newborn son.

The Sene collection includes modern popular Western songs, such as the famous Cuban song "Guajira Guantanamera" by José Fernández Díaz (no. 123) and the Mexican bolero "Cuando calienta el sol" by Carlos and Mario Fausto Rigual (no. 148), that reflect the most recent experience of Sephardi Jews in Latin American and in the United States. Emily Sene was aware of the disparate sources of her collection, ranging from the popular Moroccan-Israeli singer Jo Amar (who lived for a long time in the States) to the Andalusian singer Antonio Molina.

Many of the modern songs in the Sene collection are original and were recorded by Emily very close both in place and time to their composition. These songs reflect current social and political events and are evidence that the folk literature of the Sephardi Jews did not, as it is sometimes assumed, cease to renew itself.

Sometimes the novelty consists of the addition of new stanzas to older songs, such as song 111, which is very well documented in Saloniki. This song consists of independent mocking stanzas, one of which was obviously composed on New York City's Lower East Side, where the Senes lived throughout the 1930s:

Ke telo estas continiendo barminam.	[What are you pretending, barminam,
sos hija de un pushcarchi.	You are the daughter of a peddler.
Tu papa vende bananas aman aman	Your father sells bananas, aman, aman,
enla coner de Orchard Street.	In the corner of Orchard Street.] [10]

Emily also collected a song (no. 138) "compozada por madam Esther Cohen . . . ala melodi de eli eli" [composed by Madame Esther Cohen . . . to the melody of "Eli eli"]. This refers to the Israeli song "Halikha le-Qesaria" by Hana Senesh, music by David Zehavi. The new text by Madam Cohen is a reaction to the Holocaust: "God of heaven, watch your creatures, miserable and weeping, watch Hitler taking revenge, provide us freedom, give us a place to rest in peace." Song 139, by an anonymous author, has a strongly Zionist tone and celebrates the establishment of the State of Israel: "Let us rise the flag [of Israel] and have no other one, in the streets we shall dance, a government we have." It is properly set "ala melodi de color baleva" [to the melody of Kol 'od ba-levav], the opening words of "Hatiqvah," the Israeli anthem. One of the latest songs added to the collection treats the victory of Israel in the Six-Day War in June of 1967 (no. 143). It is set to the melody of "Nunca en Domingo" the popular theme song of the movie "Never on Sunday," by the Greek composer Manos Hadjidakis. [11]

Gender Roles in the New Sephardi Song

The repertoire collected by Emily thus reflects what can be tentatively called the "new Sephardi song." Professional Sephardi artists performed these songs at the beginning of the twentieth century with the instrumental accompaniment of Jewish and non-Jewish musicians. The contexts of their performance were the cafés and the theaters, and their songs were distributed via commercial records. The models of the songs are varied: on the one hand, there is the Turkish *şarki* and other songs in the styles affecting Turkish popular music of the period, such as the tango (see Seroussi 1990; Weich-Shahak 1995), and on the other, Judeo-Spanish versions of popular songs from France and Spain. The Sene collection includes songs from even more modern periods. These newer songs reflect the experiences of the Turkish Jews in the United States in the twentieth century, including their reactions to the dramatic events that stirred their deepest emotions: the Holocaust and the establishment of a Jewish state.

The new Sephardi song expresses the concerns of a secularized society in transition. The feminine figure appears in these songs in a new light compared with her role in traditional Sephardi society. An open discourse about all aspects of love and love relations, including explicit language about sexual relations, is found in many of these songs. The indifference and sometimes cruelty of the beloved woman toward her lover is also evident in many texts, even though in many others the woman still appears as dependent on the man's behavior. Women are thus empowered; they are no longer the object of male decisions but rather the unattained goal of their desires. Men still have the initiative in love relations, but they are desperately dependent on the responses of women.

Another theme explored in the songs is the willingness of Jewish women to enter into relations with non-Jewish men, a taboo in traditional society. Intermarriage, for example, is the subject matter of song 126, in which a Jewish woman falls in love with a Turk and flatly states: "Yo keriya ser turkita" [I wanted to be a little Turkish woman]. Sometimes, the initiative in such sexual encounters comes from a non-Jewish man. Thus, in song 96, a Turk abducts his Jewish sweetheart, who eventually chooses to remain faithful to her ancestry.

Song 66, quoted below, considers the seductiveness of female Jewish musicians in the person of a singer and ʿud player called Fortuna who started to appear in cafés in Saloniki and Istanbul at the beginning of the twentieth century. This song was published by Attias (1972, no. 48) and Levy (1973, no. 97, in a version from Sofia, Bulgaria) in shorter and less uniform versions. This fact points to the potential of the Sene collection as a reliable source for the research of the modern Sephardi song.

Primavera en Selanik	[Spring in Saloniki;
en el baile de amazili	In the dancing hall of amazili [12]

Aya avia una ija de ojos pretos	There was a lady of dark eyes
ke cantava y sona el udt.	Who sung and played the ud.
El udt tomas en la mano	You take the ud in your hand
con la grasia y la jilve [Turk.	Gently and with grace.
ğilve].	
Vas cantando vas baylando	You are singing, you are dancing
canticas de Arabistan.	Arabic songs.
Ah, no veas ke esto cantando	Oh, shall my singing not impress
	you
es ke kero yorar.	Because I want to cry.
Ya de bueno ya de negro	For good or for worse
mi ora kero pasar.	I want to pass my time.
Ah, un cuchiyo de dos cortes	Oh, a double-edged knife
en mi corasson entro,	In my heart has entered,
por una hija de hojos pretos	For a lady of dark eyes
ke tania sonava el udt.	That played and played the ud.
Ke no mankes tu Fortuna	You should not, Fortuna, be
	absent
del caffe del amali.	From the café of amali[13]
Kitas ansias de mansevos	You appease young men's anxiety
cuando cantas, sonas el udt.	When you sing and play the ud.]

A thorough inventory and full linguistic, literary, musical, and social appreciation of Emily Sene's collection is of course still due. However, even at this early stage, one can draw some tentative conclusions. First, Emily preserved a song repertoire that was meaningful to her life experience and to her social circle of secular Sephardi Jews who emigrated from Turkey to the United States. This repertoire took shape in the last few decades of the Ottoman Empire and continued to grow several decades after the immigration to the States, reflecting the concerns, the social changes, and the political events related to the Sephardi Jewish experience in their new home.

Second, this repertoire shares features with and in many cases has similar musical content as other eastern Mediterranean song traditions that persisted in exile despite major social and cultural transformations, such as the urban music of Greek immigrants in the United States. This shared musical experience represents a survival of the multiethnic tapestry of the Ottoman

Empire. While in post–World War I Turkey, ethnic diversity was being eliminated by Kemalism, in the United States Sephardi Jews and Armenian and
Greek Christians still dialogued through music.

Third, the Sene collection unravels the tendency of modern scholarship
on the Sephardi song to focus on what it considered as historically prestigious, authentic, and of aesthetic value. Paradoxically, the emphasis of scholarship on the medieval romances, the coplas, and the traditional lyric songs
dictated the agenda of the revival of the Sephardi song in the post–War II period as a mediated genre. Professional revivalist performers had access to the
printed song anthologies edited by male scholars, rather than to the handwritten notebooks written by women singers and song lovers. With very few
exceptions, the "new Sephardi song" of the interwar period, which the Sene
collection truly reflects, disappeared. Only the visionary work of a Sephardi
scholar such as Moshe Attias (1972), and to a certain extent of another Sephardi collector, Isaac Levy (1959–73), preserved some of these popular materials. All in all, the very rare 78-rpms remained the only witnesses of the
ephemeral flourishing of authentic popular Sephardi songs and of the modern transformations of some traditional songs (see Armistead, Katz, and Silverman 1981).

Emily Sene's archival work is thus a monument to this vanished voice of
Sephardi culture. The crucial role of women as transmitters of the Sephardi
song in the radically new social contexts of the twentieth century is once
again revealed. Emily's documentation differs, of course, from that of the
scholarly community in its purpose, content, and form. In spite of the "in-
accuracies" in linguistic consistency, phonetic transcription, and presentation of poetic forms found all over her collection, Emily succeeded in presenting to us one of the most unique and comprehensive documents of the
Sephardi song. Conceived and realized by a Sephardi woman without any institutional support or scientific background, this document will certainly allow us to draw a more balanced narrative of the Sephardi song in the twentieth century.

Notes

I would like to thank Dr. Judith Cohen of York University in Toronto for reading an early
draft of this chapter and for making many useful remarks. Throughout this chapter, unless
noted otherwise, translations from non-English sources are my own.

1. Como miembro de la misma comunidad hebrea, la Srta. Nahón supo valerse de amistades y lazos familiares para aproximarse a las mejores cantadoras de aquella época.

2. Ma mère nous les chantait et nous les écrivions. Nous étions toujours en famille. Comme tu sais, à Tétouan, les soirées d'hiver étaient longues et tristes. Nous écoutions toutes les mélodies du Ramadan et ça nous impressionnait beaucoup, parce que nous étions petites. Alors, ma mère, pour nous faires oublier tout cela, nous disait:—Allez, nous allons chanter.

3. [P]eut-être voulait elle aussi transmettre les chansons traditionelles à ses enfants à une epoque où leur popularité déclinait. Mais ceci est moins évident, vu l'abondance de chansons commerciales et péninsulares modernes.

4. Il contient vingt-trois *romances* et six chansons modernes, soigneusement trans-cris par des écolièrs, à l'instigation de leur institutrice, Mme Esther Benchimol de Benezri (1901–1986). . . . Mme Benchimol enseignait l'espagnol à l'école de l'Alliance Israélite Universelle de sa ville natale. Elle a dû apprécier la beauté de la poèsie traditionelle à une époque où celle-ci n'était pas encore valorisée. Aussi a-t-elle demandé à quelques-unes de ses jeunes élèves de l'école primaire de recueillir et de transcrire auprès de leurs mère et grand-mère de vieilles chansons séphardies.

5. Judith Cohen informs me that she too has in her possession two written docu-ments of songs compiled by Sephardi women.

6. Most of the information provided here derives from an interview on 14 April 1999, at Emily's home. I am grateful to the UCLA Archive of Ethnomusicology and to its curator, Louise Spear, for their collaboration in the handling of this collection. It should be noted that I am not the first scholar to visit the Sene residence. Emily and Isaac were known to Rina Benmayor and a picture of them appears in one of her books (1979). However, as far as I know, Benmayor did not use Emily's written collection in her work.

7. All the songs from the Sene collection quoted in this article preserve Emily's or-thography even at its most awkward. I have numbered the last two songs in the collection 158 and 159.

8. Cf. song 158, "Cuando salí de la Havana"; however, the appearance of Effendi in Cuba is, in my opinion, dubious.

9. Most of the information concerning the early Sephardi discography, especially the recordings by Haim Efendi, is based on the comprehensive discography being compiled by Joel Bresler (forthcoming). I am thankful to Mr. Bresler for sharing with me his valuable contribution to this rather unexplored area of Sephardi music studies. On the old Sephardi discography, see also Armistead, Katz, and Silverman 1981.

10. The Sene version opens "Una hija bova tengo barminam"; however, a more com-mon opening line is "Asi biva Ḥam Liache, bar minan" (cf. Attias 1972, no. 130). Notice the introduction to Judeo-Spanish of words of English origin: "pushcarchi" (English "push-cart" with Turkish suffix çi) and "enla coner," that is, "in the corner" (fem. form, as in Judeo-Spanish).

11. For the Judeo-Spanish version, see song 152; for another song on the Six Day War, see 119, set to the melody of the Israeli folksong "Tzena, tzena."

12. "The dancing hall of amazili" refers to Mazlum, a Jewish café in Saloniki.

13. As in the first stanza, this refers to the café Mazlum.

References

Algazi, Leon. 1958. *Chants sephardies*. London: World Sephardic Federation.

Armistead, Samuel G., Israel J. Katz, and Joseph H. Silverman. 1981. "La antigua discografía sefardí y el romancero." *La Corónica* 9 (2): 138–44.

Anahory-Librowicz, Oro. 1982. "Un manuscrito de romances sefardíes de Tetuán." *La Corónica* 11:49–51.

———. 1988. *Cancionero séphardi de Québec*. Vol. 1, *Rapport de recherche, 1986–1987*. Montréal: Collége du Vieux Montréal.

Attias, Moshe. 1956. *Romancero sefardí*. Jerusalem: Ben Zvi Institute.

———. 1972. *Cancionero judeo-español*. Jerusalem: Centro de Estudios sobre el Judaísmo de Salónica.

Atzmon, Yael. 1995. "Introduction: Judaism and the Distancing of Women from Public Activity." *A View into the Lives of Women in Jewish Societies*, edited by Yael Atzmon, 13–46 (in Hebrew). Jerusalem: Zalman Shazar Center for Jewish History.

Benmayor, Rina. 1979. *Romances judeo-españoles de oriente: Nueva recolección*. Madrid: Seminario Menéndez Pidal.

Barujel, Azibuena. N.d. "Canciones del Norte de Marruecos: Romances de Tetuán a la santa memoria de la Señora Azibuena Barujel como recuerdo para sus hijas Meriam Esther y Flora Barujel y Rachel Barujel, Tetuán Marruecos." MS., Jewish National and University Library, Music Department, Jacob Michael Collection, JMB 2235.

Baskin, Judith R., ed. 1991. *Jewish Women in Historical Perspective*. Detroit: Wayne State University Press.

Bortniker, Elijah. 1972. "Education: Middle Ages, Sixteenth through Eighteenth Centuries." *Encyclopaedia Judaica* 6, col. 403–20.

Bresler, Joel. Forthcoming. "Discography of Commercial Sephardic 78 R.P.M. Recordings." http://www.sephardicmusic.com/

Chetrit, Joseph. 1980. "Freha bat Yosef—a Hebrew Poetess in Eighteenth-Century Morocco" (in Hebrew). *Pe'amim* 4:84–93.

———. 1993. "Freha bat Rabbi Abraham—More on a Hebrew Poetess in Morocco in the Eighteenth Century" (in Hebrew). *Pe'amim* 55:124–30.

Cohen, Judith. 1980. "Le rôle de la femme-musicienne dans l'Espagne medievale, dans les communautés chretienne, juive, et musulmane." Master's thesis, Université de Montréal.

———. 1995. "Women's Roles in Judeo-Spanish Song Traditions." In *Active Voices: Women in Jewish Culture*, edited by Maurie Sacks, 181–200. Urbana: University of Illinois Press.

———. 1997. "Evolving Roles of Women in Judeo-Spanish Song." In *Hispano-Jewish Civilization after 1492*, edited by Galit Hasan-Rokem and Michel Abitbol, 81–100. Jerusalem: Misgav Yerushalayim.

———. 1998. "Women's Roles in Judeo-Spanish Sephardic Songs." In *From Memory to Transformation: Jewish Women's Voices*, edited by Sara Silberstein Swartz and Margie Wolf, 49–61. Toronto: Second Story Press.

Danon, Abraham. 1896. "Recueil de romances judéo-espangoles chantées en Turquie." *Revue des Etudes Juives* 32:102–23, 263–75; 33:122–39, 255–68.

Grossman, Susan, and Rivka Haut, eds. 1992. *Daughters of the King: Women and the Synagogue.* Philadelphia: Jewish Publication Society.

Harrán, Don. 1996. "Doubly Tainted, Doubly Talented: The Jewish Poet Sara Copio (d. 1614) as a Heroic Singer." In *Musica Franca: Essays in Honour of Frank A. D'Accone,* edited by Irene Alm et al., 367–422. Stuyvesant, N.Y.: Pendragon.

Hassán, Iacob M. 1987. "Última (?) poesía tradicional sefaradí de la zona del Estrecho." Paper delivered at the Congreso Internacional el Estrecho de Gibraltar, 16–19 November 1987, Ceuta.

Hauptman, Judit. 1993. "Women and Prayer: An Attempt to Dispel Some Fallacies." *Judaism* 42:94–103; 387–413 (reactions).

Hemsi, Alberto. 1995. *Cancionero sefardí,* edited by Edwin Seroussi in collaboration with Paloma Diaz-Más, José Manuel Pedrosa, and Elena Romero. Jerusalem: Hebrew University.

Herndon, Marcia. 1990. "Biology and Culture: Music, Gender, Power, and Ambiguity." In *Music, Gender, and Culture,* edited by Marcia Herndon and Susanne Ziegler, 11–26. Wilhelmshaven: Florian Noetzel Verlag.

Herndon, Marcia and Susanne Ziegler, eds. 1990. *Music, Gender and Culture.* Wilhelmshaven: Florian Noetzel Verlag. Special issue of the *World of Music* 33 (2).

Heskes, Irene. 1992. "Miriam's Sisters: Jewish Women and Liturgical Music." *Notes* 48 (4): 1193–202.

Jacobs, S. 1855. "Ladies' Singing in the Synagogue." *The Occident and American Jewish Advocate* 13:445–48, 492–96, 537–42.

Johnson, Barbara C. 2000. "'They Carry Their Notebooks with Them': Women's Vernacular Jewish Songs from Cochin" (in Hebrew). *Pe'amim* 82: 81–93.

Jones, L. JaFran. 1987. "A Sociohistorical Perspective on Tunisian Women as Professional Musicians." In *Women and Music in Cross-Cultural Perspective,* edited by Ellen Koskoff, 69–83. Urbana: University of Illinois Press.

Koskoff, Ellen. 1987a. "The Sound of a Woman's Voice: Gender and Music in a New York Hasidic Community." In *Women and Music in Cross-Cultural Perspective,* edited by Ellen Koskoff, 213–23. Urbana: University of Illinois Press.

———, ed. 1987b. *Women and Music in Cross-Cultural Perspective.* Urbana: University of Illinois Press.

Katz, Israel J. 1979. "Manuel Manrique de Lara and the Tunes of the Moroccan Sephardic Ballad Tradition: Some Insights into a Much-Needed Critical Edition." In *El Romancero hoy, Nuevas fronteras: 2º Coloquio Internacional,* edited by Antonio Sánchez Romeraldo, Diego Catalán, Samuel G. Armistead, et al., 75–87. Madrid: Cátedra Seminario Menéndez Pidal.

Lamphere, Louise. 1993. "The Domestic Sphere of Women and the Public World of Men: The Strengths and Limitations of an Anthropological Dichotomy." In *Gender in Cross-Cultural Perspective,* edited by Caroline B. Brettell and Carolyn F. Sargent, 67–77. Englewood Cliffs, N.J.: Prentice Hall.

Larrea Palacín, Arcadio de. 1952. *Romances de Tetuán.* 2 vols. Madrid: Instituto de Estudios Africanos.

Laskier, Michael M. 1983. *The Alliance Israélite Universelle and the Jewish Communities of Morocco, 1862–1962.* Albany: State University of New York Press.

Levy, Isaac. 1959–73. *Chants judéo-espagnols.* Vol. 1. London: World Sephardi Federation. Vols. 2–4. Jerusalem: The author.

Loeb, Laurence D. 1996. "Gender, Marriage, and Social Conflict in Habban." In *Sephardi and Middle Eastern Jewries,* edited by Harvey Goldberg, 256–76. Bloomington: Indiana University Press.

Nahón, Zarita. 1977. *Romances judeo-españoles de Tánger recogidos por Zarita Nahón.* Critical edition annotated by Samuel G. Armistead and Joseph H. Silverman with Oro Anahory Librowicz, musical transcriptions by Israel J. Katz. Madrid: Cátedra-Seminario Menéndez Pidal.

Robertson, Carol E. 1987. "Power and Gender in the Musical Experiences of Women." In *Women and Music in Cross-Cultural Perspective,* edited by Ellen Koskoff, 225–44. Urbana: University of Illinois Press.

Rodrigue, Aron. 1993. *Images of Sephardi and Eastern Jewries in Transition: The Teachers of the Alliance Israélite Universelle, 1860–1939.* Seattle: University of Washington Press.

Sacks, Maurie. 1989. "Problems in the Study of Jewish Women's Folk Culture." *Contemporary Jewry* 10 (1):95–104.

———, ed. 1995. *Active Voices: Women in Jewish Culture.* Urbana: University of Illinois Press.

Schreiber, Baruch David. 1984–85. "The Woman's Voice in the Synagogue." *Journal of Jewish Music and Liturgy* 7 : 27–32.

Seroussi, Edwin. 1990. "The Growth of the Judeo-Spanish Folksong Repertory in the Twentieth Century." In *Proceedings of the Tenth World Congress of Jewish Studies,* Division D, 2, 173–80. Jerusalem: World Congress of Jewish Studies.

———. 1995. "Reconstructing Sephardi Music in the Twentieth Century: Isaac Levy and his *Chants judeo-espagnols.*" *World of Music* 37 (1):39–58.

———. 1998. "De-gendering Jewish music: The Survival of the Judeo-Spanish Folk Song Revisited." *Music and Anthropology* 3. http//:www.muspe.unibo.it/period/MA/

Sered, Susan Starr. 1995. "Toward an Anthropology of Jewish Women: Sacred Texts and the Religious World of Elderly, Middle-Eastern Women in Jerusalem." In *Active Voices: Women in Jewish Culture,* edited by Maurie Sacks, 203–18. Urbana: University of Illinois Press.

———. 1996. "The Religious World of Jewish Women in Kurdistan." *Jews among Muslims: Communities in the Precolonial Middle-East,* edited by Shlomo Deshen and Walter Zenner, 197–214. New York: New York University Press.

Shiloah, Amnon. 1992. *Jewish Musical Traditions.* Detroit: Wayne State University Press.

Tolbert, Elizabeth. 1990. "Magico-Religious Power and Gender in the Karelian Lament." In *Music, Gender, and Culture,* edited by Marcia Herndon and Susanne Ziegler, 41–56. Wilhelmshaven: Florian Noetzel Verlag.

Weich-Shahak, Susana. 1984. "Mazal-Tov's Repertoire of Songs: Genres in Judeo-Spanish Songs from Turkey and Bulgaria." *Jerusalem Studies in Jewish Folklore* 5/6: 27–56.

———. 1989. *Judeo-Spanish Moroccan Songs for the Life Cycle.* Yuval Music Series 1. Jerusalem: Hebrew University.

————. 1992. *Música y tradiciones sefardíes*. Salamanca: Centro de Cultura Tradicional, Diputación de Salamanca.

————. 1995. "Le tango séfarade." In *Tango nomade,* edited by Ramón Pelinski, 255–69. Montréal: Tryptique.

————. 1997. "The Performance in the Judeo-Spanish Repertoire." *Musical Performance: The Performance of Jewish and Arabic Music in Israel,* edited by Amnon Shiloah, 1:9–26. Amsterdam: Harwood Academic Press.

————. 1998. "Social Functions of the Judeo-Spanish *Romances*." In *Studies in Socio-Musical Sciences,* edited by Joachim Braun and Uri Sharvit, 245–56. Ramat-Gan: Bar-Ilan University Press.

Weissler, Chava. 1995. "Women's Studies and Women's Prayers: Reconstructing the Religious History of Jewish Women." *Jewish Social Studies*, n.s., 1/2: 28–47.

8

Representations and Female Roles in the Raï Song

Marie Virolle

The musical movement called *raï* was born in western Algeria and developed chiefly in the working-class neighborhoods of the cities of Oran, Sidi Bel-Abbès, Ghelizane, Saïda, and Aïn Temouchent. It has existed for nearly a century, and its origin can be located at the junction of three musical and singing practices (Virolle 1988, 177–82): the festive gatherings of nomadic shepherds and distillery workers; leisure meetings in brothels; and urban female verses.[1]

At its outset this musical form was *badawi,* or "Bedouin" style, which uses two rural instruments: the *gellal,* a percussion instrument, and the *gesba,* a flute. The genre evolved into what is currently known as raï, which has been spread globally through the songs of Khaled. This progressive evolution was achieved by the incorporation of urban instruments: initially the violin, then, for example, the accordion, the trumpet, electric instruments, the synthesizer, and the guitar.[2] In addition, raï has drawn on the rhythms and modes of styles as varied as the oriental, Latin American, "Hindu," and Western genres such as rock or, more recently, rap.[3]

Raï was ostracized until the mid-1980s: it was never played on Algerian radio or on television and no public concert was ever staged. It was thus a marginal music, born and living on the fringes of society. In 1985, for the first time ever, a raï group, "Raïna Raï," participated in a big public event,[4] and a raï festival was also held in Oran. These two events were to trigger a "raï battle" in the Algerian media, and this once silenced music would eventually start to speak and be spoken about profusely (Virolle 1989a). It has since come to occupy an increasingly larger place on the radio waves—thanks to the initiatives of young amateurs on the French-language "channel *internationale*"—and in the daily lives of Algerians.

Furthermore, in 1986, with exposure at a soirée celebrating the Bobigny Festival in Paris during the official French-Algerian Cultural Week, raï broke through to international audiences. The genre spread to western Europe through communities of migrants, concurrently touching the entire Maghreb. Its expansion, prompted by Khaled, reached places as far-flung as Cairo, Tokyo, New York, and Bombay (Virolle 1995, 151–76). Noticeably, in its journey across the continents, raï has not "betrayed" its vernacular form, remaining close to the popular urban shape that the youth of the 1970s and 1980s had given to it in Oran, Bel-Abbès, or Temouchent. Even the most recent of the Parisian raï singers of the late 1990s, the young Faudel, remains faithful to the origins of this genre.

The Role of Women in the History of Raï

Women's contributions to raï have been fundamental at many different levels. First, women played a crucial role in the birth of this song genre. As mentioned earlier, one of the original raï movements developed in leisure places such as the *mahchachat* (cannabis dens), the brothels, and the rear rooms of cafés. These spaces were inconceivable without the presence of women, for women defined the pleasure they represented; the horizon of pleasure was sexuality, the real or imaginary availability of the female body. Women were singers, dancers, or fleeting companions. Their presence was associated with the consumption of disinhibiting substances, such as alcohol or cannabis, indispensable factors—particularly in a puritan society divided by gender—for a shift to mixed-gender moments of relaxation. The women in these "androcea" (men's gatherings for men's pleasure) were responsible for carrying—as singers or dancers—the texts and rhythms of a hedonistic song style, and for crystallizing desire.

Since independence, cabarets, noticeably the establishments of Oran's Corniche, have inherited these spaces and have become the true sites of raï.[5] Their privileged audience is made up of personalities, servicemen, and businessmen. The sums of money circulating in the soirées of cabaret are far from negligible. They sustain the system—common to various Mediterranean countries—of the "dedication" (tabriha in Arabic), an ostentatious relaunching of the song and dance prompted by money, putting into play a monetarized code of honor. In cabaret the female raï singer, the sheikha or shikha (pl. sheikhat/shikhat), is the requested and waited-for character. While any singer may animate the first part, no soirée is successful without the sheikha's presence, representing the show's climax and a catalyst of libidinous and financial energies.

Thus, the role of women in elaborating the raï text, particularly its structure, is fundamental. Raï songs present themselves as "patchworks": juxtaposed, fragmented, improvised, collagelike texts (Miliani 1992). An analysis of the texts discloses that, in general, there is a main, quite common narrative line. This theme is consolidated by given secondary topics. Together they create a canvas on which the essential characteristics of raï—namely, an existential "discourse" on one hand and a cultural referential on the other—can unfold. On a backdrop that is often little more than a pretext, a sort of embroidery flourishes, composed of the most trivial phrases taken from ordinary language. However, it also comprises recurring images and linguistic figments from popular discursive stock, and it resumes preexisting texts and citations. This is a feminine creative technique typical of the Maghreb, where it is not solely encountered in singing.[6]

The raï text is thus a divided text involving a frequently circumstantial, weak narrative aspect. It only takes, for instance, a man and a woman in the audience who have just experienced a problematic episode in their lives (imprisonment or an unhappy love affair, for example) for the improvised or recreated song to be organized around this tragedy. The circumstantial microstory forms the heart of the narrative, while the rest of the text develops around and embellishes it.

Women have also played a determining role within a particular stage of raï's diffusion: its shift from the closed and marginalized circles of male gatherings to greater social recognition. It is necessary to know that in the Algerian west groups of female singers called meddahat (lit., "laudatory singers") have existed for centuries. In family rituals like weddings or circumcisions, they traditionally sing praise songs to the Prophet and his daughter Fatima in front of female audiences (plate 13). At the time of Algerian independence, a period of "assassination of customs" caused the interdiction of the sheikhat's performances. In order to survive and to continue to practice their singing, the sheikhat introduced themselves and their secular raï repertoire into the meddahat ensembles. Gradually, the meddahat meetings during the *mahdar* of a wedding (the presentation of the bride) have become increasingly secular. During the last years of the 1980s, I witnessed numerous weddings where only two religious songs had survived: an overture and a closing number. In fact, the entire afternoon would be devoted to raï songs like the licentious and bacchic numbers performed in male gatherings. The repertoire once reserved for the "boys' night out" had become, at least for the duration of the party, a domestic female repertoire.

Concurrently, the sheikhat—who in time regained their freedom to perform outside this domestic realm—took on another function, also ritual in character but in a predominantly male environment. At rural marriages, they animate the party during the wedding night (Virolle 1995, 86–87). Their libertine, hedonistic songs can be conceived of in this context as an ode to fertility and sexuality. These "nights" have considerably enlarged the circle of raï listeners, as wedding rites attract many relatives, neighbors, and allies. In the summer—the period of weddings—outside the farms and under the stars, thousands of men gather around the sheikhat every Thursday (corresponding to the first day of the weekend). The singers are accompanied by their *berrah* (the "crier" who proclaims the dedications and collects the corresponding payments), their flautist, their percussionist, and even by a female dancer (plate 14). Only a few steps away from the nuptial couple, and not far from the "gyneceum," the female assembly is unable to see the sheikhat as they perform along the blind wall of the farm. Even today, the sheikhat still interpret the most daring of songs in the ancient Bedouin mode. During their performances, bottles of red wine circulate, the products of the soil bringing the gathering into a languid or more ardent state.

The sheikhat have also played an important role in the *wâadat,* the seasonal pilgrimages to the shrines of local saints. These big gatherings gave rise to not-so-religious side events, such as the musical presentations into which raï was introduced in the 1940s. The famous singer Cheikha Rimitti, one of the eldest sheikhat still alive, made her artistic name in that era in the *wâada* of Sidi Abed el Merja, near Relizane.[7] Raï gradually blossomed within the *wâada* environment, where it has acquired semipublic status.

Cheikha Rimitti is a very representative and yet exceptional female personality in the raï universe (Virolle 1993a, 1993b; Milani 1992). Going beyond the female poetics of the canvaslike text, which has some of the characteristics of an anonymous creativity and the joint collective repertoire, Rimitti has produced some real authorial texts. In view of the multiplicity of the themes that she has tackled—from the traditional transhumance to the airplane and the high-speed train, from the sorrow of mothers to the desire of lovers, from the moans of an orphan girl (herself having been one) to epithalamic songs, from exile to the war *baroud,* from magic spells to politics, from the alcohol that drives one mad to the pilgrimage to Mecca—she has painted a spicy fifty-year chronicle of changing Algeria. She has been most audacious in her songs, demolishing solidly anchored taboos—for instance, female virginity and the ritual fast. She has been most rebellious against situations of both individual and collective subservience, and also most provoking, well beyond the classic male stereotypes about women to which many female raï texts speak. Even in her later years, when raï was undergoing international expansion, she was able to respond creatively and to adapt to new recording techniques and other methods of distribution. For instance, in 1995, already more than sixty years of age, she mixed a record in Los Angeles, and she is also one of the first raï artists to have recorded videotapes.

Rimitti has created an important part of the larger raï repertoire, and young singers, men and women, have reprised some of her texts. The best know example is the song "La Camel," sung by Khaled on the cassette that made him internationally famous.[8] Rimitti is one of the sources of modern raï, and the *chebs* (youth) are glad to quote her as the "mother of raï."[9]

The Female Singer's Intervention Modalities

The female singer presents desire and pleasure on stage. In this way, she blurs the habitual codes of honor and, as we shall see, gender signs. She can only accomplish this double operation by losing her familial identity and by departing decisively from the patrilinear system. This allows her to place herself outside the "tribal" code of honor. First, she abandons her patronymic. She is called by first name, place name, or nickname (Virolle 1995, 81–85). She thus quits the patrilinear system in favor of mobility of residence: in fact, she does not reside with either her paternal family or, if she is married, with the family of her husband. Moreover, she never resides for long in the same place: she shifts, travels, and moves, and her personal topos is roaming.

Once completely stripped of the burden of the code of honor, she can devote herself to the "work of pleasure." However, she preserves within her repertoire an element of lament, the "work of pain" common to many female songs of the Mediterranean basin (Magrini 1998). It is one of the ways that she has of remaining feminine, clearly for her own sake but also for the image that she sends back to her male listeners. This image must underline some of the traits of traditional femininity mixed with some less classic traits.

> My heart is consumed and burned and it cooks on the embers.
> (Rimitti, "Lebnat" [The Daughters])

> Oh! My limbs come undone.
> (Fadéla, "'Atini bniyiti" [Give Me My Little Girl])

> Love is a verse which lives in one's bones.
> (Fedéla, "Nsal fik" [I've Got Rights over You])

> I have turned black, I am withering, and despair has taken hold of me.
> (Zahwaniya, "'Ana, hbibi nebgih" [My Love, I Want It])

The specificity of the raï complaint is tied to the relation operating in the texts—through contiguity—between the pain of love, social injustice, and the domination of women:

> They have suffocated me, they have wronged me, they have hurt me,
>   they have accused me.
> (Habiba el Kebira, "Hagrouni" [They Have Hurt Me])

> They told me: Swim! And I didn't know how to swim.
> (Rimitti, "Sidi 'Abed")

> Oh the mother of an only son; she dies of thirst on the roads.
> (Rimitti, "Oulidi we nkhaf 'alik" [My Son, I Fear for You])

> A woman who is without a man, it is sure that she would be held in
>   contempt.
> (Zahwaniya, "Djaw lamouni" [They Accused Me])

> Do not trust in life, it is bad and treacherous.
> (Djinya el-Kébira, "Sabbrou l Djilali" [Have Kjilali Wait])

> God of the two worlds, where is my luck?
> My luck is lost, a fish ate it in the sea.
> (Rimitti, "Ya Rebbi" [Oh My God])

They saw my shoulder going down, they crushed me.
(Djiniya el Kebira, "Wein ghachik" [Where Are Your People?])

Man is frequently presented as a selfish, manipulating, and even cruel being:

Me, my burning is unique, he, he will grow feathers.
(Zahwania, "Kayiti" [My Burning])

So sincere I am with him, yet he cheats on me!
(Zahwaniya, "Hay ʿumri" [Poor Me])

I love you, so love me, do not take me as a bird of passage!
(Sahwaniya, "Chta dani" [What Urged Me?])

He is married, why have I become a regular to him?
He has bad habits and he is debasing mine.
(Rimitti, "Ntya, ntya" [You, You])

My love whips me and my enemies watch;
All that he has done to me God will make him pay for!
(Zahwaniya, "Nerkeb hadah" [I Go Beside Him])

They have closed all the doors to me and made me drink four
    ricards.
(Zahwaniya, "Hbibi zafan" [My Love Is Angry])

By God who watches me, my love, my sins will follow you!
(Zahwaniya, "Halala lalal")

At times a miserable conscience is expressed, accompanying a feeling of personal responsibility:

Everything that has happened to me I asked for,
I wanted suffering and I suffer.
(Zahwaniya, "Chta dani" [What Urged Me?])

Our life is in our hands, it is us who kill ourselves.
Misery and suffering do not do anything to me anymore, I have
    killed myself by myself.
(Djinya el-Kébira, "Ktelna ʿamarna," [We Have Killed Our Life])

One of the recurrent themes of the female lament is the *mehna,* a polysemic concept operating a rather explosive alliance in the experiences of pain and pleasure. The root *M H N* in Arabic evokes the idea of filling something up until it cracks and overflows. It refers to the force-feeding of suffering, but also of love and alcohol. The trials recalled, of different origins, are always excessive: bereavements, serious moral wounds, unbearable material miseries. Nonetheless, the mehna derives chiefly from love: the mehna of unsatisfied love, betrayed love, misunderstood love, devastating passion. The notion of pleasure is inextricably part of this meaning. Thus one's lover will gladly be described as a mehna lover. An evening drinking binge will be called mehna. The taxi driver who takes one to meet one's beloved will be called *mul el mehna,* "the master of the mehna," as will the man whom he has taken to places of pleasure. When one drinks, when one loves, when one is happy and unhappy at the same tame, one sees "the two worlds": the one beyond and the one here, heaven and hell. The mehna is this unstable, intermediate, and paradoxical state.

> Let me drink so that I relieve myself of my lucidity.
> What is better for taking away traces than "that which erases"?
> (Rimitti, "Khallu lkas yewselni" [Let the Glass Come to Me])

> Let me [be] with those who smoke cannabis,
> You, me, and those who were blamed.
> (Habiba el-Kébira, "Hagrouni" [They Hurt Me])

> He who killed the beautiful storm, what can he do?
> You who are caught by all these misfortunes, put me in your wake!"
> (Djinya el-Kébira, "Goultou chabba" [You Found Her Beautiful])

> Oh path of torments! The path of torments takes me away
> And the other path brings me back! O path of torments!
> (Rimitti, "Trig el-mehna" [The Path of Torment])

> I'm in love with him who drags me to death
> We go to take the bus to the storm.
> (Habiba el-Kébira, "Charradni dak ezzin" [This Beauty Dragged Me to Perdition])

> Ah, how nice a good binge of whisky is!
> (Djinya el-Kébira, "Nkhaf ʿalik" [I Fear for Him])

Ah those who spend the night drinking, then the taxi comes, the
    black road.
She has laid the table. O girl, how you love the storm at the table!
(Djinya el-Kébira, "Chhal hadrou," [They Spoke a Lot])

I drank from bottles which drove the most pious mad!
(Rimitti, "Khallou lkas ywesselni" [Let the Glass Come to Me])

The raï text and performance, the "work of pleasure," noticeably feature a massive irruption of sexuality. It could even be advanced that one finds oneself
in the realm of hypersexuality. This state is brought on by the inflections in
the singer's voice, by her body, by her dance or by that of the female dancers
(*ragasa*) accompanying her, whose function is to stimulate desire, and finally
by the words pronounced.

I am yours tonight and bring me back tomorrow.
(Rimitti, "Trig el-mehna" [The Road of the Storm])

My love will come to my house and we will make love night
    and day.
(Zahwaniya, "Ghir habibi w ana" [Just My Love and I]).

I thought that kisses would make one patient, but they only
    increased my desire.
How I die for him.
(Rimitti, "Ana nebghih" [I love him])

Sleeping alone has numbed my hips, warm me and cover me!
(Rimitti, "Khallini" [Let Me])

He caressed my back and I gave him all.
(Rimitti, "A habib elhkatar" [O Treacherous Friend])

On one hand, the texts are a conventional enactment of men's fantasies: female physical beauty, accessible women, "free" love, adultery, nights of love
in a hotel, secret encounters, the pleasures of alcohol drunk in mixed company, female submission to men, and so on. On the other hand, however, and
more interestingly, as it is exceptional in the pan-Maghrebin and even in the
pan-Arab repertoires, they are an occasion for the expression of female desire
for men (Virolle 1989b). The raï singers invented, for instance, the blazons

of the male body. The whole of the Maghreb's poetics is founded on the blazons of the female body (especially the eyes, eyebrows, cheeks, complexion, hair, breasts, height, and thighs). These have provided a number of often very beautiful metaphors, which spread through the entire corpus of popular and learned poetry, in the rural and urban, as well as in the secular and religious, contexts. They could thus be applied to young men in a veiled expression of homosexuality, even to the Prophet in mystic poetry, and indeed to revered towns. Nevertheless, the male body itself is very strangely absent. Thus it is not an exaggeration to say that the raï singers have restored it—mustache, shoulders, scents, and teeth (notably, for the older men, golden teeth—to its "letters patent of poetic nobility":

> Oh mustache of a tiger and look of a lion!
> Yes, and it suits him, as does the birthmark above the mustache.
> (Rimitti, Manabrach, [I Am Not Cured])

> My love has a long neck and a large chest.
> (Zahwaniya, "Chta dani lweld ennas" [What Pushed Me toward the
>   Stranger?])

> My love is nicely proportioned and he has golden teeth.
> (Rimitti, "Ana nbghig" [Me, I Love Him])

> He is tall, it suits him, and he is well proportioned.
> (Zahwaniya, "Nerkeb hdah" [I Go Beside Him])

> The one who has a beautiful mustache has made his beautiful smile.
> (Zahwaniya, "Ana mal khouya madjach" [Why Didn't My Love
>   Come?])

> My olive-black love has adorned the table with his presence.
> (Zahwaniya, "Nerkeb hdah" [I Go Beside Him])

> My love has black eyes and languorous eyelashes.
> (Zahwaniya, "Rabbit elwalf ʿalih" [I Got Accustomed to Him])

Even the phallus is present. This last corporal element, the most important but also the most taboo, is not evoked through the denotative vocabulary but through puns, metaphors, or metonyms:

Let him play with the rearing horse.[10]
(Fadéla, "Dawni" [They Took Me])

The one I love is short and cute, in my heart he has quivered.
(Rimitti, "Trig el-mehna" [The Path of Torment])

Oh mother, a sharpened spike, torment, and love drive one crazy!
A sharpened spike and passion drive one crazy!
(Rimitti, "Sidi ʿAbed")

Another characteristic trait of the repertoire is the insistent and innovative presence of "I." *Ana* (me, I)—verse opener, reiteration, and punctuation—affirms a fully assumed individual assertion that is clearly far from the submission to the erotic imagination in use in men's gatherings. It is as if the singer had capitalized on this platform of erotic singing directed to men to deliver a message of personal freedom. The intensity of this message culminated in a song that encountered great success among all classes at the end of the 1980s. It is by a very well known local singer, Zahwaniya, "the Joyous One," and its title is the following short refrain that encapsulates its meaning: "Ma tsalunich" (Don't Ask Me for an Explanation). It is a hymn to the individual freedom of women that essentially says: "I am free to go with whom I please; I am free to waste my life if such is my desire; do not question me or judge me, as I take full responsibility for my actions." One only needs to picture a wedding in which dozens of women of all ages yell in chorus and dance to this "hit" around a stiff, still, and strained bride, to grasp the extent of the contradiction in the condition of Algerian women.

The raï singer takes upon herself—and indeed this is one of her functions—the blurring of genders. She behaves like a man as regards her spatial idiom (which is as ample as that of men and is not limited like that of women); her language (she can pronounce crude words, call out to somebody from a distance, address strangers, and she can even whistle or spit out); gestures and posture (she can occupy much more space than she is entitled to by the restrictive corporal rules for women); her behaviors (she smokes and drinks); and her voice (the majority of singers have a deep range, comparable to that of female blues singers).[11] Hers is a husky, broken voice—undoubtedly the result of alcohol and cigarettes, but also deliberate—with a register similar to that of men, all the more noticeable since male raï singers tend to cultivate registers that are higher pitched than average.

However, more than a simple inflection toward the masculine realm, the raï singer puts into work a superposition of gender-related signs (Virolle 1991). Two examples will help to make this particular *modus* concrete. The first example is that of the singer Djinya, "the She Devil," when she performs at weddings for a gathering of men. She arrives in the night from afar in a taxi (a masculine trait), but she is accompanied by two men—the crier and flautist—her close associates (a feminine trait). She sings in a deep voice some erotic texts (a masculine trait), but she wears a veil (a feminine trait). She wears a spangled dress and has naked arms (a feminine trait), but sports a tattoo on the forearm, similar to those men have done, for instance, in prison (a masculine trait). The second example is that of Rimitti on stage. She lets her opulent black hair float on her shoulders (a feminine sign) and wears a *ksiwa,* a traditional pastel dress embroidered with pearls (a feminine sign), but she sings in a male voice and intonation and drinks alcohol (a masculine sign). She salutes, and this is indeed one of her distinctive stage "tricks," standing to attention in a manly (and possibly ironic) manner. At times she commits a deliberate transgression of the division of labor in the Maghreb's instrumental domain: she plays the flute.

In these two examples—which could be multiplied—one observes a sort of construction in stages whereby masculine and feminine signs are superimposed, inverted, corresponding, and mutually nullifying. The masculine equivalent of this blurring of genders does indeed exist but is nonetheless exceptional. For instance, Sid Ahmed leads a group of meddahat in Oran and sings with them in feminine fashion. Furthermore, when Belkacem Boutelia was barely an adolescent, he replaced some female singers and was sought after for "his golden voice," although what was then emphasized was the androgyny of childhood.

Indeed, there are women who carry and take the responsibility for the blurring of genders, which tends to beget a "third gender" during the festive performative moment. This phenomenon is rare enough to make its motivations and necessity intriguing. My hypothesis is that female raï singers take charge of the bigendered catharsis generated by the festive moment that they animate. They are thus much more than female singers, for the conditions they create might be said to approximate a therapeutic domain. The female therapists in the Maghreb, whose status is often the same as that of female singers (marginalized women without men), incorporate some of the traits of masculinity (they dress like men and smoke, for example). They say explicitly that in order to be able to heal they must be men and women at the same time, and that the spirits who possess them are men. Establishing the connection between the domain of raï and that of therapy, one can suggest that this type of singing, more than others, is also a type of healing, a remedy, a *dwa*. Moreover, in the raï songs this word recurs frequently: alcohol is dwa, music is dwa, and love is dwa. What is raï a remedy for? Could it possibly be the cure for a society divided in two, where human beings find it difficult to communicate, and at times even to feel comfortable in one's own gender group?

The catharsis through singing will thus cure this disease for a while—just as therapeutic trance and clairvoyance do so temporarily. These moments shatter a representational order of things and beings and, in doing so, symbolically defuse the causes of this malfunctioning, "repairing" the subject. What are the procedures of this healing? A certain number of signs are inverted, others are hyperbolized, norms are broken in the margins, and the code is challenged. Eventually the order is allowed to reestablish itself on completion of the cathartic moment. Female singers may be said to deconstruct and reconstruct the relation between the sexes and genders, orchestrating the expression/repression of this divided society. The ideological norm is thus unshaken, but a process of reconstruction has started within the cracks.

Clearly, it consists of the enactment of a spectacle that society presents to itself, traditionally with men on one side and women on the other. Nevertheless, one of raï's innovative and specific characteristics is that the particular outburst of this tradition of separation operated in actual fact through a social practice beyond the discursive and cathartic enactment.

Sociological Implications

Since the 1980s, raï has completely abandoned the closed, nocturnal, and marginal spaces of its origin. It is now performed in stadium concerts, at public commemorative feasts, and at festivals. Its cassettes circulate in great numbers—hundreds of thousands—and are played in shops and outdoors in the streets, while young people with their transistors on their shoulders listen to raï on the beaches and in their neighborhoods. All that was previously related with reference to raï's disruption of the norms regulating the body and sexuality and the irruption of its mixed condition is hence no longer inscribed solely in borderline places and moments. Furthermore, it no longer merely takes place in the symbolic order, but indeed crosses over into the domain of the socially ordinary. This is the true impact of raï. Had it remained confined to spaces used for leisure, it would not have had any sociological implications; it would have functioned as other outlet activities do in puritan or repressive societies.

The irruption of raï into the social sphere seems, in my opinion, as important as Algeria's democratic opening. Noticeably, these two phenomena took place somewhat concurrently. The debate over raï that mobilized the Algerian press—whether raï was a "proper" art form, if it incited one to debauchery, whether the social ills that it exposed were real—preceded and, one may dare to say, even opened up the democratic debate. Raï brought under full scrutiny a society—crossed by contradictions and full of denied desires—that was unwell. The fine ideological uniqueness that prevailed after independence was shattered by the discourse of the marginalized purveyors of this song genre. They owed their words and cries only to their existential torments and desires, with no concern for their legitimization under given political or ideological labels.

A real modification of the male-female relationship and of the social representation of the female body takes place through repetition and massive divulgation, and by advertising a libidinal infringement of the norm. Women in Algeria have benefited conspicuously form the raï song. For instance, young girls can now dance in public with boys, which was unimaginable before raï gradually introduced such a custom. Their bodies—self-conscious and thus erotic—have become accepted and lawful to the eye. In addition, through raï we saw the emergence of male and female singers performing in duos. A man and a woman sing together in public—thus in front of families and people of all ages—and speak in full complicity of love and sexuality. Fadéla and Saharoaoui—a duo on stage as well as in their real-life marriage—are the most evident illustration of this.

However, Algeria is undoubtedly a country of contradictions. At a time in which Eros's quiet revolution was at work in the wake of raï, another revolution, the Islamic revolution more inclined toward Thanatos, was also in progress. As is known, some raï singers were killed, the best-known among them being Cheb Hasni. While the combat between Eros and Thanatos is still uncertain, however, it seems that nothing is capable of curbing youth's desire to cultivate their own musical expression, with its underlying rewards of freedom of expression and sexual freedom, individual affirmation, and the female conquest of spaces and behaviors. During the civil war, in a period in which individual and collective murders were at their height, RAJ, a youth association independent of all political parties and power, organized a massive raï concert in Algiers' largest stadium, attracting huge crowds.[12]

Admittedly, almost twenty years since it left its geographical and social ghetto, and approximately ten years since it achieved its status as national musical genre, raï has begun to show signs of age. It is now trying to renew itself in competition with rap, on which even in Oran, raï's birthplace, many artists have modeled their work in popular Arabic. Each year, however, a raï festival continues to take place in Oran, providing a platform where new talent can make itself known. At the international level, raï has continued its purpose as a fertile opening for other musical genres: rap, techno, reggae, and so on. Young stars like Faudel, with whom young French suburban people fully identify themselves, are replacing Khaled.

However, returning to my proposed discussion of women's place, it can be noted that female singers are practically absent from this new phase. Despite their driving role throughout the history of raï, in the present phase of incorporation of the genre into the international show business scene, women are at best mere epigones. Rimitti attempted to forge her way with recordings and videotapes. Fadéla, at Sahraoui's side, also tried without lasting success to carve her own niche. Zahwaniya, who has presently shut herself off from the rest of the world in France for security reasons, made a few appearances on television then disappeared from the public scene. Raï is only known outside the Algerian frontiers through the work of three male artists: Mami, Khaled, and Faudel. What are the roles to which women are confined in show business raï? Women are relegated to traditional roles as chorus in the records and bodies in the videos. The causes and effects of the secondary place that women have in the Western, modern, commercialized success of this song must be investigated. A few sociological considerations can clearly be reached as regards the functioning of endogenous and exogenous cultures, transplanted cultures and their social actors, and of the networks of the raï musical field. The analysis will undoubtedly tackle the feminine image promoted by the female raï singers, and the possible role of this image in spaces as ill-defined as those of Western society. Moreover, the female singers' ability to create new roles and new images in this context will be questioned. However, the fundamental question or perspective still persists. We have seen how in the sphere of musical creation a particularly hard patriarchic system did not manage to accomplish its intent of keeping women quiet. Nevertheless, will the market system of the major record and entertainment companies manage to accomplish such an aim? Will these women be reduced to silence again, and be forced to be a shady presence behind the scenes and in the ghettos?

Translation by Piera Sarasini

Notes

1. Distillery work was common, as vineyard cultivation was very developed in this region of Algeria during the colonial period. The urban verses of women are referred to by the generic term *zendali*.

2. Raï did not utilize the *ud* (lute), an instrument of the urban musical elite and so-called learned musics.

3. Music from India—popularized in Algeria through movies in the 1960s and 1970s—is referred to as "Hindu."

4. The Festival de la Jeunesse (Youth Festival) was held in Algiers on 5 July 1985 to celebrate the anniversary of independence.

5. [Corniche is the name of Oran's surrounding outskirts, where in the past the caba-rets—which have now been changed chiefly into discos or nightclubs—used to be. *Trans.*]

6. For instance, when I studied the prediction poems of the urban and rural seers, I was able to observe the same structure of canvaslike texts. It is also possible to compare the techniques used in weaving and pottery.

7. The story about her "stage name" is that when going to drink some beer in the *kantina* (the refreshment room) of the feast, she boldly ordered another round in French: "Remettez!"

8. The recording *Kutché* was created and produced in Algeria, in collaboration with the Algerian oriental jazz musician Safi Boutella.

9. The generic term *chebs* is used to designate the new generation of raï singers, as opposed to *chioukh* (sing. *sheik*, "old man" as well as "master").

10. The masculine word *zzeb*, which commonly designates the male sexual organ, is translated here as "him."

11. In fact, Chaba Fadéla has been nicknamed "Oran's Billie Holiday."

12. RAJ stands for Rassemblement Algérien de la Jeunesse (Algerian Youth Rally), and the acronym allows for a double pun: *raj* means "poison" in Arabic and, as pronounced in French, also implies "rage."

References

Magrini, Tullia. 1998. "Women's 'Work of Pain' in Christian Mediterranean Europe." *Music and Anthropology* 3. http://www.muspe.unibo.it/period/MA/

Miliani, Hadj. 1992. "Une esthétique du fragmentaire: Dame Rimitti et ses enfants putatifs." In *L'oralité africaine,* vol. 1. Algiers: CNEH.

Virolle, Marie. 1988. "Ce que chanter *eray* veut dire: Prélude à d'autres couplets." *Cahiers de Littérature Orale* 23:177–209.

———. 1989a. "Le raï entre résistance et récupération." *REMMM* 51:47–62.

———. 1989b. "Le *ray* côté femmes: Entre alchimie de la douleur et spleen sans idéal, quelques fragments de discours hédoniste." *Peuples Méditerranées* 44/45:193–220.

————. 1991. "La figure androgyne: Exemples algériens." In *Sexe et genre: De la hiérarchie entre les sexes,* edited by Marie-Claude Hurtig, Michèle Kail, and Hélène Rouch, 203–12. Paris: Éditions du CNRS.

————. 1993a. "Le raï de Cheikha Rimitti." *Mediterraneans* 4:102–15.

————. 1993b. Déchire, lacère, et Rimitti ravaudera!" *Liber* 15:16–20.

————. 1995. *La chanson raï: De l'Algérie profonde à la scène internationale.* Paris: Karthala.

9

ﯗﯗ ﯗﯗ

Poetry as a Strategy of Power:
The Case of Riffian Berber Women

Terri Brint Joseph

Although anthropological studies of the Middle East generally acknowledge the low status of Islamic women, the complex "mosaic" of national, ethnic, and tribal social organization makes it difficult to make accurate, significant statements about the area as a whole. Even when focused on a single country, anthropological accounts arrive at conflicting conclusions about the role of women. Ethnographers of Morocco like Westermarck, Coon, Hart, and Gellner have concentrated on the exercise of formal, public power and thus have stressed the hegemony of men over women.[1] This notion of monolithic masculine dominance and feminine subjugation has been somewhat modified by recent studies of women's ability to influence male decisions, a "power behind the throne" theory articulated by Roger Joseph.[2] Maser and Nelson have also argued that women wield some direct power through female systems of network and alliance. And from a different perspective, Mernissi has insisted that, with the exception of a few influential men, Moroccan males are as powerless and dispossessed as Moroccan females.[3] This variety of contradictory views makes it all the more important to engage in very specific studies that can help us ascertain the status and relative power of women in Islamic societies. The present study focuses on a delineated area, the Rif Mountains of northern Morocco; a particular people, the Riffian Berbers of the Beni-Waryaghar and Ibbucoya tribes; and a single question, the role played by the songs which Berber women compose for and then perform at wedding ceremonies. It attempts to analyze how women express themselves in a public arena within the formal, institutionalized structure of male society, rather than a female network system for covert influence. It explores the degree to which songs constitute strategic devices, weapons which can help women have a voice in the community and gain control over their lives.

Social Structure and Economy of the Berbers

The Berbers, speaking dialects of the Hamitic and unwritten language whose name they bear, form an ethnic and linguistic group within the larger Arab culture of Morocco. The indigenous inhabitants of the country, they were gradually converted to Islam between the seventh and eleventh centuries A.D. by Arab missionaries and invaders. Today they are centered in the Atlas and Riffian Mountain ranges; the latter runs south of the Mediterranean coastal plain from Tangier to Melilla, in the northern section of the country. The Beni-Waryaghar and Ibbucoya, the central Riffian tribes studied for this chapter, live in the Al-Hoceima Province, once held under the Spanish Protectorate but a part of the Moroccan regime since the country gained independence from Spain and France in 1956.

In a country noted for its poverty, the Rif is one of the poorest sections. Its comparatively mild climate is offset by deforestation and soil erosion on the slopes. The Central Rif has only two major rivers, the Nekkor and the Rhis, as its water supply, and its essential crops of barley and maize are dependent on rainfall. Since the Rif is subject to years of drought alternating with flash floods, its food supply is uncertain and, even in good years, can only support a limited number of people. Overpopulation, which has been a recurrent problem, was controlled in the pre-Protectorate days through the blood feud and since independence through large-scale emigration to the cities of Morocco, Algeria, and Europe. A settled, agricultural people, the Riffians work their steeply terraced land with hand tools, using oxen or cattle to plow only the flatter lands of the valleys. The meager crops are supplemented with vegetables grown in irrigated gardens near the rivers; nuts and fruits from orchards; and meat, cheese, and milk from the small herds of goats and sheep owned by more prosperous families. In spite of careful husbandry, malnutrition and disease are endemic in the Rif. To give but one index, at the time this field study was made the infant mortality rate, *within a week of birth,* was over 50 percent.

Women have only one access to the cash economy—the sale of eggs from their flocks of chickens and turkeys. Their days are an endless round of tasks connected with food preparation, child care, and home maintenance. Because the Riffians practice sexual segregation of women of childbearing age, these chores are associated with stages in the life cycle. From a very early age, a girl gathers firewood for her mother, assists in caring for younger children, and helps keep the house clean. As soon as she is old enough, she and her brothers take the flocks out to pasture every day, clean their pens in the household, and remove their droppings from the dirt floor. When strong enough, usually at adolescence, she gathers water from the nearest river or spring and carries it on her back in a jug which, when filled, weighs about thirty pounds. She also has increased child-care duties and plays a more responsible role in preparing meals. When she marries, a young woman will probably no longer work outside the home, unless the family cannot afford the luxury of losing some of her labor by segregating her.

Men in the Rif work in a seasonal pattern. During plowing and reaping periods, which are brief but intense, they labor for long hours in the fields. Much of their year, though, is leisurely and allows time for visiting, conversation, and forming political alliances. Women's tasks may be less intense but must be repeated on a daily basis and leave little time for relaxation; a woman is dependent socially on visits from relatives and women past menopause. Once a woman is no longer of childbearing age, her activities broaden again; meals may be prepared by her daughters-in-law, freeing her to visit neighbors and friends. Older women, especially if they are widows or have husbands who do not object to their appearing in public, may visit the women's markets and participate in religious sisterhoods.

The life of the Berber woman contrasts sharply with that of a relatively prosperous Arab woman in a Moroccan town. Whereas the townswoman will have at least one female servant and considerable leisure, which she, veiled and in her *jaballa,* devotes to visiting the mosque, the baths, her friends and neighbors, her Riffian counterpart rarely has paid help within the home, goes unveiled, has a heavy share of household responsibilities, and may have a limited circle of associates. These differences are reflections of two polarities: town/country and Arab/Berber. One explanation for the differences between Berber and Arab norms is that, until subjugated by European powers in the twentieth century, the Rif had always been *bled-es-siba,* land of dissidence, as opposed to *bled-al-mahkzen,* land of the regime or government. Because the

Riffians lived in such an isolated and impenetrable area, they could refuse to pay tribute to the sultans of Morocco or serve in their armies and could practice their own way of life. They had minimal interference from the central government and limited contact with it.

The tribal organization of the Riffians is based formally on a lineage system which establishes specific rights and obligations in a reciprocal relationship with agnatic kin and a secondary set of obligations through the affinal bonds of marriage. This lineage system is considered normative by formalist Moroccanists like Westermarck and Coon, even though it ignores the alliance relationships with neighbors, friends, and associates which Berber men devote considerable time and energy to developing, and—what is more important—takes no account of the role of women in tribal life. In "Sexual Dialectics and Strategy in Berber Marriage," Roger Joseph has questioned the normative account of mate selection in the Rif, which flatly states that fathers arrange marriages for their children and select their mates. Although this explanation would seem to be verified by the exclusive presence of males when the marriage contract is drawn up and the details of the dower, or *sadak,* recorded, Joseph has analyzed the specific behavior of both sexes and argued that the mothers of the bride and groom can exercise control over mate selection. In discussing the sexual dialectic between men and women of the Rif, Joseph characterizes the two models which have been used to study the Berbers as the "formalist" and the "interactionist." While formalists stress discrete kinship units within the segmentary lineage system that are closed and relatively stable, interactionists like Geertz focus on individuals negotiating in dyadic or face-to-face relationships which are subject to constant readjustments as each participant maneuvers for advantage and makes corresponding concessions. It is Joseph's contention that a study of both models reveals "an interplay between norms and acts" that manifests the influence of women.[4]

Joseph has emphasized the role of the mothers of the bride and groom, but not that of the potential brides and their attempts to affect the choice of their mates. It should be understood that in Berber society all able-bodied adults of both sexes are expected to conform to the Quranic injunction to marry; neither men nor women are allowed the option of remaining single. Within these limitations, however, young women are far more powerless than young men; indeed, they are usually considered the most powerless members of society except for young children. It is, in fact, through their songs that females between the ages of thirteen and twenty try to compensate for their powerlessness; they attempt to seize the initiative in courtship and to usurp their fathers' public roles as the figures who choose spouses for their offspring.[5]

Form and Composition of the Songs

Extremely brief, the Berber song is made up of a single couplet. Each of the two lines is roughly twelve syllables long, although some contain only nine and others as many as fifteen. Each song is introduced by a traditional chorus which can be repeated as often as the singers wish:

Ayah-rala boyah-ayah rala boya
Ayah-rala boyah-ayah rala boya
Ayah-ra (la) boyah [etc.]

Most Riffians interviewed for this study regard this chorus as a series of sounds with no meaning. They say it is used because "it is the custom." Several informants, however, reported that the initial *a* is a vocative like the English "oh"; *yah-rala* was said to be a form of *la la* (madame or lady), in this case the bride's mother; and *boyah* a form of *baba* (father). One anthropological account has translated the refrain as "Oh look, oh look, look at the bride."[6]

Rather than use formulaic or set material such as Lord and Parry have identified in oral narratives,[7] Berber singers engage in self-conscious composition, scrutinizing their work and subjecting it to numerous revisions. Indeed, there seem to be no Berber girls who are unable to compose and perform original songs. Composing is not only a privilege but a responsibility. It is expected that each girl will be a poet just as it is expected that each woman will bake bread for her family. One Berber song uses the complaint, "I have no songs," as a metaphor to suggest that its singer is unattractive and that no one wants to marry her:[8]

Madesrah wuware na-we thanen-awanu   [I have no songs! I'm like a rock which has fallen in a well. . . .
Ra-la thasherethine agmathunt sufero.   Oh, my friend, catch the rock with a string.]

The complaint is used ironically in a song whose very composition disproves the singer's lack of songs; in the second line, the poet asks a girlfriend to help her find a young man. Although some songs are better or worse than others according to Berber notions of poetic value, all of the women interviewed in the Rif during a period of eighteen months for this study were able to compose songs.

Although the poems are short, it is not unusual for a young woman to spend several months working on a few couplets, searching for the *mot juste* as she readies her lyrics for the weddings which occur after the harvest in late summer and early September. While going about her daily tasks, she composes her songs by singing the lyrics softly or chanting them under her breath, introducing changes by a process of conscious revision. If she replaces a word or a phrase in the lyrics, she can usually give a good reason: the revision enhances the meaning or sounds better with the other words in the song.

The Performance

Songs are performed at Berber weddings either in front of the houses of the bride and groom or on a central patio located within the walls of the house. The stage is a cleared area in front of an open fire, around which the guests are seated or stand. The audience comprises men of all ages, young women who are not yet married, older women past the age of childbearing, and young children of both sexes. Young, married women usually stay in the house itself, but they listen to the songs and watch the performance through windows if they can. The older women who stand behind the men in the audience, although they do not sing, add to the performance by ululating (making a shrill sound by trilling their tongues against the roof of their mouths) at various dramatic moments during the singing. The men in the crowd, especially the young bachelors, shout encouragement, cheer, and applaud throughout the evening.

On the first day of the wedding, the performance begins at sunset and lasts until dawn. It is then resumed on the second and third evenings, and the girls try to present a variety of songs, even though they sing several times each evening. They perform in groups of four, dressed in their finest, floor-length gowns, and wearing dark glasses which render their faces mysterious in the flickering light of the fire.[9] Although these dark glasses are supposed to function as disguises, members of the audience have no difficulty in recognizing the singers, and, in fact, much of the point of their songs would be lost were the singers to remain anonymous. It may be, however, that the glasses, operating as a fictive mask, make it easier for the girls to step beyond the role ascribed to young women of the Rif; it is this violation of normal decorum and restraint which gives the songs their particular import and potential power.

Berber women in groups of four sing the "rala boyah" chorus in unison, although each presents her own lyrics as a solo. Holding tambourines and small drums called *tabours,* the young women do a side-shuffle dance as they sing, keeping time with their hand instruments. After the chorus is completed, the first singer presents her song. If the audience likes it, the men will cheer and shout *yallah* to encourage the quartet as it breaks into another round of the chorus; the tempo quickens, and the side-shuffle gives way to the *shidhih*, in which the girls undulate, moving their hips, waists, and breasts in circular movements while the audience shouts more encouragement. After a few minutes of dancing, the tempo slows, the girls resume their side-shuffle, the second girl sings her song, and so on, until each of the quartet has performed. The girls exit to a last chorus of "rala boyah" and are replaced by a new quartet.

During this performance, the girls clearly flaunt sexual energy, perform provocative dances, and, dressed in their most seductive finery, expose themselves to public scrutiny. For the songs serve the vital function of a rite of passage for these girls within the framework of a larger rite of passage, the wedding itself. While the bride and groom are being initiated to their new status as married adults, the girls who sing at the wedding, like debutantes in Western societies, are being "presented" to the community as young women who have come of age and can be scrutinized by the parents of prospective grooms as well as by the young bachelors themselves. While the bride and groom are formally ratifying their relationship, the girls performing are setting in motion a train of events which may determine their own weddings. The Berbers themselves, of course, are consciously aware of the wedding as the context for the songs, as one lyric specifically indicates:

> Eh-ham rid gazar nunkor   [River Nekkor has risen; bringing tea
>   swatad er henne   and henna
> Wo-men gabridan saad   When luck was divided among us,
>   enesh ma tuniye.   I alone was forgotten.]

The singer associates a year of abundant rainfall ("River Nekkor has risen") with the prosperity necessary for many families to meet the expenses of weddings for their sons. The composer singles out for attention the sweet mint tea which is offered to the wedding guests, and henna, which is ritually applied to the bride and groom during the ceremonies of "the Big Henna" and "the Little Henna." In a year when all of her age mates are engaged or getting married, only the singer remains single.

The songs play their part in the very continuity of tribal society, which requires marriage, the founding of families, and the rearing of children for its survival. While the adolescent girls sing, the girls who have not yet reached puberty try to memorize the songs of the performers, waiting expectantly for the day when they, too, will be allowed to sing. They are thus going through a socialization process, receiving informal training for their own future role as women.

Songs as Social Criticism

Over and beyond their sexual and social functions, the Berber songs essentially allow young women to address the entire community. The freedom to address the tribe (*tackbitch*) or community (*dchar*) as a whole, people of both sexes and all ages, is granted to any young woman who wishes to perform; it is, however, a privilege unique to young, single women. Married, divorced, or widowed women are not permitted to perform. Men, even the most powerful leaders, cannot address the entire community. Although they utilize tribal gatherings to speak to men of all ages, they can communicate with only those women who are members of their own family or are related to them by marriage. If they wish to reach other women of the tribe, males must use their mothers, wives, sisters, or daughters as emissaries.

The songs women perform at weddings are often explicitly critical of Berber life. The range of subjects for social critique is theoretically as broad as any singer's interests; the following song, for example, attacks not only native society but the countries of Europe that hire Berber labor, create new emigration patterns in tribal life, and contribute to social upheavals:

> Afer runil ekanit Nesar   [A piece of packing cord has sullied a
>   hend g-kesan   water glass. . . .
> Ay! Alemania! nefishan   Oh, Germany! You have given illusions
>   emsan!   to beggars!]

In this song, the drinking glass, a fragile, expensive item which must be imported to the Rif, represents Germany and other European countries which send representatives to Morocco to recruit Berbers to work in their factories. The singer describes the glass as being cheapened and dirtied by a piece of packing cord, a metaphor for those Berber men, usually of poor families and low social standing in the Rif, who sign contracts and go to Europe to work. By living inexpensively abroad, these men amass what the Berbers consider a fortune, which they often use, upon their return, to buy land and to try to marry girls of proud lineage. These young men are regarded with a mixture of contempt and respect by the settled Berber community. The girl who composed this song is voicing a criticism shared by the larger Berber community when she claims that the boys are still "beggars" and their hopes of entering Berber society an "illusion." Yet emigration is a powerful mechanism in the Rif and allows young men to have greater control over their choice of spouses. With the cash accumulated abroad a young man can threaten to arrange—and pay for—his own wedding should his father be too insistent about a potential bride who is not his own choice.[10] Two other songs by Berber women attack the *makhzen,* or Moroccan government. These songs date from the time when the government pressed impoverished tribesmen into service to construct the road that cuts through the Rif from Tetuan to Mellilla. In the first, the government comes under fire for paying its workers so little that they are unable to buy the headscarves for their wives that Berber decency requires; in the second, for forcing Berber men into labor that takes them far from their homes:

E-hudem abred e-hudmen
 opeyuz
Themrarin incid quren
 suz-uzh.

[The workers who labor with
 picks on the road!
Their women must wander
 bareheaded.]

A-breth n-tumobil
 hudminth a breth-n-kum
Uk-seer thetwon the-bre-then
 red-n-hum.

[The highway? The workers must
make their own road.
The women of Tetuan aren't theirs
 and cannot be seen through
 their veils.]

The first song contrasts a Berber custom, the wearing of a headscarf by girls and women, with the Arab custom, referred to in the second, of veiling the face. Although rural Berber women tend to go unveiled, some who have moved to towns like Al-Hoceima have adopted the custom in imitation of Arab women.

In a modern song that criticizes the government for levying an admission price at a local beach in the town of Al-Hoceima, the phenomenon of tourism itself is scrutinized:

Shebab n-Al-Hoceima hisrah
 su sekn
Kenu alemanan hezrah tibe
 serkun.

[The young boys of Al-Hoceima
 dive from the shining cliffs
You, the Germans, sprawl on the
 blazing sand.]

When the Playa Quemada beach was taken over in 1966 for the use of two government hotels and a fee of one dirham was charged for admission to what had once been a public beach, the Berbers felt the fee was aimed at discouraging them from using the beach. Rather than pay admission, the Berber men perform the dangerous feat of diving from the cliffs above the beach while the tourists lie on the sand below, acquiring the suntans the Berbers, with their liking for fair skin, consider unattractive. The song's social criticism is aimed at the invading tourists and the makhzen for forcing the Berbers to pay to use their own beach. Although the song was composed by a young woman who lived in Al-Hoceima, it was taken up by the rural girls who had some contact with the town, and it became popular in the countryside, even though inlanders had little personal interest in tourists or a stake in using the Playa Quemada beach. Several informants explained its appeal in the tribal area by saying that the new admission price was similar to the government's infringements on other aspects of Berber life since Morocco's independence.

The Love Songs

The woman who performs her songs at a wedding uses them not only as social criticism but as strategies to defend herself, attack others, encourage suitors, announce an engagement, remind young men of the tribe that she is in love, shame or ridicule an unwanted swain, or justify her decision to break an engagement. Even the most ordinary love song represents a form of social criticism since it implicitly attacks three powerful stereotypes often expressed by Berber men: (1) women, especially young girls, are too foolish or uninformed to hold strong opinions about something as important as the choice of a mate; (2) they are merely pawns in the male game of strengthening past affinal relationships or establishing new ones through marriage; (3) unmarried girls, segregated from contact with nonrelated males, have no opportunity to develop positive or negative feelings toward any particular young man. Yet men not only accept these songs, they like them, memorizing their favorites to quote or chant in conversation.

Some of the most interesting and problematic songs of the Rif are addressed to young men who have already entered into successful negotiations with the composer's father. Since these negotiations will lead to marriage, the singer, if she does not care for him, must discourage the young man so thoroughly in her lyrics that he will voluntarily withdraw his offer:

A thsib-banah-tasebnath:	[I am going to wash my fringed
astsah ho fades	headscarf; I shall hang it on the
	fades bush:
Jemah sucarinik-nish d	Take your sugar away! You and I aren't
shik udentes.	good together.]

In this song, the singer places in explicit opposition the formal negotiations of the masculine world and her own, informal system for getting what she wants. The reference to sugar is an economical way of saying: "You came to my house and asked my father for my hand; he has encouraged you, accepting your proposal, but I don't want to marry you." In Berber society sugar is considered the most expressive symbol of the affection which unites an engaged or married couple. It is also used as a signal between the boy and the girl's father to open or close negotiations for a wedding. On the occasion of his first visit to the girl's home, the young man (or his representative) will present her father with five or six hard cones of tightly packed sugar. If the father is amenable to the idea of accepting the young man as a son-in-law, he will strike a cone with a hammer and break the sugar into lumps which will be used to sweeten the mint tea that he will share with the young man. If the father does not wish to encourage the young man, he will either return the cones or ostentatiously use household sugar in preparing the tea. With nothing overt having been said by either party, the young man has declared his intentions, and the girl's father has indicated his willingness or reluctance to open formal negotiations.

Moreover, by washing her headscarf, the composer of the song is metaphorically washing her hands of her lover. This cleansing is an act of purification as well; she will become a new woman who has broken with the past. The *thasebneth*, which is made of brightly colored and patterned silk with a long, soft fringe, is considered the most beautiful headscarf worn by Berber women and is worn only on special occasions when a woman wishes to be particularly attractive. The poet's use of the *fades* (*Pistacia lentiscus*) intensifies the cleansing imagery of the lyric, since ashes from the fades bush are used by Berbers to make soap. By hanging her headscarf to dry in a conspicuous location outside the home, the girl is not only rejecting her suitor but making a public declaration of the rupture and of her own freedom to consider other offers of marriage. There is also, of course, a veiled threat to use the newly washed scarf for flirtatious purposes.

The audience listening to this song would know what particular young man was seeking the singer in marriage, even though no names are mentioned in the lyric. It is unlikely that a suitor subjected to a rejection witnessed by the entire community would continue to press for marriage. Of course, the composer takes the risk that the young man will persist, that the negotiations will go through, and that she will find herself married to the butt of her song. It is only because the songs are trusted to be generally effective that a young woman can afford to gamble, wagering her desire to extricate herself from an unwanted match against the unpleasant possibility of finding herself married to a man she has spurned in public.

Berber poets exercise considerable license in their songs, in sharp contrast to the normal decorum and modesty required of a young Berber virgin. In the following song, a young woman abuses a suitor with impunity, something which she would never do to his face.

> Math zwed *el vino* nhara   [Did you drink wine today or
>   methumnat   yesterday?
> Math zwed *el vino* math   Did you drink wine glass by glass or
>   kul bid tazeyat?   the whole bottle at once?]

The singer is saying that the boy must have been drunk and, by extension, out of his mind, to have asked for her hand; he was as drunk as if he had consumed an entire bottle of wine before setting out to make arrangements with her father. Since the drinking of wine is expressly forbidden by the Quran, an injunction which rural Berbers take seriously, the singer's accusation would be an embarrassment both to the boy and to his family. It is doubtful if the young man, after this verbal face slapping, would pursue any further his plans to marry the girl.

Whatever the verbal license of the singers, the victims of their lyrics are expected to suffer in dignified silence. At a wedding which took place on the Bulma Peak in the Rif Moutains in the summer of 1966, a young man became so incensed about a song which he considered insulting that he and a group of his friends began throwing stones at the singer. The adult males in the audience quickly intervened, the boys were forcibly ejected from the compound, and the evening continued without further incident. Most of the wedding guests were shocked by the boys' behavior and observed that however insulting a girl's song might seem to any given young man she has a right to sing it. This freedom to overstep the boundary of ordinary Riffian courtesy is one of the most powerful weapons which songs give Berber women.

Many of the Berber lyrics are efforts at self-justification or defense. In one song the composer, accused of a sexual transgression, defends her own life:

Nanis eguma wutchma
   anrret a-hisen

[The boys have challenged my
   brother, "It would be better to
   kill that wanton your sister!"

anri ahzezbo huma urensen.

Then let them kill me to silence
   their lying tongues!]

A group of young men, probably disgruntled suitors, accuses the singer of sexual immorality. So serious is this allegation in the Rif that the brother would be within his rights if he defended the family honor and killed the girl. In the song, the poet shows her brother believes in her innocence, and, by openly confronting unpleasant gossip, she transforms a dangerous situation into an opportunity to defend her reputation. Only by exposing the problem to the whole community is she able to combat her accusers and maintain her good name. In another song of defense, the poet uses the public forum of the wedding to appease a fiancé who has broken their engagement because she admired the young men of Al-Hoceima on a visit to the town:

Themdenth n-Alhoceima
   arras wah ebaden
Thene esother a-lefeno
   zugen.

[The city of Al-Hoceima with its
   strong walls!
It was there I fell from the esteem
   of my darling.]

The poet admits that her head was turned by the "strong walls," or attractive young men of the town, but this public confession serves to minimize her misdemeanor. In fact, upon hearing the girl sing this song at a wedding, the fiancé decided that he had been too harsh and their marriage took place within a month. The songs are a recognized channel for redressing wrongs and for allowing the young women of the tribe to speak in their own defense. One lyric specifically mentions this function:

Suneth ezranino ashar
   riz-bubenik
Mirme gar thar-ruth wuh
   ah-wuth a wa sherenik.

[Fill your ears and your heart with
   my songs!
Tell my denouncer he lied!]

Like occidental love poetry, Berber lyrics are often songs of celebration, lamentation, and seduction. One typical love song is written as a dialogue, in which the fiancé poses a question in the first line which the composer answers in the second:

Eni mi shem rahgah a yah	[He asked me, "Where shall I put you,
denub	my poor little one?"
Donue gui a lefino mani	Put me, my darling, where you put
tigguth i-kultub.	your book.]

The singer asks her lover to place her in his hip pocket, where he carries his book, so that she can be with him all the time. *Denub,* "poor little thing," is a word that is usually used for young children and is a term of affection when applied to an adult. The other endearment in the song, *lefino,* is the first-person singular possessive of the noun *lef,* the word that signifies the trusted allies who laid down their lives for a man in the days of the blood feud; it is the strongest word for "beloved" or "darling" in the Rif and has no literal equivalent in English. In a representative example of a lament, the singer voices her loneliness for a fiancé who has gone to Europe to work in a factory:

Lefino e-sahwar ge-	[His face in the window of the photogra-
fotographia	pher's shop
Ah-we or-resewer	The portrait can't speak, but how it
afefraz-a-nita!	resembles my darling!]

Such a song, with its reference to her fiancé's passport photograph on display in the window of the photographic shop in Al-Hoceima, allows her also to remind other young men that she is engaged and is waiting for her young man to return.

Songs of seduction sung at weddings must veil their eroticism in order to be performed in public.[11] According to a Berber male informant, the following lyric is "the song most in love of any," or it is as explicitly erotic as any song which can be sung before an audience:

Ath-sarsh temese	[I shall lower a candle at the mouth of
hokahmom owahnu	the well.
Athadosun waman athaso	If the water rushes upwards, my lover
lefeno athesu.	will drink.]

The song begins with the commonplace activity of fetching water at the well, but moves into the realm of the extraordinary as the water undergoes a miraculous transformation arid becomes a fountain. The reference to a candle, which suggests that it is night rather than day, implies a tryst at the well. Even more, many Berbers claim that this lyric contains an explicit sexual metaphor: The well symbolizes the girl's vagina, the candle the boy's penis, the flame their sexual passion, and the act of drinking that of sexual intercourse. Since the lyric can be read more literally, however, it falls within the Berber concept of propriety and can be performed without causing offense.

The Songs and the Reality of Women's Lives

Although Riffians make a conscientious effort to keep adolescent boys and girls apart as part of the ideology of sexual segregation, the songs reveal that unmarried boys and girls spend enough time in each other's company to form attachments and antipathies. Since both sexes have tasks to perform which take them outside the home, parental supervision is necessarily limited. Unmarried boys make it a habit to appear at the well, river, or spring when the girls arrive to fetch water. A boy who is struck by the appearance or manner of one of the young women will accompany her part of the way to her house, staying several feet behind her; this pretense at social distance enables young people to insist that they are not together if challenged by adults. If the boy likes the girl he will begin to linger along the path just out of sight of her home in order to follow her to the well or as she goes about her errands. A few words will be exchanged, and if the girl is friendly they will walk abreast of each other when no one is in sight and perhaps disappear into a grove of olive trees to converse privately. Such encounters are "dates" in Riffian society and help young people conduct courtships and make decisions about whom they wish to marry. Despite these social patterns which have existed for at least several generations, adults, especially parents discussing their children, assume that little or no communication takes place between adolescent boys and girls. Adults maintain this social blindness because the society tries to uphold sexual segregation and clings to a formal model in which the fathers of the bride and groom arrange the marriage of their offspring. And these partial fictions are maintained in the face of the evidence from the song lyrics, heard at ten or fifteen weddings a year, which are presented and understood as true statements, not as imaginative constructs.

Although the Berbers pay lip service to a formal model in which the father of the bride arranges her marriage without consulting her wishes, the songs reveal a different world in which the bride accepts or rejects various suitors on the basis of their attractiveness to her; her father, if he appears in the lyrics at all, is a shadowy figure who simply carries out the wishes of his strong-willed daughter. One possible reason why Berber girls are allowed to expose social fictions and to challenge certain aspects of their patriarchal society may be that the performance of songs occurs during a rite of passage, what Victor Turner in *The Ritual Process* has called a marginal or liminal event (from Latin *limen,* "threshold"), in which the participants are on a threshold between two social categories and are ambiguous figures who are not fully members of either.[12] This liminality also extends to the guests at the wedding, whose own status groups are being changed by the marriage. The parents and families of the bride and groom are bidding farewell to their offspring as children and, like the elders of the community, must accept them henceforth as married adults; and the adolescent friends, the age mates of the bride and groom, must adapt themselves to the change in the couple's social role. Within the liminal event, *reversal* of social categories and *inversion,* in which the high exchange places with the low, seem to be consistent features. The Berber wedding shows a paradigm of reversal in power relationships: unmarried girls, who are less powerful in ordinary Berber life than any group except small children, suddenly become figures of authority who are allowed to address all the members of their society and to use their creativity to achieve their own ends. The powerful father of a singer (and with him, all the adult males who expect to oversee the marriages of their children) is reduced to being a passive member of the audience while his daughter is the center of attention, singing words which her audience not only carefully listens to but often actually memorizes, as she comments boldly on the attractions and weaknesses of various young men in the crowd. The girl's performance, then, allows her to play "queen for a day," but because her usurpation of power takes place within the formal structure of the marriage rites she is expected to resume her docile, obedient demeanor after the wedding, and not attempt to exercise authority until the next time she performs in public. The irony of this expectation is that the girl seizes the moment of her performance to encourage relationships which will continue after the wedding or to permanently dismiss an unwanted suitor. Her songs can have far-reaching consequences and affect the shape of her life long after the wedding is over.

The Berbers recognize that the songs are critiques of their existing mores, but when asked why such songs are allowed to be performed in public they reply in amazement that a wedding would not be a wedding without the songs, that Berber women have always sung at weddings. The more thoughtful suspect that it would be unfair to force a woman into an unwanted marriage without giving her a chance to prevent it through her lyrics. In fact, apart from the songs, a woman has no way of discouraging an unwanted or hated fiancé except by threatening or attempting suicide. However, the songs may also be perceived as a mechanism which, while giving women the impression of gaining power, ultimately supports the patriarchal system, for in spite of the rebelliousness of many of the lyrics the act of performance itself is also a mode of participation in a "marriage market," a display of wit, talent, and attractiveness to an audience that includes potential mates. Whatever the specific content of any given lyric, the singers never attack the institution of marriage itself in their songs. Their aim is to discourage unwanted suitors and to ensure engagement to their preferred young men. Notwithstanding the difficulties of determining their exact revolutionary force, the Berber songs expose the problems and deficiencies inherent in traditional views of male-female relationships in the Middle East and to the need for further, more intensive studies.

Notes

This chapter appeared originally in *Signs: Journal of Women in Culture and Society* 5, no. 3 (1980). The data on which this chapter is based were collected during eighteen months of fieldwork in 1965–66 in the Rif Mountains of Morocco. The author wishes to thank the Berbers for their patience, interest, and hospitality; Roger Joseph for his unstinting intellectual rigor and assistance; and Cheryl and David Evans, Katherine Frank Clark, Donald Heiney, James McMichael, John C. Rowe, Maria Ruegg, Barbara Herrnstein Smith, Diane Wakoski, and the anonymous reviewers of *Signs: Journal of Women in Culture and Society* for their comments and encouragement. Portions of this essay were delivered orally at the California Folklore Society (1974, 1976) and the Modern Language Association (1977).

1. Edward Westermarck, *Marriage Ceremonies in Morocco* (London: Macmillan, 1906); Carleton Stevens Coon, *Tribes of the Rif* (1931; reprint, New York: Kraus Reprint Co., 1970); David Montgomery Hart, *The Aith Waryaghar of the Moroccan Rif: An Ethnography and History* (Tucson: University of Arizona Press, 1976); and "The Land and the People" and "Social Organization," in *Morocco: Subcontractor's Monograph HRAF-62* (New Haven, Conn.: Human Relations Area Files, n.d.); Ernest Gellner, "Introduction" and "Political and Religious Organization of the Berbers of the Central High Atlas," in *Arabs and Berbers,* ed. Ernest Gellner and Charles Micaud (London: Trinity, 1973).

2. Roger Joseph, "Sexual Dialects and Strategy in Berber Marriage," *Journal of Comparative Family Studies* 7 (1976): 471–81.

3. Vanessa Maher, *Woman and Property in Morocco: Their Changing Relation to the Process of Social Stratification in Middle Atlas* (London: Cambridge University Press, 1974); Cynthia Nelson, "Public and Private Politics: Women in the Middle Eastern World," *American Ethnologist* 1, no. 1 (1974): 551–63; Fatima Mernissi, *Beyond the Veil: Male-Female Dynamics in a Modern Muslim Society* (New York: Wiley, 1975). Mernissi's view has been challenged in a review by Daisy Dwyer in *Signs: Journal of Women in Culture and Society* 2, no. 2 (1976): 470–73.

4. Joseph, "Sexual Dialects," 471.

5. Young men try to influence their fathers' decisions by threatening to divorce an

unwanted bride. Divorce is extremely easy for a man—who needs only repeat to his wife three times that she is divorced—and almost impossible for a woman to obtain. She can, however, drive her husband to divorcing her by threatening to use witchcraft against him. Such a step is rarely taken, however, since her father would have to return to the groom's family a large portion of the wedding settlement, already spent on food for the guests, and would mean that she would lose custody of all her children once they had been weaned.

6. *Morocco: Subcontractors's Monograph HRAF-62,* 178.

7. Milman Parry, *The Making of Homeric Verse: The Collected Papers of Milman Parry,* ed. Adam Parry (London: Oxford University Press, 1971); Albert B. Lord, *The Singer of Tales* (Cambridge: Harvard University Press, 1964).

8. All interpretations of the songs are based on native explications. Since they sometimes seemed far-fetched, I made it a practice to collect at least three interpretations from separate informants and found remarkable consistency in their understanding of the songs.

9. These dark glasses are obviously a recent innovation in the Rif. Although firecrackers are now used instead of gunplay to frighten evil spirits at the wedding, I was unable to determine what, if any, custom the dark glasses have replaced. It seems unlikely that they replace an earlier use of the veil, since it is always regarded as an Arab custom by the Berbers.

10. For a more detailed discussion of immigration and its impact on the Rif, see David Hart's *Aith Waryaghar,* 93–95.

11. Songs which are too blatantly sexual for the wedding ceremony are reserved for private encounters between the composer and her man. The following lyrics are two cases in point:

> Arge we-u-fen thakamun a tereyuk
> Ager wuht unbtho atere fath-e-nuk.
>
> [God, if you can find him, send me a breakfast of his kisses
> When the flowers bloom great thirst slays.]
>
> Wala mathak-e-nir menrarer thuggwazen
> Ebasheno thetfah mazwa thatubsen.
>
> [By God I swear I shall not tell all that I hide beneath my gown:
> Breasts hard and round as apples and under them, a bowl.]

A Berber bride is supposed to be a virgin at marriage, and the cloth stained with her hymenal blood is exhibited to the guests at the wedding. But if the groom has been the girl's lover, his mother will often kill a chicken and use its blood for the cloth to prevent scandal. Should his wife not be a virgin, the groom has the option of sending her back to her father's house in disgrace and reclaiming his *sadat;* but if he likes her and she can put her sexual experience with another man in a sympathetic light, he will often keep her nonetheless.

12. Victor Turner, *The Ritual Process: Structure and Anti-Structure* (Chicago: Aldine, 1969).

10

☙☙ ☙☙

Nashaṭ: The Gender of
Musical Celebration in Morocco

Deborah Kapchan

Nashaṭ is a noun that describes the attainment of a particular *ḥal,* or emotional "state" of celebration in Moroccan musical contexts.[1] Using the methodology of phenomenological description, this chapter investigates the role of gender in the creation of nashaṭ in festive situations. Nashaṭ is seen to be both an expression of the carnivalesque as well as a desirable component of Moroccan musical performance.

> *Nashaṭ:* briskness, sprightliness, liveliness, animation, vivacity, agility, alacrity, eagerness, ardor, zeal, energy, vim, activeness, activity, lively activity, action, operation; strength, power (physical and mental); vigor, vital energy, vitality.[2]

Phenomenological Description

"Phenomenology is accessible only through a phenomenological method. . . . It is a matter of describing, not of explaining or analyzing . . . [of returning] to the "things themselves" (Merleau-Ponty 1994, viii).

Scene One: Recollections of the Ethnographic Past

1982. I had just come to Morocco and was not practiced in the language. The distance of the event gives it a shadowy status in my imagination, as if I had dreamed it instead of lived it. I don't even remember how I managed to be there—in the popular section of town in the darkness. As a Moroccan friend and I walked the dusty unpaved streets to the wedding, I was aware of the Middle-Atlas Mountains looming above us, but they were invisible in the moonless night. Darkness enveloped us. The streetlights were sporadic; those that were lit flickered dimly, momentarily illuminating the half-built cinder-block buildings of the neighborhood. When we arrived at the celebration, I noticed that even the electricity in the ground-floor apartment was minimal; a single bulb dangled, unshaded, from a wire in the ceiling.

We were escorted into a narrow living room lined with stained sponge mattresses upon which people sat huddled together, the men seated together on one side of the room; the few women also pressed shoulder to shoulder, or interspersed bosom to back, on the other side of the room. It was as much separation as the cramped space allowed. I was squeezed between two heavy-thighed women, the synthetic material of their caftans swishing over me as they reluctantly ceded to their hostess's wishes to make room where there clearly was none. The sensation was sweat, sweat and noise, for blocking the entranceway now, in the only space available, were three women singers (shikhat; also sheikhat) and two men. One man held a fiddle (kamanja); another a large flat hand drum (bandir). The women also held three small finger drums (skiji). They were singing loudly in the upper parts of their throats, the force of their voices sounding like screams to my untrained ear. One by one they made their way down the narrow room, dancing, their hips undulating at the level of our faces, their turns threatening to topple the glasses set on the low round tables before us.

The guests thought these performances riotous, especially the men. Everyone was clapping. Some men tried to stand and dance with the performers. Their desire reeked of the red wine hidden behind pillows and poured discreetly into tea glasses under the table. Where was the groom, I wondered? And the bride? Perhaps they had already left to consummate the marriage. The men proffered money to the dancers, tucking bills right into their bosom and under their belts. I had the uncomfortable feeling of being where I should not be, for despite the presence of a handful of women, this space was clearly marked as male. They exhibited none of the respectful reserve I had come to expect of Moroccan men in public mixed-sex situations. Yet despite my foreign dress no one paid me any mind. The men were too carried away with their own inebriation—with the music, with the dancers—to notice my discomfort, or even my presence. This was collective seduction, my first experience of the performance of nashaṭ.

Scene Two: Female Performers and Women's Performances in the Near Past

1990. A circumcision is celebrated by an elementary school principal and his wife. They live on the school grounds. When I visit them a few weeks before the celebration, I find the wife and her sister in the courtyard with buckets of water scrubbing all the pots and pans of the household with steel wool and laundry detergent, their hands red with the effort. Preparations.

The day of the party, my two-year-old Moroccan daughter and I arrive with a small gift for the little boy. There are already thirty or some women in the classroom that they use for the party. We leave our *balgha* by the door and enter. The women range from adolescents to the elderly. Little children run mischievously across the room, escaping from the grasping arms of the playful guests; my daughter joins them impishly. Some guests sit on the foam mattresses lining the walls, others on woven mats that have been scattered on the cement. I find some friends and seat myself next to them on the floor. The hostess and her sister come around with fragrant glasses of steaming mint tea on gleaming metal trays. Minutes later, heaped plates of cookies are proffered: sugar cookies rolled in flaked coconut, cookies filled with almond paste and perfumed with orange-blossom water, cookies made with sesame paste. An abundance of sugar.

When all the women (for there are only women in attendance) have collected their cookie allotments on small foil-covered paper plates and the tea glasses have been emptied, four new women sashay into the room (plate 15). They are noisy and corpulent. Each holds a hand drum and one places a metal washbasin upside-down in the middle of the floor. A lone male accompanies them carrying a fiddle. He holds the instrument on his knee and runs the bow over the strings playing snippets of well-known pieces. The women begin to hit the small clay drums. They exchange a quick glance, listen to the lead fiddle line, and begin to sing, their voices strong and somewhat raspy.

The guests clap and sway their bodies to the music. The young girls in the crowd jump up almost brazenly and begin an undulating dance of seduction. They are dancing for themselves, but also for the eyes of the mothers of

prospective grooms. They tie scarves around their hips to accentuate the minute movements of their lower musculature, while the shikhat actively circulate among the audience members, pulling other, older, women onto their
feet. Before long the room is filled with bodies dancing energetically to the
music. Old women get up and move their hips back and forth, parodying
sexual intercourse and laughing almost hysterically. One performer jumps on
the washbasin, beating a rhythm with her bare feet. The others throw off their
headscarves, letting their long black hair go free, as they swing their heads
almost violently from left to right and right to left. This back-and-forth head
movement is an attribute of trance, and signals the group's passage from the
celebratory to the ecstatic.[3] No one is immune.

"Nashṭa mʿa ras-ak, yaki?" a family friend says to the woman on my right,
"You're pretty exuberant, aren't you?"

"Kulna nashṭin," she answers, "We're all nashṭin," and she circles away
across the room, her hips leading her in a display of nashaṭ, her face smiling
blissfully (plate 16).

Scene Three: The Ethnographic Present

1999. I am at a naming ceremony in a villa in an elite section of Marra-
kech. Early in the festivities, the guests are escorted past indoor fountains and
out into the garden where a large ram is waiting. To the pulsing beat of snare
drums, the ram is ritually slaughtered, its blood running down the blue and
white hand-lain mosaic tiles to the drain. There are sounds of joyous ulula-
tion. Blood is shed, the covenant is sealed: a new being has been given a name.

After the sacrifice, the guests are ushered back into the luxurious quarters of the villa, the women seated in the "Moroccan" living quarters on ban-
quettes, the men across the large room on Western-style leather couches. The
musical group separates us—two ud players, a drummer with a Western bat-
tery of drums, a miked darbuka player, two fiddle players. One player has
a ghaita, a double-reed woodwind, at his feet. And, of course, there is an
electric keyboard and synthesizer. This group plays all repertoires—the high
reed sounds of the Aissawa Sufi brotherhood, the sub-Saharan iron-cymbal
rhythms and snare drums of the Gnawa,[4] popular music (ash-shʿabi) as well
as the classical genre of al-malḥun, the oldest sung ballad tradition in Moroccan dialect.

The lead singer of this group is famous. He sits in the center with a microphone. The amplification is loud. It is impossible to hold a conversation
while the music is playing. So we dance. Or eat. We are served tea, nuts, cookies. We dance. Barefooted male servants offer us a choice of avocado juice or

milk blended with sugar and almonds. We dance some more. Mostly the mother of the little boy dances. She is the center of attention, celebrating the birth of her son and the sacrifice that has made his name sacrosanct. She pulls others up onto the dance floor: her sister, her aunt, her cousin, me. I am one of the few invited guests who is not a family member. This is an honor. We dance.

Soon we take our seats for dinner; first *djaj l-baldi b-zitun,* free-range chickens with olives.[5] Then a platter of freshly slaughtered and roasted lamb. After that, a steamy tagine of beef and prunes. This is followed by a huge dish of couscous layered with seven vegetables. We are served coke and orange soda throughout the meal, and hot mint tea is served at the end. After about twenty minutes, each table is presented with three bowls of homemade ice cream—hazelnut, vanilla, chocolate.

When the meal is over, the band once again begins to play. Now the music is more lively. We must dance if we are not to sleep! More family members dance: the father, the grandfather, the uncle, the great-aunt. Men and women dance together. The sweat pours down the backs of the dancers, cleaving to the satin and silk caftans, the beaded and pearled gowns of the guests. Some of the men wear dark Western suits; others are in white *faw-qiyyas,* traditional dress robes. Suddenly, without warning, one of the elder guests goes into trance, an older women who, I learn, has a history of "falling." We make room for her (one must never interrupt a trance), and her grown daughter puts a sash around her waist, gathering and holding it so that her mother's rhythmic movements can be free without the risk of her harming herself. Others continue to dance, though all watch the enraptured dancer from the corner of their eye. When the music stops, she falls to the floor and is caught by those around her and carried back to her place on the couch. She is fanned and encouraged to drink. Someone sprinkles rosewater on her to revive her with the sensation of wetness and the sweet odor. Nashaṭ has given over to *al-jadba,* trance. We have passed from the secularity of excess to the abjection of the trance state.

Nashaṭ: Excess and the Carnivalesque au Feminin

Nashaṭ is intricately related to Moroccan ludic events (*al-laʿb* in Moroccan Arabic). Imbricated in audition, it relies on the response of the audience to create feelings of consensus—literally, "feeling together" (Noyes 1993)—and ardor. Indeed, nashaṭ delineates not only a state of being, but a rhythm of being; it is a recognized performative response to a collective ambiance created in a musical environment. But it is a particularly gendered response; that is, it relies on the performance of female desire in order to be enacted at all.

That nashaṭ is related to rhythm is evidenced by another Moroccan idiom in the semantic field of celebration: *tqsira,* or "making short." Loosely equivalent to the American English idiom "to party," tqsira denotes the velocity of time as it is experienced in festive contexts. To say "Tqserna al-baraḥ f-lil" ("We partied last night," or literally, "We made [time] short last night") means that a good time was had, usually until the wee hours of the morning, and the night passed quickly in joyous and often intoxicating celebration. To party, then, is to speed up time. This is also true of the state of nashaṭ. Evoked by fast-paced music, whether acoustic or electric, nashaṭ only emerges in moments of accelerated aesthetic stimulation.

The three scenarios outlined above represent the production of nashaṭ at the level of three different social classes. The first scene is extremely popular, taking place in the poorest section of town in a cramped space, the gender separation only symbolic. Tea and a few cookies were served, and the men brought their own bottles of cheap red wine, which were barely concealed from general view. Female performers were present, and their interaction with the guests was informal and playful. These were not high-dollar shikhat, so to speak; rather performers like these are employed by the popular classes for very little monetary compensation. That they sing, dance, and often drink and smoke in these public spaces makes them the embodiment of stigma and social marginality (see chap. 8 in this volume). At this economic level, although less so now than previously, shikhat are synonymous with prostitutes (Kapchan 1996; cf. Nieuwkerk 1995).[6] They are, however, catalysts of nashaṭ insofar as they self-consciously embrace and exploit the "low" identity imputed to them by society. They become emblems of female seduction and sexuality. The men and women present interacted with their performance, getting up to dance, singing with them, clapping and generally letting themselves be taken up with the spirit of nashaṭ. The responsibility for the creation and display of nashaṭ, however, remained with the performers.

The second scenario represents a more petit bourgeois, or upwardly mobile, context.[7] The host and hostess are college-educated and live in a rapidly urbanizing agricultural center in central Morocco. The preparations for the celebration were long and arduous. The hostess herself, with the help of her female kin, spent hours baking the mounds of sweets that were served. The celebration took place in the afternoon in a respectable public setting—a schoolroom where the husband works. With the exception of the husband, who made brief appearances, and the one male band member, all the partici-

pants were women. The performers themselves enjoyed a "higher" social status because of this monosexual context. This celebration, like many middle-
class events, evidenced a close attention to decorum and propriety. The reputation of the host family was being consciously constructed in the festivities,
a reputation based on the degree of nashaṭ produced by the festive context.
Although catalyzed by the musicians, nashaṭ was enacted by the guests—in
their dance, their laughter, their parody, and their level of openness and re-
ceptivity. The guests were co-performers with the shikhat, just as bawdy and
playfully "low" as the musicians themselves, and this, no doubt, was also due
to the largely monosexual context of the performance.

The third context represents the elite sector of Moroccan society. The
food was much more copious, prepared by servants rather than the family
members themselves. The music was not just al-ʿaita,[8] or vocal shikhat music, but encompassed most all of the popular music genres heard at Moroccan celebrations. Indeed, it is fair to say that the "group" (al-juq), an amplified
band usually composed of young men and perhaps one female vocalist, has
replaced the shikhat in terms of popularity at festive events. Able to play several genres of Moroccan music, including raï (see chap. 8 in this volume), the
juq represents an interplay with global market forces, embodying the electronic aesthetic that has become an icon of modernity, while also interpret-
ing a range of regional musics for national consumption.

The group at this celebration was composed of nationally known recording artists. All men, they played to a mixed-gender audience. As mentioned
above, however, all of the guests were either extended family members or,
like me, were accorded symbolic kinship status, thus making the mixed
context more acceptable. This, added to the fact that the reputation of the upper classes is a fait accompli, and often allied with the mores of Europe,
makes the construction of public honor through gender segregation unnec-
essary. Because of these factors, the performance of nashaṭ lay entirely with
the female members of the family. They danced center stage, pulling guests
onto the floor much as the shikhat did in the first scenario. The musicians
provided the rhythm, but it was the hostesses who created the ambiance of
nashaṭ.

Observing the contexts above, it becomes clear that the production of
nashaṭ is not dependent on female musicians per se, but rather on the performance of female complicity and playfulness in a sexualized and musical
ambiance. One local criterion for evaluation of the level of nashaṭ is how
"loose" people become; the word used by most Moroccans is maṭluq. To be
maṭluq, loose, is to let go of inhibitions and to give oneself over to a collective

state of celebration (Kapchan 1996). It may have a positive or a negative connotation, depending on the context of its use.

In the first scenario—that of popular class performance—responsibility for nashaṭ was consigned to a marked and stigmatized sector of society (the shikhat), whose job it was to embody the "low" and the carnivalesque. This compartmentalization of performance repertoire in the enactment of celebration works to protect the other women of the lower classes—who are already stigmatized because of their economic status—from accusations of moral "looseness" by giving that denominator to a prescribed segment of society. (It is not necessarily immodest to be maṭluq; a shikha often exceeds the maṭluq, however, and is characterized as immodestly bold: *uja-ha mqazdar,* she is "tin-faced." Such behavior does constitute a breach of honor.) The overt flirtation of the shikhat with both the men and the women present elicited enthusiastic responses; the men interacting with the shikhat, both in terms of verbal exchange and in terms of bodily engagement in the dance. The shikhat "loosened" the atmosphere and the audience followed. In the second example—that of the more middle-class celebration—both performers and audience members were equally *muṭluqat* (fem. pl.). Responsibility for the creation of nashaṭ and the ability for the guests to be as "loose" as the performers came from the closed context of feminine celebration, licensed by the propriety of a same-sex gathering. The performance of nashaṭ played an important role, however, in establishing the reputation of the hostess, since a successful celebration is one where the all the guests are nashṭin. Finally, in the upper-class celebration, we find the performance of nashaṭ solely in the hands of the hostess and her female kin. Here there is no reputation to protect. The hostess is free to be maṭluqa without worrying about her status in the community or that of her family. The guests were considered part of an in-group with license to participate freely in the creation of nashaṭ.

Nashaṭ and Sense-Based Co-occurrence

As with any performance, there exist "co-occurrence rules" in the production of nashaṭ—factors that are present as determinants and constraints on levels of performative agency and emotion. In nashaṭ, these coeval factors are rooted in excess and grounded in the sensorium, not only in the obvious realm of sound, but also in the realms of taste, movement, and smell. Nashaṭ is imbricated in the senses, and the intensity of its emotional valence in performance is dependent on its interpolation in a larger range of (excessive) sensual experience.

Audition

Sound is the most primary requirement in the production and performance of nashat. In the above examples, there are two different kinds of Moroccan music: (1) l'ʿaita, or traditional vocal music performed by women (shikhat), often accompanied by male musicians on fiddle and drums, and (2) popular electronic music (ash-shʿabi) played by a band of male musicians, sometimes with a female vocalist. As mentioned, amplified bands are rapidly replacing shikhat in terms of popularity at festive events largely owing to their electric and modern "sound," but also to their flexibility in terms of musical repertoire. Not all the genres of music that bands play, however, lend themselves to the production of nashat. Indeed, musics that are slow—notably, love ballads in the malhun tradition and Andalusian music (choral music accompanied by a string ensemble)—while producing "other" emotional states, are not components of nashat. Nashat is a rhythmic response to a fairly fast-paced and rhythmic music—whether raï, ash-shʿabi, or l'ʿaita. Nashat is a state associated with vibrancy, with briskness, vim, and activity—adjectives that do not apply to the more meditative states brought on by slower classical genres. Thus the advantage of hiring a band or group of musicians is not only a variation of genre, but also a fluctuation in the production of emotional states. This extends also to the state of al-jadba, or trance, brought on by "beats" associated with different Sufi-influenced brotherhoods. As one band member once told me, "Hetta henaya kan diru an-nuba," that is, "We also play the turns." When I asked him what he meant, he answered, "You know, Sidi Abdelqadr, Lalla Mimouna, Sidi Hammou, Lalla Aisha Qandisha—the jinn." Some secular bands have now expanded their repertoire to include the musical progression of spirits evoked in possession ceremonies. The production of trance has become a commodity that can be marketed both locally and internationally (see Kapchan, forthcoming).

There is another component to the auditory aesthetic of nashat: volume. Whether produced by the belting voices of shikhat in close proximity to the guests or by the exaggerated amplification of the electric keyboard, the tenor of the music seems to enter the body and vibrate its very molecules. The looseness that is a quality of nashat is provoked at the microlevel of bodily movement and at the larger level of the social body (communitas). Inundated with loud sounds, the brainwaves change, the group dynamic alters, the social body is animated and revitalized.

Taste

Hospitality (*diyyafa*) is one of the most important social values in Morocco. It distinguishes families and individuals by region, by socialization, and by generosity—often measured by abundant, not to say excessive, amounts of food. It is not surprising, then, that food and drink play an essential part in all the scenarios depicted above. Even in the humblest of settings, inexpensive bakery-bought sugar cookies and sweet mint tea were served. Wine was also imbibed, though not openly "served," owing to its prohibition in Islam. In the middle-class scenario, all the food was prepared by hand—sesame seeds browned in oil-blackened frying pans, then pounded with mortar and pestle into paste for the cookies; huge batches of cookie dough mixed in large wooden tubs and baked in the public oven in batches of three or four hundred on institutional-size baking trays; hundreds of mint leaves separated and carefully washed for tea. The hostess and her family went to great lengths to create an image of themselves as cultivated and generous.

In the last scenario, food was as excessive as the rest of the festivities; we were fed huge quantities of meat. There were sheep's heads staring up at the guests from platters in the middle of each table; chickens whose skins had been carefully browned in olive oil and spices; mounds of fluffy couscous layered with lamb meat; bright orange pieces of firm pumpkin, carrots, zucchini, onions, and fava beans, seasoned with curry, fresh cilantro, and an occasional hot pepper.

Movement

Nashaṭ is a recognized performative response to a collective ambiance created in a musical environment. It is a rhythmic response, one related to velocity and the performance of feminine desire and seduction. As a reaction to music, it follows that nashaṭ includes movement, and particularly dance. In all three cases mentioned above, dance was a component—whether engaged in by the shikhat, by the guests, or by the hostess. This is not to say that dance is a requirement for nashaṭ to emerge; rather, some kind of responsive movement co-occurs with nashaṭ—whether outright Moroccan dance (characterized by rapid hip and abdominal movements and by extended and undulating arms), clapping, head bobbing, and other kinds of rhythmic bodily movements provoked by the music, or the more dramatic response of entering into trance. Nashaṭ is a participatory state; it is impossible to remain impassive and be nasht; it requires interaction and openness.

Smell

As in many cultures with a developed cuisine, smell is a sense intimately related to taste in Morocco. Hot mint and green tea is the national drink, and although the ritual of tea preparation and drinking is not as codified as it is, say, in Japan, it is just as meaningful in the cultural repertoire, symbolic of hospitality, of region (tea is made without mint in the south of Morocco, for example, and is boiled down until it is very strong and sweet), and of home and family. A good glass of tea, with just the right balance of mint, green tea, and sugar, signifies a well-cultivated and attentive hostess. Making tea for large groups requires a particular gift and is an essential aspect of celebration (see Lakhsassi 1999).

Tea was served at all the celebrations described above and always co-occurs with the production of nashaṭ. Likewise, flower water (either rose-water or orange-blossom water) is added to the sweets, giving them a distinct and pleasant odor. Incense is often burned before the celebrations; combinations of woods and resins like amber, myrrh, sandalwood, benzoin, and musk are burned on a brazier and the smoke wafted around the room in order to purify it of evil influences (the mischief of bad spirits) and to generally procure auspiciousness. This is not required, however, and occurs more in contexts of trance than in more secular productions of nashaṭ.

Defining Excess: Nashaṭ and Intoxication

The line between nashaṭ and al-jadba (from the root *ja-dha-ba*, "to attract") is thin but distinct. Someone who is entranced (*majdub*) is someone who is "attracted" to, or attracts, another entity (notably a jinn) and is inhabited (*meskun*) by that entity. There is a long history of ecstatic possession ceremonies designed to propitiate the possessing spirit in Morocco (see Crapanzano 1973; Eickelman 1976; Kapchan, forthcoming), and the aesthetics of these different rituals vary according to the sect that one affiliates with—whether the Gnawa, the Hamadsha, the Aissawa, or the Darkawa brotherhoods, to mention only the most well known. In Moroccan belief, once someone is possessed, they enter into a lifelong ritual relationship with the possessing spirit, since there is little possibility of exorcism. These ceremonies are so widespread among the various sectors of Moroccan society, that it is fair to say that

Morocco is a culture of trance, or at least a culture where an economy of trance gesture is codified and commonplace, reaching across boundaries of gender and of class.

Gestures associated with trance become signs that are then repeated and circulated in other performative contexts such as the ones above. When nashaṭ breaks into trance, as it did in the last case described, the ludic aspect of performance transforms into the seriousness of ritual, the power of seduction turns inward—the relationship of desire no longer enacted between members of the group, but rather between one individual and his or her possessing spirit(s). Such states of possession are often coded as being addictive or intoxicating by virtue of their power to seduce the individual into yet another marked state of being.[9]

In all the performances described, intoxication (al-blia) took place on one level or another and trance was signaled. In the first scene, the intoxication was quite literal—wine was imbibed by the men, albeit discreetly, and "loosened" the ambiance of the celebration. The shikhat provoked the desire of those present and a feeling of nashaṭ ensued. In the second case, the intoxication was more symbolic: at a designated moment the shikhat loosened their hair from their scarves and let it dangle before them, their chins directed toward their chests, their heads down and swinging from side to side rapidly. The vertigo induced by this act—both in the doing and in the observation—contributes to the creation of an altered state. But the movement was also a sign, one of the recognized gestures denoting the abject state of trance.[10] Possession trance is abject insofar as it "disturbs identity, system, order" and "does not respect borders, positions, rules" (Kristeva 1982, 4); uniting perceiver and perceived, subject and object, jinn and host, trance possession confounds boundaries by transcending them. This is a different experience than that of nashaṭ, where seduction depends upon the maintenance of boundaries, however fictional and ephemeral they may be.

In the third case examined—that of the elite naming ceremony—trance was actually enacted, causing a bit of alarm among the family members, and temporarily breaking the state of nashaṭ created by the hostess for her guests. Although the trance did not last long, its emergence in the context of nashaṭ elucidates the relation between the two states: both co-occur in musical contexts, relying on a certain "beat" (dukka), or rapid rhythm; both are imbricated with the senses of movement, taste, and smell (see Pacques 1991; Chlyeh 1998). Where nashaṭ is secular and carnivalesque, however—a playful mocking of serious life—trance is serious ritual, embodying the possibility of not just entering into a seductive relation of desire with the other, but of actually being inhabited by an other (a possessing spirit).

Nashaṭ connotes successful celebration. It is a performance of frivolity, a secular engagement in collective seduction that relies upon and responds to fast-paced rhythmic music and co-occurs with other sense-based experiences—notably the ingestion of food, the inhalation of specific odors, and codified movements of the body. The case studies described happened over the span of eighteen years and exemplify three different class orientations to nashaṭ. In the most popular example, the production of nashaṭ is given over to a designated category of performer (shikhat); in the more middle-class example, both performers and guests share the responsibility for the creation of nashaṭ; while in the upper-class celebration, nashaṭ is enacted by the hostess herself. All examples, however, share several performative factors: (1) nashaṭ is produced only in response to fast-paced, rhythmic music; (2) it is expressed in a gestural and verbal economy of feminine desire and seduction; (3) it is imbricated in the senses, particularly in the senses of audition, taste, smell, and movement; (4) it is a carnivalesque and ludic performance, related to intoxication, that is nonetheless in tension with the performance of trance, an intoxication of a different, more serious and ritualistic order. People in trance are never described as being nashṭin; nonetheless, people may fall into trance while in a state of nashaṭ. This transformation signals a movement out of a state of differentiation necessary to the objectification of feminine desire, and into a state of abjection, where the boundaries of the self (the desiring subject) and the object of desire (the jinn, or possessing spirit) are confounded. Because the state of nashaṭ relies on a recognition of feminine difference and desire, it instantiates gender typologies into the cultural repertoire, while at the same time producing a collective experience of festive delirium. Nashaṭ is both the measure of festive success and an example of a musical aesthetic intricately related to the performance of gender and class relations.

Notes

1. Ḥal has a secular and a sacred usage in the Moroccan idiom. Coming from the Sufi tradition, it is used to describe a spiritual state of communion with divinity. In nonreligious parlance, however, it is equated with any kind of marked (as opposed to unmarked

or usual) state of being—whether emotional, psychological, or spiritual. This is the sense in which I use the term in this chapter.

2. Cf. *Hans Wehr Dictionary of Modern Standard Arabic.* This definition is the classical Arabic definition. The Moroccan usage of this word is more specific to contexts of celebration, as delineated below.

3. Swinging the head back and forth is a common movement in trance and possession ceremonies. It is a recognized movement that connotes the state of trance.

4. The Gnawa are a subculture originating in the African countries south of the Sahara desert. They enact healing ceremonies for the possessed, invoking the spirits, or jinn (*jnun*), with their repertoire of music.

5. This is distingushed from *dajaj ar-rumi* (foreign chicken), chicken brought up on packaged feed in cages. "Foreign" chicken is cheaper, less gamy, and less succulent.

6. This was especially so in 1982 when shikhat were only beginning to launder their social image and control their value through self-conscious participation in the music market.

7. Using the categories of lower, middle, and upper class is problematic in Morocco, where *tabaqa ash-sh'abiya* (the popular class) and *tabaqa al-'aliya* (the upper class) have been the defining distinctions. The rapid influx of capitalism—evidenced by privatization, advertising, and the facility to borrow money at high interest rates—now defines a consumerist class, a class of literate and upwardly mobile working couples who embrace the ideal of the nuclear family.

8. Many shikhat song genres are defined by region; namely, *al-gharbawi, al-hasbawi, al-hawzi, al-jabli, al-j'aidan, al-mersawi, az-za'ri,* and *az-zayani.* Other genres include *al-'lawi* (song by the Beni Iznesan tribe, near Algeria), *ar-rwais* (from the Souss region), and *as-saken.* Of these, only *al-hasbawi, al-hawzi* and *al-mersawi* are considered *al-'aita,* which are *al-'anmat al-murakaba,* complex genres (Bouhamid 1995).

9. This is not an intoxication brought about by alcohol (though alcohol may play a part, as in the first scenario); rather it is a moment when ecstasy circulates among members of a group. It is an intersubjective experience, not unrelated to the concept of ek-stacy used by phenomenologist Merleau-Ponty to delineate an active movement of percipience between bodies, an act that reaches out into the world with intentionality at the same time that it draws in the world for interpretation. For Merleau-Ponty, ek-stacy is the movement of the senses outward; it is a feeling of expansiveness, as the individual body breathes through the intersubjective presence of other bodies in the world.

10. The relation between abjection and trance in Moroccan possession ceremonies is explored more fully in Kapchan, forthcoming.

References

Artaud, Antonin. 1970. *The Theatre and its Double.* London: John Calder.

Bouhamid, Mohamed. 1995. "Innahum yuriduna al-'aita ka dajijin li jam'i al-hushudi? as-sulta fi al-maghribi lam tafham 'anna ihtirama al-'aita fi-hi janibun min jawanibi al-hafidi 'ala shakhsiyatina." *Al-Ittihad al-Ishtiraqi* April 15, 6.

Crapanzano, Vincent. 1973. *The Hamadsha: A Study in Moroccan Ethnopsychiatry.* Berkeley and Los Angeles: University of California Press.

Chlyeh, Abdelhafid. 1998. *Les Gnaoua du Maroc: Itinéraires initiatiques transe et possession.* Casablanca: Éditions le Fennec.

Dermenghen, Emile. 1954. *Le culte des saints dans l'Islam Maghrebin.* Paris: Gallimard.

Diouri, Abdelhai. 1979. *Transe, écriture: Contribution à une lecture socio-sémiotique de quelques faits de culture orale et écrite au Maroc.* Doctoral dissertation, École des Hautes Études en Sciences Sociales, Paris.

Eickelman, Dale F. 1976. *Moroccan Islam: Tradition and Society in a Pilgrimage Center.* Austin: University of Texas Press.

Kapchan, Deborah. 1996. *Gender on the Market: Moroccan Women and the Revoicing of Tradition.* Philadelphia: University of Pennsylvania Press.

————. Forthcoming. *Traveling Spirit Masters: Sound, Image, and Word in the Global Marketplace.*

Kristeva, Julia. 1982. *Powers of Horror: An Essay on Abjection.* New York: Columbia University Press.

Lakhsassi, Abderahmane u Abdelhadi Sebti. 1999. *Man ash-shāy ilā al-atāy: Al'ada wa al-tarikh.* Rabat: Kuliyat al-ādab wa 'ulūm al-insaniyya.

Merleau-Ponty, Maurice. 1994. *Phenomenology of Perception.* London: Routledge and Kegan Paul.

Nieuwkerk, Karin van. 1995. *"A Trade Like Any Other": Female Singers and Dancers in Egypt.* Austin: University of Texas Press.

Noyes, Dorothy. 1993. "Contesting the Body Politic: The Patum of Berga." In *Bodylore,* edited by Katharine Young, 134–61. Knoxville: University of Tennessee Press.

Pacques, Viviana. 1991. *La Religion des Esclaves: Recherches sur la Confrérie Marocaine des Gnawa.* Rome: Vitali.

11

On Religion, Gender, and Performing: Female Performers and Repentance in Egypt

Karin van Nieuwkerk

In Mediterranean cultures, as in many other cultures, women symbolize and demarcate the boundaries of social or ethnic groups. Their sexuality and bodies have therefore been under social control for long time. In the 1960s, the concepts of honor and shame were created to investigate the issues of gender and sexuality in Mediterranean societies (see Peristiany 1965; Pitt-Rivers 1965; Abou Zeid 1965). Although the early researches of the Oxford school have been highly criticized (see Magrini's introduction to this volume; Brandes 1987; Herzfeld 1980, 1987; Gilmore 1987; Abu-Lughod 1986; Wikan 1984; Meneley 1996), and nowadays concepts such as honor and shame can be considered obsolete in many Mediterranean countries, a concern with controlling women's sexual behavior can be discerned in the Islamic world. As a result of the growing influence of Islamic fundamentalist movements, the symbolic function of the female body has regained vigor in many Muslim countries (Sabbah 1984; Ahmed 1992; Nieuwkerk 1995). Fundamentalists appear to have an "obsession with women" (Mernissi 1987).

It is no wonder, then, that Muslim women who transgress gender roles pertaining to sexual behavior are highly stigmatized. Egyptian singers, dancers, and actresses are a case in point. Belly dancers in particular are emblematic of all behaviors that women should avoid. The female body is the embodiment of seductive power, and its open expression is therefore strongly condemned in moral-religious discourses. Since the bodily dimension is focal in entertainment, it is an extremely sensitive field for women to work in. Dancers are symbols of corruption and immorality because they exhibit their sexual bodies in public to earn money. This is almost equivalent to prostitution in the eyes of many, and particularly in the eyes of the devout believers.[1]

Given the growing influence of Islamic fundamentalism in the Muslim world, several forms of art, including music and dance, are under attack (Tadros 1999; Ramzi 1999; Abu Sahdi 1999). Belly dancers are not only the target of Egyptian Muslim fundamentalists: the ultraorthodox rabbis also use their growing influence to curb this profession in Israel (NRC Handelsblad, 9 November 1988; Brooks 1998, 247). Since the late eighties, the religious battle against art has begun to affect the performers. Several famous female performers have repented and adopted the hijab, the new form of veiling. They have strongly condemned their former practices and publicly confessed their former sins. Their conversion has been capitalized upon by Islamic fundamentalists and the artists' repentance has become a symbol of the rightness of their Islamic path. The former artists are thus used in the Islamist struggle against art.

In the discourse on the "repentant artists," that is, the "born-again actresses" and "converted belly dancers" (Nasif and Khodayr 1991; Abu-Lughod 1995; Brooks 1998; Times [Cairo], 17 June 1989), an interesting and widely shared set of assumptions is discernible. It consists of the following logical deductions. The Islamic religion is all about morality. Singing, dancing, and acting is immoral. So singers and dancers are not only immoral but also irreligious. Being a devout Muslim and a practicing performer is a contradiction, particularly for women. The veiled woman and the belly dancer are antithetical symbols of the devout and the pagan person. The trend of the "born-again" Muslim performers confirms this opposition between devotion and performing. One first needs to be born again or to be converted in order to become a religious person.

In this chapter, my aim is to deconstruct this seemingly logical discourse on the contradictory nature between believing and performing. I intend to unravel the Islamist discourse on religion, gender, and performing by using the repentant artists as a case study. I compare their discourse with views of "non-star" performers in Egypt. During fieldwork on common female singers and dancers in Cairo, I discussed their opinion on being an artist and devotion. Do they perceive a contradiction between believing and performing?

The Islamic discourse on morality is highly gendered. The weight of the accusation of immorality with regard to the entertainment trade is leveled against women (Nieuwkerk 1995). Gender theories stress that in order to investigate gender one has to distinguish between three different, albeit intersecting, levels (Harding 1986, 18; Moore 1988, 12–42). First, it is important to analyze the symbolic level, that is, the ideological construction of masculinity and femininity. Second, the structural level and the differences between and within the sexes with regard to class, ethnicity, marital status, and age should be investigated. Third, it is important to analyze the individual level at which the multilayered and complex formation of identities is taking place. In this chapter, I tackle the symbolic level in particular by investigating the ideology on music, gender, and Islam. I also deal with the difference between being a star performer or a non-star performer, which is strongly related to class background. In the last section, I focus on the individual level. By concentrating on the religious identity of lower-class female performers, I analyze the ambivalent relation between religion, morality, and performing.

In the first section, I analyze the discourse on music and singing in Islam. I examine a few texts that are informative for the present Islamic fundamentalist objections against music and art. Why does the Islamist discourse "paganize" art? In the second section, I describe the recent trend of converted artists in Egypt. How are they perceived and how do they present their conversion? What does this express about the contradictory nature of devotion and being an artist? Third, I go into the religious feelings of a group of female entertainers still practicing their profession, and analyze their sense of the (in)compatibility of performing and believing.

Music, Gender, and Islam

I am currently engaged in research on Dutch female converts to Islam. For this reason, I visited the Tawheed mosque in Amsterdam. In this mosque—reputed to be very strict, scriptural, and fundamentalist—a Dutch Muslim gave a lecture on music. Speaking about music in front of a heavily-veiled audience, half of whom were Dutch converts and the other half second-generation Moroccan and Turkish women who had mastered the Dutch language, she related the following precepts. The general rule on music, singing, and listening to music is that it is *haram*, forbidden. It is a grave sin and just as bad as drinking, gambling, or adultery. We know in the West, she explained, that we forget everything when we listen to music. We forget ourselves, but more important, we forget Allah. We hang photos of our favorite pop star on the wall and adore him as a god. We all know how bad and immoral people behave in a disco. The Quran and music cannot go together in one heart. It is dangerous and one of the greatest works of the Devil. Keep away from the radio and recite the Quran instead was her advice to the audience. Several questions came up after the lecture, for example, "Is singing with children allowed?" She answered that you are allowed to sing with children but should avoid clapping hands because clapping hands is similar to a rhythmical instrument. The Dutch women silently nodded, realizing that the first song Dutch mothers teach their children, "Clap Your Hands," was haram. I was somewhat astonished to hear such a strict interpretation of music, singing, and dancing. The Dutch woman's view reminded me of fundamentalist interpretations I had occasionally heard in Egypt during my fieldwork on female singers and dancers. A few weeks later, I interviewed her and discussed, among other things, her sources for the lecture on music. She said that besides the Quran and the Hadith, an important source was her Egyptian husband.

I use this Tawheed lecture, published in part in the organization's newsletter (*El-Tawheed* 8 [90] 1999: 1–8), as an example of recent Islamic fundamentalist thinking on music, singing, and dancing. The second source I delve into is the book *Halal and Haram* by the Islamist thinker Yusuf al-Qaradawi (1984). Third, I use the research papers on religious fundamentalism from the Legal Research and Resource Center for Human Rights (LRRC) in which the views of several sheikhs, dominating the official and unofficial media, are analyzed.[2] These three sources provide insights into the different strands of present Islamist thinking: from unknown individuals such as the Egyptian husband to an acknowledged Islamist thinker, and from a range of popular sheikhs producing cassettes to official sheikhs who voice their opinions on TV. These analyses will reveal that there is no single Islamist voice, let alone one Islamic voice.[3]

In the Taweed lecture, the audience was told that Islam forbids everything that is useless. Performing innocent songs on religious feast days or at weddings is *halal* (permissible). Also songs on the unity of God, expressing love for the Prophet, or praising the benefits of Islam are halal. The *duff* (tambourine) is the only instrument that is allowed. Clapping hands and singing in the presence of the other sex are forbidden. Contemporary music and singing at weddings and parties as well as on TV and on the radio propagate sex relations by describing bodily excitement. It diverts the attention of the youth and will lead them to commit *zina'* (adultery). Not only do performers give bad habits to people; they also collect money from poor people in order to buy cars and villas in the West. Actors and actresses do the same by selling obscene films. They destroy the youth. Dancing is in all circumstances forbidden, even among women, since the female body is *'awra* (taboo, shameful) and should be concealed and protected.[4]

The analysis of why music and singing are so harmful is instructive in order to understand the strong link between music and infidelity. Music and songs may appear innocent, the audience is informed, but they bring much damage. Sheikh al-Islam ibn Taymiyah is quoted to this effect. Music is the wine of souls, and when the soul becomes like a drunkard, polytheism (*shirk*), sex, and crime will creep into the soul. Shirk, murder, and zina' are well-known crimes of musicians and their audience. Singing is perceived as an introduction to adultery. When innocent men and women start listening to music and songs, their souls will become corrupt, and finally they will commit zina'. The Devil is taking control over these people. Another authority, Ibn al-Qayyim, is also quoted in the lecture in order to stress the incompatibility of devotion and music. He states that one cannot love songs and the Quran at the same time. The one chases the other. The Quran is a burden for performers and for those who listen to songs. People who love songs do not care about their prayers, and they are indifferent and lazy when they visit a mosque.

The relationship between infidelity, sex, and music reveals the assumed incompatibility of performing and devotion. The audience is incited to forget their religion by listening to music. Performers themselves are not only accused of infidelity but even of polytheism, that is, apostasy. Whereas the interpretation of the Dutch convert and her sources, including her Egyptian husband, is very strict, this link between performance and nonbelief is also found in less strict interpretations.

The Islamist writer Yusuf al-Qaradawi, in his book *Halal and Haram,* also deals with music and forbidden things in Islam. He explains in the introduction that Azhar University asked him to write this book. According to his view, current writers on Islam appear to belong to two different categories. The first group adores the West and imitates Western habits and practices. They forget what is halal and haram in Islam. The other group is very strict and has fixed ideas about haram and halal. When this group is asked about music, singing, chess, and women showing their hands and faces, they will probably declare it haram. According to al-Qaradawi, then, the Tawheed mosque in the Netherlands would belong to this second category. Al-Qaradawi states that he himself tries not to belong to either of these groups. He intends to combine religious truth and current scientific knowledge (al-Qaradawi 1984, part 1, 8–10).

Al-Qaradawi starts his explanation by stating that singing is one of the pleasant things that satisfies the soul, entertains the heart, and caresses the ear. Islam permits singing under the condition that it is not obscene or harmful for Islamic morality. Furthermore, it is not harmful if it is accompanied by music as long as the music is not exciting. However, there are a few limitations. First, the content of the song should not contradict Islam. If, for instance, it praises wine and incites people to drink, listening to or singing the song is haram. Second, even if the content is not against Islam, the way of singing might be haram, as it would be, for instance, if accompanied by suggestive sexual movements. Third, Islam combats extravagance even in devotion, so surely in entertainment. It is not permissible to devote too much time to entertainment, as this does not leave enough time for meritorious deeds and religious obligations. Fourth, if a certain song or type of music arouses the senses and weakens spirituality, one must avoid them in order to close the door to seduction. Last, if singing goes hand in hand with activities that are haram in Islam, such as drinking, obscenity, and sin, that singing is also haram.

Al-Qaradawi does not deal with private dancing by nonprofessionals, but the status of professional dancers only needs a short exposition (1984, part 2, 162–63). Islam forbids professions that are harmful for the religion, morality, and good manners of society. Prostitution is for that reason forbidden, and by extension sexual expression in dance and other erotic activities, such as suggestive or obscene songs, provocative plays, and "any other rubbish which some people nowadays call 'art' or 'progressive.'"

Al-Qaradawi's tone is more liberal than that of the Dutch convert. Yet it should be recalled that the Islamic discourse on morality is a highly gendered discourse. If al-Qaradawi's view on the proper place of women in society is analyzed, it becomes clear that there is no space for female performers. In the section on marriage and family life, al-Qaradawi explains that Islam forbids *khulwa* (privacy) between men and women who are not related by marriage or close consanguinity. The reason for this is to protect them from wrong thoughts and sexual feelings that are naturally supposed to occur between a man and a woman in the absence of a third person. All religions forbid rape and adultery, but Islam, as the last revelation, is very strict in its interdiction on zina'. Adultery leads to uncertainty of genealogy, maltreatment of children, breaking-up of family life, bitterness in relations, the spread of venereal diseases, a general attitude of moral laxity, and an abundance of lust and self-glorification. Everything that creates passion and leads toward indecency, obscenity, and sexual relations is haram. Looking with lust at the other sex is also prohibited, because the eye is "the key of the heart" (al-Qaradawi 1984, part 2, 26). Looking at another person's ʿawra, the parts of the body that should be covered, should also be avoided, either when it pertains to the opposite sex or the same sex, with lust or without lust. According to most religious scholars, the male ʿawra includes the parts between the knee and the navel, whereas for women it includes everything except the hands and the face. Al-Qaradawi concludes that an innocent gaze at the part of the body that does not belong to the ʿawra is permitted if the gaze does not become obtrusive and is not repeated out of pleasure or lust. Watching female performers clearly does not belong to the category of "the innocent gaze."

Al-Qaradawi constructs an opposition between Muslim women and non-Muslim women. Muslim women are chaste, honorable, and modest. They hide their beauty in several ways. They cast their eyes down and do not mingle with men. Their clothes meet several conditions, such as covering the whole body except the hands and the face, while the material is not transparent and the clothes do not fit tightly. Last, Muslim women walk and talk in an honorable way, avoiding any gestures that look like flirtation. Female performers do not fit this category of Muslim women. They are antithetical to proper Muslim women. They do not hide their beauty but show their ʿawra to unrelated men. They capitalize on beauty and attraction and their ʿawra is their main productive asset. Female performers thus belong to the category of "infidels."

Our last source, the project by the Legal Research and Resource Center for Human Rights in Cairo provides another view on the Islamist discourse on gender and performing. An analysis of the LRRC research papers reveals the influence of religious fundamentalism on art, journalism, and on official governmental censorship. Marilyn Tadros describes the recent official and unofficial religious discourse concerning women and art. She describes the discourse by individuals who are given media space, such as the late Sheikh Metwali Shaarawi and Sheikh al-Ghazali. Furthermore, the views of some sheikhs whose tapes are spread all over Egypt or whose books are sold on the market but have not been given space in the media, such as Sheikh Abd el-Hamid Keshk and Sheikh Omar Abdel Kafi, are analyzed. She concludes that both discourses are similar with regard to their views on women, arts, and the media (Tadros 1999, part 3, 5).

Sheikh Shaarawi was one of the most influential authorities calling for the repentance of actresses and artists. He was particularly renowned for bringing about the repentance of the famous singer and actress Shadia. He strongly voiced the opinion that singing, dancing, and acting are haram because they excite the sexual instincts. "Then also God made the sexual instinct the only instinct that itches. Do not excite it more!" (in Tadros 1999, part 3, 2). Sheikh Al-Ghazali was known as a "moderate" but has moved to less moderate opinions recently. He has expressed the following opinion on art:

> The artistic field today in the Arab World is on very vile and im-
> balanced soil. It is strange that it is being supported by writers who
> have made pacts with the devil to fight Islam and forget God, fighting
> against everything pure and new, because under the title of secular-
> ism they are conspiring to ill this nation that seeks life under the um-
> brella of faith and steadfastness, away from all atheism and prostitu-
> tion. (In Tadros 1999, part 3, 3)

Also the following statement (written in 1992) clearly expresses his equation of art with secularism or atheism:

> In Russia where there is no religion, the arts partially took the place
> of religion, and tried to fill in the emotional space that was emptied
> by atheism. It tried to keep the hearts busy, those hearts that were
> emptied of God, busy with the different types of feelings that are
> made by music, songs, and shows. . . . But the Arab and Islamic
> nation is the complete opposite. . . . It is a nation where religion fills
> its emotion and mind with so much . . . that makes it give little time
> to madness and theaters. (In Tadros 1999, part 3, 3).

Abdel Kafi is a fervent student of Sheikh Shaarawi and Sheikh Ghazali and works as a media consultant for the Islamic World Alliance. He considers art a heretical practice and calls the cinemas "Devil homes" (Ramzi 1999, 1). He strongly supports the veiling of actresses and made the following comment on the Egyptian reaction toward the repentant artists: "When the actresses wore the swimming suits, we clapped until our palms reddened. But when she wore the veil we fought against her with the worst of methods. We all know that those who pay, usually pay for nakedness and not for veiling and the obedience of God" (Tadros 1999, part 3, 5).

Tadros concludes that women are the primary focus of the religious discourses on art. Indeed, as I have indicated, Tadros stresses that the sexual discourse is central to the religious discourse. Women exist to provoke the sexual instinct and should therefore be hidden away from sight. Art exists to provoke sexuality and thus art is an evil that requires repentance (Tadros 1999, part 3, 6).

Converted Female Performers

Since the 1980s, the growing influence of Islamic fundamentalism has been discernible in the Egyptian entertainment field. The government follows a multiple strategy with regard to Islamism. The extremists are being repressed and imprisoned, while the moderates are given the opportunity to voice their opinions. The government is partly Islamicizing its policy in order to weaken the Islamist case. The Egyptian media policy is accordingly unclear and unsystematic. The government attempts to prove that it is more "religious" than the fundamentalists and fights against the religious fundamentalists at the same time (Tadros 1999, part 1, 4). Consequently, the growing religious pressure from both sides is affecting the field of art and entertainment. The theater and media have come under stricter religious censorship (see also Abu Sahdi 1999). Religious programming has increased and some of the most fundamentalist sheikhs or Islamic thinkers are now presented on the screen. Belly dancing has been banned from TV, and it is very difficult for new dancers to obtain an official license (Nieuwkerk 1995, 63). In 1994, the religious influence was further strengthened when, in January, the State's Council announced the right of the Azhar institution to censor arts and object to broadcast views contradictory to Islamic principles and teachings (Tadros 1999, part 1, 7).

From the 1970s onward, women started to adopt the hijab, the new Islamic dress. At first it was mainly the female students at universities who started to wear the hijab, but now this practice has also spread among the women of the lower middle classes. At present, many working women are adopting the veil (see MacLeod 1991; Zuhur 1992). Abu-Lughod argues that working women are generally criticized for challenging the domestic model (1995, 57). Female performers do what an increasing number of Egyptian women have done; that is, they take on the hijab. Female stars are visible, public examples of working women. Besides, they work in disreputable fields and are accordingly under more religious pressure. Because they are so well known, their transformation has received much attention.

Islamists have capitalized on these "born-again" stars in order to support the trend toward women's veiling, particularly in their struggle against art. According to Kamal Ramzi, the extremist groups wage war against the arts at three levels. First, they attack the arts in print, publishing interviews with and booklets on repentant artists. Second, they attack cinemas and theaters as well as artists. Third, they strongly influence media and art through the rules and bylaws of censorship that are enforced by Saudi companies (Ramzi

1999, 2).[5] Here I will consider attacks in print. A booklet with the confessions of many actresses and belly dancers under the title *Repentant Artists and the Sex Stars* has been published in order to promote the case of converted artists. Shams al-Barudi's book *My Trip from Darkness to Light* includes an introduction by the Islamic preacher Zeinab al-Ghazali. Many converted dancers and actresses were invited to Sheikh Shaarawi's popular program. They distanced themselves from their former profession and received the hijab from Shaarawi, who blessed them (Brooks 1998, 242).

Shams al-Barudi was the first actress who "repented." In 1977, she retired and donned the veil. Hala al-Safy was one of the first famous belly dancers "to convert to fundamentalism" in 1986. She is reported to be active in combating dancing because she considers it totally haram and hates to remember that she used to dance. Now penitent, she has built a school for teaching Islam (*Times* [Cairo], 17 July 1989; Tadros 1999, part 4, 2). Soheir al-Babli, a star of the Egyptian theater, stopped acting in 1993 in the middle of a successful production. A week before a pilgrimage to Mecca, al-Babli was quoted as saying that actresses have nothing to repent and that "the smell of terrorist groups is rising to our noses." When she came back, she was veiled and had retired (Brooks 1998, 241; Tadros 1999, part 4, 2). Sahar Hamdi was considering retreating as well at that time; top model Gihan Babikir has also recently adopted the veil; and several Egyptian artists such as Hanan have retired (Tadros 1999, part 4, 245; *Middle East Times*, 30 May 1997; *Nisf al-Dunya*, 11 July 1999, 57–59).

Repentant artists began expressing the illegitimacy of art and the necessity for the "return to God." Religious groups promoted their conversion and remorse as exemplary to other "sex stars." The voices and choices of the repentant artists were applauded while those performers still working were condemned as pagans. According to Ramzi, it had become the norm for repentant actresses to announce that colleagues will soon join the "convoy of lights," also mentioning names of artists who had no intention of retiring. Similarly, Sheikh Shaarawi, after mentioning the veiling of a row of actresses, said: "There are others who have already taken the decision [to retire], and some of them are merely rounding up their work, especially those who do not have the means to end contracts" (Ramzi 1999, 4). This strategy put pressure on the active female performers to defend themselves.

Another example of religious pressure on performers is the refusal by the religious authorities to give famous dancers the necessary papers to perform the pilgrimage to Mecca unless they stopped performing. Even access to absolution of their "sins" is taken away from performers unless they stop their "sinful practices." This again emphasizes the idea that being a performer is antithetical to religious observance. Furthermore, the controversy over whether the money of artists can be used for religious purposes, such as distributing food to the poor during Ramadan, indicates the "paganization" of everything connected to the artists' lives.

The public reaction to the converted artists is complex, as shown, for instance, by Abu-Lughod (1995). Joy, jokes, envy, and revulsion are the artists' portion. Most intellectuals and former colleagues still working in the field of art criticized the repentant artists (Brooks 1998, 242; Abu-Lughod 1995, 64). Cynical jokes like the following are told among the Egyptian populace: "Who are the second best paid women in Egypt? Belly dancers, of course, because Saudi tourists throw hundred-dollar banknotes on their feet while they are dancing. Who are the best-paid women in Egypt? The converted belly dancers, of course, because Saudi sheikhs transfer thousand-dollar banknotes to their accounts if they stop dancing."[6] The repentant artists are accused of being only interested in money, before and after conversion. It is added that the converted stars were becoming older anyhow, and that conversion is a way of making a last big haul (Brooks 1998, 242–43; *Middle East Times,* 10 May 1997; Tadros 1999, part 4, 2). Fear of extremist attacks is said to be another reason for their conversion. A number of intellectuals and journalists have been attacked, and artists could be the next targets. Indeed Farida Seif el-Nasr—who had retired but later decided to return to show business— was attacked. Hala al-Safy recounted a dream in which she was passing a mosque and was frightened because she was not properly dressed. Suddenly a man appeared in her dream who took of his coat and covered her with it. The psychiatrist, novelist, and feminist Nawaal al-Saadawi concluded that one needs not be a psychiatrist to interpret this dream as a reaction against pressure by religious extremists (Brooks 1998, 244).

How do the stars themselves narrate their repentance? Hala al-Safi's confession is published in *Repentant Artists:*

> I confess . . . that I left my life in the hands of the Devil to play with and to do what he wanted without my feeling the sins of what I did, until God willed and desired to remove me from this swamp. . . . Just as I acknowledge and confess that I . . . regret every moment that I lived far from God in the world of nights and art and parties . . . I entrust God to accept my remorse and my repentance. (In Abu-Lughod 1995, 54).

In her confession, we see again this association of art and the Devil. The retreat of the actress Shams al-Barudi received much attention as well. Her confession is also publicized in *Repentant Artists* and contains similar motives to those found in Hala al-Safy's story. She relates how she was struck by a poem about veiling and beautiful people being duped by praise. At that moment she realized that it described her life and started to hate acting. She went to Mecca afterwards to perform the ʿumra, the lesser pilgrimage, and had a revelatory experience:

> At night I felt a constricting of my chest as if all the mountains in the world were on top of me. My father asked me why I couldn't sleep. I told him I wanted to go the Grand Mosque. He was surprised but pleased that I had requested this. When we got to the sanctuary and I greeted it and began to circumambulate, my body began to tremble. I started sweating. My heart seemed to be jumping out of my chest and I felt at that moment as if there was a person inside trying to strangle me. Then he went out. Yes, the Devil went out and the pressure that was like all the mountains of the world weighing on my breast lifted. The worries were gone. And I found my tongue burst forth with prayers for my children and my husband and I began crying so hard that it was as if a volcano had burst and no one could stop it.
>
> As I reached the shrine of the Prophet Ibrahim, I stood up to pray and recited the opening verse of the Koran as if for the first time. I started recognizing its beauty and meaning as if God has graced me. I felt there was a new world around me. Yes, I was reborn. I felt I was a bride and that the angels were walking in my wedding march. Everything around me brought me happiness.

She concludes her confession thus:

> I'll never go back to acting. I won't go back to the Devil who stole everything from me. I've tasted the sweetness of faith and closeness to God . . . just as I tasted the Devil's life. (In Abu-Lughod 1995, 55–56)

Interestingly, her story features again the connection between art and the work of the Devil. Leaving the profession is linked to a kind of exorcist ritual in which the Devil is expelled. She is born again and the opening verses of the Quran, the confession of faith, are said "as if for the first time." This is a powerful way of expressing that she is becoming a Muslim, implying she was not a Muslim before. Her story underlines the idea that leaving art is a way of moving from nonbelieving into believing.

Muhammad Ali Street Performers and Devotion

It is clear from the discussion above how the repentance of several star performers has influenced the field of art. The discourse of the repentant artists has largely converged with the Islamist paganization of art. Now we turn to how a specific group of non-star performers, the singers and dancers of Muhammad Ali Street, perceive their profession. Do they consider their profession haram? Do they experience an incompatibility between being a Muslim and being a performer? Do they feel outsiders to the community of believers?

There are three main contexts of Egyptian entertainment: first, the circuit of weddings and saint's day celebrations; second, the nightclub circuit, aimed mainly at Arab and European tourists; and finally, the performing arts circuit, the performances in concert halls, theaters, on radio and television, and so on. Whereas star performers operate within the context of art and the higher echelons of the nightclubs, the performers of Muhammad Ali Street perform at the weddings of the lower- and lower-middle classes. Many women of Muhammad Ali Street also work at saint's day celebrations but rarely work in nightclubs. The street for which this group of performers is named used to be abundant in coffeehouses and music shops, and people arranged their weddings there. Muhammad Ali Street is still the place where many performers reside, and on a Thursday evening, the evening when many weddings are celebrated, the street is crowded with taxis and minibuses that transport the performers to wedding parties all over Cairo and nearby villages.

The performers of Muhammad Ali Street and their audience belong to a different social stratum than that of the star performers, who are often of middle-class extraction. Although artists from different contexts do not mingle much, the converted stars, as prominent public figures, could influence the performers of Muhammad Ali Street. However, at the time I conducted the interviews, between September 1988 and February 1990, the theme of converted artists was not yet very prominent. It was occasionally touched upon in the interviews with Muhammad Ali Street performers, but more often an example in their own community—a dancer's daughter who had become a *muhaggaba*, a veiled girl—was mentioned to demonstrate that despite their profession they give their children a good upbringing. Nevertheless, I have two case studies of female performers who tried to stop performing and to live a religious life. From these examples, I go more generally into female performers' ideas on the sinfulness of their profession. Finally, I try to analyze the extent of their religious observance in order to draw a conclusion on the perceived (in)compatibility of religion and performing.

I met Nadia in a Cairene hotel where weddings were celebrated and where she hoped to be allowed to perform. She had just arrived from Alexandria and for that reason she did not yet have the required papers. Since she was not asked to perform, we had time to talk together. I had somehow been introduced as a psychiatrist, so she poured out all the troubles she had experienced in life. Later I visited her again in the small dirty room in a cheap hotel near Muhammad Ali Street that she occupied with another performer from the countryside trying her luck in the capital. Nadia was thirty-five years old and had been born in Alexandria into a poor family. Her father had played the accordion but died young. In order to help the family, she started to perform at weddings and saint's day celebrations when she was ten years old. She married a soldier and hoped to quit the profession, but his salary was not enough for their four children. He also insisted that she keep working because, according to Nadia, he was addicted to alcohol and hashish. She divorced and after some time remarried. After the second marriage, she stayed two years at home, put on the veil, started praying, and was very happy. She gave birth to two more children and was forced again by their financial situation to start performing. Her second husband did not like her to perform but had to admit that he could not earn enough for the family. His ambivalence about her work and probably his hurt pride made him violent: he occasionally beat her up and threw her in the street. She divorced again and continued to perform because she was responsible for six children and her mother. When she was traveling and performing, her mother would take care of the children, and when Nadia had money she would visit them in Alexandria. She was strongly convinced that her profession was haram. "We are not like the foreigners," she explained. "We have to cover ourselves. They wear shorts and such things. We have prayers and fasting and everything. Singing and dancing are haram. Even Warda's singing is haram. I don't like this work, but I have six children and my mother to care for, I have no man, no one to help me. Their father left them like this and the oldest is only thirteen." The two blessed years in which she was muhagabba and prayed were a recurring motif in her story as a paradise lost that she hoped to regain. She had heard that religious people were helping artists to leave the trade, but she was hesitant about whether this would solve her ongoing financial troubles.

Another dancer who tried to stop performing and to live a religious life is Kooka. Kooka is originally from Muhammad Ali Street and has worked most of her career in Cairo. After her second marriage, four years before the interview, she stayed with her husband in Mansoera, a small town in the Delta. I visited Kooka and her husband, a musician, at home, joined them at a wedding party in a small village, and met them again at the saint's day celebration in Dessuq. She related that as a child she loved singing and dancing. She was once sent to run an errand and came across a neighborhood wedding. She liked it a lot, used the money as a tip for the performers and even climbed on stage to dance. After her parents' divorce, she started performing at a young age. Although in the beginning she liked her work very much—the beautiful clothing she was wearing, the people applauding her, the good money she was earning—after twenty-five years she has had enough of it. In the beginning she worked as a dancer and singer, but now she only sings. She is convinced that dancing with its revealing costumes is haram. Singing is a lesser evil, since she is properly dressed. She went twice to Mecca to do the ʿumra, the lesser pilgrimage. "I went twice to do the ʿumra in order to stop performing, but I did not find another source of income and I had to work again. I wanted to veil and to stay at home, but the circumstances did not allow me to. I went to do the ʿumra, but it was useless because I had to work again. I wait until God will reward me with a source of income that is halal. Then my husband and I will leave the trade; we will go on hagg and leave it all. Everything God commands will happen."

The idea that both Nadia and Kooka express is that their profession is haram. This is also clear from an expression that most former performers use to indicate that they retired from working. "Tobt lilaah," they often said, "I repented." Moreover, people who were still working in the profession but hoped to quit often sighed, "Rabbina yitob ʿalena," that is, "May God relieve us." Another former performer related: "There were days when I was working when I would cry and say: 'Rabbina yitob ʿalayya, ya rabb' [May God relieve me, O Lord]. But it was my only salt and bread until [I repented and] God relieved me." Another retired performer stated: "I am glad I repented. I knew it was haram, but there were circumstances. I had to raise the children. But if you walk straight, God will bless you at any time. When my son started to work in the trade I was angry and sad. I ask for repentance day and night for my son." Most performers declared that their activities were sinful.

What does this conviction of their own sinfulness mean for their religious devotion? Many performers tried to observe Ramadan as faithful Muslims do. The month of Ramadan is also a month in which there is not much work. One performer explicitly said that in this month she refuses to work because Ramadan is the month for God. Several performers distributed food to the poor during Ramadan. With regard to praying, the matter was more complicated. As a recurring daily activity, it was entangled with their "sinful" work. Some dancers decided that their work invalidated the prayers and stopped praying, claiming that as soon as they stopped performing they would resume praying. One of them said: "I used to pray and go to work. Then I asked people who know a lot about religion, they said: 'It is not haram, you open your house from it and spend on your family.' But still I have the feeling that I am at fault. I stopped praying and if God relieves me I will resume praying. It is sinful because the voice is 'awra and the costume is open. For God it is haram. The feeling of guilt makes me sad." Others continued to pray, and one former performer was renowned for even praying at work. She left the stage and went inside the house of the wedding host to pray. Most performers who said they occasionally prayed performed this religious duty at home. A dancer expressed the strong contrast between working and being at home. "When I return home, I immediately wash myself and prepare for praying." In her case praying constituted a daily ritual of purifying herself from her "sins."

Several former performers of Muhammad Ali Street tried to make up for their sins by leading a religious life after repentance. Some went to Mecca; others wore a head scarf or hijab and prayed regularly. Most of them were concerned about the afterlife. That does not mean they considered themselves hopeless cases on Judgment Day. As a singer expressed: "As Muslims it is forbidden to reveal your body, but we do not know who will go to heaven or to hell. Maybe a dancer does a good deed which gives her absolution." The conviction that their activities are haram does not mean that they agreed with the soeniyyin, the religious fundamentalists. A former performer voiced the following opinion: "The soenniyyin do not like women. From a religious point of view they are right, there are vulgarities, but not by force. People want to celebrate." Another said: "It is easy for them to talk, they have better jobs. May God make things easy for them, but I am one of those who have to earn money from dancing." Another performer vehemently declared: "Fundamentalists say that we are doing things against our religion, but we eat from it. I raise my children from it. Let them provide us with another job, with enough to pay for the school and all other expenses for my children. I struggle for them."

They hope that God in his omniscience will judge them on their inner selves and will forgive their outer activities. These activities were forced upon them by economic necessity. They faced zuruf, that is, they were forced by circumstances that they could not avoid. They had to care for their families and their children and had no other source of income. "If I do not dance then my daughter will have to dance," expresses the unavoidability of their situation. They have no choice but to work as performers. By stressing their circumstances as the reason for entering the trade, by underlining the straight path they have walked during their careers, and by living a meritorious life after repentance, they hope for God's mercy.

Are the views of Muhammad Ali Street performers on the "sinfulness" of the trade the same as the religious discourse of the fundamentalists and the avowals of the repentant stars? They all agree that the trade is haram. They all perceive an incongruity between performing and religious devotion. In the Islamist discourse, devotion and art cannot go together. Artists are nonbelievers who belong to the pagan world—if not to the Devil's realm. The stars' confessions reinforce the Islamist discourse, as they represent repentance as a passage from dark to light, as a journey from nonbelieving into believing. The Muhammad Ali Street performers are also ambivalent about their religious devotion. They are concerned about their religious "sins" and the invalidation of their religious merits by their profession. Yet they do not experience a complete incompatibility between the two. Muhammad Ali Street performers do not consider themselves outside the community of believers. They do not perceive themselves as nonbelievers. On the contrary, they feel very much part of the community of believers. Precisely because they define themselves as believers, they are concerned about their afterlife. Precisely because they identify themselves as Muslims, they try to compensate for sins and to reconcile their religious practices and their livelihood.

The divergence between the religious discourse of the Islamists and the views of Muhammad Ali Street performers is perhaps not surprising. The difference between the discourse of the repentant stars and the Muhammad Ali Street performers requires an explanation. Two fundamental factors can account for the differences. First, there is a difference in class position. As explained above, Muhammad Ali Street performers are from a low-class background and remain relatively deprived. The economic circumstances of the star performers are totally different; they were usually from wealthier families and were not forced to perform. They earned a lot of money and are still well off after their repentance. That means that the argument of sinning through zuruf does not hold for the star performers. They "committed sins" in order to earn a lot of money, which is perceived as a greater sin than being forced by sheer necessity. The second factor is related to the way the discourse of the repentant artist is produced. Islamists exerted great influence on the repentance and capitalized on the converted artists. They encapsulated it in their da'wa strategy. The discourse on and of the repentant artists is part and parcel of the Islamist struggle against art.

The Islamist discourse produces a rupture between the Devil's world and religious life, between nonbelieving artists and devoted believers. This opposition between performing and believing is also inscribed in the life stories of the repentant artists, and produces the discourse of a pagan life before and a devout life after repentance. Thus we cannot hold the discourse of the repentant artists to represent the "true religious feelings" of repentant artists. We cannot simply take their accounts as truthful accounts of former (religious and artistic) feelings and activities. Furthermore, we do not know whether star performers defined themselves as Muslims at the time of performing. At the present stage in their lives as repentant sinners, they produce the rupture that is immanent in most life stories of converts: that of a radical change from bad, immoral, and pagan toward good, moral, and God-fearing. Not only at the level of the individual convert but also at the level of the Islamist discourse, only an unfaithful performer versus a devout ex-performer is functional in the battle against pagan art.

Notes

1. For an analysis of the strong connection between the female body and sexuality, and the moral-religious discourse on gender and sexuality in Islam, see Nieuwkerk 1995, 1998a, 1998b.

2. The LRRC project is called "Religious Fundamentalism: The Danger Confronting Freedom of Expression in Egypt" and includes papers by Sayed Khamis, Ali Abu Sahdi, Marilyn Tadros, Kamal Ramzi, and Osama Khalil (http://www.geocities.com/CapitalHill/Lobby/9012/Freedom/index.html).

3. For a more general account of music in Islam, see Nieuwkerk 1998a.

4. As both noun and adjective, the term ʿawra has several layers of meanings, referring to the parts of the body that must be concealed (the genitals in particular) but also more generally to women's bodies and voices (see Ahmed 1992, 116).

5. For details on the bylaws, see in particular the part entitled "Towards Violence and Terrorism" in Ramzi 1999.

6. For an interesting analysis of the reaction of Upper-Egyptian villagers toward the repentant artists see Abu-Lughod 1995.

References

Abou Zeid, Ahmed M. 1965. "Honour and Shame among the Bedouins of Egypt." In *Honour and Shame,* edited by John G. Peristiany, 243–60. London: Weidenfeld and Nicolson.

Abu-Lughod, Lila. 1986. *Veiled Sentiments*. Berkeley and Los Angeles: University of California Press.

———. 1995. "Movie Stars and Islamic Moralism in Egypt." *Social Text* 13 (1): 53–67

———. 1998. *Remaking Women: Feminism and Modernity in the Middle East*. Princeton: Princeton University Press.

Abu Sahdi, Ali. 1999. *The Influence of Terrorism and Extremism on Official Governmental Censorship over the Cinema and Television in Egypt*. http://www.Geocities.com/CapitolHill/Lobby/9012/Freedom/shadimain.htm

Ahmed, Leila. 1992. *Women and Gender in Islam*. New Haven: Yale University Press.

Brandes, Stanley. 1987. "Reflections on Honor and Shame in the Mediterranean." In *Honor and Shame and the Unity of the Mediterranean*, edited by David D. Gilmore, 121–35. Washington, D.C.: American Anthropological Association.

Brooks, Geraldine. 1998. *De dochters van Allah: De verborgen wereld van de islamitische vrouw*. Amsterdam: Ooievaar.

Gilmore, David D., ed. 1987a. *Honor and Shame and the Unity of the Mediterranean*. Washington, D.C.: American Anthropological Association.

———. 1987b. "Honor, Honesty, Shame: Male Status in Contemporary Andalusia." In *Honor and Shame and the Unity of the Mediterranean*, edited by David D. Gilmore, 90–104. Washington, D.C.: American Anthropological Association.

Harding, Sandra. 1986. *The Science Question in Feminism*. New York: Cornell University Press.

Herzfeld, Michael. 1980. "Honour and Shame: Problems in the Comparative Analysis of Moral Systems." *Man* 15: 339–51.

———. 1987. "As in Your Own House": Hospitality, Ethnography, and the Stereotype of Mediterranean Society. In *Honor and Shame and the Unity of the Mediterranean*, edited by David D. Gilmore, 75–90. Washington, D.C.: American Anthropological Association.

MacLeod, Arlene. 1991. *Accommodating Protest: Working Women, the New Veiling, and Change in Cairo*. New York: Columbia University Press.

Meneley, Anne. 1996. *Tournaments of Value: Sociability and Hierarchy in a Yemeni Town*. Toronto: University of Toronto Press.

Mernissi, Fatima. 1987. *The Fundamentalist Obsession with Women: A Current Articulation of Class Conflict in Modern Muslim Societies*. Lahore: Simorgh Women's Resource and Publication Centre.

Moore, Henrietta L. 1988. *Feminism and Anthropology*. Cambridge: Polity.

Nassif, Imaad, and Amal Khodayr. 1991. *Fannanat ta'ibat wa nijmat al-ithara!* Cairo.

Nieuwkerk, Karin van. 1995. *"A Trade Like Any Other": Female Singers and Dancers in Egypt*. Austin: Texas University Press

———. 1998a. "An Hour for God and an Hour for the Heart": Islam, Gender, and Female Entertainment in Egypt. *Music and Anthropology* 3. http://www.muspe.unibo.it/period/MA/

———. 1998b. "Changing Images and Shifting Identities: Female Performers in Egypt." In *Images of Enchantment: Visual and Performing Arts of the Middle East*, edited by Sherifa Zuhur, 21–36. Cairo: American University of Cairo Press.

Peristiany, John G., ed. 1965. *The Values of Mediterranean Society.* London: Weidenfeld and Nicolson.

Pitt-Rivers, Julian. 1965. "Honour and Social Status." In *The Values of Mediterranean Society,* edited by John G. Peristiany: 19–78. London: Weidenfeld and Nicolson.

Al-Qardawi, Yoesoef. 1984. *Halal en Haram.* Delft: Noer.

Ramzi, Kamal. 1999. *From Extremism to Terrorism: The Relationship between Religious Groups and The Arts.* http://www.Geocities.com/CapitolHill/Lobby/9012/Freedom/kamalmain.htm

Sabbah, Fatna A. 1984. *Woman in the Muslim Unconscious.* New York: Pergamon.

Tadros, Marilyn. 1999. *Women: The Perspective of Fundamentalist Discourse and Its Influence on Egyptian Artistic Creativity and Cultural Life.* http://www. Geocities.com/CapitolHill/Lobby/9012/Freedom/marlynmain.htm

Wikan, Unni. 1984. "Shame and Honour: A Contestable Pair." *Man* 19:635–52.

Zuhur, Sherifa. 1992. *Revealing Reveiling: Islamist Gender Ideology in Contemporary Egypt.* Albany: State University of New York Press.

12

Male, Female, and Beyond in the
Culture and Music of Roma in Kosovo

Svanibor Pettan

The editor of this volume, Tullia Magrini, is certainly correct in claiming in her introduction that the study of music as "gendered activity" or "gendered culture" should go "beyond the need to complete our picture of the musical world by accounting for women's musical practices." I find myself particularly intrigued by musical practices in which the binary notion of gender is questioned by individuals with "alternative gender designations" (cf. Sugarman 1997, 32).[1] Several studies suggest that such phenomena exist in various cultures of the world, among—to mention just a few—Native Americans (e.g., Hill 1935; Whitehead 1981), Tahitians (Levy 1971), Omanis (Wikan 1977), Kenyans (Shepherd 1977), Indians (Nanda 1990), Filipinos (Johnson 1997), and Turks (Stokes, chap. 13 in this volume). These studies indicate important differences among the specific cases, as well as differences in how they are perceived within their respective cultures.

In order to comprehend any alternative to the male-female duality in which sex and gender match each other, it is necessary to develop familiarity with the culture-specific data that

govern that system. This is why my discussion of a specific case of transgendered musical practices in the Balkan region of Kosovo is preceded by
discussions of music and gender in this region and among its Rom (Gypsy)
population.[2]

In this chapter, I use the past tense for two principal reasons. First, the
succession of wars that marked the breakup of Yugoslavia forced me to end
my long-term presence as a researcher in Kosovo in the summer of 1991, and
prevented me from returning to the field until late in 1999. Second, what I
found there in 1999 was an entirely different situation, particularly challenging for (the very existence of) the Roma, which turns this chapter into a document of the past that at present seems to have no chance to be naturally continued on the same soil.[3]

At the time of my research (different periods between 1983 and 1991),
Kosovo was home to seven ethnic groups (Albanians, Serbs, ethnic Muslims,
Roma, Montenegrins, Turks, Croats); three religious confessions (Islam, Or-
thodox Christianity, Roman Catholicism); and four languages (Albanian,
Serbo-Croatian, Turkish, and Romani).[4] The heterogeneous Rom communi-
ties in Kosovo considered themselves as either Roma (mostly of the Arlije and
Gurbetja branches) or members of other ethnic groups.[5] Most of them claimed
Islamic religious background and some claimed to be Orthodox Christians.
Their mother tongue in most cases was either Romani or Albanian, and many
of them were able to communicate in all four languages. The political status of the Roma as an "ethnic group" was the single lowest in Kosovo compared to the other two political categories.[6] In spite of the multifarious interactions between Rom and non-Rom communities, including recognition of
the unique Rom ability to provide musical accompaniment to certain non-
Rom dances and customs, non-Rom communities in general looked upon
Roma as an inferior group.[7]

Music and Gender in Kosovo

The level of distinctiveness and segregation determined by gender in Kosovo
was related to several factors, such as ethnic and religious affiliation of the
inhabitants, the very important rural-urban differentiation, and the regional
and local traditions. It means that, beyond the shared history of the Ottoman
Empire and patriarchal and patrilineal cultural patterns, this segregation was
more strictly observed, for example, among Albanians than among Serbs,
among Muslims than among Christians, and in the countryside than in the
cities. These claims by Rom musicians in Kosovo were confirmed by my own

observation and documentation. However, my discussion in this section of the chapter excludes the Roma, who are treated separately in the next section.

In music, one could in many cases distinguish between male and female styles and determine their particular features. Miodrag Vasiljević, who in the late 1940s collected and analyzed Kosovo songs other than Albanian, Rom, and Turkish, distinguished between "male" epic (4 + 6) and "female" lyric (5 + 5) decasyllabic models in text structures (Vasiljević 1950, 343). Similarly, Lorenc Antoni in the 1970s distinguished between the predominantly heroic male songs and the lyrical female songs among Kosovo Albanians (Antoni 1974, 109).[8] Men and women "traditionally worked and socialized in segregated groups, and developed separate repertoires of songs [that were] often performed in contrasting styles and settings" (Sugarman 2000, 987). According to Antoni, "It never happened that, for example, men sang female songs and women sang male songs. This would be considered shameful. . . . Singing together was exceptional; it may have occurred only in the cities and among the Catholics" (1974, 109).

Traditionally, the male (husband's) domain was primarily public—ranging from the customary occupations of the Kosovo countryside (agriculture, cattle breeding) to widespread guest work in the economically richer northwest of what used to be Yugoslavia, and further abroad in western European countries. The female (wife's) domain was mainly private; her duty was to take care of the household.[9] While working far away from home, men from poorer parts of Kosovo used to leave their wives and other female family members at home for long periods of time.[10] Consequently, men were those who supplied the domestic environment with novelties, while women were widely regarded as tradition keepers.[11] In some rural areas in Kosovo's mountainous south, men—unlike the women—abandoned traditional costume. If men ever practiced the traditional two-part vocal diaphony in narrow, nontempered intervals, comparable to women's singing, they no longer did so at the time of my research.[12] A man in this area dressed in a Western urban style and sang solo to his own accompaniment on a long-necked lute. His vocal quality was somewhat more sustained and smooth in comparison to the loud female singing. Since there was not much evidence about the music in Kosovo and the neighboring areas prior to the Ottoman period, there was a notion, shared by the local population and scholars alike, that the style here presented as "female, rural, and of the highlands" was in fact an old, pre-Ottoman style.[13]

The difference between the male and female domains in Kosovo was evident in the use of instruments, too. Men performed mainly on aerophones and chordophones. Aerophones included shepherd flutes (*fyell, frula; kavall, kaval*) and accordion (*harmonika*), while chordophones included plucked lutes (melodic *çifteli* and accompanying *sharki* among the Albanians, *tambura* among ethnic Muslims, *saz* among Turks) and a bowed lute (*gusle* among the Serbs and Montenegrins).[14] They were playing membranophones only within the ensembles, except for Sufi (*dervish*) gatherings among the Muslims, at which specific membranophones and idiophones were used without melody-producing instruments.

Women traditionally did not play any melodic instruments. If they used instruments at all, they just provided rhythmic accompaniment for (female) singing either on a frame drum (*def, daire, dahira*) or on an ordinary house-hold copper pan (*tepsi, tepsija*). The tepsi was used either as a drum substitute or was spun on a low round table (*sofra*), producing a low rumbling accompaniment for singing.[15]

Children of both sexes engaged in music and dance in certain traditional contexts and at school. In urban settings and to a lesser extent in the countryside, they also performed within amateur ensembles. Girls' performing in public was likely to end with marriage, except for some of those talented singers who had already achieved recognition. Several female recording artists, Kosovo Albanians, became known and respected. The 1970s were marked by Nexhmije Pagarusha, the 1980s by Shkurte Fejza, and in the 1990s the number of Kosovo Albanian female recording artists considerably increased.

Music and Gender among the Roma in Kosovo

Distinctions such as ethnicity, religion, rural versus urban setting, and regional and local traditions had the same kind of impact on gender relations among the Kosovo Roma as among non-Rom ethnic groups and musicians. Thus, sedentary Rom men were oriented toward the public domain, while women dominated the private one. The women's domain was, however, more extended than that of most non-Rom women in Kosovo, and more similar to that of Rom women in neighboring Macedonia. Based on her study of the Šuto Orizari neighborhood of Skopje, Macedonia, Carol Silverman has pointed to four rather "public" levels in which Rom women regularly participated: the larger society dominated by non-Roma, the Rom community, the extended family, and the residential family. She argued also that while macropolitics were associated with men, ritual politics were associated with women, and that rituals belonged to the "public realm involving power, economics, and performance" (1996, 64). At most feasts related to the annual cycle (e.g., Saint George's Day) and life cycle (circumcisions, weddings), Rom women took part in communal dancing in the street. Women associated with the semi-nomadic Rom branches were much more publicly exposed, in a way even more than the men, through activities such as fortune-telling, selling herbal medicines, and—in some cases—begging.[16]

Male musicians either performed instrumentally in a shawm-and-drum ensemble associated primarily with rural settings or sang within an urban ensemble, which included some of the following instruments: clarinet or saxophone, violin or electric guitar, banjo or electric bass, accordion or synthesizer, and frame drum, goblet-shaped drum, or drum set.[17] Shawm-and-drum ensembles did perform in the cities as well, although urban ensembles were seldom heard in the countryside. The audiences of these male ensembles included both men and women, separated or mixed, depending on the specific location and community.[18]

Female musicians, usually two together, sang to the frame drum accompaniment for female audiences.[19] Rom women in given circumstances accompanied singing by spinning a copper pan or by using it as a frame drum substitute. They did not use any melodic instruments.[20] Some Rom women performed in bars as singers to the accompaniment of male Rom musicians using amplified instruments. The exclusively male audiences in such bars generally regarded the morals of these singers as low, well-nigh comparable to those of prostitutes.[21]

Male ensembles usually performed in public—outdoors (on an improvised stage, for example, a terrace of a house) or indoors (in a hotel or a large city hall hired for the specific feast). Women performed in a private setting, in a closed female circle—indoors (in a room) or outdoors (in a garden). Gardens in Kosovo were usually divided from the streets by high walls. Therefore, the fact that performance took place "outdoors" did not imply its public character.

As with the non-Rom ethnic groups in Kosovo, engagement of Rom girls in music and dance within the school or amateur ensembles usually ended with marriage. I know of a young Rom woman who used to sing at weddings with an amplified ensemble and became a recording artist. Marriage ended her public musical career, although she continued to sing for family and friends.

In their adolescent years, many male Rom musicians neglected their school duties and voluntary musical involvement in amateur ensembles for the sake of paid performances at weddings and in bars. Their exposure as performers was widely regarded as engagement in regular occupation in the public domain. Although it was also acceptable for female Rom musicians to be paid for their music making, their exposure was expected to be decent, that is, within female circles only. Regional cultural patterns did allow certain variations of this rule. For instance, in the city of Pejë/Peć, female musicians would wait at the marketplace (next to male musicians) for potential patrons to hire them to perform at a feast; in the city of Prizren, however, this was considered indecent for women (though not for men), and patrons had to make arrangements at the female musician's place. In the area of Pejë/Peć it was also customary for female musicians to perform for a short while for male guests, and one of the musicians sometimes even danced. In the area of Prizren, female musicians performed exclusively for women and did not dance.

Beyond the Male-Female Duality

Three cases in Kosovo prove suitable for my discussion and two of them transcend the system of male-female duality: (1) the practice of singing to the spun copper pan; (2) the phenomenon of the sworn virgins; and (3) the role of male musicians in turning traditional female music into the popular (public) modern genre known as *talava*.

Singing to the Spun Copper Pan

Singing to the spun copper pan has been traced in Kosovo and in the related territories of Albania, Macedonia, Serbia, Montenegro, and Bosnia and Herzegovina.[22] Performers included Albanians, Serbs, ethnic Muslims, Turks, Montenegrins, Croats, and Roma; affiliates of all three major religious branches in the given territories (Islam, Orthodox Christianity, and Roman Catholicism); and both rural and urban populations. Several authors, both those native to the wider region and visitors (e.g., P. Ž. Petrović 1934; Plaku i Drenicës 1935; Šmaus [Schmauss] 1937; and Filipović 1938), researched and wrote about it. Tatomir Vukanović summarized their attempts, described the specifics concerning this practice among the listed ethnic groups, and established seven types and seven methods of—as he named it—"singing of folksongs with round a casserole [*sic*]" (Vukanović 1956).[23]

The contexts for this musical practice included both ritual and social gatherings. In most areas, it was related to weddings, but also to the other customs from the annual cycle (Bayram, Kurban Bayram, Saint George's Day), from the life cycle (e.g., circumcision among Muslims), and informal gatherings related to common work. In some parts of Kosovo, ethnic Albanian women sang lullabies to copper pan accompaniment to help their children fall asleep. According to Vukanović, in the period between the world wars in the area of Kaçaniku/Kačanik, one mother who had lost her child had sung the same lullabies on her child's grave (1956, 126). The consensus across ethnic groups was that the singing in the Albanian language was aesthetically most revealing.

The Rom women in Kosovo performed this practice regardless of their sedentary or seminomadic way of life and regardless of their rural or urban status; however, only Muslim Rom women used to do so (Vukanović 1956, 150–51).

One would expect that a copper pan, being a kitchen utensil and hence an element of the private domain, figured as an exclusively female instrument. However, according to early accounts, such was not always the case. P. Ž. Petrović, perhaps the first author to investigate the practice, related its appearance to the Ottoman restriction upon the use of the gusle, the southern Slav bowed lute. The gusle, a highly respected male instrument, was used to accompany heroic epic songs, so its replacement by the copper pan in areas under particularly strong political pressure also meant a switch in the repertoire, which already included both lyric and epic songs (Vukanović 1956, 135). Was the copper pan a double substitute—replacing the "male" bowed lute and the "female" frame drum alike? Whether it was Ottoman oppression or something else that made male and female musicians perform within the same musical idiom, and even together under given circumstances, remains an open question. Only a gender-centered investigation can lead to an answer.

Another question: Why did the Roma adopt this practice? Male Rom musicians were renowned for never adopting the villagers' old musical instruments (such as bagpipes, bowed lute, or shepherds' flutes) and for instead introducing technically superior, modern instruments (R. Petrović 1974, 157). In short, just as male musicians abandoned "instruments which do not bring money" (Pettan 1992, 152), they did not adopt the copper pan either. In fact, of all the Kosovo ethnic groups under consideration, it was only the Roma about whom I was unable to find any trace of male singing to spun copper pan accompaniment. The fact that Rom women did adopt this practice perhaps indicates difference in attitudes worthy of further exploration (plate 17).

Sworn Virgins

Sworn virgins can generally be defined as "transgendered individuals who are genetic females become social men, living masculine lives" (Dickemann 1997b, 248). They have been traced among the Albanians, Montenegrins, Serbs, Turks, and Roma in Kosovo and its wider surroundings, regardless of religious backgrounds and rural-urban distinctions.[24] The majority of documented cases originate in the mountainous border area of Albania and Montenegro (cf. Gušić 1958 and Vukanović 1961; see also the useful ethnological map in Vince-Pallua 2000). Sworn virgins have received attention from authors, both native to the wider area and foreign, since the mid–nineteenth century. In Kosovo itself, thirty-one cases were confirmed by researchers throughout the twentieth century (Vince-Pallua 2000, 145).[25]

What made these women adopt male roles? Some women became surrogate sons in their patrilineal families without male children. Some escaped undesirable marriages. Some were orphaned and took responsibility in raising younger family members. Some expressed sorrow for a fiancé who had passed away. Some were widows trying to save their property. However, others simply felt like men and preferred the male way of life (these and more causes were noted in Vukanović 1961a, 111). Evidently, it was possible to become a sworn virgin at any age, to satisfy either one's parents or oneself.

According to reports, sworn virgins shared at least some of the following characteristics: they dressed as men, had male haircuts and names, carried weapons, smoked tobacco, drank alcoholic beverages, took care of work usually associated with men, and performed music otherwise associated with men.[26] They were in most cases referred to as men, and referred to themselves in masculine terms (Dickemann 1997b, 250). The institution of sworn virgins was in general accepted by society, and such individuals appear to have been appreciated and respected.[27] This acceptance reflected the society's economic and social needs (cf. Barjaktarović 1966, 285).[28] Indeed, the sworn virgin's abstinence from sex and motherhood were rewarded by high social respect (Gušić 1976, 274).

The musical activity of sworn virgins is discussed in a relatively small number of reports (just eight, according to Vince-Pallua 2000). In the earliest of them, dating from 1905, Karl Steinmetz pointed to the virgins' knowledge of many songs thanks to their mobility, and mentioned an epic song from another part of Kosovo that the virgin he met actually sang (Vince-Pallua 2000, 35). Tatomir Vukanović mentioned a virgin from a respected family in the city of Prizren, who played "harmonika, daire, and kavala, and sang pretty well Turkish, Albanian and Serbian songs" (1961a, 97).[29] The other reports refer to the musical activity of ethnic Albanian virgins in Montenegro (Gušić 1976; Grémaux 1994) and Albania (Strauss 1997). Marijana Gušić (1976, 272–73) described an outdoor performance in which the virgin Tonë Bikaj—in front of her house and surrounded by her fellow villagers—played the end-blown flute and then performed a song topically related to her native area to her own accompaniment on a bowed lute (plate 18). René Grémaux reached the area some fifteen years after Tonë had passed away. His vivid account is based on what he heard from her younger brother and other informants: "Among the Albanians living on the Montenegrin side of the border Tonë gained considerable popularity as a singer and musician, and many people I met remember him as such. Like a genuine male he used to sing 'mountaineer songs,' holding one hand behind the ear, and he performed other traditional songs accompanying himself on the *lahutë* or *gusle,* a bow-and-string instrument. In addition, he was known to be a good player of the *fyell,* an end-blown flute. Singing and making music for an audience that included males, activities traditionally considered improper for local women, was a kind of specialty of many Albanian sworn virgins" (1994, 255).[30] Julius Strauss mentioned a case in which an Albanian sworn virgin sang in the manner customary for men, and she sat with the men at weddings when men and women sat in separate rooms (1997, 34).

Sworn virgins have been traced among the Roma in Kosovo as well. Most interesting for the present context is the case of a sedentary Muslim woman from Gjakovë/Đakovica who became a sworn virgin at the age of fifteen. When Tatomir Vukanović visited her in the late 1950s, she was fifty years old. She wore trousers, a man's shirt, and her short hair was tied up with a man's handkerchief. She lived in a household with an adopted sister. Both were musicians. They were earning money together by singing "Albanian folk songs" and beating their frame drums (Vukanović 1961b, 92).

Although we lack an explicit statement about these two musicians' audiences, it was likely that they performed for women. That is, their performance medium (singing to frame drum accompaniment) was considered acceptable for men only as a brief interlude in the context of a celebration, and only in some parts of Kosovo. At least in this particular case—in contrast to others described above, or rather as another variation of the sworn virgin phenomenon—the adoption of another gender was not paralleled by the adoption of a musical domain associated with it.

Talava

In sharp contrast to relatively numerous reports about sworn virgins, references concerning the opposite case—men associated with female gender—in the same territories are almost nonexistent. This is even more surprising if one bears in mind the extraordinary popularity of dancing boys (*köçekçe,* sing. *köçek*) within the Ottoman Empire.[31] In the first decades of the twentieth century in the city of Prizren, there was a Turkish man who usually dressed as a woman, sang Turkish songs to frame drum accompaniment, and even danced the belly dance in local bars (Vukanović 1961a, 98). In his case, the dress, instrumentation, and dance meant a clear association with the female domain.

It was in the city of Gjakovë/Đakovica in 1986 that for the first time I saw two male musicians accompanying their singing on frame drums. They were dressed as men and performed outdoors for a wedding in a Rom quarter of the town. Lyrics in the Albanian language were accompanied by various well-performed and elaborated rhythmic patterns. The audience members mysteriously smiled when I asked questions about the musicians and did not allow me to take pictures of the two. In later years, I was in a position to witness the development of this "obscure" musical practice into the dominant Rom genre in Kosovo, which became known as talava (telovas, taleva; the literal translation from Romani is "under the arm").[32]

For the present discussion, it is important to note that talava originated in the private female domain (singing to frame drum accompaniment), but by 1990 it had started to dominate the public male domain (singing accompanied by amplified instruments). How did the two otherwise largely separated musical domains come into contact?[33] My speculation is that the connection was provided by male singers to frame drum accompaniment like those mentioned above. Their physical appearance (sometimes including long hair, suggestions, not yet confirmed, that in the past they also wore a specific kind of dress), behavior (in particular verbal expressions),[34] and their musical preferences (performance in a female medium) made their audiences think of them as homosexuals. Their regional center was the city of Pejë/Peć, and their popularity was more emphasized in the western part of Kosovo than elsewhere. The lyrics they sang were in most cases in the Albanian language, less often in Romani. Local Rom audiences sometimes commented that these men were indecent and impolite, but on the other hand they gave them credit for their capability as frame drum players and especially for their excellence in creating lyrics on the spot.

The talava found its best representative in one of the two musicians I first met in Gjakovë/Đakovica in 1986. He had abandoned the frame drum and taken up the microphone instead in order to sing with the amplified ensemble of a famous male Kosovo Rom singer, who never sang to frame drum accompaniment and who was never assumed to be a homosexual himself. The singer who led the ensemble, however, had a certain affinity for the songs he had heard from his mother.[35] Their joint project meant not only a further broadening of the repertoire, but, more important, it caused a stylistic switch that altered the roles of the amplified ensemble instruments to make them resemble frame drum accompaniment. The talava quickly earned popularity

Kosovo-wide and recognition outside the province as the Kosovo Rom music. Consequently, other Rom singers and instrumentalists had to learn to perform talava in order to meet the expectations of their audiences. Thus, the shift from the female and private to the male and public domain was completed.

But talava represented more than a social shift. Musical analysis revealed the reduction of expressive means within particular musical components of the genre. This reduction was most obvious in melody, meter, rhythm, and tempo. The variety of these four musical components operating within the restrictions of singing to frame drum accompaniment gave place to a more limited number of patterns when singing was accompanied by an amplified ensemble, which in theory had greater expressive capacity. Instead of several melodies (of both Rom and non-Rom origin), often connected within the form of a medley, there was a shift to few melodic patterns, or as some informants suggested, "to a single tune." Instead of a rich variety of meters and rhythms, the amplified talava was reduced to just a few rhythmic patterns in the standardized 4/4 meter. The former variety in tempo was reduced to one steady standard tempo, usually accelerating toward the end of a block of music. The lyrics of particular tunes with occasionally improvised parts gave place to the largely improvised lyrics addressing individuals in the audience. Instead of a female dance performed by one or two individuals, the standard for the new genre became the communal round dance (*horo*), accessible to men and women alike.

Table 1 shows talava in relationship to the three domains: the female domain (female singers to frame drum accompaniment), the "transitional" domain (male singers to frame drum accompaniment), and the male domain (a male singer to the amplified ensemble accompaniment).

Male Rom musicians from Kosovo, except for those with an alleged homosexual background, did not think very highly of talava, as revealed by the interviews I conducted in 1990 and 1991. A clarinetist from the city of Prizren said: "Talava is dead music for a clarinet player—nothing for feelings, nothing for fingers." "They perform the same tune all night long," a lute player from Gjakovë/Đakovica complained, referring to the predominance of the lyrics in talava. A percussionist from Prizren criticized the attitudes reflected in lyrics: "It only takes somebody from the audience to mention his or her sick child for the singer to be ready to sing about it." According to a singer from Ferizaj/Uroševac, "These are nonsensical 'aman aman songs' using Albanian words and Rom rhythm just to extract money from the audience. Is it Rom music? Yes, it is our music here in Kosovo, but somewhere further away from here people would probably laugh at it." The statement of a saxophon-

Table 1 Domains of talava

Domain	Female	Transitional	Male
Medium	Two singers with drums	Two singers with drums	One singer with amplified ensemble
Form	Medley/Open	Open	Open
Melody	Variety	Variety	Standard
Meter	Variety	Variety	Standard
Rhythm	Variety	Variety	Standard
Harmony	None	None	Drone
Tempo	Variety	Variety	Standard
Lyrics	Set songs/ Improvised	Improvised	Improvised
Dance	Solo	Solo/None	Communal
Place	Indoors	Indoors/Outdoors	Indoors/Outdoors
Audience	Female	Female and Male	Female and Male
Function	Entertainment	Entertainment	Entertainment

ist from Mitrovicë/Mitrovica, that talava was "corrupted music enormously loved by women" pointed to the female audience largely responsible for the considerable popularity of talava.

A scholar—on the basis of listening, comparison, and analyses—is likely to sympathize with these concerns about the talava. It did reduce the performance to two basic elements: the lyrics and the rhythm that had to be suitable for dance. On the other hand, Rom women enjoyed the situation in which the music, widely considered to be related by origin to the female domain, had found its way out to dominate the general Rom music scene in Kosovo. In a way, the success of talava meant their own success in the public domain. The fact that it was not women but men, the carriers of the public domain, who performed the talava further emphasized this success (plate 19).

For more than a decade, Kosovo received international attention primarily as a region torn apart by interethnic conflicts. The analysis here does not address those political relations. My intention has been to point to the importance of gender in a cross-ethnic study that devotes particular consideration to the Roma. In the first case, singing to the spun copper pan was presented as a possible musical meeting point of two gender categories. In the following two cases—those of sworn virgins and talava—complementary associations with the adopted gender roles were discussed. The association of women with the male domain (as in the case of sworn virgins) proved to be socially acceptable to a greater extent than the association of men with the female domain (as in the case of alleged homosexuals). Bearing in mind the much greater appreciation for male children than female children in a patrilineal society such as Kosovo, the very basic explanation might be that women who associated themselves with the male gender were seen as upgrading their status, while men who adopted female roles were seen as degrading their own.

Comparison of the sworn virgins and alleged homosexual singers of talava may be key to a further understanding of gender in the contexts of Kosovo society, its Rom population, and its musical culture. Unlike the alleged homosexuals, sworn virgins were respected in a moral sense and associated with the notion of celibacy (for a thoughtful discussion on their sexuality, see Young 2000, 57–60). Most of them could be described as being "socially men" (Dickemann 1997a, 201), while the alleged homosexuals would better fit a description applied to the Omani transsexual *xanith,* who are "socially neither male nor female, but live a precariously ambiguous existence between the sexes" (Feuerstein and al-Marzooq 1978, 666). This distinction was quite evident in the domain of dress. Mostly, sworn virgins wore male clothing, while the alleged homosexuals—prior to their switch to a male performance medium, which was somehow accompanied by a switch to male dress—perhaps wore some intermediate clothing, with both male and female features.[36] Neither sworn virgins nor the alleged homosexuals did go as far as some Indian *hijras* as to remove, or change, their sexual organs (as described by Nanda 1990, 24–37). There have been reports about highly exceptional cases in which individuals "returned" to the gender denomination from which they had departed, and the key was marriage. Former sworn virgins proved their female identity by giving birth to children.[37]

Since the lack of data concerning the musical life of sworn virgins prevents me from paying it attention comparable to that of the alleged homosexuals, I conclude with remarks on the development of talava. The clear chronological order of the three stages that transformed a female indoor music performed by women for female audiences to a male outdoor music performed by men for a general audience does not imply that the initial and transitional stages became obsolete. On the contrary, female musicians who accompanied their singing with strokes on their frame drums were still in demand for female festivities in the early 1990s. Though some of the alleged homosexuals adopted accompaniment by amplified ensembles as superior to self-accompaniment on frame drums, there were still others among them who continued singing to frame drum accompaniment. Within the realm of amplified performances, most musicians were men with no alleged homosexual background who performed the talava simply because this genre was in great demand among the Kosovo audiences of the early 1990s, and it was therefore a sine qua non for Rom musicians in Kosovo.

The commercial potential of the music associated with Rom women in Kosovo was fully realized and explored thanks to the active involvement of the musicians seen as homosexuals by their own community and their change of the performance medium associated with one gender (female) to the medium associated with the other (male). During my most recent fieldwork in Kosovo in October 1999, I did find cassettes with recorded talava performances, but what I did not find were Rom musicians. The performers were ethnic Albanians, and they called their music *tallava*.

Notes

I wish to thank Karin van Nieuwkierk for her comments on an early version of this paper and Jane Sugarman for her comments on a late version. Unless otherwise noted, translations in this chapter from non-English sources are my own.

1. Two out of three case studies discussed in this chapter deal with such individuals.

2. Throughout this chapter, I use the form Kosovo (rather than either of the Albanian forms, Kosovë or Kosova, or the Serbian forms, Kosovo i Metohija or Kosmet) for the same reasons as the historian Noel Malcolm. Namely, "it is the form currently used in most English-language publications" (Malcolm 1998, xi). Geographic locations and musical instruments are specified with both Albanian and Serbian names; in a few cases Turkish and Rom names are added.

3. For the same reason, I was unable to proceed with research on this specific topic, which was only a part of my broader exploration of creativity and interactions between Rom musicians and their audiences in Kosovo (Pettan 1992).

4. Ethnic Muslims compose a distinctive Slavic group with subgroups, whose members to various extent felt related to ethnic Muslims of Bosnia and Herzegovina (Bošnjaci); the oldest subgroups in Kosovo included Goranci and Torbeši. Today, Serbian and Croatian, as well as Bosnian, are recognized as separate languages.

5. Ashkalije was the local term for the Albanian-speaking Roma who in several cases claimed Albanian ethnic identity. At the time of my research, some Roma claimed to be Egyptians (more in Duijzings 1997). Detailed lists of various Rom groups in the region can be found in Vukanović 1983 and Pettan 1992.

6. The other two categories were "nations," which encompassed Serbs, ethnic Muslims, Montenegrins, and Croats, and "national minorities," which encompassed the Albanians and Turks.

7. Only (good) Rom musicians were able to perform music for dance cycles of Albanian and ethnic Muslim men in the mountainous south of Kosovo, as well as music for

horse races and traditional freestyle wrestling in the context of rich celebrations (wedding, circumcision) within the same region (more in Pettan 2001).

8. For the similar distinctions in Albania, see Lloyd 1968, 213–16.

9. Janet Reineck (1988) has examined the dynamics of self-perception among Kosovo Albanian women from various settings.

10. This kind of situation in the region of Opojë/Opolje has been described by Reineck (1986, 35–39).

11. Sugarman properly points to the association of women with "ritual" singing and men with "social" singing (1997, 369). Of course, female songs were neither exclusively lyrical nor ritual (see Plana 1972).

12. Danish researcher Birthe Traerup has found only traces of this diaphony in the male songs during her studies in Prizrenska Gora that started in the late 1950s (1974, 213).

13. The evidence about music in the Dinaric Alps presented by Ankica Petrović (1987, 1988–89) supports the notion about a pre-Ottoman style. The distinction between rural and Ottoman-related urban music has been pointed out in several writings about music in the wider territories. For instance, Radmila Petrović distinguished between "old rural," "new rural," and "urban" music in a region in Serbia (1961), while Cvjetko Rihtman differentiated between "old Bosnian" and "small city" music in a part of Bosnia and Herzegovina (1963).

14. The tambura was increasingly being replaced by a factory-made and then modified Turkish saz. The use of the Albanian bowed lute (*lahutë*), comparable to *gusle,* was for the most part limited to western Kosovo.

15. The spun copper pan was also used to accompany dancing (as discussed by Hoerburger 1994, 59).

16. Useful comparison between sedentary and nomadic Rom women in Kosovo can be found in Vukanović (1961b).

17. Local terms for shawm included *curlë, zurla, zurna,* and *svirla.* The double-headed drum was called *lodër, goč, davul,* or *tupan.* The terms for instruments in urban ensembles were *klanet* or *saksafon, ćemane* or *gitara, cümbüş* or *bas, harmonika* or *sintisajzer, def, darabuka,* or *jazz.* Acoustic instruments were used for processions and amplified ones to accompany dance at banquets.

18. I witnessed situations in which Rom musicians performed for non-Rom audiences specific male dances (e.g., the *kalačojna* suite), female dances (e.g., *mevlana*), and those dances suitable for both sexes. I also witnessed situations in a range, from those in which within the same event, at the same time, and to the same music men danced outside and women inside the house, all the way to situations in which men and women danced together in the open circle formation.

19. Veronica Doubleday pointed to several scholars with fieldwork experience in the Middle East (such as Shiloah, Touma, and Picken) who noted "close associations" between women and frame drums. She properly emphasized that "women lack exclusive rights over any type of musical instrument, even the frame drum itself" (Doubleday 1999, 102).

20. Rom women playing melodic instruments are exceptional in general. Among the best known cases are the eighteenth-century violin player Panna Czinka in Hungary (see Sárosi 1978) and the nineteenth-century shawm (*zurna*) player Yıldız Kamer in Turkey (And 1976, 143).

21. For similar opinions in Egypt see Nieuwkerk (chap. 11 in this volume and 1995).

22. Local terms for this practice were *tue sjellë tepsin, okretanje tepsije, tepsijanje, tevsijanje* (Vukanović 1956, 153).

23. The LP *Traditional Folk Music: Songs and Dances from Kosovo Performed at the Glogovac Festival of Folklore* (PGP RTB 2510073, 1982) contains two examples of this musical practice, one Albanian and the other Serbian. In both cases the performers are women.

24. The local name for such individuals may be *vergjineshë, vajzë e betuar, mashkullore, muškobanja, ostajnica, tybeli*; Serbian researchers used Serbianized forms such as *to(m)belija* (Barjaktarović 1948, 1966; Filipović 1938, 1952) and *virdžina* (Vukanović 1956, 1961a,b, 1983). For more names see Young 2000, 67–68.

25. Publications include Miljanov [1901] 1941, Stanković [1910] 1988, Ðorđević [1923] 1984, Barjaktarović 1948 and 1966, Filipović 1952, Vukanović 1961a,b, Grémaux 1994, and Young 2000.

26. However, there was considerable variation regarding these features (Vukanović 1961a, 109; Dickemann 1997b, 250). The sworn virgins' varied self-perceptions were discussed by Gušić (1976), Grémaux (1994), and Young (2000).

27. For instance, if a girl refused to marry a certain man and became a sworn virgin instead, the man was not expected to have any bad feelings about it for his honor was not threatened by her marriage to another man (Barjaktarović 1948, 346; Vukanović 1961a, 91).

28. Vukanović also reported on the case of the so-called *beqaric*. These "divorced women and widows practice both male and female lifestyles, i.e., drink alcoholic beverages, smoke tobacco, play the tambura, and enjoy male company" (1961a, 90–91).

29. "Kavala" refers to the earlier mentioned end-blown flute, usually named *kavall* (Alb.) or *kaval* (Ser.).

30. This part of Grémaux's text was also quoted by Jelka Vince-Pallua in the section of her dissertation entitled "Virdžine i glazba" (Virgins and Music) (2000, 172–75).

31. Their "dance and external appearance suggested femininity" (see And 1976).

32. Talava in the context of the music market in Kosovo was presented in detail in Pettan 1996. A discussion of musical features was supplemented by a music transcription and recordings on the accompanying compact disc. See also Pettan 2001.

33. Some particularly popular female songs, especially those recorded on cassettes by female artists and accompanied by professional ensembles, were included in male Rom repertoires. I recorded several such songs in instrumental versions performed by shawms and drums and a brass band. More as an exception, a Rom singer with an amplified ensemble from Gjakovë/Ðakovica performed in the 1980s the Albanian female song "Kur dola të dera." Its clearly female lyrics dealt with the suffering of a young married woman, whose mother-in-law did not allow her out.

34. For instance, the use of erotic topics, which were suitable for private female circles (Pllana 1972) but not for public use and male performers.

35. Personal communication, 1990.

36. Both the shoga in Mombasa and the xanith in Sohar wore clothing that identified them to locals (Shepherd 1978b, 665).

37. In Oman "the transsexual must, like every normal bridegroom, demonstrate that he can perform intercourse in the male role" (Wikan 1977, 308).

References

And, Metin. 1976. *Turkish Dancing*. Ankara: Dost Yayınları.

Antoni, Lorenc. 1974. "Osnovne karakteristike šiptarskog muzičkog folklora Kosova i Metohije." In *Rad XIV kongresa Saveza Udruženja Folklorista Jugoslavije u Prizrenu 1967*, edited by Dušan Nedeljković, 109–22. Beograd: Savez Udruženja Folklorista Jugoslavije.

Barjaktarović, Mirko R. 1948. "Prilog proučavanju tobelija (zavetovanih devojaka)." In *Zbornik Filozofskog fakulteta Univerziteta u Beogradu*, edited by Dušan Nedeljković, 1:343–51. Beograd: Naučna Knjiga.

———. 1966. "Problem tobelija (virđina) na Balkanskom poluostrvu." *Glasnik Etnografskog Muzeja u Beogradu* 28/29: 273–86.

Dickemann, Mildred. 1997a. "The Balkan Sworn Virgin: A Cross-Gendered Female Role." In *Islamic Homosexualities: Culture, History, and Literature*, edited by Stephen O. Murray and Will Roscoe, 197–203. New York: New York University Press.

———. 1997b. "The Balkan Sworn Virgin: A Traditional European Transperson." In *Gender Blending*, edited by Bonnie Bullough, Vern Bullough, and James Ellias, 248–55. Amherst, N.Y.: Prometheus.

Đorđević, Tihomir R. 1984. "Celibat." 1923. Reprinted in *Naš narodni život*, edited by Ivan Čolović, 1:129-35. Beograd: Prosveta.

Doubleday, Veronica. 1999. "The Frame Drum in the Middle East: Women, Musical Instruments, and Power." *Ethnomusicology* 43 (1): 101–34.

Duijzings, Ger. 1997. "The Making of Egyptians in Kosovo and Macedonia." In *The Politics of Ethnic Consciousness*, edited by Cora Govers and Hans Vermeulen, 194–222. Houndmills: Macmillan.

Durham, M. E. 1928. *Some Tribal Origins, Laws, and Customs of the Balkans*. London: Allen and Unwin.

Feuerstein, G., and S. al-Marzooq. 1978. Contribution in *Man* 13 (4): 665–67.

Filipović, Milenko C. 1938. "Tepsijanje." *Prilozi Proučavanju Narodne Poezije* 5 (2): 252–54.

———. 1952. "Mirko R. Barjaktarović: Prilog proučavanju tobelija (zavetovanih devojaka)." *Glasnik Etnografskog Instituta SAN* 1:614–17.

Grémaux, René. 1994. "Woman becomes Man in the Balkans." In *Third Sex, Third Gender: Beyond Sexual Dimorphism in Culture and History*, edited by Gilbert Herdt, 241–81. New York: Zone.

Gušić, Marijana. 1958. "Ostajnica—tombelija—virdžin kao društvena pojava." In *Treći kongres folklorista Jugoslavije*, edited by M. C. Lalević, 55–64. Cetinje.

———. 1976. "Pravni položaj ostajnice-virđineše u stočarskom društvu regije Dinarida." In *Odredbe pozitivnog zakonodavstva i običajnog prava o sezonskim kretanjima stočara u jugoistočnoj Evropi kroz vekove*, Posebna Izdanja Balkanološkog Instituta 4, edited by Vasa Čubrilović, 269–96. Beograd: Srpska Akademija Nauka i Umetnosti.

Hill, Willard W. 1935. "The Status of the Hermaphrodite and Transvestite in Navaho Culture." *American Anthropologist* 37:273–79.

Hoerburger, Felix. 1994. *Valle popullore: Tanz und Tanzmusik der Albaner im Kosovo und in Makedonien*. Frankfurt am Main: Peter Lang.

Johnson, Mark. 1997. *Beauty and Power: Transgendering and Cultural Transformation in the Southern Philippines.* Oxford: Berg.

Levy, Robert. 1971. "The Community Function of Tahitian Male Transvestism: A Hypothesis." *Anthropological Quarterly* 44:12–21.

Lloyd, A. L. 1968. "Albanian Folk Song." *Folk Music Journal* 1:205–22.

Malcolm, Noel. 1998. *Kosovo: A Short History.* London: Papermac.

Miljanov, Marko. 1941. *Primjeri čojstva i junaštva.* 1901. Reprint, Beograd: Puč.

Munishi, Rexhep. 1987. *Këngët malësorçe Shqiptare.* Prishtinë: Rilindja.

Nanda, Serena. 1990. *Neither Man nor Woman: The Hijras of India.* Belmont: Wadsworth.

Nieuwkierk, Karin van. 1995. *"A Trade Like Any Other": Female Singers and Dancers in Egypt.* Austin: University of Texas Press.

Petrović, Ankica. 1987. "Oriental-Islamic Cultural Reflections on the Folk Music of Bosnia and Herzegovina, Yugoslavia." *Al Ma'thurat al Sha'biyyah* 2 (6): 10–22.

———. 1988–89. "Paradoxes of Muslim Music in Bosnia and Herzegovina." *Asian Music* 20 (1): 128–45.

Petrović, Petar Ž. 1934. "O pevanju narodnih pesama uz okretanje tepsije." *Prilozi Proučavanju Narodne Poezije* 1 (1/2): 70–74.

Petrović, Radmila. 1961. "Narodni melos u oblasti Titovog Užica." In *Rad VIII kongresa Saveza Udruženja Folklorista Jugoslavije u Titovom Užicu,* edited by Dušan Nedeljković, 95–106. Beograd: Savez Udruženja Folklorista Jugoslavije.

———. 1974. "Narodna muzika istočne Jugoslavije—proces akulturacije." *Zvuk* 2:155–60.

Pettan, Svanibor. 1992. "Gypsy Music in Kosovo: Interaction and Creativity." Ph.D. dissertation, University of Maryland, Baltimore.

———. 1996. "Selling Music: Rom Musicians and the Music Market in Kosovo." In *Echo der Vielfalt* (Echoes of diversity), edited by Ursula Hemetek, 233–45. Wien: Böhlau Verlag.

———. 2001. *Kosovo Roma* (CD-ROM). Ljubljana: Nika.

Plaku i Drenicës. 1935. "Vjersha në të sjellun të tepsis." *Leka* 7 (6): 250–51.

Pllana, Shefqet. 1972. "Këngët e martesës ndër Shqiptarët e Kosovës." *Glasnik Muzeja Kosova* 11:51–112.

Reineck, Janet Susan. 1986. "Wedding Dances from Kosovo, Yugoslavia: A Structural and Contextual Analysis." M.A. thesis, University of California, Los Angeles.

———. 1988. "Self-Perception among Albanian Women: Continuity and Change." Paper delivered at the Twelfth International Congress of Anthropological and Ethnological Sciences in Zagreb.

Rihtman, Cvjetko. 1963. "Narodna muzička tradicija istočne Hercegovine." In *Rad IX kongresa Saveza Udruženja Folklorista Jugoslavije u Mostaru i Trebinju 1962,* edited by Jovan Vuković, 75–81. Sarajevo: Savez Udruženja Folklorista Jugoslavije.

Sárosi, Bálint. 1978. *Gypsy Music.* Budapest: Corvina.

Shepherd, Gil. 1978a. "Transsexualism in Oman?" *Man* 13 (1): 133–34.

———. 1978b. "The Omani *Xanith.*" *Man* 13 (4): 663–65.

Silverman, Carol. 1996. "Music and Power: Gender and Performance among Roma (Gypsies) of Skopje, Macedonia." *World of Music* 1:63–76.

Šmaus, Alois. 1937. "Pevanje uz tepsiju." *Prilozi Proučavanju Narodne Poezije* 4 (2): 240–55.

Stanković, Todor. 1988. "Putne beleške po Staroj Srbiji." 1910. Reprinted in *Savremenici o Kosovu i Metohiji, 1852–1912,* edited by Dušan T. Bataković, 229–60. Beograd: Srpska Književna Zadruga.

Strauss, Julius. 1997. "The Virgins Who Live like Men." *Albanian Observer* 3 (2): 34.

Sugarman, Jane C. 1997. *Engendering Song: Singing and Subjectivity at Prespa Albanian Weddings.* Chicago: University of Chicago Press.

———. 2000. "Albanian Music." In *The Garland Encyclopedia of World Music,* vol. 8, *Europe,* edited by Timothy Rice et al., 986–1006. New York: Garland.

Traerup, Birthe. 1974. "Narodna muzika Prizrenske Gore." In *Rad XIV kongresa Saveza Udruženja Folklorista Jugoslavije u Prizrenu 1967,* edited by Dušan Nedeljković, 211–23. Beograd: Savez Udruženja Folklorista Jugoslavije.

Vasiljević, Miodrag A. 1950. *Jugoslovenski muzički folklor.* Vol. 1, *Narodne melodije koje se pevaju na Kosmetu.* Beograd: Prosveta.

Vince-Pallua, Jelka. 2000. "Pojava virdžine, zavjetovane djevojke, u predajnoj kulturi balkanskih naroda." Ph.D. dissertation, University of Zagreb.

Vukanović, Tatomir. 1956. "Pevanje narodnih pesama uz okretanje tepsije." *Glasnik Muzeja Kosova i Metohije* 1:117–62.

———. 1961a. "Virdžine." *Glasnik Muzeja Kosova i Metohije* 6:78–120.

———. 1961b. "The Position of Women among Gypsies in the Kosovo-Metohija Region." *Journal of the Gypsy Lore Society* 40 (3/4): 81–100.

———. 1983. *Romi (Cigani) u Jugoslaviji.* Vranje: Nova Jugoslavija.

Whitehead, Harriet. 1981. "The Bow and the Burden Strap: A New Look at Institutionalized Homosexuality in Native North America." In *Sexual Meanings: The Cultural Construction of Gender and Sexuality,* edited by Sherry B. Ortner and Harriet Whitehead, 80–115. New York: Cambridge University Press.

Wikan, Unni. 1977. "Man Becomes Woman: Transsexualism in Oman as a Key to Gender Roles." *Man* 12 (2): 304–19.

———. 1978. "The Omani *Xanith:* A Third Gender Role?" *Man* 13:473–76.

Young, Antonia. 2000. *Women Who Became Men: Albanian Sworn Virgins.* Oxford: Berg.

13

The Tearful Public Sphere:
Turkey's "Sun of Art," Zeki Müren

Martin Stokes

This chapter represents an ongoing interest in the ways in which musicians are involved in the production of cultural intimacy in the public sphere of the eastern Mediterranean's new nation-states.[1] One might determine a broad domain of music making in the region that propels figures of complex moral and aesthetic ambivalence into a sharp and often critical public light, to modernist eyes, at least. From the modernist critical perspective (almost by definition, a major source of written and archival information on the subject), these musicians, and occasionally their listeners, give tangible form to the problem of intimacy and sentiment in the wrong place. This is to say, intimacy and sentiment expressed by men, as opposed to women, and in public (in opera boxes, on television and cinema screens, and the concert stage), as opposed to in private. The connections between these forms of cultural intimacy and the institutions of and periodic crises within the modernist-rationalist nation-state form bear close examination. These states are, as many critics have pointed out, thoroughly gendered and sexualized despite their claims to universalism, and thoroughly inflected by religious forms of expression, despite their resolute, or at least, overt, secularism.

Modernist critique intrudes on ethnographic inquiry in complex ways: ethnography is after all itself a tool of modernist critique, and a number of distinctly modernist assumptions carry through into ethnographic practice. In this case, it has tended to locate matters of emotion and sentiment in a female gendered space, in structural opposition to verbal instrumental reason in the male and public domain. The issue found formal expression in the, by now much critiqued, honor and shame paradigm in Mediterraneanist studies. A more recent line of argument has been to read resistance into public, mass-mediated cultures of sentiment. While this has the virtue of seeing in sentimental publicity creative cultural "work," rather than disorder, it locates sentiment on a romantic and ahistorical margin. An implicit part of my argument would therefore be for putting aside a priori assumptions concerning the marginality of sentiment, and for attending to men's "work of pain," as well as that of women (Magrini 1998). This is not so much a matter of redressing an imbalance, but a challenge to consider some of the theoretical issues involved in understanding sentiment in modern contexts of mass-mediated publicity, and particularly that of the modern nation-state.

A more pressing and personal project will be to revise some of my own accounts of queer and transgendered performers in Turkey. In particular, *The Arabesk Debate* (Stokes 1992) was informed by a somewhat crude pressure-valve theory, in which I came to see an entire field of cultural production, Arabesk, as a discursive complex shaped around notions of gendered, sexualized, and ethnicized alterity. These discursive constructions, I argued, were explicitly located in a Turkish premodernity, a pernicious "Orient" still lodged deeply and inexplicably in the heart of the modern nation-state. Despite its temporal othering, I argued (in this respect, I believe, entirely correctly) that Arabesk was a distinctly modern phenomenon. It drew effortlessly on vernacular religious practice, whose repression in official discourse was particularly marked at the time.[2] It adapted well to the lives of professional musicians pursuing somewhat precarious and marginal lives in the city, and translated easily into a local industry–generated cassette and music-film culture. Arabesk was at the same time sufficiently flexible, as a discourse, to allow for its appropriation by the generals who supervised the coup of 12 September 1980, who banned much else deemed counter to the Ataturkian westernizing and secularizing political heritage. Conceivably, they themselves saw in Arabesk a useful device for alleviating social and political anxiety while never speaking overtly of class or ethnicity. But the discursive construction of Arabesk as a music of outcasts and marginality was sufficiently strong for a later generation of liberalizers (in the wake of structural adjustment) to gain political capital by "bringing it in from the margins," and reversing a tradition of cultural dirigisme. While a strong language of marginality and even deviance undoubtedly existed in the prorepublican circles in which I moved, focusing on Arabesk in general, and figures such as Zeki Müren in particular, it was a language I took rather uncritically, and in some respects at face value.[3]

I take my lead in this chapter from Norwegian anthropologist Anne Ellingsen, whose brilliantly counterintuitive suggestion that we look at Turkish singers in terms not of deviance, but of normativity, of gendered decency (Ellingsen 1997), has been immensely useful. My own analysis differs from hers in some respects. It is certainly important, as a corrective, to establish the hypernormativity of singers such as Zeki Müren, and to complicate the kinds of models that would assign such singers, unproblematically, to the margins. But is also necessary to probe this hypernormativity for the contradictions and tensions that lie within it. In exploring these tensions and moving, in the process, from the sociological to the aesthetic and back, this kind of inquiry may provide an angle on some pervasive issues concerning the relationship of kinds of sentimentalism to kinds of modernism within specific national projects. The sentimental, with its commitment to the democratic ("love knows no bounds") and its affinity with forms of mass-media circulation, lies at the heart of the formation of national publics. Yet the fact has been persistently misrecognized by cultural elites wedded to forms of modernist theory implacably hostile to "the sentimental." Sentimental culture bears the marks of, and struggles with, this contradiction, though in various and complex ways. The Turkish case, as we shall see, is peculiarly revealing.

Zeki Müren

Zeki Müren was born in the provincial city of Bursa on 6 December 1931; he died on 24 September 1996 to national mourning, more or less a household name in Turkey as a singer, composer, and film star.[4] He was primarily associated with the light classical ("nightclub," or *gazino*) genre, but moved closer to Arabesk in his later career. His father was a moderately well-off tobacco and timber merchant in Bursa, in northwestern Turkey. Bursa nurtured a large number of well-known popular classical musicians. The city's prosperity rested on its rich agricultural hinterland, industrial development during the early republican years, and proximity to Istanbul's markets. This nourished an energetic and urbane bourgeoisie, with close ties to cultural life in Istanbul. Zeki Müren's father's partner was a successful Istanbul businessman,

Ihsan Doruk. Doruk was married to fledgling film star Cahide Sonku, who costarred with Zeki Müren in his first film, *Beklenen şarkı* (1953) and provided him with his contacts in the film world after his initial success as a radio singer. Proximity and close cultural ties with Istanbul meant that Zeki Müren's father was able to consider sending his only son to the city to complete his education. Zeki attended high school as a boarder at Istanbul's Boğaziçi Lise in 1946–47, and began to take classes with Serif İçli, Kadri Sençalar, and Agapos Efendi, the first two being particularly noted members of the Turkish Radio Art Music Orchestra, located nearby in Harbiye. An early composition of Zeki Müren's was sung by Suzan Güven on Turkish Radio in 1949 or 1950; an invitation to audition for the Turkish Radio followed from Radio director Refik Fersan, and his first live broadcast took place on 8 April 1951 (Hiçyılmaz 1998, 41). His program presented a diverse range of music, including sternly classical pieces from Sadullah Ağa and Ismail Dede, more contemporary pieces from Şevki Bey and Salahattin Pınar, a *maya* (a vocal improvisation in a quasi-folk idiom, akin to the *gazel*) and a piece of his own, "Yalan dünya, senden bezdim." Though Zeki Müren sang less and less of his own compositions as time went on, this diversity of repertoire was typical, not only of him, but also of many of the other great singers of his generation.

A regular series of Saturday night radio concerts followed. He registered at the Fine Arts Academy in Istanbul following his first radio appearance, cultivating a reputation not only as a musician, but also as a writer. His first recorded hit in 1951, "Bir muhabbet kuşu," was the beginning of a long association with RCA Victor (His Master's Voice) in Istanbul. Film work followed: he participated in some eighteen musical films, from *Beklenen şarkı* of 1953 to *Rüya gibi* in 1971, and on the back of this, from 1955 onward, a lucrative career as a nightclub singer. In the 1950s and 1960s, a time of increasing market-fuelled prosperity and rural-urban migration, Istanbul's nightclubs were palaces of elaborate and conspicuous consumption, maintaining orchestras of highly paid musicians (many of whom also worked at the Turkish Radio).[5] They provided a stage for elaborate battles for prestige and attention among the great singers of the time, which dominated the popular cultural journals of the period. This was a stage on which Zeki Müren soon came to occupy a central position, through an unrivaled and often innovatory command of performance detail, genteel high camp—his costumery took a decisive turn after seeing Liberace on an American trip in the 1960s[6]—and astute tactical moves. Zeki Müren's rivals in the nightclub world (among whom one would include Alaattin Yavaşca, Mualla Mukadder, Adnan Pekak, and others) soon began to disappear into the background. By this stage, an older generation of singers, including Safiye Ayla, Munir Nurettin Selçuk, Hafız

Burhan, and Müzeyyen Senar, had evidently lost either the energy or the taste for this kind of cutthroat competition.

Hiçyılmaz provides an interesting example of Zeki Müren's astute tactics in these gazino wars. An elaborate press campaign stoked up the rivalry between Zeki Müren and Mualla Mukadder for the 1959–60 New Year's Eve party in rival establishments. Mualla Mukadder was, reputedly, planning a quasi-dramatic musical in which she would play the part of Venus in Botticelli's painting, rising from the waves on an oyster shell. All manner of camp fireworks were surely expected from Zeki in response. Zeki Müren's coup lay in realizing that the Gregorian calendar's new year coincided, in this particular year, with Regaip Kandilli, a minor festival connected calendrically to Ramadan, and observed, significantly, mainly by women. Zeki Müren's program took place in an austerely decorated gazino, the music restrained, classical, and severe. Not only did Zeki Müren outwit his rivals by staging his meta-awareness of the rules of this particular form of competition (cf. Herzfeld 1985), but also by demonstrating a capacity for sensitivity to the rival demands of "Christian" and Islamic calendars. Prime Minister Menderes's conservative reaction to the secular reforms of the 1930s and 1940s had not yet reached their abrupt conclusion in the military coup of 1960.[7] Müren's move in acknowledging religious decorum was very much of its time. More particularly, his awareness of and sensitivity to women's religious practice, a complex and contradictory field during this period of aggressive secularization and Islamist reaction, allowed him to cultivate a female audience at matinee performances as no other nightclub singer had previously succeeded in doing.

Zeki Müren's cultivation of female fans provides an interesting vantage point on the mechanisms at work in manufacturing a reputation in the world of Turkish nightclub superstardom. On the one hand, Zeki Müren positioned himself as an active player in a world of spectacular professional rivalry. On the other hand, he assiduously cultivated an image of decorum and respectability. Müren's success lay in the way he could bring the two together in a delicate tension. This enabled him to construct for himself a complex but compelling public persona, one of decency pushed beyond its boundaries by a harsh and uncomprehending world (a story told over and over again in his films). It also allowed him to cultivate a fan base among women of all ages across Turkey. While Zeki Müren has been the subject of criticism from many quarters, it is important to grasp that this criticism has never been directed at the singer as a figure of outrage, shame, deviance, or any other sort of moral outsidership, as appears to be common in a number of other Middle Eastern and Mediterranean cases.[8] We must therefore be extremely cautious about assigning Zeki Müren to the cultural margin. Some of the reasons for this may be clear already: his elite musical training, bourgeois provincial upbringing, religious sensitivity, and so forth. However, Zeki Müren's homosexuality, and his turn to a self-evidently "marginal" musical genre, Arabesk, in the late 1970s, need to be considered first.

Zeki Müren's Homosexuality

Zeki Müren's sexuality is an obvious, though complex, topic of discussion. When I began research in the early 1980s, Zeki Müren was living openly with his long-term male partner, Fahrettin Arslan, in semiretirement in the Turkish seaside town of Bodrum. This was unremarkable to almost everybody I spoke to. The "unremarkable" here, as elsewhere, contained within it contradictions, which began to unravel in public after his death. A long interview with Fahrettin Arslan, published very shortly after his death, explicitly likened their partnership to the male-male partnerships canonized in classical Sufism. Zeki Müren himself apparently likened himself to the medieval mystic Celaleddin Rumi, and Fahrettin Arslan to Rumi's constant companion and inspiration, Şems. A nostalgic argument has, in some quarters, come to be spun around Zeki Müren. This is that Zeki Müren and other queer singers represent a continuous Middle Eastern tradition of gender ambiguity and deviance, nourished by the Ottomans, but forcibly repressed by obsessively heteronormative republicans in the early twentieth century. For them, "the freedom of women" was a key rallying point, and westernization was constantly imagined in terms of the "hygienic" and "efficient" nuclear family. Queer critique in Turkey on the subject of popular culture, as on Islam and globalization, sees the late Ottoman period as a model of cosmopolitan civic, political, and cultural virtues in the light of the bankruptcy of the republican tradition.

Others have, by contrast, explicitly sought to heterosexualize the memory of Zeki Müren. One might refer in particular to Ceyhan Güç's imaginative pseudoautobiography (written in the first person), *Şimdi uzaklardaysın* (1996), and Ergün Hiçyılmaz's more scholarly *Dargınım sana hayat: Zeki Müren için bir demet yasemin* (1997), on which text, I gather, a musical revue has been constructed. Ceyhan Güç's tactic is to stress an overintense relationship with his mother (who is, by contrast, almost entirely absent in Hiçyılmaz's book), and a childish but unconsummated love affair in Bursa. These two facts are used to account for his delicate artistic spirit (*ince ruhlu* being the regularly used Turkish phrase) and his inability to establish long-term relationships with other women. Hiçyılmaz launches a more spirited attack on

Zeki Müren's queer apologists. A lengthy scene depicts Zeki Müren's adolescent visits to the brothels of Karaköy, and he attempts to account for the 104 women with whom Zeki Müren reputedly slept. He interprets Zeki Müren's long-term relationship with Fahrettin Arslan as one of a number of merely *platonik* relationships he had with a number of other men and women, meriting only passing comment. Unfortunately, some of Zeki Müren's well-documented but understandably evasive responses to prurient journalistic inquiries add credence to these simplistic heterosexualizing tactics. In one remarkable exchange, journalist Halit Çapan asked Zeki Müren about his clothes. The conversation dwelt briefly on the subject of Yavuz Sultan Selim's earring.[9] Zeki Müren had commented on the absurdity of somebody's claim that he had already had a sex-change, on the basis of his androgynous dress sense ("if women wear trousers, does this mean they are all going to have sex-change operations too?"). Halit continued with these words: "But Zeki Bey, if a man goes on stage wearing women's clothes, hasn't he lost something of his manhood?" Zeki replied: "I don't wear women's clothes. I wear the kind of clothes Ceasar, and Baytekin, and Brutus wore." Halit went on: "So how does your nakedness (*çıplaklığınız*) make you feel on stage?" to which Zeki replied "Like a wrestler going out to wrestle in swimming costume (*mayo*)" (Hiçyıl-maz 1997, 51). Photographs of him dancing with, or locked in embrace with well-known female stars, float on this sea of journalistic testosterone. There is much to be said, of course, about the ways in which Zeki Müren positioned himself in relation to these discussions. His mastery of the sartorial repertoire contains more than a hint of the diva's disdain for those with more limited viewpoints, who would insist on seeing the apparel of Caesar, Baytekin, and Brutus as "women's clothes," and fail to grasp their wider historical and cultural resonance. At the same time, his apparent endorsement of the presuppositions of his interlocutor, that wrestlerlike masculinity is never to be lost or compromised, is striking. He was evidently as much caught up in the contradictory representations that surrounded him as were those journalists and cultural commentators who sought to "explain" him.

Zeki Müren's Voice

The second area in which Zeki Müren might be considered, by critics, to be occupying clearly oppositional ground is in his embrace of Arabesk, a genre excoriated by the intelligentsia and marginalized from its inception by the state media apparatus. His 1979 recording *Kahır mektubu* involved an explicit adoption of 1960s Egyptian models of popular song style. The composer of the piece, Muzaffer Özpınar, had himself encountered Umm Kulthum's later song style (the *ughniyāt* recorded with her erstwhile rival Mohamed Abd al-Wahhab) through recordings while in Paris in the 1970s.[10] Thoroughly inspired, he set out to write his own Turkish version, and *Kahır mektubu,* a thirty-minute piece with a recurrent refrain (as in Abd al-Wahhab's *Inta 'Omri,* for example), and lavish orchestration, was the result. Zeki Müren's moves in and out of Arabesk did not, however, seem to attract a great deal of attention, let alone condemnation. Partly this was a matter of the ways in which this move was perceived, or not perceived, by those who might have commented. Both light nightclub classical and Arabesk had a proletarian fan base who were, as far as one can be aware, unconcerned by matters of genre definition. Arabesk and gazino styles blended into one another and merged: the musical language, in crucial respects, was largely the same. For the intelligentsia, both light classical and Arabesk were neither progressive nor "properly Turkish," and both were ideologically tainted as a consequence. This was, after all, the most recent of a number of effortless and undemonstrative embraces of distinctly foreign musical styles (including tango and an earlier generation of Egyptian film musicals). The move to Arabesk was, then, a matter of relative insignificance for most people.

Changes of repertory were irrelevant as long as Zeki Müren's extraordinary voice provided aesthetic continuity. The admired qualities of his voice, in turn (as with Umm Kulthum in Egypt) rested on the quality of his diction.[11] Zeki Müren's spoken, written, and sung poetry was of an elevated quality, of a kind that has no counterpart in spoken Turkish except in poetic recitation. Though difficult to characterize to somebody who has never heard Zeki Müren speak or sing, it could be described as being marked by slight swells and tremors, particular attention to consonants normally swallowed or elided, and a tendency to make absolutely clear the distinction between back and front vowels. Words can indeed be heard clearly throughout Zeki Müren's songs. When they are blurred or violated, this blurring or violation has a clear expressive and dramatic purpose. Many professional musicians who remember that period remark that Zeki Müren was the first person to understand the full expressive potential of the microphone, effecting a revolution in popular musical expression akin to Bing Crosby's crooning technique.[12] "Good Turkish" evokes class, status, and prestige, despite the fact that nobody would dream of imitating the way Zeki Müren spoke in everyday life. To speak good Turkish, for most Turks today, is to speak clearly and directly, to connect signified with signifier by the most direct possible route. It is not to beat about the bush, as foreigners, particularly their southern and western neighbors, are assumed to do. The everyday, nonelite language of the

Anatolian inhabitants of the Ottoman Empire was indeed the master signifier of the Turkish revolution in the early twentieth century, evoking clarity, functional communicative efficiency, democracy, and, of course, ethnic homogeneity. Zeki Müren's "good Turkish" was a, if not the, crucial component of his high prestige. It overrode the significance of his flirtation with Arabesk, to such an extent that at the height of the Turkish Radio and Television's media battle against Arabesk in the mid-1980s, Zeki Müren could be invited to perform as a special guest star on the TRT New Year's Eve program. Even people who intensely disliked his music would, in conversation with me, invariably add "but I do love the way he speaks." He instilled notions of "correct pronunciation" that few other people could achieve. His cassettes carried "good Turkish" into homes and hearts in ways in which Turkish primary school teachers in remote Kurdish villages, and the neologism-laden jargon of the state news broadcasts in the early 1980s, could never hope to do.

Zeki Müren's voice was a national institution, but it contained within it some illuminating tensions. These say much about the politics of language in the 1950s and 1960s. One might note, for example, a significant discrepancy between the language he used in his journalistic writing in fashion magazines and the like, and his poetry.[13] His published poetry (in the volume *Bildircin yağmuru*) was in a self-consciously simple style. It is not difficult to detect the underlying influence of poets such as Orhan Veli, and other leading modernists cultivated during the early republican period. His written articles, on the other hand, contain many echoes of the official language of the Menderes era, during a period of reaction to the republican reforms. This writing, to be found in magazines such as *Artist, Yeni Yıldız,* and *Dedikodu,* demonstrate a more self-consciously "complex" literary character, making expansive use of the flowery Arabic and Ottoman register purged by the language reforms of earlier decades. One can pursue this ambiguity into the heart of Zeki Müren's singing, by detour of some of his own reflections on what makes for a great voice among his immediate forbears and contemporaries, in conversation with the journalist Ayda Özlü Çevik (Hiçyılmaz 1997). The old republican favorites, Munir Nurettin and Safiye Ayla, with their literary lyrics and crystal clear diction, are rejected. His preference is clearly for singers such as Müzeyyen Senar and Hafız Burhan (Munir Nurettin's main rival), for whom the literary value of the texts was not particularly significant, and the words, such as they are, are there to be swallowed up by the voice.

"When I was at middle school in Bursa, I only had one of Munir Nurettin Bey's records. I one had one of Safiye Ayla's, too. But I had thirty-eight of Müzeyyen Senar's. The kind of voice which makes the hairs on the back of your neck stand up, which makes you have a drink to disperse your sadness, that's Müzeyyen Senar's voice. They say Bülent Ersoy's voice is like Müzeyyen Hanım's. True, the style is the same, but the sound is quite different. If you put a Müzeyyen Hanım LP on the turntable, and play it at a slower speed, you get Hafız Burhan. His old 78s still move me. Munir Nurettin Bey never did" (Hiçyılmaz 1997, 113).

This does not, of course, tell the whole story. There are, for example, good grounds for thinking of Zeki Müren as Munir Nurettin's most worthy and faithful successor. Despite his criticism of Munir Nurettin, Zeki Müren took on, and applied to the limit, Munir Nurettin's aesthetic program: one of obsessive attention to visual detail in musical performance (dress, in particular), of high literary ambition and reverence for the Turkish language. Like Munir Nurettin, he evidently saw himself as a modernist and progressive, even though his music was being criticized from many quarters for its reactionary nature.

So there are grounds for taking these comments with some caution, and for understanding them as reflecting a certain "anxiety of influence." This both conceals distinct continuities with an earlier generation of singers, and also asserts a sovereign capacity to play the gamut of musical expressivity, not restricted to a particular school—something that could not, he implies, be said of his famous rival, Bülent Ersoy. But what does emerge from this complex process of self-positioning is the way it was structured by, and reframed, some of the key contradictions of this particular period. On the one hand, Zeki Müren's was a vocal art of literary ambition, progressive, comprehensible, and eminently rational in its aesthetic purpose. On the other hand, it was also a vocal art of emotional persuasion, of *tarab,* to appropriate, only slightly out of place, the term Jihad Racy identifies at the heart of vocal and instrumental music elsewhere in the Levant during this period (Racy 1988). Through distinguishing Müzeyyen Senar and Munir Nurettin in this particular way, Zeki Müren distinguished and made much of the tension between the two aesthetic principles. Any effort to understand Zeki Müren as "marginal," pure and simple, will thus not only lack historical and sociological acuity, but also fail to grasp an important aesthetic dynamic at work in his vocal style.

"The Comparison between Bülent Ersoy and Zeki Müren"

Bülent Ersoy, already mentioned in relation to Müzeyyen Senar's influence on Zeki Müren, is Turkey's most famous living transgendered singer.[14] The comparison, in some respects, is thus obvious and inevitable. There is a problem, however, to which I alert readers by placing the heading to this discussion in quotation marks.[15] This is that this comparison was a constant and insistent subject of journalistic inquiry during Zeki Müren's own lifetime. One cannot compare without taking into account that the comparison existed, and that it clearly affected the way in which the singers viewed themselves and one another. The fact that the comparison was constantly made means that there are no neutral grounds on which an abstracted comparison can be made. We might, though, try to read this comparative case against the grain to yield some rather different insights into Zeki Müren's public persona.

An early and in some respects typical example of "the case of Bülent Ersoy versus Zeki Müren" can be found in Cemal Süreya's *99 yüz* (Süreya 1989, 136). For him, the contrast had simple modernist-enlightenment parameters. One at least knew (and I paraphrase Süreya) what Bülent Ersoy was. He declared himself, loudly. The transformation of man to woman may have crossed a moral boundary, but it had a certain legibility to it: the legibility of modernist self-fashioning.[16] Bülent Ersoy declared himself a woman, and thus became a woman. Zeki Müren, on the other hand, made no such declaration concerning his sexuality. On the contrary, he equivocated endlessly. As Cemal Süreya puts it: "however famous he was it was just fame. The 'Muhabbet Kuşu' lived comfortably, running from success to success. . . . There was no need to display bravery in any area. He wasn't even able to defend his homosexuality" (Süreya 1989, 316). Süreya's words speak eloquently about the ways in which the Turkish social democratic left grappled with the complex and turbulent worlds of mass-mediated identity politics in a state that recognized no category of belonging other than that of "the citizen." There is no problem in being the way you want to be, he says, as long as you have the courage of your convictions to declare it and argue it out in public. What is central to the construction of this case ("Bülent Ersoy versus Zeki Müren") is a kind of social-democratic assumption. This is that identities are only identities if they are declared, and that these declarations have to conform to criteria of theoretical transparency in order to be translated into a coherent political/legal program, of the kind, say, that has been pursued by a number of queer and transsexual groups in Turkey over the last five or six years. According to these criteria, one party (Bülent Ersoy) succeeds while the other one (Zeki Müren) fails.[17]

One gets a sense from Süreya of the ways in which the comparison between the two singers became an important component of public discourse on gender, sexuality, and the wider issue of identity politics in Turkey. Some of the significance of this case can be sensed when one considers the relative ease with which this topic could be discussed, and the relative lack of public discussion of the war taking place in the southeast of the country. One might debate the extent to which the Bülent Ersoy/Zeki Müren issue acted as a metaphor, or provided a kind of displacement mechanism for other identity struggles (arguably of more direct material and political consequence). This line of thinking suggests that the form of the case study and the nature of its circulation in public space are in many respects more significant than the "content" of the case study itself. For those of us reading the comparison in terms of what we might learn specifically about Zeki Müren, though, there is a problem. This is simply that the comparison suggests that Zeki Müren is little more than a failed Bülent Ersoy, according to criteria of success and failure, both aesthetic and political, that may be entirely irrelevant to the older singer. My own comparison in the following paragraphs will, by contrast, try to show that Zeki Müren and Bülent Ersoy are rather different kinds of figure. Culturally and historically speaking, they cannot be compared on the same terrain, or, at least, the terrain that is conventionally mapped for the purpose.

First, what one comes to know about both singers is formed in quite different ways. In comparison to Zeki Müren, Bülent Ersoy presents complex biographical problems. One can legitimately and publicly come to "know about" Zeki Müren. There are biographies, fictionalized autobiographies, Web sites, entries in music encyclopedias, documentary film programs, and a stage musical.[18] He also left behind a substantial body of his own writing, in the form of poems and journal articles. Bülent Ersoy is famous, but in a very different way. She recorded some of the best known cassettes in the 1980s, and is now well beyond the routine drudgery of the nightclub circuit. However, she occasionally makes appearances at large civic festivals (such as the midsummer Gülhane Park festival in Istanbul) to connect with a huge audience of proletarian fans. The distinctive sound of her voice is almost an atmospheric property of the city's streets, bars, and taxicabs, but she is a curiously absent presence, and has left little written trace. The singer rarely gives interviews; she and her entourage at Raks Müzik (with whom she now records) actively discourage researchers. There are no books, documentary films, official Web sites, or stage reviews, to the best of my knowledge. In some senses, therefore, there is not much to "know" about her, although this lack is, of course, a social fact in its own right.

What people in Turkey know about Bülent Ersoy is known primarily through the tabloid press. Press releases document a vaguely implausible, but no doubt sincere quest for bourgeois respectability (Bülent Ersoy, wearing headscarf, renounces all musical activity for the month of Ramadan; Bülent Ersoy plans engagement, and is assembling her dowry; Bülent Ersoy, finally, gets married in Izmir). Her insistent heteronormative fantasies always raise a smile, for most Turkish observers, but little more, even though her uncertain gender status has been a matter of high-level legal and political concern. Media coverage has by no means all been of a prurient nature. Turkey's intelligentsia continue to see the legal and political status of transsexuals as a matter of serious concern (Roberts and Kandiyoti 1998). Bülent left the country to undergo sex-change surgery in London in 1981, after which a highly publicized debate took place as to whether the singer would thereafter perform as a man or a woman. Women (but not men) require a special police permit to perform in public; this, in the event, was not forthcoming, although the precise grounds are unclear to me and those I have discussed the matter with. Bülent, or her managers, were evidently not prepared to make the argument that she was really a man, and as a consequence, she spent several years in virtual exile.

It is hard to assess the exact motivations involved. Clearly, life in Germany presented more opportunities for a singer during the harsh years of cultural, economic, and political austerity that prevailed in Turkey after the 1980 military coup. In 1986, Turkey's new liberal leaders were already signaling the need for cultural change with reference to Bülent Ersoy and other banned and marginalized artists.[19] If her exile years were years of Arabesk, her return to Turkey was marked by recordings in a severely classical style. *Konseri* (ca. 1987), *Alaturka 1995,* and her recent *Orkide* series have large string orchestras, but otherwise are self-conscious in their classicism, involving long and academic *taksim* improvisations, and a slow and sober pace, quite removed from Arabesk's general hustle and busyness. The quest for legitimacy, both sexual and cultural, therefore, has clear career motivations in the context of the liberalization of the Turkish political and economic system during these years. But they cannot absolutely be reduced to this. At any rate, interested observers do not have much to go on. Tabloid journalism, humorous gossip, and conjecture shape the circulation of knowledge about the star.

Second, Zeki Müren and Bülent Ersoy are not often compared as musicians. A musical comparison reveals some interesting points of convergence and divergence. Bülent's performance style draws on similar roots as Zeki's, in particular the early guidance and inspiration of Müzeyyen Senar, and the later mentorship of Muzaffer Özpınar. Both musicians can move fluently between classical and popular repertories, though Zeki Müren's movements are relatively unmarked, while those of Bülent Ersoy are marked and self-conscious.[20] Bülent Ersoy's voice, however, owes much more to Müzeyyen Senar's than to Zeki Müren, his own comments notwithstanding. Sighs, gasps, and groans obscure or interrupt words. Indeed, for many fans, the "meaning" (*mana*) and expression (*ifade*) of her performance reside in the interruption and fragmentation of the verbal text. What is meaningful for fans is precisely this affective violation: signs of an intention to mean, and not an underlying (and verbalizable) "meaning" amenable to some kind of analysis or interpretation. This interruption and fragmentation has a sexual dynamic. This fact emerged most strikingly when Bülent filled in the sound of the call to prayer in a recording of the 1940s Munir Nurettin number "Aziz Istanbul" with a "real" call to prayer, which she sung herself, attracting a certain degree of hostile commentary from Istanbul's Islamists. It is not easy to contrast their vocal styles, since both derive from similar sources. But one could focus on the ways in which both singers "mark" the Turkish language. For Zeki Müren, the primacy of language was never doubted, and attention to prosody (*prozodi*) a taken-for-granted hallmark of good musicianship. For Bülent Ersoy, evidently, good musicianship resided in expressive deviation, of fragmenting and dispersing texts to such an extent that their verbal intelligibility is easily lost.

My own "cross-grain" reading of this overworked comparison suggests the relatively unmarked nature of Zeki Müren's attachment to the nation-building project, at least, as it appeared to many in Turkey in the 1950s and 1960s. Contradictions are expressed but resolved within what could (at least then) be unproblematically perceived as a "Turkish" musical style. It also stresses the strongly marked nature of Bülent Ersoy's detachment from the nation-building project, and the ways in which this shaped and was shaped by the more fragmented political context of the 1980s and 1990s. The public presentation of gender transformation, the handling of the Turkish language, and the self-conscious shifts between "Turkish" and Arabesk repertories speak strikingly in this regard.

A Surplus of Affect

The most striking feature of a wide range of sentimental musics in the Mediterranean region—here I might tentatively throw in the musics associated with Mohamed Abd al-Wahhab, Ferid al-Attrache, Abd al-Halim Hafiz—is its surplus of affect (to appropriate Appadurai's useful phrase), its superabundance. This is almost a tautology, at least to modernist eyes, for whom "sentiment" and "surplus" are almost synonymous. Modernist rationalists everywhere deplore inefficient communication, which is precisely why they identify excess in this music, and then explain it away. The grain of this kind of thinking is rather hard to escape. We have, then, to find a slightly more oblique angle on the issue. A useful starting point may be to consider super-abundance and semiotic surplus as itself meaningful and significant, and not just as excess baggage.

One might pursue this idea in relation to sound, visual representation, and narrative employment. One is the bigness of the sound—a vague formulation, but it might capture the significance of vast, overwhelming, overpowering voices, so rich and multilayered in physical texture, that the listener has no option but to loose him or herself in it. The volume of Arabesk and popular classical music in live performance in Turkey should be emphasized here. The voice is not only heavily amplified, but richly overlaid with reverb. The only possible condition of listening is one of closeness, of engulfment.[21] Critical distance is out of the question. The "meaning" of the voice does not lie in signs that await decoding under the surface, so to speak, but in a sensuous rhetoric of meaning-making on that very surface. One can only point to it and sigh, as indeed most of my friends would do when talking about Zeki Müren, or, indeed, Bülent Ersoy. The visual imagery is also one of insistent superabundance. Not just taste, but too much taste. Not just elegance, but too much elegance. Not just luxury, but too much luxury. Not just flowers, but buckets and buckets of flowers. The narrative modalities are varied, finding expression most characteristically in music film, and related forms of popular culture (*foto-roman,* once, in Turkey, and now music videos, which present three-minute versions of entire Arabesk movies). These differ according to gender and age, though it seems characteristic of this cultural formation that the most significant stars are young men. They invariably depict refined decency or sensitivity operating under impossible strain or adversity. What varies, and is the subject of imaginative handling on the part of movie scriptwriters, is the circumstance that flings the protagonist into a situation in which his or her reserves of decency are not enough to save him from exposure and inevitable humiliation. While the moment of humiliation is invariably the crux of the drama, and the moment at which the tears begin to flow and the very best songs emerge, we are never allowed to forget, even at this moment of sympathetic identification, that it is all the protagonist's own fault. The effort to be decent, beyond all reasonable expectations, is act of a fool who doesn't realize that modern life simply has no room for this kind of affective baggage. The films might be described, in other words, as dramas of moral surplus.

This narrative production of moral surplus has clear consequences for the way in which gender is organized and portrayed. Most particularly, I would argue, it loosens the reciprocally structured relationship between morality and gender. In short, one cannot, in the moral calculus of the musical film, act morally and gender-appropriately. There is no sentimental "solution" to the dilemma, in the Turkish musical film. There is no possibility of developing and sustaining a different kind of subjectivity, with clearly and coherently gendered correlates (as, for example, in the sentimental novels and dramas of late-eighteenth-century Europe). In the context of Turkish musical film, the futility of a gendered moral code becomes more and more apparent. There is a two-way process at work here. Gendered morality becomes too big for the subject, supplying implausible and self-destructive solutions to complex moral dilemmas. On the other hand, the subject becomes too big for conventionally gendered morality, while failing to find any form of coherent expression, or self-actualization, in the narrative telos.

Another way of framing my argument would be to say that the musical drama turns gender into hypergender. A reading of Baudrillard's influential notion of hyperreality might be useful here. For Baudrillard, the hyperreal presented itself as exaggeration, artifice, and fantasy. Its purpose, he argues in his famous analysis of Disneyland, is to shore up "the real," a notion which becomes ever more notional as the Saussurean sign is stretched to and finally beyond its breaking point. "Reality" no longer "is" its representation (qua McLuhan), but has been replaced by it. Only if it looks like what it looks like on TV can we be sure it is "real," as he never tires of telling us. Might something similar be involved in the display of gendered opulence, luxury, and superabundance we are discussing here? There are grounds, I believe, for bringing his point to bear on converging lines of thought elsewhere, in particular queer theory and an older tradition of Mediterranean ethnography. Queer theory stresses gender and sexual performativity. Gender and sexuality are their enactments, and queer theory's own canon of spectacular media stars operate semiotically "by making gender so fabulously artificial [by] showing up the artifice of gender" (Morris 1995, 583).

Mediterranean anthropology and ethnomusicology have also had a tradition of thinking about the agonistic, enacted quality of personhood in which gender and sexuality are central (see Herzfeld 1985, Cowan 1992, and Sugarman 1988 for recent examples). It has also focused ethnographic attention on moments of representational crisis in which the very frames within which gender and sexuality are enacted themselves come into focus as an object of moral anxiety. Older ways of narrating gendered selfhood make less sense, for example, in modern Crete, according to Michael Herzfeld, in a classic study (Herzfeld 1985), where "real men" no longer need to steal sheep to access a more powerful form of cultural capital: money. They make less sense in northern Lebanon, according to Michael Gilsenan (1996), where men risk ridicule if they attempt to adhere to an outdated honor ethic, and struggle to cope with the exigencies and performative dynamics of new political and economic realities. In these, the tractor becomes more important than the gun and urban real estate supplants agricultural land as the basis of wealth and prestige. The old is easily exposed as "fantasy," as "theater" and artifice, no longer delivering on what it once promised. New forms of mediated consciousness come into existence, peripheral in Herzfeld's 1985 study, but central to Gilsenan's Lebanese study (1996), working at this gap between gendered performance and what "performance," now seen as such, so visibly fails to achieve.

The coincidence of forms of hypergendered musical performance with the political traumas of modernity (from masculinist/modernist state formation to the violence of structural adjustment) in many large southern and eastern Mediterranean locales is, in my view, hardly fortuitous. A common set of circumstances prevail: a quasi-colonial relationship that prevails between north and south, the systematic and ongoing underdevelopment of major regions across southeastern Europe and the Middle East, and inevitably, unstable state structures with authoritarian political cultures. The effects of these circumstances on productive and reproductive roles within and outside the household have been extensively documented, albeit in ways which have tended to reproduce local modernist elites' anxiety about "the position of women." Their effect on masculinity is significant as well. Labor markets within and outside the Mediterranean world increasingly turn to casualized women's labor in service sectors as the Fordist economy is dismantled across the old industrialized first world. The masculinist/modernist state projects which dominated the political landscape of the eastern Mediterranean for the middle fifty years of the twentieth century (those of Atatürk, Hoja, Nasser, Metaxas, Tito, and so forth) have run aground, in some cases with catastrophic consequences. As Zeki Müren's case shows eloquently, musical figures of hypergendered cultural intimacy have provided important ways of imagining the nation as a space of shared sentiment. But they are an ambiguous and often poorly understood comfort from those who invest most heavily in imagining the nation-state as a big happy family under the rule of a benevolent paterfamilias. They thrive, after all, in conditions of representational crisis in which they actively participate. They give shape and compelling affective form to a nagging question. What happens when that fundamental "Mediterranean" certainty, "being a man," collapses?

Notes

This chapter has gone through various incarnations. It was read, first, at the meeting of the ICTM Mediterranean study group in Venice 1998. Discussion of the paper with Martha Feldman, Eddie Seroussi, Karin van Niuewkerk, Marie Virolle, Phil Bohlman, Tony Langlois, Piera Sarasini, Svanibor Pettan, Joaquina Labajo Valdes, and the organizer, Tullia Magrini, on that occasion initiated the first major rethink. I have given papers based on versions of this chapter at Harvard, New York University, and the Turkish Circle at the University of Chicago. Comments by Virginia Danielson, Kay Shelemay, Gage Averill, and Hakan Özoglu have been much appreciated. The chapter benefited greatly from a read at a late stage by my reading group colleagues at the University of Chicago, David Levin and Martha Feldman.

I would like to thank Anne Ellingsen for her generous sharing of thoughts and materials over the years, in relation to Zeki Müren in particular. Many of the articles and books referred to here came into my hands through her, and many of the interviews referred to here were conducted jointly. Ted Swedenburg's e-mail missives on queer Turkey over the years have been invaluable. I would also like to thank Ayşe Draz, who told me about and then passed on her copy of Hiçyılmaz's detailed biography of Zeki Müren at a particularly timely moment.

Finally, a word on translations: unless otherwise noted, all translations from non-English sources in this chapter are my own.

1. Feld 1982 and Abu-Lughod 1986 on the social and cultural productivity of emotion are crucial points of reference. Berlant 1997, Ellison 1999, Middleton 1992, and Herzfeld 1997 recast the problem with reference to modernity, citizenship, and the nation-state; this is my more specific point of departure.

2. The practice was, though, ambivalent. See Stokes 1992 on the so-called Rabita affair, in which the Turkish general's complicity in sponsoring Islamist projects among Turks in Germany came to light.

3. Hann (1994) is surely right to detect in this the "ghost" of "Orientalism." If this inheres in some of the writing on Turkey produced in these years, the answer may lie in the ways in which researchers wittingly or unwittingly reproduced the dominant discourse of the period, assuming that it was the most powerful "reality producer" at the time, and that the equations it made (for example, "Orient" equals "deviance") either were, or became, the way things were.

4. Zeki Müren gives his own birth date, in his poem "Biyografım" (1965, 127) as 6 December 1933. It is difficult to know whether this rewriting is a matter of authorial vanity or reflects a confusion over birth dates engendered by the common practice of announcing dates of birth later than their actual occurrence, the overt rationale for this being that families have the productive and emotional resources of their male children in the family for a longer period of time than would otherwise be the case. Adulthood begins when obligatory military service ends. The date 1931 comes from Rona 1985.

Cemal Süreya's brief article on Zeki Müren in *99 yüz: Izdüşümler/söz senaryosu* (Süreya 1989, 315–17), in the context of people and names who have shaped the end of Turkey's twentieth century, observes, simply, that "there is nobody more famous in Turkey than Zeki Müren," adding, "though taken seriously by none." This grudging recognition encapsulates the ambivalent response of the Turkish intelligentsia to Zeki Müren's fame, an uncomfortable but inescapable fact.

5. Hiçyılmaz records the names of the musicians employed by Küçük Çiftlik Parkı in Istanbul, including Salahattin Pınar, Şadi Işılay, Ismail Sençalar, Yorgo Bacanos, Kadri Şençalar, Şükrü Tunar, Necdet Gezen, Sevgi Aslangil, and Hakkı Derman—a who's who of popular classical musicians in the 1950s and 1960s. The main gazinos were Türkuaz, Beşiktaş Bahçesi, Tepebaşı, Küçük Çiftlik, around the European district of Beyoglu and the Bosphorus shore. Later in the 1960s, gazinos were put up in the old city districts of Aksaray and Yenikapı, notably Yenikapı Çakıl *gazinosu,* and in and around Bebek, further up the Bosphorus.

6. The term "camp" is often taken to imply a degree of self-awareness and ironic distance, and this is, perhaps, not the most appropriate way to approach Zeki Müren, who, beyond managing his career with enormous skill, was not always absolutely in control of his self-presentation. His rather elliptical responses to journalists, discussed below, might be seen in this light, at least.

7. For a valuable analysis of the continuities underpinning Islamist and secularist politics in Turkey during this period, see Keyder 1987.

8. The moral language of honor and shame is particularly inappropriate. The semantic universes evoked by the deployment of words such as *ayıp* (*'ayb*) and *haram,* or *rezil/rezalet,* are far away. See, for example, Karin van Nieuwkerk's contribution to this volume (chap. 11) and 1995. I never heard Zeki Müren or Bülent Ersoy, at least, discussed in these terms.

9. The sultan reputedly wore an earring to remember a promise. "Kulağım küpeli olsun" (may my ear have a ring it) is still used to tell somebody that you sincerely intend to remember a promise made to them. In the late 1980s, very few Turkish men wore earrings. If they did, the automatic assumption made by most was that they were homosexual. I had taken my own earring out before living in Turkey, but the hole in my ear was clearly visible—there was no disguising the fact! It was thus a constant topic of conversation. The story of the Sultan's earring came up frequently, partly to structure discussion about "modern life" and its foibles in Europe. Partly, though, it also seemed to evoke memory of a prerepublican time when different and in some respects more complex gendered expressive styles were legitimate and respectable.

10. This and other observations in this section are drawn from interviews with Muzaffer Özpınar with Anne Ellingsen and myself in August 1996.

11. The ability to speak good and clear Turkish was a fairly unambiguous index of national aspiration and national participation on the part of most Turks, at least until the mid-1980s.

12. Cem Karaca, interviewed by Anne Ellingsen and Martin Stokes, August 1996.

13. From the early 1950s on, he composed less and less of the music that he himself recorded. The media corporations in Turkey, then, as now, provided an elaborate network of composers, lyricists, producers, and arrangers. Singers, by and large, just sang. Those, like Orhan Gencebay, who chose to set up their own labels, did so, among other reasons, in order to be able to compose their own music. *Berdüş* (1957) was the last film for which

Zeki Müren wrote the music, though, his first hit, "Bir muhabbet kuşu" (1951) had been written by his clarinettist, Şükrü Tunar, and his first film had music composed to it by Şadi Işılay. In both cases, his immediate entourage provided him with compositions in the early years. After turning to Arabesk, he struck up a close working relationship with Ilham Behlül Bektaş (lyricist) and Muzaffer Özpınar (composer and arranger), who followed him from Türküola to Raks Müzik in the 1990s.

14. A major transgendered/transsexual scene used to revolve around Tarlabaşı and Ilker Sokak, near Taksim in the center of Istanbul.

15. My concern with the necessity of grasping the historical and cultural formulation of "cases" draws on Chandler 1999. The formation and public circulation of "the case of Bülent Ersoy versus Zeki Müren" is in some respect more significant than the "content" of the case study itself. In this situation, one might stress the ways in which the public discussion of citizenship in Turkey increasingly found a focus in sexual politics during the 1990s. It is difficult to say whether this is a displacement of, or metaphor for, more nationally pressing questions of identity and citizenship, namely, the devastating military operations against Kurdish villages in the southeast of Turkey during this period. On the general issue of sexual politics in this period, see Roberts and Kandiyoti's analysis (1998).

16. A point Sander Gilman emphasizes in *Making the Body Beautiful* (1999). Transsexuals are modernists through and through.

17. The irony would be that most "out" queer activists have nothing but contempt for Bülent Ersoy. Demet Demir, a transsexual prostitute and well-known queer activist, felt that Bülent Ersoy was an opportunist (interview with Anne Ellingsen and Martin Stokes, August 1996). The total inability of many of her clients to comprehend their own homosexuality and act intelligently on this knowledge, she felt, had some connection to the Bülent Ersoy phenomenon. She herself identified strongly with pop and rock.

18 See, respectively, Rona 1985, Hiçyılmaz 1997, Güç 1996, Show TV's Aynalar documentary (which can be found on www.showtv.net), and Dedeman Topluluğu's review, *Bir demet yasemin*.

19. These included Arabesk singers such as Orhan Gencebay and Ibrahim Tatlıses to radical rock singers such as Cem Karaca.

20. The titles of his cassettes often refer to genre. Before you hear a note, you are aware of being in the semantic universe of Arabesk, or of Turkish classical. The Arabesk cassettes have poetic titles, usually the name of a song. The classical recordings have some abstract term followed by a number (e.g. *Orkide 1, Orkide 2*), or imply genre explicitly (e.g. *Alaturka 95*) or implicitly (*Konseri,* for example, is likely to refer to an art music concert, rather than anything else).

21. One should note here that Zeki Müren pioneered the use of a T-shaped stage, which allowed him to walk right out into the heart of the auditorium.

References

Abu-Lughod, Lila. 1986. *Veiled Sentiments: Honor and Poetry in a Bedouin Society.* Berkeley and Los Angeles: University of California Press.

Baudrillard, Jean. 1983. *Simulations.* New York: Semiotext(e)

Berlant, Lauren. 1997. *The Queen of America Goes to Washington City: Essays on Sex and Citizenship.* Durham: Duke University Press.

Chandler, James. 1999. *England in 1819: The Politics of Literary Culture and the Case of Romantic Historicism.* Chicago: University of Chicago Press.

Cowan, Jane. 1992. *Dance and the Body Politic in Modern Greece.* Princeton: Princeton University Press.

Danielson, Virginia. 1998. *The Sound of Egypt.* Chicago: University of Chicago Press.

Ellingsen, Anne. 1997. "Ibrahim Tatlıses and the Popular Music Genre Arabesk in Turkey." *Studia Musicologia Norvegica* 23:65–74.

Ellison, Julie. 1999. *Cato's Tears and the Making of Anglo-American Emotion.* Chicago: University of Chicago Press.

Feld, Steven. 1982. *Sound and Sentiment: Bird, Weeping, Poetics, and Song in Kaluli Expression.* Philadelphia: University of Pennsylvania Press.

Gilman, Sander. 1999. *Making the Body Beautiful: A Cultural History of Aesthetic Surgery.* Princeton: Princeton University Press.

Gilsenan, Michael. 1996. *Lords of the Lebanese Marches: Violence and Narrative in an Arab Society.* Berkeley and Los Angeles: University of California Press.

Güç, Ceyhan. 1996. *Simdi uzaklardaysın.* Istanbul: Ad.

Hann, Christopher. 1994. "The Ghost of Orientalism in Recent Writing on Turkey." *Journal of the Anthropological Society of Oxford* 24 (3): 223–43.

Herzfeld, Michael. 1985. *The Poetics of Manhood: Context and Identity in a Cretan Moutain Village.* Princeton: Princeton University Press.

Herzfeld, Michael. 1997. *Cultural Intimacy: Social Poetics in the Nation-State.* London: Routledge.

Hiçyılmaz, Ergün. 1997. *Dargınım sana hayat: Zeki Müren için bir demet yasemin.* Istanbul: Kamer.

Keyder, Calgar. 1987. *State and Class in Turkey: A Study in Capitalist Development.* London: Verso.

Magrini, Tullia. 1998. "Women's 'Work of Pain' in Christian Mediterranean Europe." *Music and Anthropology* 3. http://www.muspe.unibo.it/period/MA/

Middleton, Peter. 1992. *The Inward Gaze: Masculinity and Subjectivity in Modern Culture.* London: Routledge.

Morris, Rosalynd. 1995. "All Made Up: Performance Theory and the New Anthropology of Sex and Gender." *Annual Review of Anthropology* 24:567–92.

Müren, Zeki. 1965. *Bildircin yağmuru.* Istanbul: Istanbul Matbaası.

Nieuwkerk, Karin van. 1995. *"A Trade Like Any Other": Female Singers and Dancers in Egypt.* Austin: University of Texas Press.

Racy, A. Jihad. 1988. "Sound and Society: The Takht Music of Early Twentieth-Century Cairo." *Selected Reports in Ethnomusicology* 7:139–70.

Roberts, Mary, and Deniz Kandiyoti. 1998. "Transsexuals and the Urban Landscape in the Istanbul." *MERIP* (Middle East Research and Information Project) 28 (1): 20–25.

Rona, Mustafa. 1985. "Zeki Müren". In *20 yuzyilin turk musikisi ansiklopedesi.* Istanbul: Çagloglu.

Stokes, Martin. 1992. *The Arabesk Debate: Music and Musicians in Modern Turkey*. Oxford: Clarendon.

Sugarman, Jane. 1988. "Making Muabet: The Social Basis of Singing among Prespa Albanian Men." *Selected Reports in Ethnomusicology* 7 : 1–42.

Süreya, Cemal. 1989. *99 yüz: Izdüzümler/söz senaryosu*. Istanbul: Kaynak.

Select Discography of Zeki Müren Recordings

Bir tatli tebessüm. HMV/Sahibin Sesi recordings from the 1950s. Coşkun Plak KB.94.34.U.044.008, 1994.

Türk sanat müziği konseri. HMV/Sahibin Sesi recording, c. 1960. Coşkun Plak 93.34.U.044.005, 1993.

Kahır mektubu. Türküola 1979. Türküola LC 2955, 1991.

Aşk kurbani. Türküola c. 1986. Lider Plak KTB.90.34.U.083, 1990.

Helal olsun. Lider Plak KTB 87.34.U.083.03, 1987.

14

"And She Sang a New Song": Gender and Music on the Sacred Landscapes of the Mediterranean

Philip V. Bohlman

The king entered
With many knights and servants.
The count's wife had already been received
With the playing of the string instrument.
There she played on the lute
With words full of joy.
The pagans announced in full voice
That they had never heard anything better.

The monk was seated at the head table.
She did it with love and respect.
Fish and game were served to him
And everything his heart might desire.
When she observed this,
She gathered her courage.
"It is happening so well,
That my undertaking is bound to go well."

So she played on the harp
And she sang a new song,

Full of courtliness and artistry,
That which resounded through the palace.
The pagans would release him
Once night had fallen.
For during these events
The count received word of his fate.

"The Count of Rome" (ca. 1600), verses 15–17
(Bohlman and Holzapfel 2001, 90–102)

Music and gender are inextricably bound together in the allegory "The Count of Rome," textually and historically the oldest ballad to map the sacred landscape of the Mediterranean. The ballad's narrative depends on the confusion and inversion of gender roles, especially the ability of a woman to play social roles usually restricted to men. In several crucial ways, music sets the stage for the transformation of gender roles, by providing the common ground shared by the ballad's major players. Music also sets the stage for the sacred journeys that provide further narrative fabric for "The Count of Rome," and it is hardly surprising that this ballad, sung in innumerable variants, would enter song repertories throughout the Mediterranean. Already by the turn of the seventeenth century, "The Count of Rome" was a song about the Mediterranean as a region where music and gender would serve as allegories for the struggle to transform the Mediterranean's sacred landscape into the common ground of Mediterranean history.

There is nothing simple or singular about the presence of gender in the ballad. At a critical moment in the middle of the narrative, the eponymous "count of Rome," captured by a Muslim Mediterranean king while on a pilgrimage to the Holy Sepulchre in Jerusalem, is rescued by his wife, who has disguised herself as a Christian monk. The rescue is possible because the count's wife is a musician, and at the turning point in the verses transcribed above, the woman/wife/monk/musician draws us into a moment of musical power and musical invention. Having played the lute to enchant the "pagans" (*hetens*) at the Ottoman court, she now plays her harp (*Do schlug sie auff der harpffen*) and succeeds in winning the release of her husband, the count, by singing a new song (*mach ein frysch gesanng*).

Music and religion form the common signature of the feminine in "The Count of Rome." The count's wife acquires the power to rescue her husband only as a musician bringing a music new to the Muslim courtiers along the Mediterranean pilgrimage route. The count himself, however, remains deaf to the music and blind to the presence of gender. After his release, he completes his pilgrimage and then returns to Rome, only to castigate his wife for doing nothing to win his release. To reveal to her husband that it was she who had risked her life for his, "she went immediately to her room, she took the monk's habit, and she took up the strings of the lute and harp that she had played so well" (verse 28). The traces of conflicting identities are stripped away from her true self as "she entered through the door with music" (*sye tradt hynein mit schalle*). She becomes a monk and a musician to reveal the power of a woman to challenge the power of male-dominated courts. It is only at the allegorical juxtaposition that the gendered presence of music is made visible, which is to say audible, for the listener.

The Mediterranean in the ballad, too, seems cloaked by layers of conflicting signification. The version of "The Count of Rome" quoted above is a translation of the earliest surviving print of the ballad (see Bohlman and Holzapfel 2001, 99–100).[1] The medieval Germanic language (*Mittelhochdeutsch*) of the text notwithstanding, its provenance remains Mediterranean (Süß 1980). Not only did it appear in northern Italy, but it is printed in Hebrew orthography. Those two facts are not particularly unusual, for many printers of Hebrew books, pamphlets, and broadsides settled in northern Italy after Jews were expelled from the Iberian peninsula in 1492. The ballad and its symbols chart a landscape where historical narratives from different parts of the Mediterranean converge. Though the text bristles with Christian symbols—the count undertakes a Christian pilgrimage, and his wife disguises herself as a musician-monk—it also juxtaposes narratives of the Mediterranean as the historical border between Christianity and Islam. The combination of literary languages from northern Europe (Middle High German) and the Mediterranean (Hebrew words, not just Hebrew spellings) also locates the song in a border region of historical contestation and conflict. A welter of symbols collapses in upon the historical space of the song, and a new historical space, somewhere in the eastern Mediterranean, is opened, entered by a woman making music and singing a new song.

Gender and the Sacred Spaces of Music in the Mediterranean

Historically speaking, traditional approaches to the Mediterranean enforce notions of sharp separation and the concomitant dichotomies: north and south; Europe and Africa; Europe and Asia; the first world and other ordinally distinct worlds; Christianity and Islam; people with history and those without. In religious and aesthetic domains, there has been no less a tendency to view the Mediterranean as a dividing line, thereby reinforcing historical dualities. The visual arts in the Christian north have a complex representational vocabulary, whereas in the Muslim and Jewish south representational imagery is eschewed. The development of harmony from tonality in Europe spawns a different music history from the persistence of modality in North Africa and the Middle East. Mirroring the dualizing tendency in other cultural domains, representations of gender, too, have traditionally relied on sharp divisions between male and female, for example, in the threadbare tropes of male "honor" and female "shame" used to frame the tension between men and women in Mediterranean society. It is these essentializing dichotomies that Tullia Magrini dismantles in her introduction to this volume.

In this chapter, I turn to the complex presence of gender in Mediterranean song repertories, specifically in sacred music and musical practices, to suggest why the categories of male and female cannot simply be reduced to dualities in the Mediterranean. The many sacred musical practices where both male and female are found, moreover, are also spaces where sharp distinctions between many dualities blur and dissolve. Gender distinctions are not somehow eliminated or neutralized, rather they are remixed and reconfigured. The relation between male and female may be turned on its head or inside-out, but it is significant that the relation does not simply disappear.

Sacred song is a particularly resonant and powerful medium for the processes of remixing and reconfiguring difference on the imagined and real landscapes of the Mediterranean. Sacred song unravels the sharp dichotomies that dominate the discourses about the aesthetics of Mediterranean cultures. In so doing, song opens up spaces that are no longer just male and female but may mix male and female musical practices or even, in some cases, become androgynous. Traditional and postmodern musics of the Mediterranean may display the outward appearances of androgyne. *Raï* in Algeria and Morocco has become a postmodern case in point (see Virolle-Souibès 1995 and chap. 8 in this volume). The traditional cabaret or club milieu of raï is a space rendered male by the extensive presence of women. Raï itself marks this new gendered dependency through its aesthetics of male singers valued for their effeminate voices and female singers who have succeeded because of their low voices and masculine performance style, giving new gendered meaning—and aesthetic "indeterminacy," as Marc Schade-Poulsen refers to it—to the social space in which raï is performed and heard (Schade-Poulsen 1999, 141).

Raï is in many respects quintessentially Mediterranean, for the ways it juxtaposes gender and Islam underscore colonial and postcolonial histories, not least among them the presence of Algerian guest workers and immigrants in France and elsewhere (see Gross, McMurray, and Swedenburg 1996). Raï further sharpens the focus of this chapter because its aesthetic and reception histories are both secular and sacred. The rise of raï has paralleled the rise of Islamism in Algerian society, despite its mixing the male and female roles of musical production and consumption. Indeed, the paradox is at first glance perplexing because one might expect the critical message of raï to be anti-Islamist. The rhetoric of raï, however, does not contradict the rise of Islamism in Algeria, and therefore it acquires the potential to complement religious fundamentalism. Raï and Islam do not so much occupy the same space as draw a cluster of public discussions and debates about gender into the same discourse (Schade-Poulsen 1996, 148–53; cf. Bohlman 2000, 293–96).

As I briefly sketch the gendered space opened by raï, it is the presence of Islam that seems strangely out of place. How can there be a religious dimension to a music that wantonly flaunts the conventions of religion, and whose texts, with few exceptions, knowingly violate Muslim tenets? The answers to such questions are many and complex, but most critical is the fact that it is precisely the complex issues of gender—whether primarily questions of family structure or voiced and unvoiced questions of sexuality—motivating the Algerian public's intensified affiliation to Islamic practice in a postcolonial Algeria that raï maps through performance. Such questions of gender, Schade-Poulsen observes, are not Western, however the surface elements of the music (e.g., Western instruments) may make them sound as if they were (1996, 142). The sacred dimensions to raï's aesthetic space are therefore fundamentally Muslim, which in turn contextualizes that aesthetic space as Mediterranean, not Western and not global.

The representational symbolism of the Mediterranean's sacred landscapes are crucial for the poetics of sacred song because it provides a space or place that processes of gendering open through the performative acts of worship and music making. Worship and music interact to create specific, culturally determined "senses of place" as Steven Feld and Keith Basso would refer to them:

> Senses of place: the terrain covered here includes the relation of sensation to emplacement; the experiential and expressive ways places are known, imagined, yearned for, held, remembered, voiced, lived, contested, and struggled over; and the multiple ways places are metonymically and metaphorically tied to identities. (Feld and Basso 1996, 11)

Intensifying the sense of place that maps the sacred song in the Mediterranean, both locally and regionally, is the way in which religious practice and musical practice situate memory and through performance empower it to give meaning to place. A shrine, for example, condenses many different levels of memory—historical, genealogical, ritualized, political, sacred—but it is the interactive performative acts of music and worship that reveal specific sets of memories. Music and worship, through performance, instantiate place itself (see Feld 1996).

The music and the musical practices "envoiced" through sacred song are not symbolic and abstract, but real and realizable through spaces of performance such as those Elaine Marks recognizes in her use of the *marrano* as a metapor for the feminine aspects of Jewish experience (Marks 1996). The *juifemme* (lit., Jew-woman, or "Jewoman") has a distinctive set of experiences, but they are necessarily Jewish experiences. The spaces in which they transpire possess the attributes of "both-and," whereby female and Jewish need not contradict each other, even when they constantly respond to changing cultural contexts. Like the marrano in the metaphor, Iberian Jews who chose conversion over death by the Inquisition after Spain and Portugal expelled the Jews in 1492, Marks's juifemmes have the potential to intensify Jewish experience by adapting it to so many different places.

The power to shape and reshape the gendered conditions of Islam in Bedouin society lies at the core of Lila Abu-Lughod's discussion of poetry and the meanings of veiling. When veiled, a woman does not abandon her sentiments—experiences of autonomy, modesty, or sexuality—but she reconfigures their social presence through the complex poetics of North African Bedouin women. The veil does not hide them through its enforcement of modesty; rather it resituates them within a social space with an aesthetic context of its own (Abu-Lughod 1986).

Gender proves crucial to an aesthetic understanding of the Mediterranean's sacred landscapes. It becomes even more crucial when religion shapes the musical practices in the poetics of memory, transforming it into a sacred poetics. In all the dominant religions of the Mediterranean, religious practices magnify rather than ameliorate gender distinctions. Men and women worship in different ways and often in different places, and their religious practices map their lives in very different ways. When one speaks about "the music" of Islam, Judaism, or Christianity in the Mediterranean, it is necessary to distinguish between men's and women's practices and repertories before any kind of meaningful discussion can even begin. The danger that such seemingly clear distinctions pose is one of essentialism. The critical issue is that, though often separated, the sacred musical practices of men and women are not isolated from each other. Meaningful discussion must ultimately lead beyond traditional gender categories to examine the places male and female practices intersect. It is into these spaces that notions of sense and sentiment, poetics and aesthetics, move and unleash alternative forms of gendering musical and religious expression.

Sacred Song and Gendered Narratives

> Have you a scripture that promises you whatever you choose?
> Or have We sworn a covenant with you—a covenant binding till
> the Day of Resurrection—that you shall have what you yourselves
> ordain?
>
> Quran, sura 68:37

Narrativity lies at the core of the poetics of sacred song and gender, and the musical practices that inscribe the Mediterranean's sacred landscape are overwhelmingly narrative. The particular components of narrativity that are crucial to the sacred poetics are (1) the capacity to tell stories and recount history, (2) mediation by those who perceive and receive sacred messages to those for whom those messages are intended, and (3) creating a layered texture of sacred meaning by juxtaposing different musical genres. Such characteristics of narrativity are, in themselves, not unique, but their concentration in the different musical genres and practices of the sacred poetics is, thus empowering music through performance—the enactment of narrative—to create a sense of place.

Story and history intersect in the narrative genres constituting sacred song. Sacred sites often form because of particular events—an act of martyrdom or miracle—and these in turn provide the basis for the histories of those sites. As songs come into existence to recount the origins of the sacred site, they acquire their meaning through processes of narration: they tell not only of the original events, but they layer subsequent events specific to the sacred site on top of the initial narratives. Within the songs, stories accrue in such a way that together they represent the history of the sacred site. In this way, narrativity begins locally. It may also have more expansive origins, especially when musical genres are created to narrate the events and genealogies of a much larger history. Epics, for example, possess this type of narrativity. Within epic cycles, individual songs and even individual genres parse history from within, framing the events and lives that made history.

The sacred songs that are so distinctively Mediterranean are fundamentally narrative, as are ballads such as "The Count of Rome." Even more significant are the *romance* and *romancero* ballad repertories of the Sephardic diaspora in the Mediterranean, which are almost entirely a musical practice maintained by women (cf. Armistead and Silverman 1971, 1986; Hemsi 1995; Seroussi 1998). It is because of the essential narrativity of the foundational texts of the major religions in the Mediterranean, the Hebrew and the Christian Bibles, and the Quran, and especially because of the rich presence of metaphor in those texts that they, too, contribute specific texts to the articulation of local musical practices at shrines or pilgrimage sites.

Music's power to mediate assumes many forms in the sacred songs of the Mediterranean. Sacred texts are often transmitted and perceived through intermediary voices. The foundational texts of the three dominant religions are either partly or, in the case of the Quran, entirely revealed and mediated. Ontologies of music, too, depend on an understanding of voice being "received" and then transmitted. The recitation practices of Judaism, Christianity, and Islam all interpret the musical context of text as a vessel (e.g., *kle* in Hebrew), a means of making the text clearer and more meaningful through melody. In the poetics that comes to embody the musical practices at many local sacred sites, gender heightens the role of mediation. In Christian pilgrimage, for example, Marian apparitions are the primary media for connecting worshipers to the word of God. Paradoxically, whereas the bodies of males more often serve as evidence for miracles and martyrdom, it is women who acquire religious significance through their mediation of these experiences. Gender leaves its mark on mediation through a complex calculus of performance that opens the spaces of the Mediterranean's sacred landscape (cf. Christian 1992).

The presence of gender in narrative genres inscribes a wide range of meanings on the Mediterranean's sacred landscapes. Extensive border-crossing is abundantly evident in "The Count of Rome." The musical repertories sung by pilgrims or for saint veneration, too, rely on complex degrees of layering. The Jewish women whose songs venerate Moroccan saints tap repertories of *qasīda,* reinscribing a popular Arabic genre on the genealogy of their own Jewish saints. Christian pilgrims turn to Marian songs at critical historical moments, transforming the symbolism of traditional repertories into contemporary meaning. Gender, particularly because of the ways song repertories express religious imagery and practices that rely on both separation and juxtaposition of male and female, shapes the ways in which sacred spaces come into being through performance.

Gender and the Performance of Sacred Space

> I shall continue to sing,
> To gladden my burnt heart
> And request what I crave
> And the saint is he who shall cure me,
> Dear Rabbi Shalom Zawi.
>
> "Tsaddiqim el-ʿzaz," or "The Beloved Saints
> (Ben-Ami 1998, 109–10)

The expressive meaning of gender is most powerfully inscribed through the performance of faith at the shrine. Therefore it is hardly surprising that the Mediterranean, with the remarkable density of shrines constituting its sacred landscape, is made legible through sacred song. The shrine is a local site of worship, and it traces its origins to events and individuals of local significance. The significance of a shrine, nonetheless, is not delimited by local practice. Quite the contrary, worshipers from elsewhere visit the shrine, transforming its local meanings into international, even occasionally panreligious, significance. Male practices of Islam in North Africa, for example, rely on a network of Sufi shrines. Whereas individual saints are celebrated at individual shrines, it is only together that these shrines come to embody the larger genealogy of saint veneration expressing North African Sufism. Marian shrines in Greece and the Aegean have similar functions, intensifying the local but contributing an essential link to a larger Catholicism.

Performance may take place in many different ways at a shrine. First of all, it is possible to say that the shrine itself "performs." Marian images or icons often speak to or otherwise communicate with worshipers, whether through voices, songs, or symbolic events (e.g., the tears of a weeping icon). The worshiper comes to the shrine as a spectator or auditor, expecting to witness performance. Second, it is crucial for worshipers not to limit their responses to a passive encounter but to enter into a performative dialogue with the shrine itself. The apparitions that appear at Christian shrines, in particular, address their audiences with questions or with requests that the worshipers undertake something on their behalf. The worshiper becomes the agent of faith because the enshrined saint cannot. Third, the performative experience at the shrine grows stronger through *communitas*. It is important to the ritual practices of the shrine that individual encounters and dialogues with saints extend to the community that forms through worship at the shrine (see Turner and Turner 1978). Entire repertories of song, such as the *piyyutim* of

Moroccan Jews (Ben-Ami 1998) or Marian songs, connect individual experiences to a larger community, proffering that community a new liturgical identity. Finally, the geography of the shrine and its environs are made meaningful primarily through performance. At certain moments of intense meaning, shrines accommodate the visits and worship of large numbers of pilgrims, and it is only when these worshipers are kept in motion—through processions, through visits to ancillary shrines, through the formation of communities with specialized functions—that the shrine effectively serves the needs of the faithful in attendance. The sacred landscape of the shrine can and does accommodate the needs of many worshipers, becoming the site for a polyphonic texture of liturgies, healing practices, and saint veneration.

Gender marks shrines in the Mediterranean at virtually every level. The communities and cults that venerate saints usually do so for reasons that reflect gender distinctions within society and within individual ritual practices. Catholic shrines, at least on their surfaces, are gendered female. Many shrines are dedicated to the veneration of the Virgin Mary or woman saints; pilgrims in many parts of the Mediterranean are overwhelmingly female; and many song repertories suggest a distinctively female dimension of worship, for example, in Marian songs. Women are much less likely to participate in the veneration of Sufi saints, who are almost exclusively male. Jewish saints in North Africa, too, are largely male. However, even at Muslim and Jewish shrines, women play a role in saint veneration that is arguably more significant than that of men, both because women participate more actively in the performance of music at the shrines and because their musical practices are more accommodating, thus investing shrines with a more expansive, flexible capacity for sacred time.

The musical practices of a shrine, however their surfaces are gendered, are also sites for the leveling of gender distinctions. Thus, the Jewish women who sing in Hebrew and Arabic to venerate Moroccan saints do so in public, ostensibly violating the principles of orthodoxy. Similarly, the music of Catholic shrines may afford women opportunities for expressing their personal needs through worship and song that are otherwise inaccessible in the hierarchy of the Church (Magrini 1998). Indeed, the roles of men and women as music makers within a Catholic context are inverted at shrines. Unlike participation in the public mass and in the liturgy of the Catholic Church, where women play a subsidiary role at best, the musical leaders of ritual practices at many Catholic shrines are women. In Balkan pilgrimages, for example, women control all aspects of musical performance, from chanting the rosary during extensive foot pilgrimages to distributing the printed texts sung at different shrines along the longer journey (Bohlman 1999, 38–39). The crucial point is that the shrine, as a site of sacred performance, gives voice to those otherwise silenced because of gender restrictions. Sacred song at the shrine not only reorders the presence and expression of gender, it does so in a visible, public way (see Dubisch 1995, 193–228).

Paradoxically, whereas it might seem natural that Catholic shrines, so often devoted to Marian worship, would attract women as performers to abandon the space of the liturgy in the church for a more exclusively female space in the shrine, that is not entirely the case. During the month of May, for example, when worship of Marian imagery is most intense, men are often more visible in public forms of Marian worship than are women. Song performance at such shrines often involves prolonged contemplation of images of the Virgin Mary, with sacred time articulated through the singing of songs from special hymnbooks for the Marian month. Marian contemplation requires the male gaze upon the female object, but within the shrine itself it is the connection within the space that engenders Marian songs.

The veneration of saints among Moroccan Jews has developed into an extraordinarily complex sacred space for gendered performance. Three types of songs are drawn from the Moroccan Jewish liturgy for singing at the graves of saints. The first is the *piyyut,* a composed song, performed entirely in Hebrew and by men. Piyyutim are not limited to the Moroccan-Jewish tradition, but are traditional within other Jewish communities. Literacy and the maintenance of manuscripts undergird the piyyut tradition. There is a second type of composed song to extol saints at the shrines devoted to them. Also a type of piyyut, these songs contain alternating Hebrew and Judeo-Arabic verses; only men sing the former, but women may sing the latter. Finally, Moroccan Jews perform songs from the widespread Arabic genre qasīda, which have Arabic texts, especially Judeo-Arabic texts. Qasīdot are sung almost entirely by women, though men are not excluded from the tradition and may join in singing under special circumstances (Ben-Ami 1998, 105–6).

Sacred song in the Moroccan-Jewish tradition has even broader dimensions, for saint veneration is a practice that Muslims and Jews in North Africa share. There are some saints, for example, whom both Muslims and Jews venerate. Muslim and Jewish traditions overlap, and the song repertories used to extol saints musically open spaces where songs in both Hebrew and Arabic coexist, or where the two languages alternate within the same songs (Ben-Ami 1998, 131–46). The poetic spaces in which Judaism and Islam overlap, furthermore, exhibit gendered qualities, for men more commonly sing in Hebrew and women in Arabic. These intersecting performance practices reflect specific historical conditions of identity for Moroccan Jews, previously in Morocco and increasingly, in the final decades of the twentieth century, in

Israel (Seroussi 1986). The veneration of Moroccan-Jewish saints therefore takes place on many musical levels, but the songs associated with the saints inflect each level through distinctive expressions of gendered worship (Ben-Ami 1998, 125–30).

Sacred Song and Sacred Journey

> There the goddess took her place, and cried out a great cry and terrible and loud, and put strength in all the Achaians' hearts, to go on tirelessly with their fighting of battles.
>
> *Iliad,* book 11

Sacred journey charts the historical landscapes of the Mediterranean. It is through this constant passage that the religions of the region weave a fabric of intersecting histories. Religious sojourners follow the routes to the sacred sites in the eastern Mediterranean where earlier soldiers and saints traveled. The Mediterranean thus both "orients" the major religions, directing their historical journeys toward Jerusalem and Mecca, and reaches toward those places in the western Mediterranean, such as the pilgrimage site of Saint James, Santiago de Compostela, where the world once came to its end.

Through sacred journey, no less dense and seamless in the lives of Muslims, Jews, and Christians at the beginning of the twenty-first century than during the spread of Islam across North Africa in the ninth century, the Crusades in the eleventh century, or the Sephardic diaspora in the fifteenth century, the Mediterranean becomes not just a map *for* but a map *of* Judaism, Christianity, and Islam. Sacred song articulating the historical journeys of the Mediterranean's religions cuts across the borders of those religions. Sacred song does not so much unify them as provide common ground, and a poetics of commonality is critical to the history of the Mediterranean that must survive the confrontation and conflicts of its disparate parts.

The sacred landscapes of the Mediterranean have historically unfolded through epic, not least among them the five-book epic cycle of the Torah, the Books of Moses in the Hebrew Bible. Through performance, epics pose complex questions of gender. On their surfaces, Mediterranean epics point to indices that are overwhelmingly male. The eponymous figure in many epics — Moses, Odysseus, El Cid, Orlando — is male; in the performance practices associated with most Mediterranean epics, the singer and, to a large degree, his audience are male. If the historical agency of epics is strikingly male, the narration of specific historical moments frequently admits women actors to the historical drama of the epic. Women often problematize the epic's narrative, whether appearing in the classical figure of Helen of Troy in the *Iliad* or the modern entry of women as religious-musical specialists into the synagogue, where they then give (female) voice to the epic of Moses. By problematizing the epic's narrative, women transform its relation to the public spaces in which it is performed.

Diaspora turns in on diaspora in the Mediterranean, tracing and retracing ancient and modern sacred journeys; beginnings and endings overlap, as if to become indistinguishable. Just as its epics distinguish the Mediterranean, so too do its diasporas. So distinctive of the Mediterranean is diaspora that the very historiographical models with which we interpret diaspora originate in the Mediterranean. The dispersion of a nation or people, on one hand, draws upon the spread of the Greeks through the Aegean and beyond. The exile of a people from their homeland, on the other, has long taken the diaspora of the Jewish people as its model. The Mediterranean therefore becomes a space of intersecting diasporas, and it is from spaces formed by these historical intersections that sacred song is given voice.

Gender transforms the historical geography of diaspora. Families and communities may be broken as departure from the homeland begins, but they may also be reconstituted in the lands of diaspora. The narratives of guest workers from the Mediterranean take as their central trope the problem of reconstituting broken families and suturing the lives of decaying communities in the industrial neighborhoods of the north. Women enter the music culture of the diaspora in ways that were unknown prior to departure from the homeland. In Berlin's Kreuzberg district or in the Paris suburbs with growing Maghrebi populations, women perform genres that had traditionally been restricted to males. In the social organizations of such diaspora communities, mixed choruses sometimes form, reconstituting the community away from the homeland but also using music to mix genders in ways unimaginable in the homeland (see, e.g., Reinhard 1987).

Pilgrimage also makes the Mediterranean's sacred journeys audible through song. There are not only pilgrimage songs connected to specific places and events, but those that accompany pilgrims on their journeys. Pilgrimage songs lend order to time and history. Individual songs serve to memorialize those who have passed along the sacred journey before, and singing them draws each pilgrim into the community of faithful whose lives enter the narrative space between the sacred journey and history. The music of pilgrimage negotiates between past and present, making the past physical and real in the border spaces between sacred and historical time (Bowman 1991; Christian 1992; and Bohlman 1996).

Pilgrimage songs usually depend on extraordinary juxtapositions of gender. Within the contexts of religions constituted by male hierarchies, the miracles and messages that attract pilgrims most often depend on female agency. Pilgrimage songs empower women to participate in moments of crisis and to enter upon the contested landscapes of the Mediterranean. When they do so, they are singing, be it in the domestic ritual of the Passover seder or in the repertories of qasīda performed at the tombs of Maghrebi Muslim saints. The sacred poetics of the pilgrim's space depend on music to confirm the spiritual transformation of the present and to give voice to the voiceless, thus giving them a place in a sacred landscape. That landscape is contested as much at the beginning of the twenty-first century as in those distant moments that engendered the first pilgrimages and yielded a sacred identity to the Mediterranean.

Medjugorje: Sacred Song in Time of War

> We pray to the Mother,
> > to the Mother, the Blessed.
> Oh, hear our songs,
> > as we journey together.
> Ave, Ave, Ave Maria, Ave Maria, Maria.
>
> You, Queen of Peace,
> > grant us your atonement.
> We are all your people,
> > oh, Mother, the Blessed.
> Ave, Ave, Ave Maria, Ave Maria, Maria.
>
> "The Medjugorje Song" (late 1980s)

Sacred spaces continue to open throughout the Mediterranean region, and music and gendered musical practices continue to participate actively in the opening of sacred spaces. I turn to one of the most recently transformed sacred spaces, formed at the interstices of the Balkan conflict: the pilgrimage site of Medjugorje, near Citluk, Bosnia-Herzegovina. Medjugorje has engendered a series of sacred practices that stretch beyond its remote location, and its sacred poetics have become meaningful throughout the Mediterranean and beyond. It would be tempting to interpret sacred song at Medjugorje as globalized and postmodern, but that would be minimizing its true meaning for the many for whom the sacred journey to and the experience of Medjugorje's shrines open a sacred door to the future.

Medjugorje's history as a sacred site began on 24 June 1981, when the Virgin Mary appeared to six children living in the hilly region of southern Bosnia-Herzegovina, about thirty kilometers from the border with Croatia and about thirty kilometers from Mostar. Medjugorje lies in a historically contested region, yet the site where the Marian apparitions took place is remote. After the initial apparition, the Virgin Mary appeared on each of the next six days, affirming to the six children to whom she first appeared and then to growing crowds that she was, indeed, Mary, the mother of Jesus. She spoke to the six children, initiating a maternal dialogue, in which she established herself as a mother concerned with their well-being and their future. Most who came to witness Mary in the first week did not see her, but they came to believe that she was indeed in their midst. The children saw Mary day after day, and she has continued to appear until the present. Her most recent appearance was at 9:55 A.M. on 18 March 2000, two days before I wrote these lines.

The apparitions of Our Lady, Queen of Peace, in Medjugorje are neither vague nor nebulous: not only does she appear to several individuals at once, including entire congregations, but she speaks to them clearly, and she communicates a sacred message at regular intervals, which she delivers clearly and distinctly. During the 1980s, the Virgin of Medjugorje appeared most regularly on Thursdays, speaking briefly to the growing staff of clergy and laypeople who maintained the nascent pilgrimage site. The so-called Thursday messages were gathered and disseminated, for example, through pamphlets, books, and broadsides, and as sound cassettes distributed throughout the world (cf. Rupčić 1989 and *Donnerstag-Botschaften*). A complex, yet distinct, discourse emerged from the many messages communicated by the Marian apparitions. One of the most recent messages mediated through an apparition at Medjugorje is that of 25 February 2000:

> Dear children!
> Wake up from the sleep of unbelief and sin, because this is a time of grace which God gives you. Use this time and seek the grace of healing of your heart from God, so that you may see God and man with the heart. Pray in a special way for those who have not come to know God's love, and witness with your life so that they also can come to know God and His immeasurable love. Thank you for having responded to my call. (http://www.medjugorje.hr/ezadnpor.html)

The sacred messages mediated through the Marian apparition at Medjugorje have a rich, polyphonic texture and a distinctive discourse of gender.

The forms and genres within this discourse arise from specific themes, and the ways in which they are mediated rely on the interaction of music and gender in complex ways. From the beginning of the apparitions, it became clear that the Virgin Mary was an emissary for five themes that would be developed systematically through variation of the discursive polyphony. These five themes leave their marks on Medjugorje worship, for they are revealed again and again to the faithful. In the order of their revelation, the five messages constituting the palimpsest of Medjugorje's sacred poetics are (1) peace, (2) faith, (3) conversion, (4) prayer, and (5) fasting. The discourse that spins out from the five messages always weaves them into a tight fabric, in which each message comes to depend on the other four for its meaning. Fasting intensifies prayer, conversion intensifies faith, and all the messages intensify the first, peace.

A web of gendered meanings and acts always shapes the core of Medjugorje's sacred aesthetics and song repertories. It is her "voice" that witnesses hear, though she often speaks for others and usually insists that she is no more than a mediator, the one designated to deliver the message. The apparitions and messages stress community and commonality, but they do so by insisting on the metaphor of the family. Mary may be many things—"a teacher, a leader, a beautiful woman"—but most of all "she is a mother" (*Donnerstag-Botschaften,* n.d.). Her presence as a mother is crucial for the ways in which the Medjugorje experiences are shaped by gender. Women are the most powerful interpreters of the messages, and women experience apparitions far more often than men.

The pilgrims who gather at Medjugorje to witness the power of peace, moreover, are overwhelmingly female, though until 1996 it was exceptionally dangerous for women to make the pilgrimage through war-torn areas of Croatia and Bosnia. The gendered qualities of Medjugorje's sacred landscape contrast in every way possible with the ongoing conflicts in Bosnia and the other areas of the former Yugoslavia, defined as they are by the male patriarchies of the Balkans.

Sacred song provides a crucial medium for the representation of gender at Medjugorje. Soon after the first seven Marian apparitions, Marian songs were being mustered to remember the apparitions using the voices of past pilgrims. The themes of Marian songs were remarkably close to those expressed in the "Thursday messages." In particular, the theme of Mary as the "Queen of Peace" resonated with the first of her key revelations. New Marian songs quickly followed, first as traditional songs were adapted to heighten their local meaning, and then as composers and arrangers within the Catholic mystical traditions recognized that the Medjugorje messages could contribute to the growing repertory of songs created to narrate the experiences of modern pilgrims. "The Medjugorje Song," which appeared on pilgrimage cassettes first in the late 1980s (e.g., *Maria, Königin aller Heiligen*), quickly spread throughout Europe and the world, giving the Medjugorje pilgrimage an international context, and adding it to a much more extensive sacred landscape in the new Europe (see Bohlman 1996).

Song transforms the sacred poetics of pilgrimage to Medjugorje, where the symbols of gender transform worshiping pilgrims into families capable of reproducing peace at the heart of a war-torn region. The musical life at Medjugorje is ongoing, performed continuously for and by the pilgrims who visit the sacred site. If tens of thousands make music in Bosnia itself, far more experience the music issuing from the pilgrimage site through broadcasts on "Radio Station 'Mir' Medjugorje," which is accessible through both radio and the Internet (http://www.medjugorje.hr/eradio.html). Masses, recited rosaries, and the performances of visiting pilgrims may be heard in live radio broadcasts, or listeners and worshipers may download them from indirect access sites. The Medjugorje songs find expression in most European languages, and various Web sites make the countless songs of pilgrims quickly available to all who wish to enter the sacred landscape of Medjugorje.

With musical practices dependent on the dissemination of audiocassettes, as well as on radio and Internet dissemination, it might seem as if Medjugorje were a postmodern version of such historical pilgrimage sites as Lourdes or Fátima. Medjugorje, however, lies in the midst of a zone of conflict, and it emerged as a pilgrimage site during a period of escalating tensions and expanding war. Its transformation into a sacred landscape, therefore, is not simply a random geographical fact; that landscape provides an alternative to the Balkan conflicts whose human victims are countless (cf. Manuel 1992 and Bax 1995). Since March 1999, the messages from Medjugorje have increasingly included appeals for humanitarian assistance for the residents of Kosovo and for the Kosovar refugees. The Kosovo war and even more recently the Macedonian conflict, therefore, have entered into the polyphony of sacred song at the pilgrimage site, which consciously crosses religious borders by recognizing fully that Islam is the dominant religion of Albanians in both Kosovo and Macedonia. The songs of Medjugorje thus do not shut out those of other faiths whose lives are endangered, but rather expand sacred space to accommodate an ever more complex polyphony giving voice to the voiceless.

Gender and Music on the Landscapes of War and Peace

> Atop a hill in Galilee
> A guardsman sits, and merrily
> He plays upon his flute a song
> To lamb and kid the whole day long.
>
> There was a giant of sturdy stock;
> He cleft the cliff, he moved the rock.
> With a song of life the conqueror
> Defeated hordes in ruthless war.
>
> "'Tis good," he said, "to die at the post,
> To give to our land our uttermost!"
> There was a giant formerly,
> A mystic man—one arm had he.
>
> "Alei giv'a, sham Bagalil," or "Atop a Hill in Galilee"
> (Nathan 1994, xvii, 16–17)

This essay closes as it began, with a sacred song in which gender and music join to remap the Mediterranean. In many ways, however, "The Count of Rome" and "Atop a Hill in Galilee" are the same only because they are mirror images: Each contains the inversion of the other. Music afforded power to a woman in "The Count of Rome" and to a man in "Atop a Hill in Galilee." The historical goal of the pilgrims from Rome is now claimed for the future by the pioneer settlers in Galilee. The woman makes music work by donning the habit of a monk, whereas the man cloaks his ability to change the land in the mystery of a body magnified by the loss of an arm. The common ground in both songs, nonetheless, remains the sacred landscape of the Mediterranean, and its commonality is only enhanced because, in neither song, has that landscape fully been realized by the Jewish communities in which these songs of the Mediterranean circulated. The sacred landscape, in the end, remains an ideal, approached by extraordinary male and female figures, whose gender, forged and narrated through myth, allows them to use music to rise beyond the ordinary to transform the place of the sacred in the Mediterranean.

It is telling, moreover, that neither song truly occupies the sacred landscape of the Mediterranean that it attempts to claim. "The Count of Rome" served as an allegory for late medieval and early modern movement across the Mediterranean, recognizing the places of disjuncture opened by religious difference. The ameliorative intervention by the gendered allegory on the power of music rerouted the ballad's major characters, but it failed to allow them—and by extension, the Jewish singers and publishers who produced the version discussed in this chapter—a place of their own. "Atop a Hill in Galilee," its appropriation of mythical masculine power notwithstanding, did not describe a real, historical Galilee inhabited by Jews. Settling the sacred landscape of Palestine in the 1930s, when this song passed between oral and literate tradition, had amassed a surfeit of highly gendered images, which filled the repertory from which this song came, one of the first to use the modern Hebrew language consciously. The land itself was feminine, but its builders were masculine; the past was evoked through the mythological presence of female symbols, but the struggle to defend the present was possible through historical male actors. The distinction between male and female would seem to drive a wedge through these so-called *shire chalutzim* (songs of the pioneers), but music—as allegory, as weapon, as historical narrative—created a common space for male and female in the songs, which circulated between Palestine and the diaspora in the late 1930s, even as the specter of the Holocaust loomed (see the anthology published as Nathan 1994).

The role of gender in the Mediterranean that I have explored in this chapter has been present in sacred song itself. The repertories I have used to illustrate narratives about the Mediterranean, historical movement across and about the Mediterranean, and responses to war and peace have formed at moments of crisis and as responses to historical change. As song repertories they function to accommodate those responses, and primary among those responses has been the evocation of Mediterranean landscapes where music served as a tool to realize the unimaginable. These landscapes are abundantly evident in Mediterranean ballads, in the networks of pilgrimage routes and saints shrines, in the performance of contemporary popular song as sacred, whether in Islamist urban styles from North Africa or orthodox Christian and Jewish rock styles from the Levant. On these sacred landscapes, music endows men and women with power to reimagine the sense of place in which they live, and to rechart a different Mediterranean, a Mediterranean of difference, by singing a new song.

Note

1. Unless otherwise noted, all translations from non-English sources in this chapter are my own.

References

Abu-Lughod, Lila. 1986. *Veiled Sentiments: Honor and Poetry in a Bedouin Society.* Berkeley and Los Angeles: University of California Press.

Armistead, Samuel G., and Joseph H. Silverman. 1971. *Judeo-Spanish Ballads from Bosnia.* In collaboration with Biljan Sljivic-Simsic. Philadelphia: University of Pennsylvania Press.

————. 1986. *Judeo-Spanish Ballads from Oral Tradition: Epic Ballads.* Vol. 1. Berkeley and Los Angeles: University of California Press.

Bax, Mart. 1995. *Medjugorje: Religion, Politics, and Violence in Rural Bosnia.* Amsterdam: VU Uitgerverij.

Ben-Ami, Issachar. 1998. *Saint Veneration among the Jews in Morocco.* Detroit: Wayne State University Press.

Bohlman, Philip V. 1996. "Pilgrimage, Politics, and the Musical Remapping of the New Europe." *Ethnomusicology* 40 (3): 375–412.

————. 1999. "(Ab)Stimmen der Völker in Liedern—Musik bei der Neubelebung der Frömmigkeit in Südosteuropa." In *Musik im Umbruch: Kulturelle Identität und gesellschaftlicher Wandel in Südosteuropa,* edited by Bruno B. Reuer, 25–44. Munich: Verlag Südostdeutsches Kulturwerk.

————. 2000. "Ethnomusicology and Music Sociology." In *Musicology and Sister Disciplines,* edited by David Greer, 288–98. Oxford: Oxford University Press.

Bohlman, Philip V., and Otto Holzapfel. 2001. *The Folk Songs of Ashkenaz.* Recent Researches in the Oral Traditions of Music, no. 6. Middleton, Wis.: A-R Editions.

Bowman, Glenn. 1991. "Christian Ideology and the Image of a Holy Land: The Place of Jerusalem Pilgrimage in the Various Christianities." In *Contesting the Sacred: The Anthropology of Christian Pilgrimage,* edited by John Eade and Michael J. Sallnow, 98–121. New York: Routledge.

Christian, William A., Jr. 1992. *Moving Crucifixes in Modern Spain.* Princeton: Princeton University Press.

Deutsches Volksliedarchiv. 1935. *Deutsche Volkslieder mit ihren Melodien: Balladen.* Vol. 1. Berlin: Walter de Gruyter.

Dubisch, Jill. 1995. *In a Different Place: Pilgrimage, Gender, and Politics at a Greek Island Shrine.* Princeton: Princeton University Press.

Feld, Steven. 1996. "Waterfalls of Song: An Acoustemology of Place Resounding in Bosavi, Papua New Guinea." In *Senses of Place,* edited by Steven Feld and Keith H. Basso, 91–136. Santa Fe, N.M.: School of American Research Press.

Feld, Steven, and Keith H. Basso. 1996. Introduction to *Senses of Place,* edited by Steven Feld and Keith H. Basso, 3–11. Santa Fe, N.M.: School of American Research Press.

Gross, Joan, David McMurray, and Ted Swedenburg. 1996. "Arab Noise and Ramadan Nights: Rai, Rap, and Franco-Maghrebi Identities." In *Displacement, Diaspora, and Geographies of Identity,* edited by Smadar Lavie and Ted Swedenburg, 119–55. Durham, N.C.: Duke University Press.

Hemsi, Alberto. 1995. *Cancionero sefardí.* Edited by Edwin Seroussi, in collaboration with Paloma Diaz-Mas, José M. Pedrosa, and Elena Romero. Jerusalem: Magnes Press of the Hebrew University.

Lachmann, Robert. 1978. *Gesänge der Juden auf der Insel Djerba.* Yuval Monograph Series, no. 7. Jerusalem: Magnes Press of the Hebrew University.

Magrini, Tullia. 1998. "Women's 'Work of Pain' in Christian Mediterranean Europe." *Music and Anthropology* 3. http://www.muspe.unibo.it/period/MA

Manuel, David. 1992. *Medjugorje under Siege.* Brewster, Mass.: Paraclete.

Marks, Elaine. 1996. *Marrano as Metaphor: The Jewish Presence in French Writing.* New York: Columbia University Press.

Nathan, Hans, ed. 1994. *Israeli Folk Music: Songs of the Early Pioneers.* Foreword and afterword by Philip V. Bohlman. Recent Researches in the Oral Traditions of Music, no. 4. Madison, Wis.: A-R Editions.

Reinhard, Ursula. 1987. "Türkische Musik: Ihre Interpreten in West-Berlin und in der Heimat." *Jahrbuch für Volksliedforschung* 32 (1987): 81–92.

Rupcić, Ljudevit. 1989. *Erscheinungen unserer lieben Frau zu Medjugorje: Eine theologische Bewertung und Augenzeugenberichte.* Jestetten: Miriam Verlag.

Schade-Poulsen, Marc. 1999. *Men and Popular Music in Algeria: The Social Significance of Raï.* Austin: University of Texas Press.

Seroussi, Edwin. 1986. "Politics, Ethnic Identity, and Music in the Singing of Bakkashot among Moroccan Jews in Israel." *Asian Music* 17 (2): 32–45.

———. 1998. "De-gendering Jewish Music: The Survival of the Judeo-Spanish Folk Song Revisited." *Music and Anthropology* 3. http://www.muspe.unibo.it/period/MA

Süß, Hermann. 1980. "'Der Graf von Rom,' ein altes deutsches Volkslied und sein jiddischer Druck aus dem 17. Jahrhundert." *Israelitische Kultusgemeinde Fürth,* September, 18–24.

Virolle-Souibès, Marie. 1995. *La chanson raï.* Paris: Karthala.

Discography

Donnerstag-Botschaften der Mutter-Gottes in Medjugorje. Augustinus LP 3886, n.d.

Maria, Königin aller Heiligen: Die schönsten Wallfahrer-Lieder mit alten Melodien und alten Texten. Augustinus LP 4086, n.d.

Internet Sources

Annual Apparition to Mirjana Soldo on March 18, 2000. http://www.medjugorje.hr/enajnovo.html

Medjugorje and Our Lady Queen of Peace. http://www-cs-students.Stanford.EDU/~marco/medjugorje

Radio Station "Mir" Medjugorje. http://medjugorje.hr/eradio.html

Svetiste "Kraljice Mira" Medugorje. http://www.medjugorje.hr

Caroline Bithell is lecturer in ethnomusicology at the University of Wales, Bangor. The main focus of her research to date has been the island of Corsica, where she has conducted fieldwork since 1993. Particular areas of interest include polyphonic singing traditions, musical revival, and the professionalization of traditional musics, music and politics, and gender issues. She has had work published in journals in the United Kingdom, Italy, and Georgia and is currently coeditor of the *British Journal of Ethnomusicology*.

Philip V. Bohlman is professor of music and Jewish studies at the University of Chicago. His research ranges widely across geographical areas and theoretical approaches, among them music as a constitutive process in religious change and nationalism. Among his recent publications are *World Music: A Very Short Introduction* (2002) and *Music and the Racial Imagination* (2000), coedited with Ronald Radano and published by the University of Chicago Press. With Bruno Nettl, he is coeditor of the series Chicago Studies in Ethnomusicology.

Gail Holst-Warhaft is a writer, musicologist, and an adjunct professor of classics and comparative literature at Cornell University. She is the author of *Road to Rembetika* (1975), *Theodorakis: Myth and Politics in Contemporary Greek Music* (1980), *Dangerous Voices: Women's Laments and Greek Literature* (1992), and *The Cue for Passion: Grief and Its Political Uses* (2000).

Terri Brint Joseph was for many years professor of English and comparative literature at Chapman University. Her most recent work was *Ezra Pound's Epic Variations* (1995). Professor Joseph died in the spring of 2002, just as this book was going to press.

Deborah Kapchan is associate professor of anthropology at the University of Texas at Austin. She is the author of *Gender on the Market: Moroccan Women and the Revoicing of Tradition* (1996), as well as numerous articles on narrative and performance. Her second book, *Traveling Spirit Masters: Sound, Image, and Word in the Global Marketplace,* is a study of Moroccan Gnawa music and musicians and their collaborations with American and French artists in Morocco, France, and the United States.

Joaquina Labajo teaches ethnomusicology at the Autónoma University of Madrid. Her research interests include the construction of Spanish musical stereotypes and the ideological aspects of urban traditions. Besides other works, she has published *Aproximación al fenómeno orfeonístico en España* (1987).

Tullia Magrini is associate professor of ethnomusicology and anthropology of music at the University of Bologna. She is the founder and chair of the Study Group on Anthropology of Music in Mediterranean Cultures of the International Council for Traditional Music. She has published books, collections, articles, CDs, and CD-ROMs on a wide range of topics, including analysis and anthropology of music, and music as representation of gender. Among her most recent publications is *Universi sonori: Introduzione all'etnomusicologia* (2002). She is the founder and editor of the Web journal *Music and Anthropology.*

Karin van Nieuwkerk is lecturer in social anthropology of the Mediterranean and the Middle East at Nijmegen University, and currently a postdoctoral fellow at the International Institute for the Study of Islam in the Modern World, Leiden. Her main fields of research are art and entertainment in Egypt, conversion to Islam, and Islam and migration. She is the author of *"A Trade Like Any Other": Female Singers and Dancers in Egypt* (1995).

Svanibor Pettan is associate professor in ethnomusicology at the University of Ljubljana and also teaches at the Universities of Maribor and Zagreb. His research interests include Rom music in southeastern Europe, music in relation to politics and war, music of minorities, and applied ethnomusicology. Among his most recent publications is the CD-ROM *Kosovo Roma.*

Goffredo Plastino is lecturer in world musics at the University of Newcastle. He has done fieldwork in southern Italy and in Spain and has published on ethnomusicology, organology, rap, opera, jazz, and photography. He is currently editor of *Italian Treasury,* a CD series in the *Alan Lomax Collection.* Among his publications are *Tambores del Bajo Aragón* (2001), *Mappa delle voci: Rap, raggamuffin, e tradizione in Italia* (1996), and as editor, *Mediterranean Mosaic: Popular Music and Global Sounds* (2002).

Piera Sarasini lectures in ethnomusicology at Maynooth College and is completing her Ph.D. in anthropology at Queen's University, Belfast. She has written articles on Murid ritual music. Her present work is a study of rock music–making in Dublin.

Edwin Seroussi is professor of musicology and director of the Jewish Music Research Centre at the Hebrew University of Jerusalem. He has researched Jewish musical traditions in North Africa and the Middle East and Israeli popular music. His publications include *Spanish-Portuguese Synagogue Music in Reform Sources from Hamburg* (1996) and the *Cancionero sefardi* (1995) by Alberto Hemsi.

Carol Silverman, associate professor of anthropology and folklore at the University of Oregon, is involved with Rom music and culture as a researcher, teacher, and performer. Focusing on Bulgaria and Macedonia, she has investigated the relationships between music, politics, identity, and gender. Among her recent published articles is "Rom Music" in *The Garland Encyclopedia of World Music* (1999).

Martin Stokes is associate professor of music at the University of Chicago; he is the author of *The Arabesk Debate: Music and Musicians in Modern Turkey* (1992), and editor of *Ethnicity, Identity, and Music: The Musical Construction of Place* (1997) and other collections.

Jane C. Sugarman is associate professor of music at the State University of New York at Stony Brook, and specializes in the music and dance of southeast European communities. Her book *Engendering Song: Singing and Subjectivity at Prespa Albanian Weddings*, published by the University of Chicago Press, appeared in 1997. She is currently researching the diasporic Albanian popular music industry.

Marie Virolle is an ethnologist responsible for research at the French Centre National de la Recherche Scientifique. She has published several articles on oral tradition in Algeria, noticeably on rituals and sung poetry, in specialized journals, and is author of *La chanson raï* (Paris, 1995) and *Rituels algériens* (Paris, 2001). Until 1998 she codirected the Research Group on the Songs and Musics of the Maghreb and of Immigration (GERCHAMM) at the Maison des Sciences de l'Homme, Paris.

Abadzi, Rita, 173–74, 183
Abu-Lughod, Lila, 275, 277, 334
A Cumpagnia, 52, 62n.22
advertisements, flamenco entertainers and, 69
A Filetta, 56, 57
Africa. *See specific countries; specific cultures*
"A habib elhkatar" (O Treacherous Friend), 223
Ahmed, Sid, 226
Albania. *See* Prespa Albanian culture
"Alei giv'a, sham Bagalil" (Atop a Hill in Galilee), 346
Algeria: gender roles, 225–26, 228; raï and, 9, 16, 23, 215–16, 228. *See also* Maghreb
Algerian Youth Rally. *See* RAJ
Ali Pasha, 97–98
amanes/amanedhes. *See* cafés-aman
A Mannella, and Corsican traditional songs, 46–47
Amar, Jo, 205
Amaya, Carmen, 75, 76, 82–83
"'Ana, hbibi nebgih" (My Love, I Want It), 220
Anahory-Librowica, Oro, 199, 210n.3
"Ana mal khouya madjach" (Why Didn't My Love Come?), 224
"Ana nebghig" (I Love Him), 223, 224
Andalusia, 68, 69, 80, 81
Andreas (flutist), 204
Angel, Isaac, 205
Angelova, Lisa, 142n.25
Anghjula Dea, 57

Antoni, Lorenc, 289
Arabesk music, 308–9, 313–14, 321, 326n.19
"Arapines" (Arab Girls), 185–86
archivists, 14, 27, 197–204, 209
Armenia, 189n.10
arts. *See* public performers
"Asi biva Ḥam Liache, bar minan," 210n.10
A Testa Mora, 53
"'Atini bniyiti" (Give Me My Little Girl), 220
Attias, Moshe, 209
audiences: at bouzouki clubs, 187; for çengi entertainers, 100; communication with by flamenco dancers, 74; gender roles and, 2, 8; for köçek entertainers, 96–97; in Kosovo, 291, 295, 301n.18; raï, 332; Turkish musical culture and, 311, 321, 326n.21
auditory senses, 259–60, 263
"Aziz Istanbul," 320

Babikir, Gihan, 276
Babli, Soheir al-, 276
Baka, Amalia, 189n.10
Baka, Diamando, 189n.10
Balkan culture: amplification in instrumental performances, 122; belly dance in, 124; çoçek dance in, 7; čoček dance in, 129; dancing as source of income for women, 14–15; köçek entertainers in, 97–98; line dance in, 89, 126–27; men's dance performances, 126–27; musical culture of, 46, 342, 345; professional entertain-

Balkan culture (*continued*)
ers in, 124–25, 141n.10; sexual integration and, 126–27; social dancing
and, 92; sworn virgins, 10; transsexual
singers and, 10; war and, 342, 345;
women's dance performances, 14–15,
126–27; women's vocal performances,
142nn. 24, 25. *See also specific countries;
specific cultures*
Balkan Muslim Rom culture: belly dance in,
129, 141n.15; Bulgaria and, 140n.2;
celebrations, 125; courtship practices,
126; ethnic identity, 300n.5; gender
identities in, 133–35; henna ceremony,
123, 128, 140n.5; honor and shame
theory of Mediterranean cultures, 131–
33, 141n.20; men's dance performances,
126; men's instrumental performances,
140n.4; men's role in, 133–35; men's
vocal practices, 133, 142n.23; sexual
segregation in, 122–25; sterotypes
of women performers, 139; wedding
celebrations, 122–23, 132, 141n.21;
women's dance performances, 120–22,
126, 137; women's instrumental performances, 120–22, 140n.4; women's role
in, 131–32, 133–35, 139; women's vocal performances, 120–22, 133–35,
139, 142nn. 23, 24, 25. *See also* Balkan
culture; Dutch Muslim culture; Islam;
Muslim culture; Rom culture
ballad singing, 3–5, 29n.3, 37, 198, 205, 331
ballos (dance), 24
Balogh, Jozsel, 142n.25
Balouch, Aziz, 72
Baroja, Julio Caro, 84n.4
Barudi, Shams al-, as repentant artist,
276–79
Barujel, Azibuena, 200
Basso, Keith, 333
Batis, Yiorgos, 176, 182
Bat Sheva (singer), 204
Bayiaderas, 184
Bedouin culture, 112, 215, 218
Bellou, Sotiria, 10, 174–76, 186, 187
belly dance: in Bulgaria, 130, 139, 141n.18;
at Bulgarian Rom music festivals, 129,
141n.15; history of, 92, 104, 124; Is-
lamic fundamentalist opposition to, 23,

268, 275; in Macedonia, 130, 141n.18;
and self-stereotypification among Roma,
130; ultraorthodox opposition to in Is-
rael, 268; in Yugoslavia, 141n.16
Benchimol, Esther, 199
Benchimol, M. José, 199
Benitah, Perla Boaknin de, 199, 210n.2
Beni-Waryaghar (tribe), 15, 234
Berber culture. *See* Riffian Berber culture
berrah ("crier"), raï and, 218
Bey, Enderunli Fazil, 96
Bikaj, Tonë, 294, 295
Boaknin, Luna Benaim de, 199
"born again" artists, Islam and, 268, 275–79,
283–84
Borrow, George, 72
Boutelia, Belkacem, 226
bouzouki clubs, 171, 179, 187, 188
bouzouki music, 169, 175, 176, 178, 188,
190n.15
Brandes, Stanley, 12
brothels, 215. *See also* prostitution
Brown, Catherine, 124, 141n.8
Bulgaria: and Balkan Muslim Rom culture,
130, 140n.2; belly dance in, 130, 139,
141n.18; čoček dance in, 128–30;
daire playing, 121; polyphonic singing, 54, 61n.2; women's dance performances, 121, 127–30; women's vocal
performances, 142nn. 24, 25

cabarets, raï and, 217, 230n.5
cafés-aman, 170, 173–74, 189n.7
Café de Chinitas (film), 72, 78, 80
Calabria, Italy, 163n.1
Calabrian culture: amplified musical performances in, 150–51, 164n.13; gender
identities in, 18; gender roles in, 6–7,
154, 157–60, 161–62; men's dance
performances, 157–60, 164n.17;
men's instrumental performances, 157,
164n.13; men's role in, 18, 161; men's
vocal performances, 16–17, 29n.5;
musical culture, 148–49, 150–51,
157–60, 164n.14, 165n.23; pilgrimages and, 149–50, 164n.12; professional entertainers, 159; religious music, 150–51; Rom musical culture in,
164n.19; serenades of love and disdain,

16–17, 29n.5; sexuality and, 159–60;
tarantella and, 6–7, 16, 154, 157–60,
163, 164nn. 15, 17, 165nn. 22, 24;
tarantelle music and, 164n.14; women's
dance performances, 157–60, 164n.15;
women's instrumental performances,
162, 165n.27; women's role in, 16, 148,
161–63; women's vocal performances,
16–17, 29n.5, 162. *See also* Calabrian
festivals
Calabrian festivals: of Madonna della Montagna at Polsi, 149–50, 164n.7; of Saint
Rocco at Gioiosa Ionica, 157–60, 162,
163, 165nn. 22–24; of Saints Cosimo
and Damiano at Riace, 153–56,
164n.18
çalapara, çampara (wood or metal clappers),
92, 114n.13
čalgija entertainers, 121, 122
Camaron, 79
cannabis, use of, 216
Canta u Populu Corsu, 51, 52, 56–57,
64n.32
Canta u Populu Corsu: Eri, oghje, dumani, 51
Canti corsi in tradizione, 53
Cantu nustrale (De Zerbi), 47
Caracol, Manolo, 77
Carmen (Bizet), 74–75
Carmen (film), 75
Carmen (Mérimée), 69, 72, 74
Casabianca, Gigi, 63n.29
Casalonga, Nicole, 52, 63n.29
Casa Musicale, 57
Catholicism. *See* Christianity
Catinchi, Philippe-Jean, 59
Çelebi, Evliya, 92, 93–94, 114n.8
celebrations: in Balkan Muslim Rom culture,
125; in Kosovo, 290–91; men's instru-
mental performances, 125–27; in Mo-
rocco, 247n.7, 252, 255–61, 264n.5;
raï and, 215, 217–18, 230n.4; religious, 82, 121; Sephardi, 203; and
nashaṭ, 252–56; women's dance performances, 125–27. *See also* wedding
celebrations
Cellier, Marcel, 54
çengi entertainers: history of, 92, 94–95,
98–102, 105, 114n.11, 115n.21; and
homoeroticism, 97; in Kosovo, 105,

115n.21; and Macedonian culture,
99–100, 115n.21; men's dance performances, 92, 98–102; and Muslim culture, 105, 115n.21; and Ottoman
culture, 92, 94–95, 98–102, 104,
114n.11, 115nn. 15, 16, 124; payment
of, 100–101, 115n.15; professional
status of, 125; prostitution and, 101,
115n.16; and Rom culture, 95, 96,
99–100, 101–2, 115n.16; and Serbian
culture, 99, 105, 115n.14; and tawa'if
of northern India, 97; women's dance
performances, 92, 94–95, 97, 98–102,
104, 114n.11, 115nn. 14, 15, 124; in
Yugoslavia, 104–5, 115n.21. *See also*
çoçek/čoček (dance)
Çenginame (Book of Dancing Boys) (Bey), 96
Centre d'Art Polyphonique, 63n.30
Cesari, Michéle, 52, 62n.21
*Chant corse: Manuscrits fraciscains, XVII–XVIII
siècles,* 62n.22
chanteurs de charme, 47
"Charradni daz ezzin" (This Beauty Dragged
Me to Perdition), 222
chebs, 219, 230n.9
"Chhal hadrou" (They Spoke A Lot), 223
children, public performances of, 290
chjam'è rispondi singing, 36, 40–41, 61nn.
8, 9. *See also* polyphonic singing
choirs, and Corsican women's vocal performances, 46, 57
Chrisafakis, Manolis, 190n.26
Christianity: and characterization of çengi
entertainers as decadent, 101–2; conflict with Islam, 21; musical culture of,
334–35, 336; paneyiri festival, 24; pilgrimages, 29n.10, 336, 340–41, 342;
role of women in, 21, 29n.6; social
dance and, 103–4
"Chta dani" (What Urged Me?), 221, 224
čiček (dance), 103
çiftetelli (dance), 92
Činčirova, Zlatka, 142n.25
Cinqui Sò, 56
cocaine, use of, 182
çoçek/čoček (dance): Albanian culture and,
107; Balkan culture and, 7, 129; in Bulgaria, 128–30; as expression of sexualized femininity, 88; history of, 88, 92,

çoçek/čoček (dance) (*continued*)
102–3, 105, 115n.17; line dance and,
107–11; in Macedonia, 88, 102–3,
128–30; men's instrumental performances, Prespa Albanian, 106; music
for, 113n.1; Muslim culture and, 7; Ottoman culture and, 7, 92, 107; Prespa
Albanian culture and, 106, 107–11;
professional performances, 129; in Romania, 129; Roma women's performances of, 7, 107, 115n.22; as solo
dance, 128–30; in Toronto Prespa
Albanian culture, 87–88, 107–8; Turkish influence, 108; at wedding celebrations, 129; women's dance performances, 7, 87–88, 105, 106, 107,
127–30, 141nn. 13, 14; women's
dance performances, Turkish, 105,
109–10, 115n.21; and women's vocal
performances, 106–7, 115n.17. *See
also* çengi entertainers
Cohen, Esther, 206
Cohen, Judith, 197–98
commercial entertainers, 47–48, 56, 130,
141n.18. *See also* public performers;
world music markets
commercial songs, 199, 206–9
copper pan (musical instrument), 292–93,
302nn. 22, 23
Corsica: Chants polyphoniques, 52
Corsica: Women's Polyphonies, 63n.29
Corsican culture, 48, 62n.17; folklore entertainers in, 47; gender roles, 47, 56; lament tradition, 22, 36, 42–43, 44–45,
47; lullaby singing, 43–44; men's vocal
performances, 8–9, 34, 36–40, 46–
48, 56–60, 61n.3, 62n.17, 64n.32;
musical culture of, 33–36, 45–60;
paghjella singing, 34, 36–37; polyphonic singing, 8–9, 53, 56, 62n.18;
riacquistu movement, 51; song schools,
56–58, 61n.3; and stage performances,
54–56; traditional songs, 46–47, 53,
54, 55, 57; vendetta in, 43; women's
role in, 15, 38, 49–50; and women's vocal performances, 33–36, 42–43, 47–
49, 51–53, 57–60, 61n.3, 62nn. 16,
20, 63n.31
Corsica sacra, 63n.29

"Count of Rome, The," 329–31, 336,
346–47
courtship practices, 108–9, 126, 236,
242–43, 247–49, 249n.5
Cowan, Jane, 13
Crawford, Cindy, 88, 110, 111
Crete, 17–18
"Cuando calienta el sol," 205
čuček (dance), 127. *See also* çoçek
cultural intimacy, in Turkey, 307–8, 323
çyçek (dance), 92. *See also* çoçek/čoček

daire (musical instrument). *See* frame drum
Dalipova, Ramiza, 142n.25
dance songs, in Prespa Albanian culture, 89,
90–91, 110–11, 116n.24
*Darginim sana hayat: Zeki Müren için bir demet
yasemin* (Hiçyilmaz), 312
Davis, John, 13
"Dawni" (They Took Me), 225
def (musical instrument). *See* frame drum
Defter-i Aşk (Book of Love) (Bey), 96
"Delgadina," 205
Delgras, Gonzalo, 72
Delias, Anestis, 176, 190n.15
De Mille, Cecil B., 75
Demir, Demet, 326n.17
"Dervisena" (Dervish Woman), 185, 192n.33
dervish, song lyrics specific to, 182, 186
devadasi entertainers, 112
devolliçe (dance), 90
De Zerbi, Ghjamana, *Cantu nustrale,* 47
"Dhe me stefanonesai" (You Won't Marry
Me), 186
diaspora, musical culture and, 341
Diaz, José Fernández, 205
Di li venti, a Rosula, 62n.21
diversification, cultural, 20–23
divorce, in Riffian Berber culture, 249n.5
"Djaw lamouni" (They Accused Me), 220
Djinya (the She Devil), 226
Dobreva, Binka, 142n.25
domestic (nonprofessional) entertainers:
daire performances and, 121; flamenco
and, 67, 68, 81–82, 84n.3; raï and,
215, 217–18, 230n.1; in Rom culture,
125–27; in Sephardi musical culture,
203–4; and sexuality, 132. *See also*
professional entertainers

Donnisulana, 52, 53, 54, 56, 62n.22
Đorđević, Tihomir, 99
Doubleday, Veronica, 140n.3, 301n.19
double gender identity, 10–11, 326nn.
     14–16
drugs, illegal, 180–82, 183–84, 216
Dutch Muslim culture, 269–71
dyshe (dance), 98, 114n.13, 115n.22

écoles de chant, 56–58, 61n.3
economics of performing: çengi entertainers
     and, 100–101, 104, 115n.15, 124;
     gender roles and, 291–92; and public
     performers, 277, 279, 280, 282–83;
     tipping as degrading, 133, 141n.22
ecstatic possession ceremonies, Moroccan,
     261–62, 264nn. 4, 9
E Duie Patrizie (The Two Patrizias), 51, 52.
     See also Les Nouvelles Polyphonies
     Corses
Effendi, Haim, 204–5, 210n.8
Egypt: belly dance and Islamic fundamental-
     ism in, 23, 268, 275; class differences
     among dancers, 283–84; dance and
     sexual immorality in, 111–12; and hi-
     erarchy of professional entertainers,
     142n.27; hypersexualizing of dance in,
     112; religion in, 268–83; repression of
     public performers in, 275; women's
     dance performances and, 111–12;
     women's role and Islamic fundamental-
     ism in, 27
"Eleni," 180, 190n.22
Elías, Francisco, 75
"Elli," 179–80, 190nn. 18–21
El Tenazas de Morón, 72
Ersoy, Bülent, 11, 316–20, 326n.17
Eskenazi, Roza, 173, 174, 182, 183
"Esma–Ensemble Teodosievski," 135, 138
Esse, 52
ethnomusicology studies, 2
Europe, musical culture and, 9–10, 80
Evliya, Efendi [Çelebi], 92
E Voce di u Cumune, 52
"Eyer karalik," 205

Fadéla, Chaba, 220, 225, 228, 229, 230n.11
Falireas Brothers, 191n.27
Falla, Manuel de, 71–72

Farrar, Geraldine, 75
Faudel, 9, 229
Fejza, Shkurte, 290
Feld, Steven, 333–34
fencing dance (sherma), 164n.17
Fernanflor, Isidoro Fernández Flórez,
     79–80
festival of Madonna della Montagna at Polsi,
     149–53
festival of Saint Rocco at Gioiosa Ionica,
     157–60, 165nn. 22, 23, 24, 25, 26
festival of Saints Cosimo and Damiano at
     Riace, 153–56, 164n.18
fighouradzis (poseur), 176, 190n.15
"Figouradzis," 190n.15
films, Turkish, 321, 322
flamenco entertainers: advertisements using,
     69; Balouch on flamenco singers, 72;
     domestic entertainers and, 67, 68, 81–
     82, 84n.3; gender identities and, 26;
     gender relationships and, 7, 77–79, 83;
     gender roles and, 76; guitar playing,
     76–79, 80; history of, 67–69, 72–73;
     and homosexuality, 71–72, 177; men's
     dance performances, 7, 84n.2, 177;
     men's instrumental performances, 68,
     77, 79; men's role, 71–72, 73; men's
     vocal performances, 26, 68, 69–71, 72,
     73, 77, 78, 80–81; Moneleón on, 70,
     80; myths, 68, 69, 78, 79–83; Papa-
     pavlou on, 177; professional entertain-
     ment and, 67, 68, 81–82; in religious
     celebrations, 82; Rom culture and, 15,
     68, 73, 74, 75, 76, 80–81; Spain, 67–
     69, 72; stereotypes and, 67, 68, 74, 75,
     79–83; transvestitism and, 71–72, 76;
     voices of, and sexuality, 71–72, Washa-
     baugh on, 171; women's dance perfor-
     mances and, 26, 68, 73–75, 76, 78–
     79, 82; women's vocal performances
     and, 26, 69, 71, 77–78, 80
folklore entertainers, 46–47, 104–5
folksongs, 27, 197–98, 199, 204–6,
     210nn. 2, 3
"Fonias tha yino" (I'll Become a Murderer),
     181
forbidden lifestyles, 173–74, 178, 179–85,
     216
Fortuna, 207

frame drum (def, daire), 120–22, 140n.3, 296, 299, 301n.19
fundamentalism, Islamic: belly dance and, 23, 268, 275; raï and, 228, 333; women's role, 27, 267. *See also* Islam

gara poetica, 61n.8
Garbiz ('ud player), 204
Gattaceca, Patrizia, 33, 51, 52, 55, 63n.29
Gautier, Théophile, 74
Geertz, Clifford, 236
gender identities: female sexuality, 132–33; flamenco entertainers and, 26; line dance and, 88–91; musical culture and, 5–6, 287–88; religion and, 21–23, 28; women's dance performances and, 111–12. *See also* transsexual singers; *specific countries; specific cultures*
gender relationships: in bouzouki clubs, 187; and café-aman entertainment, 174; and dances, 6–7, 76 (*see also specific dances*); in flamenco, 7, 77–79, 83; and musical culture, 5–6; raï and, 227; rebetisses and, 185–88; and Riffian Berber marriage customs, 236; in tarantella, 6–7. *See also specific countries; specific cultures*
gender roles: of audiences, 2; ballad singing and, 3–5; çoçek and Prespa Albanian women, 106; and Corsican polyphonic singing, 56; defined, 1–2, 28n.1; diaspora and, 341; in epics, 340–41; flamenco entertainers and, 76; and gusle, use of, 293; Hanna, on dance and, 6, 161; honor and shame theory of Mediterranean cultures and, 12–13, 131, 267; men's instrumental performances and, 291, 301n.18; musical culture and, 1, 2, 3, 8, 47, 308; and pilgrimages, 342; raï and, 27, 225–26, 227, 332–33; in Sephardi songs, 207; shrines and, 338–39; tarantella, 26, 147–49, 161–62; in tavala evolution, 299–300; women's vocal performances, 71
Geronimi, Marie-Ange, 63n.29
ghawazi entertainers, 111
Ghazali, Sheikh al-, 274
"Ghir habibi w analogical thought" (Just My Love and I), 223

Gilmore, David D., 39
"Giramondu," 55
Gogos, Dimitris, 184
gomenes, 184
Goodwin, Sarah Webster, 71
"Goultou chabba" (You Found Her Beautiful), 222
Granitu Maggiore, 63n.30
Greece: bouzouki music, 188; forbidden lifestyles as entertainment in, 182; gender identities and, 170–71; lament tradition in, 44; line dance, 89–90; paghjella singing, 44; paneyiri festival, 23–24; rebetika entertainers, 179, 186, 187; rebetisses, 179–88; social dancing in, 92; urban culture and, 170; women's vocal performances, 15, 63n.23, 186, 187; zebekiko, 7–8, 24
Greek-Turkish culture, zebekiko (dance), 24
Grémaux, René, 294–95
"Guajira Guantanamera," 205
Güç, Ceyhan, *Şimdi uzaklardaysın,* 312
Guelfucci, Petru, 56
guitar playing, 76–79, 80
Gušić, Marijana, 294
gusle, gender roles and use of, 293
Gypsy culture. *See* Rom culture
Gypsy dance style, and Roma culture, 14–15, 73, 74, 76

Habiba el Kebira, 220
Hadzidakis, Manos, 176, 177, 179, 187, 206
"Hagrouni" (They Have Hurt Me), 220, 222
"Halala lalal," 221
Halal and Haram (al-Qaradawi), 270, 271
"Halikha le-Qesaria," 206
Hamdi, Sahar, 276
Hanan (artist), 276
Hanna, Judith Lynne, 6, 161
hanoum/hanoumi/hanoumaki/hanoumissa, rebetika song lyrics and, 180, 181, 182
hasapiko (dance), 177–78
hashish, in rebetika song lyrics, 180–82, 183–84
hasiklis. *See* hasiklou
hasiklou, 183
Haskil, Stella, 175, 186, 187
Hasni, Cheb, 23, 228
Hayk (violinist), 204

"Hay ʿumri" (Poor Me), 221
Hazan, Victoria, 189n.10, 205
"Hbibi zafan" (My Love is Angry), 221
Hebrew songs, 20, 204
Hélène, 54
henna ceremony, 123, 128, 140n.5, 239
heroin, use of in Greek urban culture, 182
Hiçyilmaz, Ergün, 312–13
hijab (women's dress), 275
Hiotis, Manolis, 176
homoeroticism, 97, 177–78, 188n.2
homosexuality: flamenco entertainers,
    71–72, 177; köçek entertainers, 96; in
    Kosovo musical culture, 299; Müren
    and, 312–13; raï , 224; rebetika, 176,
    177; tavala, 10–11, 122, 296, 299; in
    Turkey, 313, 317, 325n.9, 326n.17
honor and shame theory, 11–18, 39, 83,
    84n.4, 131–33, 141nn. 20, 21, 267
Hungarian culture, and women's vocal per-
    formances, 142n.25
hyperreality, and Turkish musical culture,
    28, 309, 320–22
hypersexuality, 28, 112, 130, 223, 322, 323

Ibbucoya (tribe), 15, 234
I Chjami Aghjalesi, 52
illiteracy, 196–97
immorality. *See* sexual immorality
India, 97, 112, 114n.11, 198
In paradisu, 63n.29
intermarriage, and Sephardi musical culture,
    207. *See also* marriage customs
intimacy, cultural, 307–8, 323
Islam: ʿawra, 271, 273, 284n.4; in Bulgaria,
    130, 140n.2; class distinctions among
    performers, 283–84; conflicts with
    Christianity, 20–21; ethnic identity,
    Rom, 300n.5; gender identities and,
    132–33; gender roles and, 269; hijab,
    275; in Macedonia, 130, 140n.2; mu-
    sical culture, 269–72; pilgrimages,
    29n.10, 276, 340; prostitution, 272;
    public performers, 272, 274, 283–
    84; raï and, 9, 16, 23, 215–16; sexual
    immorality, 268, 269, 271, 273–74,
    284n.4; sexual segregation, 272; wom-
    en's role in, 22, 267–68, 334. *See also*
    Balkan culture; Balkan Muslim Rom

culture; Dutch Muslim culture; funda-
    mentalism, Islamic; Muslim culture;
    Rom culture
Israel, musical culture in, 11, 22, 268
Italy, musical culture in, 2, 3–5, 16–17,
    29nn. 3, 5, 37

Jag, Kalyi, 142n.25
Japan, solo dance and sexual immorality, 112
Jašarov, Ilmi, 88
Java, solo dance and sexual immorality, 112
Jewish communities: musical culture of, 98,
    189n.10, 195–96, 204, 346, 347. *See
    also* Sephardi culture
jinn, and nashaṭ, 259, 263, 264n.4
Joseph, Roger, 233, 236
Judaism, 21–22, 29n.6, 268, 334–35, 336,
    340

kafaenas, entertainment and, 102–3
Kafi, Omar Abdel, on public performers and
    Islam, 274
"Kai i gomernes," 191n.32
Kalčeva, Ruska, 142n.25
Kanto, 104
Kapetanakis, Kimon, 175
"Kapnoulou Mousterian industry omorfi"
    (My Beautiful Smoker), 184
Karafezieva, Maria, 142n.25
Karipis, 176
karşilama (dance), 92
karsilamadhes (dance), 24, 29n.11
Kasimatis, Zacharias, 175–76
"Kayiti" (My Burning), 221
kcim (dance), 105
Kébira, Djinya el-, 220, 221, 222, 223
Kébira, Habiba el-, 222
kechekides entertainers, 104
Keddie, Nikki R., 13
Kerala culture, archiving of, 198
"Ke telo estas continiendo barminam," 206,
    210n.10
Khaled, 9, 215, 216, 219, 229
"Khallini" (Let Me), 223
"Khallu lkas yewselni" (Let the Glass Come
    to Me), 222, 223
Kiromitis, Stelios, 175
kjuček (dance), 127, 129
köçek entertainers: audiences and, 95, 96–
    97; in Balkan culture, 97–98; history

köçek entertainers (*continued*)
of, 92, 93–94, 96, 104; homosexuality
and, 96; Jewish musicians, 98; men's
dance performances, 93; Ottoman culture and, 94, 95, 97–98, 114n.8; Roma
culture and, 98, 114n.12; solo dance,
96; in Turkey, 98; women's dance performances, 97–98. *See also* çoçek/čoček
kols, 93–94, 95–96
Kooka, subject of case study, 280–81
Koskoff, Ellen, 3
Kosovo, 288, 300nn. 4, 6; celebrations and
women's dance performances, 290–91;
çengi entertainers, 105, 115n.21; daire
performances, 121; gender-based restrictions on female performers, 291–
92; gender identities, 28, 288–90,
301n.18; gender roles, 290, 291, 292,
298–99, 301n.11; homosexuality, 299;
marriage customs, 290, 291; men's
dance performances, 301n.18; men's
instrumental performances, 289–90,
291, 301nn. 14, 15, 17, 18; men's vocal
performances, 301nn. 11, 12; musical
culture, 10, 28, 122, 150–51, 288,
293–95, 299; public performances ,
290, 291; sexual segregation in musical
culture, 289–90; social dancing, 105;
song lyrics and gender in, 289; sworn
virgins, 10, 293–95, 299; transsexual
singers, 293, 302nn. 27, 28; Vaseiljević
on song lyrics, 289; wars and musical
culture, 345; women's dance performances, 301n.18; women's instrumental performances, 291, 292–93, 294,
301nn. 19, 20, 302nn. 22, 23, 29;
women's role, 290–91; women's vocal
performances , 116n.23, 291, 301n.11
Koštana (Stanković), 101
"koutsavakis, The" 190n.16
"Ktelna ʿamarna" (We Have Killed Our Life),
221
Kunstler, Agnes, 142n.25
Kutché, 230n.8
Kutev, 54
kyuchek (dance), 92

La Argentinita, 71
"La Camel," 219

La Macarron, Juana, 76, 77
lament tradition: of cafés-aman, 173–74,
189n.7; in Corsican culture, 15, 42–
45, 47; raï and, 219–23; in Riffian Berber culture, 246; and vendetta, 42–43;
women's vocal performances, 15, 36,
42, 43, 44, 80; and "work of pain," 22,
219
languages, and Mediterranean ballads, 331
Latin America, Sephardi culture in, 205
"Lebnat" (The Daughters), 220
Legal Research and Resource Center for Human Rights (LRRC), 270, 273
Les bals de l'Opera, 74
lesbianism, 10, 174–75, 176
Lesbos, Greece, 23–24
Les Nouvelles Polyphonies Corses, 51, 55,
56, 59, 63n.25. *See also* E Duie Patrizie
(The Two Patrizias)
L'Événement, 56
Levy, Moshe, 209
line dance: Albanian culture, 108; Balkan
culture, 89, 126–27; çoçek and, 107–
11; gender identities and, 88–91;
Greece and, 89–90; in Macedonia, 87–
88; men's dance performances, 87–88,
115n.16; in Muslim culture, 115n.16;
in Prespa Albanian culture, 87–91; and
Prespa Albanian dance songs, 89, 90–
91, 113nn. 3, 4; in Rom culture, 88–
89; women's dance performances, 87–
89, 128
literacy, 196–97
Loeb, Laurence D., 196
Lorca, García, 71–72
love songs, Riffian Berber culture and, 246
Lucia, Paco de, 79
lullaby singing, 36, 43–44, 47
lyra (musical instrument), 104
lyrics. *See* song lyrics

Macedonian culture: Balkan Muslim Rom
culture, 140n.2; belly dance, 130,
141n.18; çengi entertainers, 99–100,
115n.21; čiček , 103; čoček dance in,
88, 102–3, 128–30; daire performances and, 121; Islam in, 130, 140n.2;
line dance in, 87–88; paneyiri festival,
23–24; social dancing in, 92, 105; solo

dance in, 87–88; wedding celebrations, 125–26, 141n.11; women's dance performances, 127–30; women's vocal performances, 121–22, 142nn. 24, 25
Machado, Antonio, 73
Madam Cohen, 206
Madonna, 11, 112
Madricale, 56, 60
Madrigalesca, 63n.29
"Maghissa tis Arapias" (Enchantress of Arabia), 185
Maghreb: musical culture and, 9, 23, 228. *See also* Algeria; Morocco; Tunisia; *other countries; specific cultures*
magical songs, 121
Mairena, Antonio, 73, 80
makam system, 121
Malayalam, archived folksongs, 198
Mami, Cheb, 9, 229
"Manabrach" (I Am Not Cured), 224
manges. *See* rebetika entertainers
Maria de la O (film), 75
Marian apparitions, 336
Marian shrines, 336, 337, 338, 339, 342–45. *See also* shrines
"Marika hasiklou," 183–84
"Maritsa sto haremi" (Maritsa in the Harem), 186
marketing, 120, 130–31, 137, 139
Markos Vamvakaris 1932–40, 191n.32
Marks, Elain, 334
Maroniti, Angeliki, 174
marriage customs, 207, 236, 290, 291
"Ma tsalunich" (Don't Ask Me for an Explanation), 225
Mayesh, Jack, 205
Mecca, pilgrimages to by performers, 276, 281
meddahat singers, 217
Mediterranean cultures, 18–28; gender roles, 2, 8–11, 329–35, 347; honor and shame theory of, 11–18, 83, 84n.4, 131–33, 141nn. 20, 21, 267; men's roles, 322–23; musical culture, 2, 23, 329–31; sacredness in, 334–35, 336, wars and musical culture, 345–47; women's role, 13, 22, 23, 29n.9; women's vocal performances, 15. *See also specific countries; specific cultures*

Medjugorje: apparition of Mary, 343–45; "The Medjugorje Song," 342, 345; music and war in, 342, 345
melodic instruments, played by women, 301n.20
men's dance performances: çengi entertainers, 92, 98–102; čiček, 103; flamenco entertainers, 7, 26, 77–79, 83, 84n.2, 177; line dance, 87–88, 115n.16; physical nature of, 7; solo dance, 92, 93–94; tango, 177; tarantella, 154, 164n.17; zebekika/zebekiko, 7–8, 178, 190n.15. *See also specific countries; specific cultures*
men's instrumental performances: amplification, use of, 122, 291; audiences in Kosovo, 291, 301n.18; bouzouki clubs, 171, 179, 187, 188; bouzouki music, 175, 176; café-aman, 173; at celebrations, 125–27; and çoçek, 106; flamenco, 68, 77–79, 82; gender roles and, 291, 301n.18; henna ceremony and, 123; Morocco and, 257; and nashaṭ, 252, 253, 254, 259–60, 263, 264n.4; rebetika entertainers, 169
men's role: as archivists, 27; in Calabrian culture, 18, 161; and flamenco, 71–72, 73; in Mediterranean cultures, 322–23; in Morocco, 233; pilgrimages and, 340; in Rom culture, 133–35; in Sephardi culture, 27; stereotypes in Mediterranean cultures and, 169–70; tarantella, 161
men's vocal performances: amplification of, 321; ballad singing, Italian, 3–5, 29n.3, 37; café-aman, 173, 189n.7; chjam'è rispondi singing, 36; dance songs, Prespa Albanian, 89; flamenco, 68, 69–71, 72, 73, 77, 78; flamenco song lyrics and, 80–81; monophonic singing, 35t; and nashaṭ, 254; polyphonic singing, 8–9, 34–35, 59–60, 61n.2, 64n.32; raï and, 9, 229, 332; rebetika entertainers, 9–10, 170–71; transgendered individuals, 10–11. *See also specific countries; specific cultures*
meraklou, 183
Mérimée, Prosper, 69, 72, 74
Merleau-Ponty, Maurice, 264n.9

"Mes tis Polis to hamam" (In the Baths of Constantinople), 182
"Mes tous Zambikou" (At Zambikos's), 183, 191n.29
Micaelli, Jacky, 52, 63n.29
Middle Ages, and music of Mediterranean cultures, 19–20
Middle East, women's role in, 23, 233. See also specific countries; specific cultures
"Missirlu," 205
mizrakhit (music), 20
modern commercial songs, 199, 206–9
Molina, Antonio, 205
Molina, Miguel de, 71
Moneleón, José, 70, 80
Morocco: archivists, 198–200; Berber culture in, 234; class and celebrations, 255–57, 263; entertainers and the media, 141n. 16; food, 261, 264n.5; gender relationships, 252–53; men's instrumental performances, 257; men's role in, 233; musical culture, 254, 257, 259, 264n.8; and nashaṭ, 8, 27, 252–56, 260, 263; women's role in, 233, 235, 258; women's vocal performances, 15, 257. See also Maghreb
"Mortissa hasiklou" (Dope-head Dropout), 184
Moslem society. See Muslim culture
movement, aspect of nashaṭ, 260–61, 263
Msika, Habiba, 196
Muhammad Ali Street (performance group), 279–83
Müren, Zeki: and audience cultivation, 311, 326n.21; biography, 309–10, 324n.4, 325n.6; composers and, 310, 325n.13; education of, 310; film career, 310; homosexuality, 312–13, 316–17, 318; musical career, 309, 310–11, 313–16, 319, 325n.6; and religious calendar, 311; Turkish language mastery, 314–15, 320, 325n.11; and Turkish politics, 320; vocal art of, 314–16
musical instruments: amplification and, 122, 291, 296; çalapara, 92, 114n.13; copper pan, 292–93, 302nn. 22, 23; female sexuality and, 132; frame drum (def, daire), 120–22, 140n.3, 296, 299, 301n.19; guitar, 76–79, 80; lyra, 104;

melodic, played by women, 301n.20; in Morocco, 254, 257, 259; raï and, 215, 218, 226, 230n.2; sworn virgins and, 295; tavala entertainers and, 295, 296. See also men's instrumental performances; women's instrumental performances
music anthropology, 2
Muslim culture: belly dance in, 130; çengi entertainers, 101–2, 105, 115n.21; çiçek, 103; çoçek, 7; ethnic identity, Rom, 300n.5; gender roles in, 268; line dance, 115n.16; musical culture, 121–22; raï and, 9, 228; solo dance in, 103–4; and women as public performers, 271, 273, 274; women's dance performances, compared to prostitution, 268; women's role in, 267–68; women's vocal performances, 189n.10. See also Balkan culture; Balkan Muslim Rom culture; Dutch Muslim culture; Islam; Prespa Albanian culture; Rom culture
Mustafov, Ferus, 88, 141n.18
Mystère des voix bulgares, 9, 54
myths, flamenco entertainers and, 68, 69, 78, 79–83
My Trip from Darkness to Light (al-Barudi), 276

načnis entertainers, 112
Nadia, subject of case study, 280, 281
Nahón, Zarita, 198, 210n.1
nashaṭ, state of: and celebrations, 252–56, 263; class and, 256–57, 263; description, 251–55, 263; as intoxication, 253, 256, 262, 263, 264n.9; men's instrumental performances, 252, 253, 254, 259–60, 263, 264n.4; men's vocal performances, 254; the senses in, 258–61, 263; and sexuality, 257, 263; sheikhat entertainers and, 252, 254, 256, 263, 264n.6; women's dance performances, 252–55, 260; women's instrumental performances, 252, 253, 263; women's vocal performances, 252, 253, 263
Nasr, Farida Seif el-, 277
"Nea meraklou" (Young Bon Vivant), 183, 191n.30
"Nerkeb hdah" (I Go Beside Him), 221, 224

"Never on Sunday," 206
Nikolesco, Lili, 176
Ninou, Marika, 175, 187
"Nkhaf 'alik" (I Fear for Him), 222
North Africa, dance and and sexual immorality, 111–12
Novo, Pineda, 76
"Nsal fik" (I've Got Rights over You), 220
"Ntya, ntya" (You, You), 221
"Nunca en Dominga," 206

"O boufedzis" (The Buffet Man), 182, 191n.27
"O! ke meuve mezes" (Oh! These Nine Months), 205
Oldenburg, Veena Talwar, 97
opera singers, Corsican, 47
oral tradition, and Italian ballad singing, 3–5, 29n.3
Organum (ensemble), 62n.22
Ottoman culture: çalapara musical instruments, 92; çampara musical instruments, 92; çengi entertainers, 92, 94–95, 96, 98–102, 104, 114n.11, 115nn. 15, 16, 124; çoçek, 7, 92, 107; gender roles, 96, 114n.10; homosexuality in, 96; köçek entertainers and, 94, 95, 96–98, 114n.8; musical culture, 208–9; solo dance, 92–106, 114n.7; women's dance performances, 94, 107
"Oulidi we nkhaf 'alik" (My Son, I Fear for You), 220
Oxford school, and honor and shame theory, 11–13, 16, 18, 84n.4, 267

Pagarusha, Nexhmije, 290
paghjella singing, 36–37, 38–39, 44, 49; ballad singing compared to, 37; chjam'è rispondi singing compared to, 41; in Corsican culture, 36–40, 61nn. 6, 7; men's vocal performances, 36–40, 44, 50–51; and women's role, 34, 38, 58. See also polyphonic singing
Palti, Sara, 204
paneyiri (festival), 23–24
pantomime (dance), 103
Papagika, Marika, 174, 181, 189n.11
Papaioannou, Yiannis, 176, 185, 187
Papapavlou, Maria, 177
Papazoglou, Vangelis, 174, 183, 185

Papazova, Pepa, 142n.25
Payioumdzis, Stratos, 176
Peña Flamenca femenina de Huelva, 84n.3
Per Agata, 53
Pérès, Marcel, 52
Peristeris, Spyros, 175
Peristiany, John G., 11–12
Petropoulos, Ilias, 177
Petrović, Ankica, 301n.13
Petrović, Petar Ž., 293
Petrović, Radmila, 301n.13
phenomenology, 251–52
pilgrimages, 29n.10; in Calabrian culture, 149–50, 164n.12; Christianity and, 340; gender roles and, 336, 340–41, 342; Islam and, 276, 340; Judaism and, 340; men's roles, 340; musical culture, 336, 338–39, 340–42; public performers and Islamic, 276, 281; raï and, 218
Piraeus, musical culture, 7–8, 9–10, 24, 169, 171, 185–87
Piraeus Quartet, 169, 176, 187
Pitt-Rivers, Julian, 11–12, 83
"Più chè u sole," 64n.32
Poletti, Jean-Paul, 57, 63n.30
Poli, Lydia, 63n.29
Poli, Patrizia, 51, 52, 55, 63n.29
Politissa, Marika, 182
Polsi, pilgrimage to , 16
polyphonic singing: by Bulgarian performers, 54, 61n.2; Centre d'Art Polyphonique, 63n.30; chjam'è rispondi singing, 36, 40–41, 61nn. 8, 9; Corsican culture and, 8–9, 53, 56, 62n.18; Corsican entertainers, 56; Gattaceca on, 33; gender roles and, 56; Les Nouvelles Polyphonies Corses, 51, 55, 56, 59, 63n.25; men's vocal performances, 8–9, 59–60, 61n.2, 64n.32; women's vocal performances, 9, 34. See also E Duie Patrizie (The Two Patrizias); paghjella singing
Polyphonies corses, 59
Prespa Albanian culture, 113n.2; çoçek dance, 107–11; courtship practices, 108–9; dance songs, 89, 90–91, 110–11, 113nn. 3, 4, 116n.24; gender identities and, 88–91; hypersexuality, con-

Prespa Albanian culture (*continued*)
cern about, 112; line dance, 87–91,
108; men's vocal performances, 89;
public performers in, 106–7; social
dancing, 92; solo dance, 87–88, 105,
107–11; women's dance performances,
7, 87–88, 105–7, 112, 127–30; wom-
en's çoçek performances, 7, 87–88,
105–7; women's vocal performances,
89, 106–7, 142n.25
"Primavera en Selanik," 207–8, 210nn.
12, 13
processional dance, 126; festival of Saint
Rocco at Gioiosa Ionica, 157–60,
165n.25; festival of Saints Cosimo
and Damiano at Riace, 155–56, 162,
165n.20; women's dance performances,
128
professional entertainers: belly dance, 130,
141n.16; in Calabrian culture, 159;
čoček, 129; Egypt, and hierarchy of,
142n.27; festival of Saint Rocco at Gioiosa Ionica, 159, 165n.26; flamenco,
67, 68, 77, 79, 81–82; Islam and, 272;
in Sephardi culture, 207; solo dance
and, 92, 93–94; women's dance performances, 124–25, 141n.10; women as,
in Roma culture, 133. *See also* domestic
(nonprofessional) entertainers; *specific
entertainers*
prostitution, musical culture and, 101,
115n.16, 215, 268, 272, 291
public arenas, women's role in, 123–24,
140n.7, 235, 240, 248, 290–91
public performers: case studies of, 280–81;
children as, 290; conflict of profession
and religion, 269, 277, 279, 280, 282–
83; Muhammad Ali Street, 268–83;
pilgrimages by to Mecca, 276, 281; and
religious authorities, 275–76; repentant
artists, 275–76, 277–78, 281–82. *See
also* commercial entertainers; world
music markets; *specific countries; specific
cultures; specific religions*

Qaradawi, Yusuf al-, 270, 271–73
Qayyim, Ibn al-, 271
queer theory, 11, 322
Quilici, Félix, 34

"Rabbit elwalf ʿalih" (I Got Accustomed to
Him), 224
Raffaelli, Michel, 53, 62n.21
raï: Algerian culture and, 9, 16, 23, 215–16,
228; audiences, 332; Bedouin culture
and, 215, 218; berrah performer, 218;
cabarets, 217, 230n.5; and cannabis,
216; celebrations, 215, 217–18,
230n.4; domestic entertainers, 215,
217–18, 230n.1; and fundamentalism,
Islamic, 228, 333; gender roles affected
by, 27, 225–26, 227, 228, 332–33;
history of development, 215–16,
230n.3; homosexuality in lyrics, 224;
hypersexuality and, 223; Islam and, 9,
16, 23, 215–16; lament tradition and,
219–23; Maghreb and, 9, 228; men's
vocal performances, 9, 229; musical
instruments, 215, 218, 226, 230n.2;
in Muslim culture, 9, 228; pilgrimages and, 218; prostitution and, 215;
public performers, 216, 227–29;
sheikhat entertainers, 217, 218; song
lyrics and, 217, 219–25, 230n.6; as
therapy, 227; urban culture and, 215,
230n.1; wedding celebrations and,
217, 218, 226; women's dance performances, 218; women's instrumental performances, 226; women's role
and, 216–19, 225, 230n.6; women's
vocal performances, 9, 218–19, 229,
257
Raïna Raï, 216
RAJ (Rassemblement Algérien de la Jeunesse),
228, 230n.12
rakkas entertainers, 92
Ramzi, Kamal, 275–76
rebetis/rebetes, 170, 179, 180, 182, 184
rebetika (songs): Bellou, 10, 174–75; bouzouki music and, 169, 175, 176, 179,
187–88; café-aman, 170, 174; description of, 170; Greece and, 186, 187; history of, 169, 172, 176; homoeroticism
and, 177–78; homosexuality and, 176,
177; men's dance performances, 177–
78, 190n.14; men's instrumental performances , 169; men's vocal performances, 9–10, 170–71; Piraeus as
origin of, 9–10, 169, 171; sexual im-

morality associated with, 10; song lyrics, 169, 170, 171, 179–88, 189n.3; women's dance performances, 26–27; women's role, 188; women's vocal performances, 9–10, 170, 173–74, 175–76, 186, 187

Rebetiko (film), 173, 188

rebetisses, 179–88

Redžepova, Esma: belly dance and, 130; biography, 133–35; career, 14, 119–20, 135–38; dance performances of, 137; and marketing of self, 120, 137; marriage, 135–36, 138, 142nn. 25, 26; on sexual segregation at wedding celebrations, 122–23; on solo dance, 129–30; stereotypes of Rom women and, 120; vocal performances of, 120, 133–35, 138

Redžepova, Sajka, 134

refugees, and music from Asia Minor, 172

religion: gender identities and, 20–23, 28; public performers and, 269, 275, 277–78, 281–82, 283; raï and, 224; repentant artists 268. *See also specific countries; specific cultures; specific religions*

religious celebrations, 82, 121. *See also* celebrations

religious music, Calabrian, 150–51

repentant artists: class distinctions among, 283–84; Islam and, 268, 275–79, 283–84

riacquistu movement, 51

Riffian Berber culture, 234–36; courtship practices, 236, 242–43, 247–49, 249n.5; divorce practices, 249n.5; gender relationships and, 236, 248, 249; gender roles and, 235; henna ceremony, 239; lament tradition, 246; love songs, 246; marriage customs, 236; public arenas and women, 235, 240, 248; seduction songs, 246–47; sexual immorality and, 244–45; sexual segregation in, 247; song lyrics and, 237–38, 240–47, 250n.8; stereotypes of women in, 242; wedding celebrations, 244, 247–48, 250n.11; women's role in, 235, 238–40, 248, 250n.9; women's vocal performances, 15, 27, 234, 237, 238–40

Rigual, Carlos Fausto, 205

Rigual, Mario Fausto, 205

Rihtman, Cvjetko, 301n.13

Rimitti, Cheikha, 218–25, 229, 230n.7

rites of passage, and Corsican paghjella singing, 50–51

ritual songs, 22, 121. *See also* folksongs

rizitika songs, 17–18

Rochi, Anna, 64n.32

rock music, 326n.19

Rom culture, 119, 140nn. 1, 2, 300n.5; belly dance, 104; çengi entertainers in, 95, 96, 99–100, 101, 115n.16; çoçek, as performed by women in, 7, 107, 115–16n.22; domestic entertainers in, 125–27; economic aspects for women performers, 14–15, 73, 74, 81, 121; ethnic identity, 300n.5; flamenco entertainers, 15, 68, 73–76, 80–81; gender identities, 28, 133–35; gender roles, family fiestas and, 81–82; guitar playing, 78; Gypsy dance style in, 14–15, 73–76; hypersexuality of female form in, 130; köçek entertainers, 98, 114n.12; line dance, 88–89; men's instrumental performances, 74, 80–81, 119; men's role in, 133–35; men's vocal performances, 68, 73; musical culture, 10–11, 28, 119, 122, 140nn. 1, 2, 164n.19, 288, 289, 300n.7; myths, flamenco entertainers and, 68, 69, 78, 79–83; public and private arenas in, 123–24, 140n.7; religious celebrations, 82; sexual immorality and, 101, 115n.16; stereotypes of Rom women, 120, 130–31, 139; tavala entertainers, 297–98; women's dance performances, 7, 68, 74–76, 80–81, 107, 114n.12, 115n.22, 128; women's role in, 133–35; women's vocal performances, 14–15, 121–22, 133–35, 142n.25. *See also* Balkan culture; Balkan Muslim Rom culture; Dutch Muslim culture; Islam; Muslim culture

Romania, čoček and, 129

romantic songs, Sephardi culture, 198

Rossi, Annabella, and tarantism, 28n.2

Rossi, Tino, 47

Roukounas, Kostas, 175, 183–84
"Run and Ask, Mangas," 186

Saadawi, Nawaal al-, 277
"Sabbrou I Djilali" (Have Djilali Wait), 220
sacred songs, 57, 63n.29, 334, 336, 347
Safy, Hala al-, as repentant artist, 276–79
Saharoaoui, 228, 229
Sahwaniya, 221
Salonikios, 173
Samarel, Nahman/Nathan/Nat, 204
Santavuglia, 63n.29
santouri (musical instrument), 173
Sardinia, chjam'è rispondi singing in, 61n.8
scherma (fencing dance), 164n.17
schools of songs, 56–58, 61n.3
Schwartz, Martin, 190n.26
scole di cantu, 56–58, 61n.3
Scuprendu l'alba corsa, 52
"Seda amarilla," 205
seduction songs, Riffian Berber culture and, 246–47, 250n.11
Seigel, Jerrold, 171
Selam/Selomo, Tio, 204
Semsis, Dimitrios, 173
Sene, Emily, 14, 27, 199–206
Sene, Isaac, 201, 202
Senesh, Hana, 206
Senr, Müzeyyen, 315–16
senses, and nashaṭ, 259–61
Sephardi culture: archivists, men as, 27; archivists, women as, 14, 27, 197–204, 209; ballads, 198, 205; Benitah folksong collection, 199; folksongs, 199, 204–6; Hebrew religious songs, 204; intermarriage theme of songs in, 207; Latin America and, 205; literacy, 196–97; men's instrumental performances, 201, 202, 204, 207; men's vocal performances, 204–5; modern commercial songs, 199, 206–9; musical culture, 203–4, 207, 208–9; professional entertainers, 207; romantic songs, 198; U.S. and, 205; women's dance performances, 201; women's role in, 196–97, 198–200, 204; women's vocal performances, 205, 207; Zionist songs, 206, 210n.11. See also Jewish communities

Serbian culture, 92, 99, 105, 115n.14, 141n.10
serenades, of love and disdain, 16–17, 29n.5
Sevengil, Refik Ahmet, 97
"Sexual Dialectics and Strategy in Berber Marriage" (Joseph), 236
sexual immorality: ʿawra and, 271, 273, 284n.4; çengi entertainers, 101, 115n.16; Islam and, 268, 269, 272; and musical culture, Turkish, 311, 322, 325n.8; rebetika entertainers, 10; Riffian Berber culture and, 244–45; solo dance, 111–12
sexual integration, 126–27, 128
sexuality: in Calabrian processional dance, 159–60; in çöçek dances, as performed by women, 88; flamenco entertainers and, 71–72; men's dance performances and, 7; raï and, 223–29, 230n.10; rebetika entertainers and transgressive expressions of, 10–11; in solo dance, 96; women's, as concern of Mediterranean cultures, 267; women's dance performances, 96, 111–12, 132, 139; women's instrumental performances, 132; women's vocal performances, 132
sexual segregation: in Balkan culture, 126–27; in Balkan Muslim Rom culture, 122–24, 125; at celebrations, Moroccan, 252, 256, 257; Islam and, 272; in Kosovo musical culture, 289–90; Loeb on Yemen and, 196; and Riffian Berber courtship tradition, 247; at wedding celebrations, 122–23; women's dance performances and, 128. See also specific countries; specific cultures
Sfax, Lila, 196
Shaarawi, Metwali, 273–74, 276
Shahe (çengi entertainer), 100
sheikhat entertainers, 111, 217, 218, 252, 254, 263
shoga entertainers, 302n.36
shota (dance), 107
shrines, musical culture and, 334, 336, 337–40, 342–45
"Sidi ʿAbed," 220, 225
Şimdi uzaklardaysin (Güç), 312
singing schools, 56–58, 61n.3
Sintineddi, 64n.32

sirtos (dance), 24
social dancing, 92
Soledonna, 63n.29
solo dance: in Albanian culture, 105, 108, 115n.18; Christianity and, 103–4; çoçek and, 107–11; čoček and, 128–30; men's dance performances, 92, 93–94; in Muslim culture, 103–4; in Ottoman culture, 92–106, 114n.7; in Prespa Albanian culture, 87–88, 107–11; professional entertainers, 92, 93–94; Redžepova on, 129–30; sexuality and, 96; urban culture and, 103–4; women's dance performances, 87–88, 92, 93–96, 103–4, 107–12, 127–30
song lyrics: in courtship practices, 242–43; flamenco, 80–81; Hebrew, in mizrakhit music, 20; Kosovo gender roles, defined by, 289, 301n.11; modern commercial song, 199, 206–9; in musical culture of Islam, 272; rebetika, 169, 170, 171, 179–88, 189n.3; Riffian Berber, 237–38, 240–47, 250n.8. *See also specific types of songs*
Spain, musical culture, 67–69, 72, 74, 80
spun copper pan. *See* copper pan
Stanković, Bora, 101
Steinmetz, Karl, 294
stereotypes: of flamenco entertainers, 67, 68, 74, 75, 79–83; marketing usefulness in Rom culture, 130–31, 139; of rebetika, 169–70; in rebetika song lyrics, 188; Redžepova on Rom women and, 120; of Riffian Berber women, 242; of Rom women, 120, 130–31, 139; tango dance and, 188n.2
Strauss, Julius, 295
Sufiism, 337, 338
Süreya, Cemal, 317
sworn virgins, 10, 20, 23–25, 293–95, 299, 302nn. 27, 28
syncretisms, cultural, 20, 23–25

Tadros, Marilyn, 273, 274
"Ta hanoumakia," 181–82, 183, 190n.26
Taktsis, Kostas, 178–79, 187
talava, 295–98
taledhek entertainers, 112

tango (dance): homoeroticism and, 188n.2; men's dance performances, 177; in Sephardi musical culture, 207
tarantella: in Calabrian culture, 6–7, 16, 154, 157–60, 164n.15, 164n.17; and gender relationships in Polsi, 6–7; gender roles and, 26, 147–49, 151–53, 161–62; men's dance performances, 154, 164n.17; men's role, 161; women's dance performances, 16, 164n.15; women's role, 16, 147–49, 161–62, 163n.4
tarantelle music, 164n.14
tarantism, 2, 28n.2
Tavagna, 56, 60
tavala entertainers: and alleged homosexuality, 296, 299; amplified musical instruments and, 296; gender roles and, 299–300; men's dance performances, 295–96, 302n.31; men's instrumental performances, 295, 296; men's vocal performances, 296, 302nn. 33, 34; musical culture and, 10–11, 28, 122, 295–98; in Rom culture, 297–98; women's vocal performances, 296, 302nn. 33, 34
tavşans, 95
tawa'if entertainers, 97, 112, 114n.11
Taymiyah, Sheikh al-Islam ibn, 271
Teatru di a Testa Mora (The Moor's Head Theater), 53
Teodosievski, Stevo, 135–38
Tetuán, women as archivists in, 198–200
therapy, raï as form of, 227
Thiers, Jacques, 51–52
tipping, of entertainers, 133, 141n.22
Tognotti, Dominique, 53
Tomasini, Joëlle, 63n.29
Tomboulis, Agapios, 173
"To neo hanoumaki," 181, 190nn. 24, 25
"To omorfopedho" (The Handsome Fellow), 186
Toronto Prespa Albanian culture, and çoçek, 87–88, 107–8
Toundas, Panayiotis, 173, 182
traditional songs, Corsican culture and, 46–47, 53, 54, 55, 57
trance, Moroccan culture of, 255, 261–63, 264n.3

transgendered individuals, 10–11,
326nn. 14, 15, 16
transsexual singers, 10, 11, 293, 302nn. 27,
28, 37, 316–20, 326n.16
transvestitism, flamenco entertainers and,
71–72, 76
"Trekse manga nationalism rotisis," 186,
192n.34
"Trig el-mehna" (The Path of Torment), 222,
223, 225
"Tsaddiqīm el-ʿzaz" (The Beloved Saints), 337
tsamiko (dance), 89–90
Tsarouchis, Yiannis, 177
tsifteteli (dance), 92, 177
Tsitsanis, Vassilis, 173, 175, 176, 185, 186,
187
Tunisia, 22, 196. See also Maghreb
Turkey: belly dance, 104, 108, 124; çoçek,
108; cultural intimacy in, 307–8; gender identities, and musical culture of,
11, 28, 317, 322; homosexuality, of
Mùren and Ersoy and, 313, 317,
325n.9, 326n.17; hyperreality and,
309, 320–22; hypersexuality and, 323;
köçek entertainers in, 98; language,
and musical culture of, 314–15, 320,
325n.11; men's vocal performances,
310–11, 313, 317, 325nn. 5, 9,
326n.17; musical culture of, 207, 208,
308–9, 310–11, 314, 320–22, 325n.5,
326n.20; nation-statehood and musical
culture of, 307–8, 320, 326n.15; social
dance in, 92; women's dance performances, 108; women's role in, 22; ze-
bekika/zebekiko, Greek-Turkish influence on, 24
Turkish Jewish community, women's vocal
performances, 204

U cantu prufondu, 62n.21
U cantu prufondu 2, 62n.21
"Una hija bova tengo barminam," 210n.10
"Un dia yo bezi," 205
United States, musical culture, 205, 207,
208–9
urban culture, music and, 103–4, 170–71,
182, 215, 230n.1, 235

Vamvakaris, Argyris, 176, 184–85, 186
Vamvakaris, Markos, 169, 176

Vaseiljević, Miodrag, 289
Vembo, Sophia, 175
vendetta, Corsican, 42–43, 62nn. 11, 12
Victor, 180
Vlora, Ekrem Bey, 98
Voce di Corsica, 56, 60
voceri. See lament tradition
Vukanović, Tatomir, 292–93, 294

wars, musical culture and, 46, 342, 345–47
Washabaugh, William, 171
wedding celebrations: in Balkan Muslim
Rom culture, 122–23, 132; čoček and,
129; in Macedonia, 125–26; raï and,
217, 218, 226; Redžepova on sexual
segregation at, 122–23; in Riffian Berber culture, 244, 247–48, 250n.11;
and Riffian Berber women's role, 238–
40, 250n.9; virginity of brides, 132,
141n.21. See also celebrations
"Wein ghachik" (Where Are Your People?),
221
"Widow and the Hashish, The" 184
"Woman Dervish, The" 186
"Woman Satrap," 186–87
women's dance performances: celebrations
and, 125–27; çengi entertainers, 92,
94–95, 97, 98–102, 104, 115nn. 14,
15, 124; čiček, 103; çoçek, 7, 87–88,
105, 106, 107–11, 115n.21; čoček,
128–30; flamenco entertainers, 7, 26,
68, 73–75, 76, 77–79, 83; köçek entertainers, 97–98; in Kosovo, 290–91;
line dance, 87–89, 128; and nashaṭ,
252–55, 260, 263; processional dances,
128; raï and, 218; and respectability,
74, 111–12; sexual integration and,
128; sexual nature of, 88, 96, 131, 132;
solo dance, 87–88, 92, 93–95, 103–
4, 105, 107–11, 127–30; tarantella,
164n.15; zejbeks entertainers, 101–2.
See also specific countries; specific cultures; specific dances; specific performers
women's instrumental performances: čalgija
entertainers, 121; daire, 121; guitar,
flamenco, 76–77, 80; melodic musical
instruments, 301n.20; and nashaṭ, 252,
253, 263; raï and, 226. See also specific
countries; specific cultures

women's role: as archivists, 14, 27, 197–204, 209; honor and shame theory of Mediterranean cultures and, 11–18, 131–33, 141n.20; and literacy, Sephardi culture, 196–97; in Mani's ballads and laments, 189n.3; and nashaṭ, 253–54; raï and, 216–19, 225, 230n.6; in rebetika entertainment, 188; and rebetika song lyrics, 169, 170, 185, 189n.3; in Riffian Berber wedding celebrations, 238–40, 250n.9; tarantella and, 16, 147–49, 161–62, 163n.4; women's vocal performances, Corsican, 33–34. *See also specific countries; specific cultures*

women's vocal performances: and audiences in Kosovo, 291; ballad singing, Italian, 3–4, 37; café-aman, 173–74, 189n.7; as čalgija ensembles, 121; at celebrations, Sephardi, 203; chjam'è rispondi, 41, 61n.9; çoçek, Prespa Albanian, 106–7; čoček and, 115n.17; in Corsican choirs, 46; daire and, 120–22; of dance songs, Prespa Albanian, 89; flamenco, 69, 71, 77–78, 80, 82; in folkloric ensembles, Corsican, 46–47; gender roles, transgressed through, 10, 176; guitar, flamenco, 80; Joseph on, 15; lament tradition and, 15, 36, 42–43; lullaby singing, Corsican, 43–44; monophonic singing, 35t; and nashaṭ, 8, 252, 253, 263; polyphonic singing, Corsican, 9, 33, 34, 35t, 56, 59, 60, 62n.18, 63n.29, 64n.32; polyphonic singing, Prespa Albanian, 61n.2; and professional entertainers, Jewish, 196; raï and, 9, 218–27, 229, 257, 332; and rebetika, 9–10, 169, 173–74, 179–87; Redžepova, 133–35; respectability and, 71, 132, 291; Sephardi culture and, 205, 207; stage performances, 54–56; at weddings in Kosovo, 290, 291. *See also specific performers*

world music markets, Corsican musical culture and, 54, 55–56, 59. *See also* commercial entertainers; public performers

xanith entertainers, 299, 302n.36
Xenakis, Iannis, 53–54
"Ya Rebbi" (Oh My God), 220
Yemen, 196
Yiorgakopoulou, Ioanna, 187
"Yo keriya ser turkita" (I wanted to be a little Turkish woman), 207
Yugoslavia, 105, 115n.21, 121, 135, 136, 141n.16

Zahwaniya (the Joyous One), 220, 221, 223–25, 229
zebekika/zebekiko, 7–8, 24, 178–79, 190n.15
Zehayi, David, 206
zejbeks entertainers, 101–2
Zionist songs, in Sephardi culture, 206, 210n.11